CONTENTS

Foreword   xiii

Introduction and acknowledgements   xv

CHAPTER 1   The problem   1
Background   1
The unequal balance   2
Reported fraud and its cost to companies   2
Attitudes to corporate fraud   6
Benefits from controls and loss reduction   11
Conclusions   13

CHAPTER 2   Essential theories and classifications of fraud   14
Theories in criminal motivation   14
    Organized criminals   14
    First-time offenders   15
    Acceptable crime   17
    Motivation for computer abuse   18
    Aspirations and practical theories of motivation   21
    External pressures and motivation   22
The corporate position   22
Essential theories on fraud   23
    Differential of opportunity theory   23
    Theory of concealment   25
    Theory of deviations   27
    Theories of minimum and general collusion   28
Divisions in fraud   28
    Internal criminals   28
    External criminals   29
Subdivisions in fraud types   30
    Category A1   Internal—management—larcenous   30
    Category A2   Internal—management—misrepresentative   32

Category A3   Internal—management—manipulative   33
Category B1   Internal—operations—larcenous   37
Category B2   Internal—operations—misrepresentative   38
Category B3   Internal—operations—manipulative   41
Category AB4   Internal—management or operations—extorsive   42
Category C1   External—business contacts—larcenous   44
Category C2   External—business contacts—misrepresentative   45
Category C3   External—business contacts—manipulative   49
Category D1   External—opportunist—larcenous   50
Category D2   External—opportunist—misrepresentative   51
Category D3   External—opportunist—manipulative   53
Category E1   External—organized—larcenous   56
Category E2   External—organized—misrepresentative   58
Category E3   External—organized—manipulative   59
Category CDE4 External extorsive   60
High risk areas of fraud   63
Conclusions   67

CHAPTER 3 Records and essentials of computer processing

CHAPTER 3 Records and essentials of computer
processing   69

Accounting records   69
  Final accounts   69
  Day-to-day records   74
  Double entry accounts   74
  Impact of fraud on final accounts   77
  Stock records   78
  Transportation and other records   78
  Statistical records   78
  Correspondence, personal travelling expenses and telephone billing
      records   80
  Informal and personal records   80
Computer processing   80
  Basic operations   81
  Operating systems   81
  Application programs   83
  Data files and data bases   85
  Terminals and remote access   86
  Passwords   87
  Queuing, spooling and printing   87
  Systems console and journalling   88
  Job accounting   89
  Machine failures   89

Correction of errors and adjustments   89
Back-up media and programs   90
Conclusions   90

CHAPTER 4   Elements of fraud: theft act and conversion   91

Fraud elements   91
Theft acts   92
  Unconcealed theft acts   92
  Concealed theft acts   96
Conversion   96
  Cheque conversions   96
  Conversion of false accounting credits   98
  Conversion of stolen goods   99
  Other symptoms of conversion and theft   104

CHAPTER 5   Elements of fraud: concealment   105

Manipulation   105
  Primary manipulation   105
Secondary concealment: avoidance of blame   130
Plausible excuses   132
Conclusion on manipulations   132
Misrepresentation   133
  Misrepresentation of physical realities   133
  Misrepresentation of personal realities   137
  Misrepresentation of commercial realities   137
  Conclusions on misrepresentations   138

CHAPTER 6   Computer related fraud   139

Background   139
A misunderstood problem   140
  Definition of computer fraud   140
  Fear of the unknown   141
  When in doubt: panic   141
  Dracula in charge of the bloodbank and vested interests   141
  Watch the machine: forget the man and his motivation   143
  Concentration and bottlenecks   143
The starting point   143
The nature of risks in computer systems   144
  Divisions in covert risks   145
Mainstream methods of fraud   146
  Access or way in   146
  Mainstream manipulation methods   156

Other methods of fraud in computer systems   183
    Extortion and sabotage   183
    Privacy infringements   184
    Theft of resources   184
Conclusion   187

CHAPTER 7 Detection techniques   188

The purpose and benefits of fraud detection   188
Basic rules   189
Critical or key point auditing   191
    Problems arising from the use of the technique   191
    Probability of detection   192
    Planning for the audit   193
    Method of approach   195
Job sensitivity analysis   218
    Method of approach   218
Vulnerability charts   222
    Columns 1 and 2a   225
    Column 2b   225
    Columns 3 and 4   226
    Column 5   227
    Columns 6 and 7   227
    Column 8   228
    Column 9   229
    Columns 10 and 11   229
    Columns 12 and 13   229
    Column 14   230
    Example of the use of a vulnerability chart   230
Invigilation and created checks   231
    Method of operation and problem areas   233
    Preventive invigilations   238
Observation   239
    Methods and problems   240
    Observation equipment and records   246
Undercover investigations and informants   248
    Roles of undercover investigators   250
    Getting the investigator to work   251
    Liaison between the agent and the company   253
    Company informants   253
    Conclusions on undercover investigations   253
Business intelligence   254
    Passing off or forging products   254

Psychological sabotage   255
Blackmailing key employees of the victim   255
Blocking the victim company's communication channels and
  disrupting work   255
Taking unjustified legal action against the victim   255
Headhunting   255
Unfair trading and external frauds committed by competitors
  which put the victim at a disadvantage   256
Spot checking   257
  Use of spot checks   257
  Selection of areas for checking   258
  General principles   258
  Checks on the movement of goods   260
  Checks on the completeness of recorded income   261
  Checks on commercial and personal realities   262
  Checks on physical realities   264
  Spot checking through staff rotation   266
  Conclusions on spot checks   267
Criminal targeting   267
  Methods of investigation   268
  Conclusions on criminal targeting   269

CHAPTER 8   Investigations   270

Setting the objectives of an investigation   270
  Prosecution   273
  Civil action   277
  Negotiation   278
  Fidelity insurance   278
  Dismissal   279
  Defensive action   280
Factors to be considered in setting objectives   280
  Company politics   280
  Adverse publicity   281
  Police involvement   281
  Investigative resources   283
  Employee morale   283
  Consider the worst case   284
  Acquisition of records   284
  Admissibility of evidence   285
  Analysis of exposure points   286
  Analysis of weak points in the victim's case   286

Methods of investigation 287
Acquisition and analysis of documents 288
Analysis of deviations 292
Surveillance 293
Expert witnesses and forensic examination 295
Pretext investigations 296
Interviews 296
Reviewing investigation results 318
Report 318
Original exhibits 319
Copy exhibits 319
Filing papers 320

CHAPTER 9   Defensive systems 321

Defensive rationale 321
Company policy and strategy of control 322
Responsibilities for security 323
Budgets for security and controls 325
Minimum standards of protection 326
Conduct of investigations 326
Company-wide procedures 326
Employee selection 326
Personnel policies and procedures 343
Protection of information 347
Reporting losses and other incidents 349
Fidelity insurance 350
Emergency planning 351
Preventive security 352
Physical security 353
Security systems 359
Conclusions on preventive security 359
Accounting controls 360
The role of accounting systems in fraud prevention 360
The scope of accounting controls 361
Defined systems 361
Physical controls 362
Controls over inventories and the movement of goods 364
Accountability 365
Consistency and uninformity 366
Record integrity 366
Rotation of duties 368
Separation of duties 368

Third-party intervention and corroboration 370
Authorization 371
Exception reports 371
Disbursements 372
Incoming funds 372
Contracts and tenders 373
Enforcement 373
Special defences against misrepresentations 374
Defences against commercial misrepresentations 376
Defences against personal misrepresentations 377
Defences against physical misrepresentations 378
Conclusions on defences against misrepresentations 379
Detection 379
Conclusion 380

CHAPTER 10   Computer security and fraud defences 381

Perceptions of risks and controls 381
Risk evaluation: background and methods 381
Risk identification 384
Risk quantification 385
Principles of risk management 387
Recommended method of approach 388
Appointment of a computer security project team 388
Eclectic risk evaluation 389
Selection of controls 394
Baseline controls 394
Computer audit 400
Conclusions 406

APPENDIX A   Corporate fraud checklist 407

APPENDIX B   Job sensitivity analysis 421

APPENDIX C   Recommended security policy 431

READING LIST 434

GLOSSARY 436

INDEX 443

Foreword

Officers and directors of financial institutions and corporations are under attack. Business competition, economic conditions and a fundamental change in the philosophy of personal accountability are profoundly affecting businesses and the potential liability of their officers and directors. As the financial arena grows more complex and profits are more easily lost than gained, no company is immune to the dangers of fraud, conflicts of interest and negligence. Stockholders, regulators and even the institutions themselves are holding directors and officers to unprecedented standards of knowledge, responsibility and performance. These developments signal the need for people managing the affairs of corporations to be keenly aware of the consequences of their omissions and the methods available to protect their institutions, and ultimately themselves, from liability.

Executives are being personally held liable for failing to establish a thorough system of risk management, a program for detection of dishonesty, procedures for investigation and adequate insurance portfolios to protect from the catastrophic losses which can be occasioned by fraud.

Fraud, its implementations, detection and prevention are highly specialized complex areas as are the legal and moral questions raised.

While this is touted as the communication age, the unspoken truth is that its bastard by-product, corporate fraud, is the real growth industry of the 1980s. The computer is its greatest asset and its nemesis.

It is necessary to keep in mind that 'computer fraud' is really 'computer assisted fraud'. The prevalent attitude in most companies whose executives are of the pre-computer generation is that computer related risks can be eliminated by restricting physical access to the computer room through an elaborate series of sophisticated locks and coded magnetic cards. This is all done under the mistaken belief that if the computer room is protected so is the computer system. This combined with the ideas that 'our employees are all honest' or 'our fraud prevention systems have always worked and therefore will continue to perform' are dangerous fallacies.

The truth is that fraud related risks simply cannot be completely eliminated by internal or external means.

Experience has shown that these vital issues are addressed only in isolated technical publications and very few individuals have the dedication or experience to understand thoroughly this evolving area. Fewer still have the ability to explain lucidly these complex risks to the corporate executives. Michael J. Comer has, for the second time, demonstrated these unique skills. His 1977 publication, *Corporate Fraud*, which has become a standard reference, was years ahead of its time in expounding principles for the survival of the corporate executive.

Michael J. Comer raises the consciousness of the executive while educating in a forceful, creative, interesting and intelligent manner. If fraud is the growth business of the 1980s, then this publication is the survival handbook for the time.

Wildman, Harrold, Allen, Dixon, & McDonnell

Patrick M. Ardis

Memphis, Tennessee

Introduction and Acknowledgements

It is about 10 years since writing began on the first edition of this book. Since that time, there have been many dramatic changes.

The boom years of the early 1970s were quickly replaced by a global recession encouraging previously honest people and companies to see fraud as the easy answer to their economic survival. Computers are increasingly becoming the targets for economic and violent attack. Encouraged by the lenient sentences imposed for non-violent crime, organized criminals have recognized that fraud is big business. The boom in fraud has arrived.

In the intervening 10 years my own views of fraud have changed and become even more cynical. Over 15 years in government service and with a major international oil company had provided what I believed in 1974 to be a fair insight into the problems of corporate fraud. However, in the five years of running a consulting practice in computer security and fraud investigations, horizons have been extended. Assignments with Network Security Management Limited have allowed me the privilege of working for a large number of companies and financial institutions, many of which would be rightly regarded as leaders in technology, management, security and controls.

Experience of fraud investigations (amounting to over US$150 million per annum) and preventive assignments in a wide cross-section of industries and countries has reinforced my opinion on the scale and diversity of commercial dishonesty. It has also demonstrated where and why fraud occurs and how it can be prevented, detected and investigated. Lessons have been learned the hard way, from my own and other people's mistakes.

Client confidentiality naturally prevents discussion of individual assignments although the lessons learned from them are included.

The major revisions in this edition include three important theories which help to predict where fraud will occur, a more practical analysis of computer fraud and defences, new coverage on risk evaluation, interviewing, investigations, bribery and corruption, contract auditing and on the management, strategy and mechanics of control.

The case studies used as illustrations have, in the main, been extracted from the *Computer Fraud and Security Bulletin*, published by Elsevier International Bulletins of Oxford, for which I have been editor for the past six years.

I remain deeply indebted to the many people who helped and encouraged me in the production of the original version of *Corporate Fraud* and to my colleagues in Network Security Management Limited whom I regard as among the best commercial fraud investigators in the world. It is a delight to work again with McGraw-Hill in Maidenhead.

I am grateful to many clients, whose names cannot be mentioned, to friends in government service and law enforcement, and to the authors who kindly allowed me to quote from and learn from their works.

My final thanks must go to the thousands of fraudsmen and women I have dealt with over the past 20 years for providing me with the insight on which this book is based and the need for its publication.

1. The problem

Rule 1:   The essence of successful fraud is that honest people should not suspect
Rule 1a: Which honest people?

Background

When in the past few years a President and a Vice-President of the United States of America, Crown Princes, Prime Ministers, a brace of British politicians and a host of chief executives from major companies have fallen from power as a result of fraud no one could argue that the bells have not been rung.

Dramatic headlines cry out for attention and yet few people understand fraud, believe that they could be its victims, or take on the responsibilities of prevention and detection.

Fraud is a grey subject, surrounded by mystique and too often by apathy. Whereas society seems outraged, and rightly so, at overt acts of violence and terrorism and is prepared to devote attention and resources to their solution, covert and possibly in the long term more damaging losses through deceit escape attention and succeed by default.

Fraud may be defined as any behaviour by which one person intends to gain a dishonest advantage over another.* This is not a legal definition and it is not intended to be. It is adequate to embrace the subject matter of this book and to include such diverse acts as petty theft, pilfering, extortion, embezzlement, forgery, unfair competition, commercial espionage and other white collar, blue collar and computer crimes.

In recent years, prompted by an increase in international violence, corporations have sought to improve physical security. While this drive for protection against overt loss has spiralled, attention has been deflected from silent risks—from the disloyal or subverted employee, dishonest business contact or competitor, industrial spy or organized criminal.

The very stealth of fraud avoids attention. It is like a malignant cancer eating away at commercial enterprise. Through this erosion, society as a whole suffers.

This book attempts to identify the problems of corporate fraud and to offer practical solutions. It is possible to take the view that, in discussing the subject at all, fraud will be encouraged, or that the problems are exacerbated by drawing attention to them. This view is very wrong.

* A glossary of the technical terms used in this book will be found on page 436.

1

The unequal balance

It has been said that for every credibility gap there is a gullibility fill: too many fraud victims are taken by surprise, unaware of what might happen. It is often an unequal fight between naive, honest and well-intentioned management with limited resources to devote to security and well-informed criminals with limitless time to scheme and plunder. The essence of successful fraud is that honest people should not suspect; evil triumphs when good people do nothing.

There is abundant evidence that criminals are often extremely well informed. A number of publishers of underground books specialize in providing manuals for the would-be and existing criminal. The *Check Book*, from the Eden Press of California, sets out a detailed methodology of defrauding banks. Under the expert eye of the author, called Hot Ralph, the would-be fraudsman is taken from NSF schemes through to multi-million dollar lapping frauds with the float periods of the various Federal Reserve districts clearly explained.

Jails are also an excellent school for criminals, equal in their own ways to Eton, Harrow, Oxford, Yale or Cambridge. In an article for the *Computer Fraud and Security Bulletin* measures to prevent wire tapping were discussed. The editorial office received a letter from a prisoner in an American jail stating that the article 'wasn't bad as far as it went'. He then continued to set out a scheme for wire interception that was so advanced that a decision was taken not to publish it.

Honeywell, the giant American computer manufacturer, set up a scheme to train prisoners in computer sciences. Courses were run at Framlingham Prison, Massachusetts for about 650 prisoners. The scheme was halted when the prison was raided by the local police. Five prisoners were arrested on suspicion that they had used the prison computer to run an illegal gambling racket and a drugs distribution scheme. To make matters worse, the convicts failed to disclose their income to the Internal Revenue Department and were additionally charged with tax evasion!

Rather than to encourage crime, the main purpose of this book is to alert management to the dangers and mechanics of fraud and to tell managers what can be done to prevent it. When a potential perpetrator and a potential victim are equally well informed about the possibilities of fraud, the initiative rests with the defender. The essence of successful fraud is that honest people should not suspect.

Reported fraud and its cost to companies

Statistics summarizing reported and prosecuted crimes are an inaccurate measure of the scale and scope of corporate fraud. Estimates suggest that less than 15 per cent of discovered cases are reported to the police. The reasons for non-reporting vary from the reluctance of victims, and particularly banks, to admit that they have been defrauded to failure to recognize that losses were dishonest.

Other victims are dissuaded against taking action out of misguided sympathy for the perpetrator, lost management time in attending courts, or in the belief that funds cannot be recovered. The cause and effect of these and other attitudes are discussed later.

It is also important to recognize that in some cases frauds cannot be prosecuted as crimes. The criminal law has failed to keep pace with changes in technology and in business generally. There is no crime of industrial espionage in the UK; the perpetrator may or may not be liable to prosecution depending only on the method used to steal information. If a vital conversation is monitored on a tape recorder there is unlikely to be any criminal penalty. If the same conversation is monitored on a radio transmitter, there is a criminal offence under the Wireless and Telegraphy Act for using a radio transmitter without the appropriate licence! but the penalties are derisory when measured against the potential rewards.

Similarly many acts of computer abuse cannot be prosecuted because the criminal law's definition of property is ambiguous and may not cover intangible electronic impulses on magnetic media. Also, the astute criminal will choose to commit his fraud across international boundaries. In doing so he will exploit conflicts in jurisdiction always to his own advantage.

Until recently, the Director of Public Prosecutions in the United Kingdom was reluctant to prosecute even clear-cut cases of non-violent crime providing both the victim and the perpetrator were other than British nationals. In fairness, this incredible ruling was changed, but for a time the UK threatened to become the fraud haven for international criminals.

What official crime statistics truly represent was nicely put by Gwynn Nettler.*

> Getting arrested is an interactional process. The police force, the policeman, and the offender do make a difference—up to some limit—in determining what is recorded as crime. The question is whether this interaction systematically biases the official statistics of a particular jurisdiction for a particular period. The best answer seems to be that official records in the democracies reflect the operation of a judicial sieve. What are counted, finally, as crimes are the more obvious offences, the more serious offences, offences whose victims have brought complaints, and offences some of whose victims are dead—those crimes, in short, for which the public put pressure on their police to make arrests.

* _Explaining Crime_, McGraw-Hill, New York, 1974.

Given these limitations, reports on corporate crime grossly understate the scale and nature of corporate fraud.

There have been very few studies which shed light on the scale and cost of fraud as opposed to the much more restricted problem of prosecuted crime. The exception was a report produced by the US Chamber of Commerce 1974 in the *Handbook of White Collar Crime*. It was based on official crime figures supported by interviews with victims (who had not reported) and perpetrators (who had not been caught). Although the figures, which are shown in Table 1.1, are now out of date, they show an interesting pattern.

Table 1.1   Analysis of fraud types: US study

Type of fraud		Annual loss ($ billions)	% of total
Bankruptcy frauds		0.08	0.19
Bribery, kickbacks, etc.		3.00	7.18
Computer related frauds		0.10	0.23
Consumer fraud			
private victims	5.5		
business victims	3.5		
government victims	12.0	21.00	50.26
Credit cards and cheques		1.10	2.64
Embezzlement		3.00	7.18
Pilferage		4.00	9.57
Receiving stolen property		3.50	8.37
Insurance frauds		2.00	4.79
Securities fraud and forgery		4.00	9.57
		41.78	100.00

The vast majority of frauds were in the consumer area and relied on personal deception rather than the manipulation of accounting records. These differences and the significance of them are described in Chapter 2. The very low proportion (0.23 per cent) of computer fraud arises from two reasons: confusion over definitions and, more importantly, from the fact that in 1974 computers were less pervasive than they are today.

An internal report produced for fidelity insurance underwriters suggested that the workforce in the 'average commercial enterprise' could be divided into three distinct sections (Figure 1.1).

To many managers it would be unthinkable that 25 per cent of their colleagues could be dishonest, but practical experience indicates the figures are more likely to be correct than not.

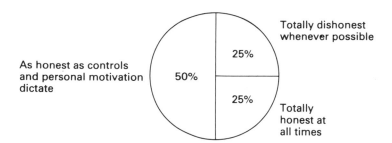

Figure 1.1   Breakdown between honest and dishonest employees

The definition of workforce is also wider than most people appreciate; it includes all company employees, from the senior board director down to the lowly manual worker. Most managers assume that fraud, if it occurs at all, does so at levels below them in the organization. This is seldom the case: the most dangerous frauds are those which occur at higher management levels.

Other research organizations have made predictions on the scale of corporate fraud as follows:

- crime is said to cost the UK over 2.5 per cent of its gross national product;
- in the UK one man in three and one woman in eight will be convicted of a standard list (criminal, non-motoring) offence;
- 30 per cent of all American company liquidations are said to be as a result of fraud;
- the average embezzlement continues for $3\frac{1}{2}$ years before it is uncovered, usually by chance;
- FBI figures indicate that bank losses from fraud are five times greater than losses through robberies and violence;
- polygraph tests on American bank and retail shop employees showed that between 40 and 70 per cent had stolen from their employer.*

Reliable estimates suggest that the 'average company' loses between 2 and 5 per cent of gross turnover as a result of fraud. For example, in 1978 a UK government department carried out an audit of a British public company and reported losses from fraud as great as 16 per cent of turnover in some distribution depots.

It is unlikely that fraudulent losses will diminish in the foreseeable future since there is every indication that the younger generation is possibly more criminally inclined than its predecessors. More than half of the people arrested for indictable offences in London in 1983 were under 21; almost one-third of that number were between the ages of 10 and 16.

---

* *Explaining Crime*, McGraw-Hill, New York, 1974.

Disruptive behaviour in schools, now running at an alarming rate, is an ill omen for future employers.

A survey conducted by the London School of Economics revealed that nine out of ten schoolboys admitted stealing by the time they had left school:

- 88 per cent had stolen from school
- 70 per cent had stolen from a shop
- 33 per cent had stolen from a store or barrow
- 25 per cent had stolen from a car or lorry.

Students at universities and polytechnic colleges are often brought up with ethical standards which immediately conflict with those of their future employers. Computer freaking, games playing and illegal penetration of systems to which they are denied legitimate access are accepted, if not encouraged. A lecturer at a London college told a third year class in computer studies that they had all failed their final examinations. He added that the results were held on the college's computer system and if any student could access the computer files and change his grades he would accept that their technical skills must be sufficient to warrant a pass. None of the students failed.

This may appear to be harmless fun but the exercise reinforces ethical standards of conduct which could be disastrous in the business environment.

In the final analysis, each organization faces unique risks and varying degrees of dishonest losses, depending to a large extent on the nature of the business and the attitude of its senior management to business ethics and controls.

Attitudes to corporate fraud

There are probably no aspects of commercial life more contentious than security, fraud prevention and detection. It is a fact that in some areas fraudulent behaviour is openly tolerated if not institutionalized. The belief that each job has its hidden benefits is ingrained and it could be argued that management should do nothing to interfere with this secondary economy; that the allowance of small 'fiddles' encourages the workforce to work harder.

The problem with this view is that there is no such thing as a small fraud. It is difficult to convince an employee that by taking £10 per day he is defrauding the company of £3000 per annum. Fraud is contagious and corrosive; allow small frauds to escape unpunished and they will soon grow. Allow one section of the workforce to take unauthorized benefits and everyone will expect the same. Multiply the costs over all the workforce throughout the year and it becomes clear that fraud cannot be tolerated.

The scale of fraud in an organization is a reflection of the ability of its managers to manage. Often people would prefer to be deceived than to be perceived as distrustful. Dealing with fraud calls for a tough, yet fair, unambiguous policy by top management that dishonesty will not be tolerated. It is essential that the policy is applied consistently to all employees, including the top managers themselves. Chapter 9 addresses these policy areas.

Experience indicates that management fails to exercise control for one of a number of reasons:

1. *Management does not understand the risks* It is not surprising that an honest manager should believe that his colleagues and subordinates should follow similarly honest standards. The reverse is certainly true; ask a criminal about fraud and he will tell you that everyone is dishonest. Quite rightly good managers are risk takers—they take risks in every aspect of their business—but the difference with fraud is that seldom do they know the adverse consequences of the risk being accepted. The old saying 'whoever saw the calculations that went with the calculated risk' is certainly true when it comes to fraud.

   In most aspects of business, managers have some direct personal experience of the matters at issue and, if they do not, will call for expert professional advice. The need for controls against fraud is often decided on a subjective guess, in the belief that most people are honest, and without any determination as to what the risks in their organizations might be.

2. *It can never happen to us* There will be cases where this attitude is undoubtedly true. Some companies, although it is difficult to imagine what they might do and where they are, would be safe in this opinion and in taking it obviously save on the cost of controls. It is far more likely that the opinion is wrong and self-defeating.

   Generally the organizations that believe it can never happen to them are unaware of the risk. Because of this, their controls are inadequate, which is a fact quickly spotted and exploited by criminals. In short, the organizations which believe it can never happen to them, present themselves as precisely the sort of soft targets that criminals choose to exploit.

3. *We cannot afford the cost of controls* This argument is an indication of naivety rather than of good commercial sense. Security costs are made up of two elements: the cost of losses and the cost of controls. Money is not saved by abandoning security; in fact, the reverse is usually true.

   All companies will lose a percentage of turnover through fraud and this is the first element in calculating the cost of security; the cost of losses. The second element is the cost of controls and prudent management should ensure, as far as possible, that they are commensurate with the risks and that they are cost effective (Figure 1.2). Thus the object of security is to reduce the *combined* cost of losses and control to the minimum possible level.

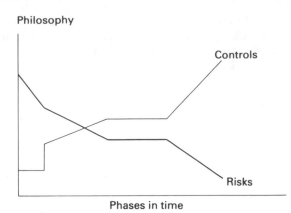

Figure 1.2   Over- and under-protection

4. *Management has no confidence in controls*   It is certainly far more simple to design bad controls than good ones. Often security is ignored because recommendations for controls lack credibility. Effective security usually means:

- identification and quantification of the risks;
- a clear strategy for control set at the most senior level, incorporated into a policy which is disseminated to all employees so that they know what is expected of them;
- assignment of responsibilities;
- an integrated system of controls, commensurate with the risks, which are either:
  - totally self-enforcing,
  - understood and supported by all employees at all times,
  - delegated to specialist staff who have powers of enforcement;
- personal penalties for non-compliance.

Too frequently organizations fail to understand the risks, overlook strategy and management direction and then criticize *ad hoc* controls when they fail.

5. *Security is bad for employee morale*   Frequently security and personnel issues appear to conflict; security managers may seek immediate dismissal of employees suspected of dishonesty, or press for screening of job applicants prior to engagement or other issues which are not pleasant from a personnel point of view.

It is easy to give priority to the rights of criminals while overlooking the obligations to honest employees and shareholders. The effect that failure to investigate a suspected fraud case, or to prosecute the person responsible has on honest employees is difficult to determine, although experience suggests it is demoralizing and far reaching.

At what point a company draws the line between personnel and security issues should not be left to the manager of either function to decide, but should be set down as company policy at board level.

6. *Our auditors would detect fraud* Most auditors would disagree most strongly with this opinion. External public accountants are not expected to uncover dishonesty and in fact will usually make this fact abundantly clear in engagement letters and reports. In the UK the obligations of the statutory auditors are to:

- make a report to the members on accounts examined by the auditors (and on every balance sheet, profit and loss account and group accounts laid before members in general meeting during period of office);
- state whether accounts have been properly prepared in accordance with current legislation;
- state whether a true and fair view is given on the company's state of affairs as at the end of its financial year;
- state whether a true and fair view is given of the company's profit and loss;
- state whether a true and fair view, so far as concerns members of the company, is given of the company's and subsidiaries' state of affairs and profit in the case of consolidated accounts;
- carry out such investigations as will enable the auditor to form an opinion as to whether proper books of account have been kept by the company and proper returns adequate for their audit have been received from branches visited by them;
- carry out such investigations as will enable the auditor to form an opinion as to whether the company's balance sheet and (consolidated) profit and loss account are in agreement with the books of account and returns;
- state whether proper books have not been kept;
- state whether accounts are not in agreement with records and returns;
- state that they have failed to obtain all the information and explanations necessary for the purpose of the audit, if such is the case;
- provide details of loans to officers if such information is not given in the accounts;
- provide particulars of remuneration to directors and certain employees if such information is not given in the accounts;
- state whether there are, or are not, circumstances connected with his resignation which he considers should be brought to the notice of creditors;
- report departures from standard accounting practice.

The accounting profession has gone through much soul-searching on what should be achieved in audits. Richard Briston, Professor of Accountancy at Strathclyde University, suggested in the *British Accountancy Journal* that British companies spent over £250 million per annum on irrelevant audits. He stated:

- Traditional audits, required by law, are irrelevant and should be abolished.
- The accounting profession should try to work out new approaches to audits.
- Neither shareholders nor management derive obvious benefits from the audit process.
- Audit reports are rarely informative. Such qualifications as are normally made seem calculated to protect the auditor from claims of negligence and libel rather than to protect shareholders.
- All large companies should be required by law to maintain an internal audit team which would report to a supervisory board, thus giving the internal auditors independence.

A report for the Institute of Internal Auditors by Brian Ruder of the Stanford Research Institute showed that most senior managers believed that internal auditors were responsible for fraud detection, although less than 20 per cent of auditors shared this view.

A study conducted for the *Computer Fraud and Security Bulletin* showed that frauds were detected by the methods shown in Table 1.2.

Table 1.2 Methods by which frauds are detected

Accident	51%
Auditors	19%
Management controls	10%
Disgruntled mistresses	20%

On this basis it could be argued that it would be more effective to fire most internal audit departments, encourage key employees to take on mistresses and then disgruntle them: what's more, it would be much more fun!

Yet it would be unfair to criticize auditors for failing to detect fraud. Audit fees have generally been cut back by clients eager to save costs and seldom are internal audit departments given the responsibility and the authority to detect and investigate fraud.

The prevention of fraud, like security generally, should start with senior management; it is a top responsibility.

Benefits from controls and loss reduction

Legislation places clear obligation on the fair and accurate recording and reporting of transactions. Additionally, company directors have a clear fiduciary duty to protect the assets entrusted to them. But seldom has the law been the driving force for changing ingrained patterns of behaviour; it has tended to follow and codify accepted practice rather than to derive effective changes.

The criminal courts have often been scathing about the lack of security in companies. A good example was reported in the *Financial Times* on 28 October 1973; the case involved the Ford Motor Company:

> The Judge said in passing sentence that there was such laxity in security and controls that the Company positively invited the dishonest conduct. There had been no proper control of stock of scrap metal and no periodical stock taking. Had there been a regular check on stocks the fraud could not have persisted as it did for well over two years.
>
> More revealing was the evidence of a buyer, a Ford employee who at the end of 1969 made a written report to his superior, a senior buyer, as a result of having been shown some of Ford's valuable scrap metal lying at the scrap metal emergency yard. The report was destroyed and no further investigation took place nor were the Police called in until the fraud had reached such proportions at the end of 1971 that a blind eye could no longer be turned.
>
> No reason was given for the refusal to unearth the fraud but there was a hint that Fords feared worsening industrial relations should employees be subject to criminal investigations. This behaviour resulted in the Court refusing to make any order of compensation. The Judge said that if the victim of fraud actively encouraged dishonesty he could not expect the criminal courts to come to his assistance so readily.
>
> The Ford case poses a major question to the criminal law. How should the law regard the victim of fraud if his knowledge or attitude is conducive to his own loss. The commission of crime is no isolated accidental act. It is the culmination of a process in which many factors are at work; there are few genuinely random victims of crime. The householder who is a victim of burglary has, as often as not, paid too little heed to the state of his locks, left windows unfastened or gone on holiday and advertised his absence by omitting to cancel deliveries of milk. The motorist who leaves a camera or a briefcase exposed on the seat of his car is asking for someone to break in and steal it.
>
> Victims sometimes go beyond being just careless over their property. Often they suffer as a consequence of their own cupidity and foolishly

entrust property to confidence men who assure them blindly that some financial venture is about to produce a fantastic profit.

How does all this apply to the huge industrial organisation? That such firms as Fords are prone to large-scale defalcations is obvious. During the trial, one witness who was described as THE investigator (the emphasis was supplied by him when describing his job) gave a clue to the problem for a company like Ford. He said with refreshing candour that the Ford Motor Company allocated so much of their budget to security and that was that. The amount of money allowed by the company was to provide a token security force, which could not operate as anything more than a very mild deterrent to determined pilfering. Apart from the most casual and sporadic visiting by members of the security force, there was no surveillance of the pig field from which it is said the bulk of the losses occurred.

The Judge posed the question 'has the time come in the development of our society when some system of security needs to be imposed by legislation? Would it be an intolerable imposition upon management in industry to be made to allocate a percentage of the total turnover to the protection of **property from** thefts both by customers and staff? At the very least one is entitled to expect that the large companies will have a system which has a reasonable prospect of uncovering any large-scale fraud, even if no preventive action can be fulfilled.'

It is doubtful that penalties under the law or criticism by judges will cause companies to improve controls. Cases brought by shareholders alleging negligence against officers whose companies have lost and sometimes been bankrupted by fraud have succeeded but do not provide the stimulus necessary to tackle fraud.

Successful companies usually have one major reason for preventing and recovering from losses and that is because it is profitable to do so; particularly when markets cannot be expanded easily and profits are hard to earn.

The true benefits of fraud prevention can be illustrated from the following example:

Company A has a turnover of £20 million and gross profits of £2 million (10 per cent). Losses from dishonesty could, on average, be expected to amount to £600 000 (3 per cent). A decrease in losses to 1.5 per cent of turnover would produce savings of £300 000 which would make a contribution to profits equal to an increase of £3 million in turnover. The gearing is in favour of preventing losses.

A second reason why management should take a direct interest in security is to ensure the stability and long-term survival of their organizations in a hostile business world; the major undisclosed liability of many organizations is their inadequate security. Problems which are not dealt with seldom go away.

Conclusions

This book is presented to enable managers to review the risks from fraud in the organization for which they are responsible; it describes essential factors about fraud and the motivation of perpetrators, the nature of concealment and high risk areas. Chapter 9 sets out major strategic issues and policy matters: These are developed into individual controls both inside and outside the computer environment. Chapter 7 gives techniques for detecting fraud in situations where no suspicion exists. Chapter 8 deals with the difficult problem of investigations.

2. Essential theories and classifications of fraud

Rule 2: When two people meet to discuss money belonging to a third, fraud is inevitable

Fraud appears to be an intangible, amorphous thing, confounding comprehension and belief. The newspapers, radio and television reveal complex embezzlement, long firm frauds, commercial and organized crimes, and laymen can only stand back in amazement at the apparent ingenuity of criminals.

Although its intricate workings are limited only by human imagination, it is nonetheless true that frauds fall naturally into identifiable categories. There are few 'new' frauds, merely old ones given new leases of life by particular embellishments and the continuing gullibility of victims.

This chapter introduces a number of important theories through which the mechanics of fraud can be understood. It begins with probably the most important aspect, i.e., motivation.

Theories in criminal motivation

It would be simple to take the view that thieves are born dishonest and nothing that society can do will reform them. It would be equally unrealistic to assume that all criminals are socially deprived misfits who deserve nothing but understanding and compassion. Somewhere between these two extremes, the truth may be found.

ORGANIZED CRIMINALS

Organized criminal groups, such as the Mafia, have long recognized the benefits to be extracted from non-violent crime; particularly credit frauds, investment scams and the laundering of funds through apparently genuine companies. Threats of violence against members of the public, co-conspirators and employees of victim organizations have often been used to open up opportunities otherwise not available.

Recent years have produced two important developments. The first is the entry of lower echelon, but violent, criminal gangs into the fraud scene, no doubt encouraged by the ease of commission and the desultory penalties if caught.

It is significant that the largest bank robbery was about 1 per cent of the largest known fraud and that the total of bank losses from fraud is approximately 50 times greater than those from all other crimes combined.

The second innovation of organized criminals is the creation of spurious commercial disputes (breaches of contract, etc.) between their front companies and third parties. For example, a front company might order a large quantity of goods from a genuine supplier. Proper contracts are drawn up and advance payment made. Pressure is then applied to an employee of the supplier resulting in a failure to deliver at the right time, at the right price or in the correct quality or quantity. Civil action will be taken against the supplier, usually involving a claim for damages. Frequently litigation will be settled out of court, much to the advantage of the criminals.

FIRST-TIME OFFENDERS

A high proportion, if not the majority, of corporate criminals can be loosely defined as 'first-time offenders'. The definition is loose because criminals are seldom caught on their first outing, though they will usually suggest that this is the case. The term 'first-time offender' simply refers to a person who has not been caught before.

It is important to understand what leads people into corporate fraud. Two American criminologists, Edwin O. Sutherland and Donald R. Cressey, have examined the motivation of criminals in depth. Although their research produced somewhat differing conclusions, their opinions when taken together provide a possible explanation of the motivational forces behind corporate fraud.

Sutherland's theory of 'differential association' has been widely accepted as being highly relevant to white collar crime.* He asserted:

> A complete explanation of white collar crime cannot be derived from available data. The data which are at hand suggest that white collar crime has its genesis in the same general process as other criminal behaviour, namely differential association. The hypothesis of differential association is that criminal behaviour is learned in association with those who define such behaviour favourably and in isolation from those who define it unfavourably. A person in an appropriate situation engages in such criminal behaviour if and only if the weight of the favourable definitions exceeds the weight of the unfavourable definitions.

Sutherland did not suggest that the hypothesis covered all cases, or was a universal explanation of all white collar crime.

What can be deduced from Sutherland's work is that where a company

---

* Edwin O. Sutherland, *White Collar Crime*, CBS, New York, 1961.

condones or takes a weak attitude in dealing with crime it encourages others to follow. Where senior management engages in unethical conduct, accepts sloppy controls, wastes assets and talents, it encourages others to follow: crime is contagious. Conversely, and this is possibly the greatest value of Sutherland's work, a company that creates a climate of honesty can reduce losses. It can ensure that the factors unfavourable to crime exceed those favourable to it.

Although Sutherland's theory of differential association may not explain the lone embezzler or forger, the theories developed by Cressey do. Cressey suggested that:*

> Trusted persons become trust violators when they conceive of themselves as having a financial problem which is non-shareable, are aware that this problem can be secretly resolved by violation of the position of financial trust, and are able to apply to their own conduct in that situation verbalisations which enable them to adjust their conceptions of themselves as trusted persons with their conceptions of themselves as users of the entrusted funds or property.

A recent case illustrates this theory:

> Super salesman John O. has a steady well-paid job and thought his marriage was sound. But when he discovered letters to his wife written by another man and suspected that she was having an affair, he employed a firm of private investigators and they worked on the case for varying periods over nine months. The bills were heavy and Mr O. began taking sums of money from the accounts of the firm. He soon found he was getting deeper and deeper into debt and began to use the company's money to gamble in the hope that he could repay his employer from his winnings. Mr O. took £47 000 and most of it went on horse race betting. Mr O., the father of two children and now divorced, was jailed for 4 years when he admitted 10 charges and asked for 76 more to be taken into consideration. He claimed dishonesty had been forced on him.

The factors which enable a criminal to justify his dishonesty are often complex.

Many thieves who steal from their large multinational employer might never consider defrauding a small shopkeeper or colleague. If the organization is distant or big enough, popular guilt about stealing from it diminishes. Further, many thieves do not see their dishonesty for what it truly is and often minimize the significance of criminal behaviour.

In other cases, Sutherland submitted, the stigma of criminality is lacking

---

* Donald R. Cressey, *Other People's Money*, Patterson Smith, New Jersey, 1973.

when certain laws are violated. Evasion of income tax, customs duty, computer program and video piracy are examples of 'acceptable' crimes.

ACCEPTABLE CRIME

Frauds committed by senior managers, supposedly in the best interests of their companies, are also examples of acceptable crime.

The US bankruptcy court asked serious questions following the collapse of a company which twelve months earlier had reported profits of US$12.4 million. This is what happened to S, a division of a giant New York based office equipment manufacturing group.

The court heard that inventory was controlled on a perpetual system and that physical stocks were regularly checked and recorded on special tags. The tags would be submitted to data processing where they would be key-punched and an 'unpriced' inventory report produced. The unpriced report would be returned to the initiating department for checking against its own manual records, so that any input errors could be corrected.

When the unpriced run was finally agreed, it could be further processed against a master pricing file. The priced output was never sent back to the initiating department but was instead used by the financial control section to update the general ledger and prepare monthly and annual accounts.

The problems of S arose because of serious and allegedly delicate adjustments introduced after the final unpriced run had been agreed. The bankruptcy examiner found that in one case, an unpriced listing was increased from what should have been a true face-value of $89 million to $182 million. Items which were never included on the unpriced runs suddenly appeared on the priced version.

So great were the inflations that the company did not have the physical warehouse space to store the goods. In one case substantial inventories were shown as being located in a warehouse which has been closed down since 1977. Apparently, it escaped the attention of the auditors who conducted their checks on the unpriced runs.

Members of the data processing department were said to have been involved in the manipulation and received substantial bonuses for their assistance. It was also alleged that fictitious general ledger entries were made: expenses would be mysteriously reduced and sales inflated. The manipulation was made in such a way that balances appeared to agree, but the perpetrators believed that there was always the chance that auditors would hit upon the intermediate tapes used to produce the false results.

Computer operations staff overcame this possibility by giving many of the working tapes dates such as 33 December or the 0 June which were obviously excluded from all library listings. Once the final adjusted files had been prepared, the working tapes were destroyed.

It was alleged that the president and chief executive officer had almost total control of the division and strongly resisted interference from other board members. The agendas for board meetings were not prepared until the last minute, thus reducing the possibility of embarrassing questions. Accounts were similarly released at the last minute and in such volume that it would take a superman to wade through them. Information asked for by the other directors was simply not delivered.

This case is far from unusual and illustrates the dangers which are ever increasing of collusion between senior board members and data processing staff.

Challenge or revenge may also provide the motive for crime or the justification for dishonesty:

A former employee of M Limited, who stole over £2000 worth of valuable electrical equipment as a protest was jailed for four years when he appeared before Chelmsford Crown Court.

The man had pleaded guilty to stealing 50 computer memory banks and an oscillator. Defending counsel said that the man had stolen the parts as a 'protest'. He was upset at the immoral attitude of M Limited in making components for both sides in the Middle East war and the only way of making his objections known was to take some items and hide them.

MOTIVATION FOR COMPUTER ABUSE

Computer technicians have different thought processes from most employees and are often far removed from the general managers supposed to control them. 'Computicians' are normally young, highly intelligent questioners of authority, marked by an ability to think of ways around problems, used to taking short cuts and often resentful of what they perceive as artificial barriers imposed by more senior employees who don't understand modern technology. Their motives for what others might consider to be deliberate abuse can be strange indeed:

A young programmer was dismissed from his job for playing cricket in the computer centre. He had considered appealing to the industrial tribunal for unfair dismissal on the grounds that he had only used a soft ball which was unlikely to damage computer equipment. In the end common sense prevailed and he began working for a new company but he found it difficult to forget Jane, a computer operator with his ex-employer.

His attempts at telephoning her, waiting for her to leave the premises and writing all failed to establish contact and the cause of true love seemed lost. Then, out of the blue, Jane phoned him at home, saying that she had a problem with the system and was unable to contact any of the current staff. She asked for his help. Tongue tied at the very thought of speaking to his goddess, he told her how to correct the faulty system, but forgot to ask her for a date.

Kicking himself for an opportunity missed he considered other ways of establishing contact. He thought 'although I can't phone her, I can gain access to her computer. Why don't I simply mess around with some of her programs and sooner or later she will phone me again.'

In a quiet moment the programmer dialled into his ex-employer's computer, the number had not changed nor had his old passwords and access codes been invalidated. He attempted to access Jane's program but the system reported an attempted security violation and disconnected his terminal.

Then he remembered the special lines of code which were called 'The Universal Key' and in a flash he gained free access to Jane's programs and listed them out. He made a number of unauthorized changes to the coding and logged off sure that the system would fail and, when it did, Jane would phone him. That evening he stayed at home waiting for the call for help, but it did not come.

A few days later he tried again and it became a regular practice for him to dial into his ex-employer's system and make unauthorized changes to online programs.

Unbeknown to him, the ex-employer was distraught and had called in both hardware and software experts to try to resolve the unexplained crashes. Eventually the programmer's efforts were detected and during an interview he quickly admitted responsibility.

'Look' he said, 'if I had really wanted to sabotage the system, I could have done much better than I did. This was the only way I could get Jane to telephone me. I am no crook, it was their fault they should have let me speak to her.'

The cost to the employer—in reconstructing damaged files and processing delays—was over US$50 000 but the programmer simply could not understand why his ex-managers were so upset and he referred to their concern as 'small minded'.

In many cases of computer abuse this disregard for other people's property coupled with a disrespect for senior management's lack of technical knowledge has been a factor. This is not difficult to understand. Until a few years ago, technical competence and seniority more or less were directly proportional. A new accountant joining the company would have a depth of skills less than the people meant to control him. It was also likely that the extent or width of his knowledge was exceeded by management and thus if he needed advice, his managers could assist. The surplus of management's technical knowledge was both a reason for respect and a means to control (see Figure 2.1).

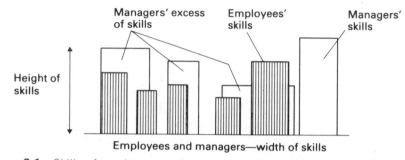

Figure 2.1   Skills of employees and managers: in the past

In computing the opposite position usually applies; junior members of data processing, fresh from college, have technical skills more current and at higher levels in specialist subjects than established managers. They often lack the width of knowledge or maturity to apply their skills in a broad commercial environment (Figure 2.2).

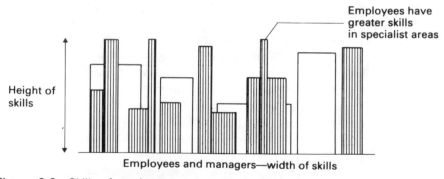

Figure 2.2   Skills of employees and managers: in the future

This produces two dangers: the first is that junior employees can 'look down' on their managers and challenge their authority generally. More importantly, managers are unable to check the work of their subordinates in these specialist areas; honesty and accuracy have to be taken on trust.

Management should recognize the difficulty of controlling specialist staff (this is referred to in detail in Chapter 9) and their individual aspirations.

ASPIRATIONS AND PRACTICAL THEORIES OF MOTIVATION

Emile Durkheim, whose work is summarized in Gwynn Nettler, op. cit., put forward the theory of anomie which is highly relevant to the management of technical and professional staff.

Durkheim reasoned that where a person's aspirations are balanced by opportunities available for achievement, a state of contentment exists. On the contrary, he suggested that crime breeds in the gaps between opportunities and aspirations. Where aspirations cannot be fulfilled through legitimate opportunities, unconventional methods will be sought.

Clearly, only a proportion of people to which the theory applies will be tempted to commit crime against their employer. Others may take up all-consuming interests outside the workplace, where aspirations and opportunities are in balance, while others may find a new employer.

There is a lesson here for managers of highly intelligent staff whose career paths may terminate at relatively lowly positions in an organization. It is possible, that the high turnover rate in many data processing departments arises not from some inherent failing among computer men that drives them to chop and change, but is more the responsibility of employers who often fail to consider technicians for higher managerial posts or refuse to guide them to realistic aspirations.

While recognizing that every employee will at some stage come to a halt it may be that data processing people reach their ceilings too quickly or fail to understand the reasons why their aspirations cannot be fulfilled. Controlling technicians calls for honest and fair personnel policies.

It is clearly very difficult to generalize about any aspect of human behaviour and the various theories on motivation are not totally compatible nor relevant to the technological era.

The cases handled by Network Security Management Limited have identified the following patterns of motivation in white collar and computer fraudsters:

— envious and resentful of the success of their organization and their colleagues, they believed that their contributions had not been recognized and that they were therefore entitled to benefits of their own choosing;
— high personal expectation of financial rewards, bordering on selfishness;
— disregard for the feelings of others often coupled with a disrespect of their colleagues, their managers and other people's property.

Frequently perpetrators were seen by management as hard workers but with limited chances of advancement: perpetrators often believed their managers were 'stupid', 'weak' and 'amoral'.

EXTERNAL PRESSURES AND MOTIVATION

Motivation, like all aspects of human behaviour, changes and is subject to external social forces. An honest person one day may be a criminal the next; having overstepped the line, he is likely to repeat his behaviour. The effects that social pressures have on personal motivation cannot be quantified although research suggests that rapid changes in the structure of society and in crime run on parallel lines.

It is not an objective of this book to enter the debate on the rights and wrongs of social change but it is necessary to try to determine what effects such changes might have on the protection of corporate assets and on crime rates generally. Professor Dahrendorf of the London School of Economics identifies a breakdown in the social rules, or social fragmentation. He argues that high rates of inflation, international terrorism and deterioration in international relationships are evidence of a war of all against all.

Certainly there are grounds for believing that society is becoming more expectant, more materialistic and its members more eager to put personal gain and greed before collective interests.

The changes in society may be, and usually are, argued from extreme positions. It could be said that all change is for the good; that fraud is merely a redistribution of wealth; that protests, riots and bombings are no more than expressions of freedom. The argument might be advanced that people should be allowed to do exactly as they please without constraint or obligation to others.

Another way of looking at changes is to believe that they could be worse. Or that, given time, they will naturally get better; that the ills in society will automatically correct themselves. This optimistic view is rarely borne out by events. In the absence of positive action, situations tend to determine rather than improve.

In a climate of rising expectations, unemployment and permissiveness, more and more people are able to justify dishonesty and to see crime as an answer to their problems.

Whatever the truth in these diverse arguments may be, there is a danger that companies get caught in the cross-fire. The pressures which employees, business contacts and competitors are subjected to as members of society may cloud their attitude to crime, their expectations and honesty at work.

The corporate position

Possibly the only conclusions that can be drawn from these opposing arguments is that companies, as well as individuals, should remain alert to pressures and actions that might prejudice their interests. This is the view taken in this book. The proprietors of a business have the right to protect it and the obligation to manage it in the most effective and honest way.

Essential theories on fraud

The difficulties that confront thieves should never be underestimated. They do not operate in an environment entirely of their own choosing; they are constrained; there are things that they can do with reasonable chance of success and others that spell their doom.

The interplay between an organized commercial society and criminal behaviour sets up wave patterns, creates practices, defines courses of action from which general deductions can be made.

There are four theories which assist in an understanding of fraud:

Differential of opportunity (see Figure 2.3)
Theory of concealment
Theory of deviation
Theory of minimal and general collusion

These and the practical lessons that can be drawn from them are discussed below.

Figure 2.3 Differential of opportunity

DIFFERENTIAL OF OPPORTUNITY THEORY

All people have the opportunity to commit fraud:

— against their employer
— against suppliers and customers of their employer
— against third parties
— against government departments

which is governed by three factors:

- the access the perpetrator has or can contrive to premises, accounts, assets and, increasingly more important, to computer systems
- skill in identifying the opportunity and exploiting it
- time in planning and committing the fraud

These will obviously differ from one person to another and from one time to another.

Of these factors, access is possibly the most important and will be achieved under one of two conditions (see Table 2.1).

Table 2.1 Access to fraud opportunities

Access level	Fraud achieved by
Authorized access granted through employment	Breach of trust
No access	Access contrived by skill or collusion

The majority of corporate frauds occur through breaches of trust by employees and others to whom access is granted. In this respect many companies are negligent in failing to check the backgrounds of potential employees. Statistics from the *Computer Fraud and Security Bulletin* show that more than 30 per cent of major losses could have been prevented if the victims had simply checked into the backgrounds of potential employees and persons to whom they advanced funds.

The largest number of frauds are committed by people using low skill levels: although they may not account for the largest losses (see Figure 2.4).

In the same way that social pressures may increase the justification for crime, changes in the complexity of commerce affect criminal opportunities. The speed and efficiency of international communications mean that a fraud

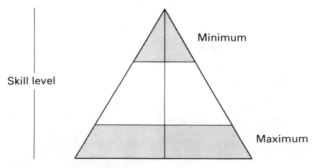

Figure 2.4 Minimum and maximum collusion

that has been successful in Washington can be copied the next day in London or Zurich. The last decade has seen the development of the international criminal—the forger, the securities or insurance thief and commodity fraudsman, all of whom have been able to manipulate boundaries and laws to their advantage.

THEORY OF CONCEALMENT

Reduced to its basic level, fraud is simple and its objective—to gain a dishonest advantage by reducing the victim's assets—patently clear. Confusion is deliberately introduced by the thief before, during or after an act of theft, to conceal it, or to assist in its commission.

This confusion does not alter the fact that a loss, or more precisely a debit to net worth, is created each time a *real* asset is stolen. It is a shortage that can be replaced only if the asset or its equivalent is returned. Concealment may divert attention from the shortage; disguise, confuse or delay its discovery; or prevent identification of the thief.

But in all frauds, the hard truth—the debit to net worth—remains and, in well ordered companies, should quickly come to notice.

The greed of thieves is such that, having arranged, or more usually been given, an opportunity for crime, they will exploit it, and having exploited it once, will strive to increase and extend it. Fraud follows an incremental, if sometimes erratic pattern limited only by the thief's greed, accidental or contrived opportunities, and his success in concealing previous losses. There are seldom small frauds, merely large ones given insufficient time to grow.

Whereas greed motivates criminal exploitation of opportunities, self-preservation is all-important when it comes to concealment. The thief will usually try to hide the loss and the evidence which indicates that he is responsible for it. He will strive to conceal the fraud in the best way available to him—to adopt what may be called the optimum concealment course.

Concealment of fraud is dealt with in detail in Chapter 5 but some discussion is necessary at this stage. When a theft of a real asset is not concealed, a discrepancy between a physical inventory and its related accounting record (an account/inventory discrepancy) will arise.

Thefts may not be concealed for one of two reasons:

1. Concealment is not necessary because:
   - the victim's records will not disclose the loss; or
   - although the loss may be uncovered, the records are insufficient to identify the thief (there is no audit trail); or
   - the victim condones the theft.

2. Concealment is not possible because the thief has no concealment course available to him.

Concealment is an essential ingredient of most systematic frauds. It can be defined as a manipulation of an accounting record or misrepresentation of a physical, personal or commercial reality intended to:

- hide, disguise or alter an account/inventory discrepancy before, during or after a theft act;
- disguise, confuse or delay the recognition of the thief's guilt (to avoid location of blame) or to establish a plausible excuse for dishonesty;
- enable the thief to obtain, or to continue to obtain, a dishonest advantage by deception

When an account/inventory discrepancy is concealed, the thief need not be too concerned about his responsibility being identified. As a general rule, discovery of a loss is the starting point for an investigation.

To conceal an account/inventory discrepancy in a closely controlled real account, the thief must either reduce the book value of the asset or inflate the value of the physical inventory so that they appear to agree. This apparent agreement can be achieved by:

- misrepresenting the value of the physical inventory
- manipulating the account

as shown in Figures 2.5 and 2.6. In Figure 2.5 the account/inventory discrepancy is concealed by misrepresenting the value of the asset, e.g., adding an empty box to the stock.

In Figure 2.6 the account/inventory discrepancy is concealed by the posting of a false credit to the real account. The result of making this false entry—the consequential debit—will be discussed later.

Throughout this book, misrepresentation refers to the falsification of a personal, physical or commercial reality before, during or after theft, either to assist its commission or to conceal a loss. Manipulation refers to the falsification of an accounting record. The falsification is documentary, before, during or after a theft and is intended to conceal a fraud or to assist in its commission.

The following examples show the fundamental difference between manipulation and misrepresentation.

> A cashier at a petrol station took £20.00 from the till and altered the records to show a fictitious sale to a credit customer whom the cashier knew was soon to go into liquidation, and whose debts would never be paid.

This is manipulation. The impact of the loss (discrepancy between the cash in the till and the account) is transferred to debtors and, if unchecked would be

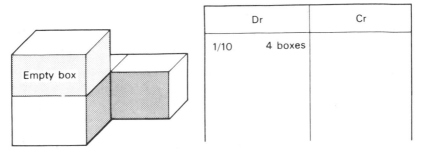

	Dr	Cr
	1/10 4 boxes	

Figure 2.5 Concealment of a loss by physical misrepresentation

written off to bad debts. The aim of the manipulation is to conceal the loss. If it comes to light the cashier's blame may be obvious.

This contrasts with the effects of misrepresentation:

> A forecourt employee at a service station did not record £100's sales on the cash register. At the end of the night shift he stole £100 and wound back the recording meters on the petrol pumps by gallons equivalent to a value of £100.

The debit to net worth is transferred from the sales/cash discrepancy to a stock shortage. The loss is disguised, and identification of the person responsible made more difficult.

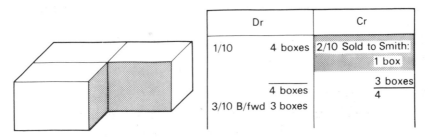

	Dr	Cr
	1/10 4 boxes	2/10 Sold to Smith: 1 box
	4 boxes	3 boxes
		4
	3/10 B/fwd 3 boxes	

Figure 2.6 Concealment of a loss by manipulation

THEORY OF DEVIATIONS

Fraud is a deviant behaviour; criminals are limited in the opportunities available to them and the ways in which they can conceal their guilt. These limitations and the pressures criminals apply to overcome them frequently result in plausible deviations from accepted behaviour and procedures.

Often deviations from accepted procedures are the first sign of fraud. Chapter 8 shows their significance in investigations.

THEORIES OF MINIMUM AND GENERAL COLLUSION

Collusion is a factor in many frauds and far more common than most honest people suspect. It usually occurs under two distinct circumstances:

- to provide the necessary opportunities, resources or skills to commit a fraud (minimum collusion)
- to share the benefits of low skill frauds among the maximum number of people (institutionalized fraud or general collusion)

which can be of major significance in conducting investigations (see Figure 2.4).

Minimum collusion

Opportunities for fraud are extended by collusion. Specialist skills might be required to commit a particular act or to obtain access to premises or records. Collusion of this type usually applies to high level manipulative frauds and will be limited to the smallest number of people absolutely necessary for the fraud to succeed.

Maximum or institutionalized collusion

In many industries and companies frauds involving low levels of skill are ingrained; books on institutionalized crime have been written on the bakery industry, by milkroundsmen and attendants at petrol filling stations. In these cases, collusion takes place to the greatest extent possible so that all employees are 'in the same boat' and united in a common criminal pursuit. This reduces the dangers of detection and the risks of one employee giving information on another.

These theories have important consequences in the investigation of fraud and are discussed further in Chapter 8.

Divisions in fraud

The first division in the apparently heterogeneous mass of frauds is based on the differential of opportunity theory and is made according to the source of the threat.

INTERNAL CRIMINALS

A criminal on the victim company's payroll will, during the course of his everyday employment, have access to certain company assets and to some company records. The amount of access to either assets or records will be determined by his function within the organization. A blue collar—or operation—worker will have regular access to physical inventories, measuring equipment and source documents or records of original entry, such as invoices, delivery notes or stock records.

An employee at the first level of supervision may have less routine access to physical inventories, but greater control over accounting records. At a higher level, managers may have few constraints placed upon their access to records, but limited control over inventories. An operations worker does not have the same opportunities to commit major manipulative frauds. But he may be able to conceal fraud by interfering with mechanical measuring equipment (weighbridges/flow meters/cash tills) which normally come under his control. He may also be able to alter, add, or remove source documents, or misrepresent the volume or value of physical stocks.

EXTERNAL CRIMINALS

This definition applies to all thieves who are not employed by the victim company.

A company's business contacts (suppliers, customers, agents) and their employees have access to certain assets and accounts. This depends on the extent and nature of their business relationships. It is usually significantly less than that granted to company employees, but more than for external criminals and opportunists.

Members of the public who are neither employees of the victim company, nor business contacts have virtually no access to accounts and assets. Opportunities may be limited almost entirely to unconcealed frauds.

Organized criminals are in a class by themselves and represent a risk which most companies—acting independently—are unable to counter. When organized criminal conspiracies include or involve company employees, opportunities and concealment courses are virtually unlimited and are often based on extortion.

The risk sources and their interrelationships are shown in Figure 2.7.

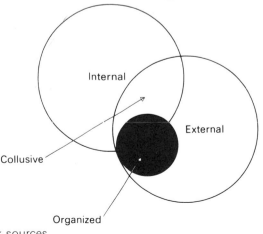

Figure 2.7   Risk sources

Subdivisions in fraud types

Although it is possible to make a division between one-time and systematic frauds, classification on this basis is not particularly meaningful. It is more practical to distinguish frauds according to their method of concealment.

Manipulative frauds can usually be regarded as 'on book' since they involve deliberate changes to accounting records although the impacts are often predictable and obvious.

The second type of concealment relies on misrepresentation of a physical, personal or commercial fact; they are usually 'off book' with limited impact on accounting records.

Thus, based on the method of concealment used and the position of perpetrator in relation to the victim, the 17 categories of fraud as depicted in Table 2.2 can be defined.

Table 2.2 Fraud categories classified according to the source of risk and concealment course

Source and type	Concealment course			
(Source: type)	Larcenous (no concealment) 1	Misrepresentative (falsified reality) 2	Manipulative (accounts) 3	Extorsive (force) 4
A Internal: management	A1	A2	A3	AB4
B Internal: operations	B1	B2	B3	
C External: business contact	C1	C2	C3	
D External: opportunist	D1	D2	D3	CDE4
E Collusive: organized	E1	E2	E3	

It is not necessary, at this stage, to examine the table in detail. It is included here to provide a framework for examples taken from recent press reports. The examples are arranged under the appropriate category headings and are prefaced by definitions. The characteristics of each category are also noted. All the definitions are made from the position of the victim of a fraud: internal or external, depending on the normal relationship of the thief.

CATEGORY A1 INTERNAL—MANAGEMENT—LARCENOUS

Definition Frauds committed by employees of the victim company who have general access to and control of accounting records but whose regular access to physical assets and measuring equipment is limited.

The frauds are simple and unconcealed because:

— the loss will not be recognized or, if recognized, suspicion will be directed away from the thief, or

- concealment is not possible because the thief does not have access to an available concealment course, or
- the victim condones the theft.

Examples

Salesman was his own rival

A salesman who ran a spare time design company 'in competition with his employers' lost his claim that he had been unfairly dismissed. The court heard that the salesman did his work in secrecy. It was clear that he put himself in a position where he might be tempted to consider his own interests instead of those of his employers.

This is a case of a person, in a managerial position, who was able—through a conflict of interest—to put his private business ahead of his employers. He obtained an intangible and unconventional 'asset'—paid company time.

Men talk their way into court

A young night auditor with a motor hotel decided to use his employer's telex and telephones to contact his family and friends in New Zealand. The man clocked up calls while working at the hotel. He admitted dishonestly using a total of £341.64 worth of electricity and was fined a total of £80 with £179.17 compensation and £20 towards legal aid.

In this case, concealment was not necessary because the telephone account was not closely controlled.

Vanished films used to make pirate copies

Detectives who began an investigation into the disappearance of two films uncovered a nationwide pirating swindle.

The swindle involved the theft of films and copying them for redistribution. This happened without the knowledge of the film companies.

Five men pleaded guilty to conspiring to defraud major film companies by the unlawful copying and distribution of films and the breaking of copyright. One of the accused admitted borrowing films over a long period and passing them to another man who copied them.

The case involved an unlisted asset—unauthorized copies. The removal of the conventional asset—the film—was temporary. The permanent theft of the data on the film was intangible and its loss unnoticed. Concealment was unnecessary.

Characteristics of frauds in category A1

- These frauds consist either of petty theft of tangible assets, to which the thief has normal access but no direct responsibility or accountability, or substantial theft of intangible or unrecorded assets, whose loss can escape without notice.
- Such frauds are usually small in any well-ordered company, but their prevention is important since the thief can readily graduate to larger frauds having once overstepped the line between honesty and dishonesty.
- The thefts may escalate into manipulative frauds if the thief finds a concealment course.
- The thief is exposed to detection during the theft act or while the stolen goods remain in his possession. There is seldom any audit trail after the event.
- The frauds usually result in a daily erosion of profit rather than a high impact or spectacular loss.
- They differ from category B1 (operations—larcenous frauds) only in the type of assets at risk.

Other frauds in category A1

- conflicts of interests (theft of company time)
- misuse and theft of office supplies and equipment
- misuse of computer time
- misuse of secretarial services

CATEGORY A2   INTERNAL—MANAGEMENT—MISREPRESENTATIVE

Definition   Frauds committed by employees of the victim company who have general access to and control of accounting records but whose regular access to physical assets and measuring equipment is limited.

The frauds involve misrepresentation of a physical, personal or commercial reality before, during or after a larcenous theft, to assist in or to conceal its commission. Without concealment the loss and the guilt of the thief may be obvious.

Examples

Fruit machine man hits jackpot

The sales manager of a company letting out gaming machines on hire to public houses, cafés and clubs hit on a scheme to defraud his employer, a court was told.

It was alleged that the man deliberately manipulated the cash meters on certain machines, under-recorded the takings, and split the profit with dishonest operators.

Essentially a misrepresentation of a physical reality: the reading and integrity of the cash meter.

Bank clerks ran own firm in £10 000 swindle

Two bank clerks formed their own company and invested £358 000 in bonds for customers of a branch of Bank X where they worked. They opened a bank account—with Bank Y—for their own company and accumulated in that account over £10 000 commission on the sale of bonds, that should have been payable to Bank X, their employer.

In a six-month period, 96 transactions were made with customers of Bank X. The customers would write out cheques payable to the bond company thinking they were conducting business through Bank X. The clerks paid these cheques into their own account. They would then send one of their cheques to the bond company—less 3 per cent handling commission—which was retained in their account.

Misrepresentation of a commercial reality concealed Bank X's loss of £10 000. The investors did not lose.

Characteristics of frauds in category A2

- Usually the object of the misrepresentation is to assist in the commission of the fraud (and is contiguous with the theft act) or is designed to point suspicion away from the thief.
- The loss (account/inventory discrepancy) usually remains unconcealed or the theft of intangible assets escapes attention.
- The frauds may be long or short term.
- Normally they involve the misrepresentation of a physical or commercial reality.
- The misrepresentation is invariably restricted to an event to which the thief is a party. These events are substantially different from those involving operations employees (category B2).
- The thief is most exposed at the time the misrepresentation is made. He is often able to provide a plausible excuse for possession of stolen goods.

CATEGORY A3   INTERNAL—MANAGEMENT—MANIPULATIVE

Definition   Frauds committed by employees of the victim company who have general access to and control of accounting records but whose regular access to physical assets and measuring equipment is limited.

The frauds involve manipulation of accounting records before, during or after a larcenous or misrepresentative theft, to assist in or to conceal its commission. Without concealment the loss and the guilt of the thief may be obvious.

Examples

Manager accused of £4000 fraud

The branch manager of X Limited—a retail shop multiple—was accused of manipulating cash receipts and bank records. It was a rob Peter to pay Paul fraud, said the judge.

Prosecuting counsel said that the fraud began when the manager tried to cover genuine cash shortages but events soon got out of hand and he panicked. He delayed the submission of daily sales returns to his head office and was able to use cash received on subsequent days to cover earlier shortages.

The fraud came to light when the manager disappeared and auditors were called in.

Table 2.3 Example of a 'lapping' fraud

	Takings		Adjustments			Banked
Date	Total amt received (£)	Stolen in the day (£)	Amt removed to make up earlier shortages (£)	Balance of cash left over (£)	Date	Amount (£)
Dec.					Dec.	
1	700	—	—	—	1	700
2	850	—	—	—	2	850
5	1000	300	—	700	—	nil
6	520	—	300	220	6	1000
7	950	200	300	450	7	520
8	1200	400	500	300	8	950
9	520	100		420	—	—
12	800	100	480	220	12	1200
13	1000	300	300	400	13	520
14	1700	500	400	800	14	800
15	1000	200	200	600	15	1000
16	1700	850	—	850	—	—
19	400	100	250	50	19	1700
20	900	900	—	—	—	—
	3950					
	50					
	4000					

This is a typical example of a 'lapping' or 'teaming and lading' fraud. Such frauds are generally short term but can involve large sums of money. The thief must be able to gain access to cash or cash equivalents and to accounting records.

In the case reported, sales and banking were as shown in Table 2.3. The shortages on previous days are made up with current cash. For example, the theft of £300 on 5 December is made up by taking an equivalent amount from cash received on 6 December; leaving that day's bankings short.

Sometimes the cash received is not sufficient to make up a shortage. On 8 December, allowing for thefts and previous deficiencies, only £300 of £1200 was left. Takings on 9 December of £520 less £100 stolen (i.e., £420) was held back until the banking for 8 December could be made good with cash received on 12 December (£480).

Lapping can be achieved without holding back cash or bankings and can be far more complex than the example quoted. For example, when the thief has access to cash and to the sales ledger he is able to conceal cash shortages by making fictitious postings to customers' accounts (i.e., debtors). The shortage in cash (asset) versus banking records (accounts) is concealed as a fictitious build-up in debtors' balances, as Table 2.4 shows.

When the thief disappears the victim is left with uncollectable balances in his debtors' accounts.

Table 2.4 Impact of lapping frauds on debtors' balances

Takings			Falsely posted to trade debtors (£)	Banked	
Date	Amt (£)	Stolen (£)		Date	Amt (£)
Dec.					
5	1000	300	300	5	700
6	520		—	6	520
7	950	200	200	7	750
8	1200	400	400	8	800

Jail for the big spender

A £5500 a year sales manager who stole more than £25 000 from his employers over nine months spent it on gambling and nightclub hostesses. The man pleaded guilty to nine charges of stealing a total of £8926 from his employer and he asked for 32 similar offences, involving £16 942, to be taken into consideration. The trial judge said that the man was living in a Walter Mitty world.

Prosecuting counsel said that the man joined his employers a month after finishing a three-year sentence for embezzling money from a previous employer. The cash he received was between £22 000 and £24 000 but the total loss to the company was £41 900 because Mr X sold electrical parts to a customer at below price. The money he received was not paid to the company.

The fraud was concealed by a manipulation. Sales invoices—for sales paid for in cash—were destroyed. Further manipulation of accounts was unnecessary, although the shortage in stock should have become obvious.

Note (a) that the sales manager had regular access to all copies of the sales invoices and (b) that he had been previously convicted of fraud.

Characteristics of frauds in category A3

- This category covers the most prevalent and costly management frauds.
- The frauds can be long or short term.
- Manipulation is normally intended to conceal the loss (when the thief has control over the asset prior to the theft) or to assist in and prepare the way for a larcenous fraud (when the asset is beyond his domain). Avoidance of blame, should a loss come to light, is normally a secondary and sometimes unobtainable objective.
- Manipulation may be positive (when a false record or fictitious entry is made) or negative (where an entry or record is omitted or destroyed).
- Negative manipulations rarely conceal a shortage but may disguise or confuse the responsibility for it. (See Chapter 5 for definition of negative manipulations.)
- The manipulated records are those to which the thief has access. The difference in the type of record available for manipulation draws the dividing line between this category and category B3 (operations—manipulative).
- The manipulation may involve suppressed sales or liabilities or inflated expenses or assets.
- The impact of a manipulation is often obvious in non-financial, managerial or statistical records, to which the thief has no access.
- The concealment itself exposes the thief to detection. He is also at risk when he attempts to convert stolen goods into cash.
- Concealment frauds leave a permanent audit trail.

Other frauds in category A3

- embezzlements
- computer frauds involving input, program patches, amendments to master files and output

- expense fiddles
- false purchases
- false performance reports (either internal or external to the company) to increase a share in profits or bonus or to hide inferior results.

CATEGORY B1   INTERNAL—OPERATIONS—LARCENOUS

Definition   Frauds committed by employees of the victim company who have general access to and control of physical assets and measuring equipment but whose access to accounting records is limited.

The frauds are simple and unconcealed because:

(a) the loss will not be recognized or, if recognized, suspicion will be directed away from the thief, or
(b) concealment is not possible because the thief does not have access to an available concealment course, or
(c) the victim condones the theft.

Examples

An iron nick (ironic) case

Earl F. Lorence, director of security for the Metropolitan Tobacco Co., New York, reported an interesting case in his chapter for the book *Internal Theft and Investigation Control.**

'Some years ago the head of a giant plant engaged in Government contract work wanted a publicity picture of thousands of employees coming out of the main gates at quitting time. To set the scene the gates were locked and camera men were stationed at the watchman's tower. The workmen, however, did not know what was planned. The rumour was that the FBI was going to search them all for stolen parts and tools.

When the picture was snapped, the gates were opened and the workmen left for home. On the floor where they had been standing were over 4000 items of tools, parts, scrap, soap, towels and even a 15-pound sledge-hammer—all left behind by a few thousand good, honest, hard working people who had intended to take these articles without permission.'

This is by no means an uncommon example. It illustrates the scale of dishonesty.

Magpie postman stole parcels worth £17 000

A postman described as being like a magpie stealing bright shiny objects, took 100 postal packets a week for a year and he had property valued at

---

* Security World Publishing Co., California.

£17 000 hoarded in his home when he was arrested. The man, who was said to have stolen more property than any other postman in the history of the Post Office, was jailed for five years.

In a statement the man had said, 'I don't know why I did it. It was just a habit.'

This case is typical of many opportunist thefts where the motive is not primarily financial necessity.

Characteristics of frauds in category B1

- Such frauds generally consist of the theft of tangible assets, such as tools and stock, to which the thief has normal access but no direct responsibility or accountability.
- Although they are usually small, their prevention is important to a company since a thief can readily graduate to larger frauds having once overstepped the line between honesty and dishonesty.
- The thefts may escalate into manipulative frauds if the thief finds a concealment course.
- The thief is exposed to detection during the theft act or while stolen goods remain in his possession. There is seldom any audit trail after the event.
- The frauds usually result in a daily erosion of profit rather than in a high impact or spectacular loss.
- They are different from frauds in category A1 only in the type of goods at risk.
- The theft act may take place on or off company premises.

Other frauds in category B1

- use of company machines, equipment or time to perform private or conflicting work
- theft of rools, raw materials and working stocks

CATEGORY B2 INTERNAL—OPERATIONS—MISREPRESENTATIVE

Definition Frauds committed by employees of the victim company who have general access to and control of physical assets and measuring equipment but whose access to accounting records is limited.

The frauds involve misrepresentation of a physical, personal or commercial reality before, during or after a larcenous theft, to assist in or to conceal its commission. Without concealment the loss and the guilt of the thief may be obvious.

Examples

Eight jailed in fuel fraud conspiracy

Eight men who admitted charges of conspiring to cheat and defraud the Customs and Excise of about £200 000 duty on a million gallons of diesel oil were sentenced at the Crown Court. The amounts mentioned in the charges were estimates and it was quite impossible to say exactly how much money and oil had been involved.

Two loaders at the installation devised ways of stopping a red marking dye being injected into the oil as it was being loaded into the tankers. The marker dye was an indicator that duty had not been paid.

The great fuel swindle ended abruptly when 120 customs officers and 40 regional crime squad police officers made simultaneous raids on 60 garages, coach operators, taxi firms and haulage contractors.

The fraud involved a (physical) misrepresentation: the integrity of the dye injection equipment.

Ford fiddle men share £10 000 in scrap plot

Four men at Fords Dagenham factory shared £600/£700 per week for 'swinging the bridge'—the name given to four swindles they operated for two years.

Swindle number 1 involved a swinging weighbridge. Advantage was taken of a defect to register a heavier weight when scrap was delivered.

Swindle number 2 involved making duplicate tickets when heavy loads arrived and using the second ticket for lorries with lighter loads.

Swindle number 3 was the enhanced weight fiddle. A screw on the weighbridge was manipulated to give a heavier reading.

Swindle number 4 was a double weight fiddle. Drivers went on to the weighbridge then drove around without tipping and returned to be weighed again. Dealers in on the fiddle were credited and paid for delivering heavier loads; 21 men were originally accused in the plot. Lorry drivers in on the fiddle would drive up to the office and, while the clerk was dealing with documents, another member of the weighbridge staff would collect an envelope containing money from the driver.

This is typical of frauds involving physical misrepresentations (i.e., falsifying the accuracy of control hardware and machinery).

£¼ million haul by label switch parcel gang

Members of a gang which stole at least £250 000 worth of goods by re-addressing parcels at British Rail and British Road Services depots were jailed for between 15 and 30 months at the Old Bailey.

It was alleged that the two ringleaders, who worked at London depots, kept stocks of labels on which they had printed an address used as a pick up point, said the prosecuting counsel. When consignments that seemed valuable arrived at the depots the labels were stuck over the genuine names and addresses. The parcels were then left to take their normal course in the delivery system. British Rail and British Road Services were used to deliver the goods to premises rented by the gang leaders under false names. Dishonest handlers collected the goods—which included ladies' knickers, trousers, dictation machines, typewriters and stereo equipment—and sold them as bargains in pubs and on market stalls.

Both the ringleaders had used aliases and bogus references to get the jobs with British Rail and British Road Services. Transport police estimate the value of the goods stolen in two years to be at least £250 000. That is to say nothing of the number of consignors who no longer have confidence in the services and are not prepared to use them for fear of losing their goods.

The detective investigating the case said, 'Had it continued for another six months, I doubt whether we could have discovered it at all, because the system would have been perfected by then. The labels used were extremely good and very convincing.'

Although documents (falsely addressed labels) were used, the fraud was achieved by misrepresentation (part personal, part physical) of the true identity of the recipients.

Characteristics of frauds in category B2

- The most prevalent and costly operations frauds fall in this category.
- The frauds may be long term and often involve collusion.
- Usually the misrepresentation involves a physical reality and is intended to disguise a loss or to achieve a theft. Such misrepresentations rarely conceal a loss.
- The misrepresentation is invariably restricted to a reality over which the thief has control. These realities are fundamentally different from those involving management employees (A2).
- The thief is most exposed at the time the misrepresentation is made. He is often able to provide a plausible explanation for the possession of stolen goods.

Other frauds in category B2

- false accident claims (compensation or insurance)
- falsification of clocking-in cards (time clocks) and other control machinery
- stock/inventory misrepresentations

CATEGORY B3   INTERNAL—OPERATIONS—MANIPULATIVE

Definition   Fraud committed by employees of the victim company who have general access to and control of physical assets and measuring equipment but whose access to accounting records is limited.

The frauds involve manipulation of accounting records before, during or after a larcenous or misrepresentative theft, to assist in or to conceal its commission. Without concealment the loss and the guilt of the thief may be obvious.

Example

Rail dining car staff jailed for 'mean' fraud

A number of British Rail employees were sentenced to imprisonment and fined at the Old Bailey. The men were employed as waiters and dining car staff by British Rail and were responsible for serving meals and collecting fees from passengers. Prosecuting counsel said the fraud was done with the aid of a bogus rubber stamp almost identical to the official one used by British Rail for stamping receipts of money from dining car services. At the end of each journey cash should have been handed in at the station. Instead it was pocketed by members in the swindle who accounted for it using forged receipts stamped with the fake stamp.

Frauds in this category are distinguishable from those falling in A3 by one thing only: thieves employed in management positions have greater access to accounting records and may have a wider choice of manipulation courses than operations thieves. In the example, the operations employees had regular access only to sales vouchers. Bearing this fact in mind, they had a limited choice of concealment courses. They could:

(a) *Reduce the value of sales income by*—
    (i) making sales to customers without issuing sales vouchers
    (ii) reducing the value on the copy sales vouchers handed in
    (iii) under-recording the total of the individual sales vouchers by falsifying an adding machine tape (see page 112)
    (iv) using unofficial sales vouchers or out of series vouchers
    (v) recording thefts as cash shortages

(b) *Inflate amounts of cash accounted for by*—
    (i) falsifying the cashier's receipt (this was the chosen course)
    (ii) reusing old receipts

The method chosen by the gang, (b)(i) above, was, although they did not realize it, short term, since the loss would eventually become obvious.

Although the men had countless opportunities to steal cash, their concealment courses were all unsatisfactory. They were foolish to try!

Characteristics of frauds in category B3
- The frauds can be long or short term.
- Manipulation is normally intended to hide or confuse a loss (when the thief has control over the asset prior to the theft) or to assist in and to prepare the way for a larcenous or misrepresentative fraud, when the asset is beyond the thief's domain. Concealment of the thief's guilt is often a secondary consideration.
- Manipulation is normally restricted to source documents over which the thief had ready control and is more often achieved by negative rather than positive manipulation.
- Manipulation normally involves a suppression of sales income.
- The impact of manipulation is often obvious in higher levels of financial accounts or management and statistical records—over which the thief has no control.
- The thief is most exposed to detection in the concealment phase (where he has no or little excuse). He is also at risk when he attempts to convert stolen goods into cash.
- Concealment frauds leave a permanent audit trail.

Other frauds in category B3
- payroll padding
- false cash purchases
- false expense claims

CATEGORY AB4   INTERNAL—MANAGEMENT OR OPERATIONS—EXTORSIVE
Definition   Frauds committed by employees of the victim company and involving force, coercion or blackmail. They may or may not be concealed.

Examples

Mr Ali's overtime cost him £800 in 13 years of tips to foreman

A steelworker was counting the cost of working overtime. In 13 years he reckons he has handed over to his foreman nearly £800 for the privilege of working extra hours.

At the Crown Court the foreman was jailed for three years after pleading guilty to charges of corruption going back as far as 1958. The foreman's levy on Mr Ali and other workers varied between £2 and £20 a time.

Social workers and union officials expressed their concern about what they are convinced is the widespread accepted practice of foremen, who have sole control of allocating overtime, demanding a levy from immigrants. In many cases the immigrants, who are often sending money abroad, are reluctant to report the cases because they might lose not only the extra cash but their jobs as well. In other instances the immigrants have only a slim grasp of English and accept the practice as normal.

Mr Ali joined the company in 1958 and was told almost immediately by his fellow immigrants that to work overtime a fee was due to the foreman. At the time, he said, he spoke no English and simply paid up. Later he realized the payments were totally illegal. He claimed he went to the management and police to complain but was unable to persuade fellow workers to back him. However, he persuaded two of them to come forward and substantiate his evidence. His persistence forced the police to act and two marked £1 notes handed over to the foreman by Mr Ali produced the necessary evidence.

There was now damaging documentation of extortion. According to the management there was no hint of what had been going on until last June. A spokesman said that about three months before the charges were made a complaint was put forward.

Sabotage check at car firm

Suspected sabotage at a car plant in Liverpool was investigated by the police. Pieces of metal and steel tubing were found lodged in the machinery of an assembly line during the night shift and brought the line to a halt nine times.

A spokesman for the company said that shop stewards and convenors were cooperating with police in the investigation.

This case, viewed against the background of militancy and disruption in the car industry, illustrates how extortion could result in serious financial loss.

Suspended sentences for pickets

Five 'flying pickets' who swarmed across the building sites in Shropshire during the 1972 building dispute, terrifying workmen and residents, received suspended prison sentences at Shrewsbury court.

Prosecuting counsel said the pickets had damaged property and machinery and had intimidated and terrified building workers and residents.

The people involved in this case were possibly motivated by political or financial gain which, through extortion, they proposed to achieve. People who wished to continue working were forced to stop.

Characteristics of frauds in category AB4

- The application of force or blackmail overcomes the normal constraints on theft opportunities and concealment courses.
- Threats—from internal sources—are *normally* directed towards the proprietors of the victim company:
  - the loss is overt and involves a confrontation/dilemma;
  - the act may or may not constitute a criminal offence.
- When a threat is directed against another company employee or a third party:
  - the loss will be short term unless the victim fails to call for assistance and has a concealment course available to him;
  - the threat may relate to an event or area over which the thief has routine control;
  - the impact of the fraud may be obvious in behavioural patterns or business trends.
- In all cases the thief is exposed to risk of detection if the subject of extortion calls for assitance before the fraud comes to a natural end.

CATEGORY C1   EXTERNAL—BUSINESS CONTACTS—LARCENOUS

Definition   Frauds committed by suppliers, customers, agents, contractors and all employees of such enterprises who through a commercial relationship with the victim company have limited access to premises, assets or accounts.

The frauds are simple and unconcealed because:

(a) the loss will not be recognized or, if recognized, suspicion will be directed away from the thief, or
(b) concealment is not possible because the thief does not have access to an available concealment course, or
(c) the victim condones the theft.

Examples

Shoplift gang's £250 000 M and S fiddle

Shoplifter's Unlimited, a bizarre 'company' trading in crime went into compulsory liquidation last night. For nine 'directors and staff' it meant the crash of an organization which had a turnover estimated at up to £250 000.

The gang traded for more than a year on Marks and Spencer's proud boast 'We will always exchange an article or give a cash refund'. Their system was simple. The gang shoplifted an item then took it back and demanded a refund, posing as bona fide customers.

This is an interesting example of conversion of stolen goods into cash, using the victim's own system against him.

Business contact was established when refunds were claimed on goods that had been previously stolen.

A real let down

Motorway police stopped to examine an abandoned butcher's van—with two flat tyres—and discovered more than they had bargained for. In the back they found two sheep's carcases, half a cow, and two dozen pigs' feet; all of which should have been delivered to X Limited, a wholesale meat provisions company.

The driver was traced and admitted short delivering the meat. He said his van had broken down *en route* to a private customer who had agreed to buy all 'extras' off him, for cash.

The driver was fined £200 and ordered to pay costs. In mitigation the man's boss said that he had been an excellent employee who had been tempted into crime by customers' laxity in checking their orders. He said the whole affair was a big let down.

The short delivery of commercial goods is a prevalent type of fraud involving operations workers (drivers) employed by business contacts. The victim is the company who has to pay for the short delivered goods.

The frauds may be achieved by or concealed through the misrepresentation of a physical reality; either by inflating the goods on board the vehicle prior to delivery or by concealing goods left on board after delivery (category C2).

They may also involve collusion with people working for the victim.

Characteristics of frauds in category C1

- These frauds consist mainly of petty theft of tangible assets in which the thief—as a result of his normal business relationship with the victim—has access. Accountability may be vague.
- The thefts may escalate into misrepresentative or **manipulative** frauds if the thief finds a suitable concealment course.
- The thefts may be outside the victim's premises (on the way to or from).
- The thief is exposed to detection during the theft act or conversion, or while the stolen goods remain in his possession.
- When a loss comes to light, the guilt of the thief is often obvious.
- C1 frauds differ from category A1 and B1 frauds only in the source of risk and in the nature of normal fraud opportunities.

CATEGORY C2 EXTERNAL—BUSINESS CONTACTS—MISREPRESENTATIVE

Defintion Frauds committed by suppliers, customers, agents, contractors and all employees of such enterprises who through commercial relationship with the victim company have limited access to premises, assets or accounts.

The frauds involve misrepresentation of a physical, personal or commercial reality before, during or after a larcenous theft, to assist in or to conceal its commission. Without concealment the loss and the guilt of the thief may be obvious.

Examples

Orange grove investors 'ended up with jungle'

Investors who paid out £130 000 for fertile orange groves in British Honduras—said to have been producing rich crops—were sold 'good old-fashioned jungle', it was said at the Old Bailey yesterday. The three men who sold the land with the aid of an attractively produced brochure did not have the title to sell it anyway, said prosecuting counsel.

This case involved misrepresentation of a physical/commercial reality.

£7.5 million farm fraud swindles

Unscrupulous businessmen have swindled the EEC Community Farm Fund out of millions, the Director General of the Market's Financial Control Department told journalists.

One recurrent form of fraud was carried out with barges loaded with feeding stuffs and grain sailing round Europe's mainland waterways without ever unloading their cargoes.

The cargo was declared as for export outside the Community. Before sailing from Antwerp, for instance, the traffickers would collect one export subsidy.

Once arrived in Rotterdam or Amsterdam they would repeat the export formalities and cash in a second time on the subsidy.

The trick would be re-enacted in Denmark and perhaps a couple of times more within the Community.

Viewed from the position of the EEC, the victim, the fraud falls into category C2: falsification of a commercial reality.

Cheque card Charlie

Scotland Yard has urged the police all over the country to catch a cheque book thief who has defrauded the big four banks of £80 000 in a few months. If the thief, nicknamed 'cheque card Charlie', is not found he will become a millionaire in about five years. His activities have caused the banks to think again about their cheque card system.

Charlie's technique is to steal a cheque book and cheque card which authorizes withdrawals of up to £50 with a guarantee of payment by the issuing bank. Each cheque book with 30 cheques is then cashed quickly for £900. He is said to be a brilliant copier of handwriting and signs the cheques with a copy of the signature on the cheque card.

The police think that Charlie may be receiving only about half of the total sum of the fraud. He may be buying some of the cheque books from thieves rather than stealing them all himself.

Although they involve forgery (misrepresentation of a physical reality), at the heart of such frauds is a personal misrepresentation.

A cutting tale

Company X sold its products throughout Europe at varying prices, depending upon market competition, income levels and other marketing factors. Prices in Sweden, for example, of certain brands of razor blades were less than one-third of the UK domestic price and less than one-sixth of the price for the same article in the US.

Company Y purchased X's products in Sweden and shipped them to the US, therefore undercutting company X's parent company, causing loss of market stability and profit.

When Company X's Swedish agent, at the request of the parent company, refused to supply Company Y, Company Y purchased further supplies through an intermediary, stating that the products were destined for sale in Australia, where X was not represented.

This is not necessarily a criminal offence; it is a misrepresentation of a commercial reality.

£130 000 fraud on insurance company

A report is being sent to the Director of Public Prosecutions about 20 fraudulent claims totalling £130 000 on the Dominion Insurance Co.; this fraud was first detected at the company's Swindon branch office.

The report follows nine months of investigations in the Plymouth area by Devon and Cornwall's fraud squad. The claims related to cars, caravans and other property reported lost or damaged in storms in the West Country last year. Investigations have also been made in Hampshire, Dorset and Wiltshire.

Some of the vehicles claimed for never existed, police say. They suspect a 'wheel conspiracy', with one man at the hub.

This involved misrepresentation of a physical reality: the existence of crashed cars.

Credit card swindler's 300 names

Using 1000 credit cards which he obtained in fictitious names, a New Jersey man raised loans of £330 000 which he squandered on the stock market.

Investigators say John L. Spillane, 31, had 300 different identities over a five-year period. So complex was his multifaceted life that Spillane could not remember all his transactions.

Investigators say that Spillane first set up several fraudulent businesses, secured post office boxes for their mailing addresses and ordered telephones in the names of various companies.

He then persuaded five banks in New Jersey to give the 'businesses' loans.

This was a personal and commercial misrepresentation.

Characteristics of frauds in category C2
- This category includes several of the most prevalent and costly frauds.
- They usually involve misrepresentation of a commercial or personal reality to assist in a larcenous fraud.
- The business relationsip is often established with fraud as the main objective, misrepresentation of a personal or commercial reality is often contiguous with the opening of the business relationship.
- The loss (account/inventory discrepancy) usually remains unconcealed.
- The aim of concealment is the avoidance of blame or the creation of a plausible excuse.
- The frauds are essentially short term (in relation to one victim); victims may be changed to extend the fraud.
- The misrepresentation is in an area over which the thief has control or an event to which he is a party.
- The thief is most exposed in the act of theft or at the time the misrepresentation is made. The chance of his identification or detection after the event is less likely.

Other frauds in category C2

Description	Reality falsified
– long firm (credit) frauds	commercial
– credit card frauds	personal and commercial
– cheque frauds	personal and/or commercial
– insurance frauds	personal, physical or commercial
– busts, scams and con games	personal or commercial
– pyramid frauds ⎫ – franchise frauds ⎭	commercial
– property/investment frauds	commercial, personal or physical
– short delivery frauds	physical

CATEGORY C3 EXTERNAL—BUSINESS CONTACTS—MANIPULATIVE

Definition Frauds committed by suppliers, customers, agents, contractors and all employees of such enterprises, who through a commercial relationship with the victim company have limited access to premises, assets or accounts.

The frauds involve manipulation of accounting records before, during or after a larcenous or misrepresentative theft, to assist in or to conceal its commission. Without concealment the loss and the guilt of the thief may be obvious.

Examples

Washington MICR deposit slip fraud

A depositor exchanged blank deposit slips on the counter in the bank with his own MICR coded slips. He accumulated $250 000 in four days from other people's deposits (which were credited to his account). He then withdrew $100 000 dollars, disappeared and has never been caught.

In this case the manipulation was an essential part of, and preceded, the theft act. The fraud was possible because the victim company's (i.e., the bank's) accounts were available to the thief.

18 sent to jail for Navy '5 per cent drop' catering fraud

A lieutenant in the Royal Navy whose greed ended one of the biggest naval frauds in history—estimated to have involved more than £250 000—was jailed for 4 years. Prison terms totalling 25 years and 9 months were imposed on 18 in all—6 Navy officers, 8 chief petty officers and 4 civilian suppliers. Another 63 people, including Navy personnel, and two companies were fined a total of £23 625, making a total of 81 sentenced. The judge said the case had disclosed the horrifying picture of blatant and downright fraud.

The frauds were so widespread and had gone on for so long that it had been impossible to estimate accurately the total involved, although from the evidence it was clear that they had covered a period of nine years.

The frauds involved submitting false invoices for food and general goods supplied to ship and shore establishments after catering officers and civilian firms collaborated together to make extra money. The proceeds were divided 75 per cent to catering officers and 25 per cent to civilian suppliers. It brought the officers an additional £2000 per year. They passed over varying sums to catering branch chief petty officers involved in the fiddle.

The fraud came to light when a newly appointed catering officer was appalled at the size of amounts on invoices. He told superior officers and the police were informed.

The background to the matter, it has been said, was that for as long as anyone can remember it had been general, though not universal, practice in the Royal Navy for civilian suppliers to pay catering officers a commission of 5 per cent on goods sold.

Concealment was achieved by false/inflated supplier invoices aided by a misrepresentation of a physical reality (quantity and quality of stock).

Characteristics of frauds in category C3

- Manipulation is usually confined to those documents and accounts that pass between the victim and the thief as a result of their business relationship.
- The frauds are usually long term.
- The manipulation is mainly used to create the opportunity for a larcenous fraud.
- The symptoms of the fraud are often obvious in non-financial, management or statistical records.
- If the loss is discovered, the thief has only a slight chance of avoiding blame; his escape usually relies on false identification or a plausible excuse.
- The thief is most exposed to detection in the concealment phase, provided he can be properly identified and traced.

Other frauds in category C3

- false investment data:
  - profit manipulations prior to takeovers
  - inflation of results to increase bonus payments/dividend claims
  - suppression of reserves or provisions to manipulate profit results prior to loan applications, takeovers or investments
- false credit and hire-purchase applications

CATEGORY D1   EXTERNAL—OPPORTUNIST—LARCENOUS

Definition   Opportunist frauds committed by members of the public and the business community—including competitors—who are neither employees nor business contacts of the victim company and who have no regular access to its assets or accounts.

The frauds are simple and unconcealed because:

(a) the loss will not be recognized or, if recognized, the thief cannot be identified, or
(b) concealment is not possible because the thief does not have access to an available concealment course, or
(c) the victim condones the theft.

Example
Pop record pirates hit industry

Record pirates who make long-playing discs from illicit recordings of live pop concerts are costing the record industry millions of pounds a year, a record company spokesman said.

The industry is seriously worried by these bootleg manufacturers who pirate the work of famous recording artists and pay nothing to either song writers or artists. A spokesman for one of the major record companies explained that bootleg records are cut at private pressing plants—the kind of firms which make recordings for private families to send to relatives abroad.

Recently a number of bootleg records which are suspected of having been made on the Continent have appeared in British shops.

Fraud by a business competitor, involving an intangible asset—copyright. Viewed from the buyer's position such frauds would be of the 'passing-off' type and would, for him, have the characteristics of a fraud in category C2 (business contact—misrepresentative).

Characteristics of frauds in category D1
- The opportunity to steal tangible assets has to be created by the thief, either by trespass or by altering his status to that of a business contact.
- Such frauds consist mainly of petty or once-off, high-impact theft of tangible assets, for which no concealment course is available. They may also involve intangible assets where concealment is not necessary.
- Category D1 frauds differ from categories A1, B1 and C1 in the nature and type of opportunities.
- After successful commission of the larceny, the thief is at little risk of identification or apprehension; his anonymity and lack of company connection act in his favour.
- The thief is exposed to detection during the time he is on the victim's premises, while engaged in the theft and while stolen goods remain in his possession. There is seldom any audit trail after the event.

Other frauds in category D1
- robbery
- burglary
- hold-ups
- walk-in office/factory thefts

CATEGORY D2 EXTERNAL—OPPORTUNIST—MISREPRESENTATIVE

Definition Opportunist frauds committed by members of the public and business community—including competitors—who are neither employees nor business contacts of the victim company and who have no regular access to its assets or accounts.

The frauds involve misrepresentation of a physical, personal or commercial reality before, during or after a larcenous theft, to assist in or to conceal its commission.

Examples

Lorry firms forge permits for Europe

Forged road haulage permits are being used to carry thousands of pounds worth of British goods into Europe. Even some large lorries, carrying £30 000 loads are crossing the channel on forged permits that cost less than 5p to print. Road haulage permits are issued by agreement in Britain, France, West Germany and Italy to limit the number of foreign lorries travelling on each other's routes.

The holders of the forged permits were given a dishonest advantage: they were able to conduct business while honest competitors—whose permits had been exhausted—could not. The forged permit amounts to a physical misrepresentation.

A sharp operator

Company X sought damages against Company Y. It was alleged that Company Y:
- obtained substandard packing material from Company X's suppliers and used it to counterfeit Company X's products;
- called on Company X's customers and offered goods which they misrepresented as being Company X's at less than half of Company X's regular prices.

Company X claimed damages for loss of business and reputation.

Not necessarily a criminal offence, this case involves intangible assets (market share). The conversion symptoms (sales to a third party) by Company Y may carry an impact in Company X's marketing and statistical records.

Director faces bribe trial

The head of an advertising firm was remanded on a £100 bail charged with offering a £2000 bribe to a council official.

This case should be viewed from the position of the agent's competitors. Had the bribe been accepted, they would have been put at a commercial disadvantage when bidding for council business.

The concealment of the bribe payment to a third party would have amounted to a misrepresentation of a commercial reality so far as competitors were concerned.

Hoover declares war on the cheats

The giant domestic appliance firm of Hoover is waging a day-to-day campaign against teams of men and women throughout the country who are giving the impression that they are the company's official representatives and often charge exorbitant prices for repairs to washing machines and vacuum cleaners. On many occasions repairs are not even done, and some that are leave the machines in a dangerous condition. The company is now so worried about the damage to its reputation and the way in which its authorized dealers and genuine repairers are being hurt that it has a lawyer and a number of senior executives working on the problem.

What occurred was a misrepresentation of a commercial or personal reality.

Characteristics of frauds in category D2

- This category covers the most prevalent and costly type of opportunist frauds, where the thief may be a business competitor.
- These frauds normally involve misrepresentation of a commercial reality— directed at a third party—resulting in a loss of an intangible asset to the victim (e.g., market share, competitive position).
- The fraud may be long or short term.
- The misrepresentation is normally before or continguous with the theft act.
- The thief is exposed to detection in all phases of the fraud, although may not be at risk of criminal prosecution.
- The loss is rarely noticed by the victim.

Other frauds in category D2

- most, if not all, passing-off offences
- bribery of connected organizations by business competitors where the reality falsified is commercial: free and fair competition.

CATEGORY D3 EXTERNAL—OPPORTUNIST—MANIPULATIVE

Definition Opportunist frauds committed by members of the public and business community—including competitors—who are neither employees nor business contacts of the victim company and who have no regular access to its assets or accounts.

The frauds involve manipulation of accounting records before, during or after a larcenous or misrepresentative theft, to assist in or to conceal its commission. Without concealment the loss and the guilt of the thief may be obvious.

Examples

Fraud everywhere in Bordeaux wine, judge told

Fraud is rife throughout the Bordeaux wine trade, one of 18 accused declared when the French 'winegate' trial opened. The accused said: 'In 30 years in the trade I have seen fraud practised everywhere—among owners, dealers and professional associations. Baptizing, as we in the trade call it, is a common practice. Some dealers make a speciality of transforming poor wines into better ones.'

The prosecution was based on a 55-page report prepared by the Finance Ministry fraud inspectors. They made three basic accusations:

1. Red wine shipped from Provence and bottled as Bordeaux red with the *Appellation Controlée* label.
2. Large stocks of poor wine, 'unfit for consumption', which had been chemically treated to alter its colour, taste and smell, were found.
3. Documents essential to the inquiry were destroyed.

The switching operation enabled an ordinary table wine to be passed off as a red Bordeaux. This involved obtaining an officially authorized and sealed stamping machine and inserting details of one wine on the official certificate and details of another wine on the corresponding stub.

Basically this was misrepresentation of a physical reality, supported by the manipulation of records.

Company offshoot accused of US customs evasion

Signalling a drive to crack down on satellite plants established by US companies abroad to take advantage of lower labour rates, the administration has filed charges of conspiracy to evade £86 400 in customs duty against a subsidiary of Company X. It is alleged that Company X undervalued computer circuits assembled in its factory in Mexico and then sent them into the US.

This involved documentary undervaluation on customs records. Viewed from the position of a competitor, the practice reported gave Company X an unfair competitive advantage.

Check on wave of outlaw trade directory firms

Scotland Yard is intensifying enquiries into bogus trade directory firms using high pressure selling techniques. The firms are sending companies 'adverts' which look so much like outstanding bills that many are tricked into paying them as bills. One firm is estimated to have made £200 000 in the past few weeks. The technique is to send an invoice to a company for the cost of appearing in the directory. On the bottom of the invoice, or on the back it is stated there is no necessity to pay. Many companies assumed the invoice to be bona fide and paid without further checking. Many junior clerks would probably accept these bills as genuine invoices.

This is essentially an opportunist fraud, relying for its success on a misleading accounting document; when the 'account' is accepted and paid the thief becomes a business contact of the victim.

Oil company faces £100 million accusation

The chairman of an oil company together with the company itself was accused of defrauding the public for failing to disclose contracts which could reduce its net income by more than £100 million. The suit was filed in New York and alleges that the company made fraudulent statements in public offerings in the summer of 1971 when it was seeking new capital.

It alleged that the company failed to tell investors that—because of fear that Libya would cease crude oil production—the company had tripled its tanker fleet to be ready to carry supplies from the Persian Gulf. The increase in the size of the fleet exposed the company to losses, it was alleged.

The victims in this case were the stockholders.

Characteristics of frauds in category D3
- These frauds may be long or short term.
- They involve a manipulation of records outside the ownership, custody or control of the victim company (i.e., the thief's or a third party's).
- The manipulation may be positive—when a false record is created—or negative—when a record is omitted or destroyed.
- The loss to the commercial victim is usually in an intangible asset or interest.
- The impact of the fraud is often obvious in the victim's statistical or management records.
- The manipulation is normally directed at assisting the theft act.
- The manipulation may be designed to conceal a loss when the thief or fraudulent company would otherwise be readily identifiable and traceable.

Other frauds in category D3
- consumer frauds assisted by false documentation
- false investment manifestos and prospectuses

– false documentation frauds committed on third parties (including government departments)

CATEGORY E1 EXTERNAL—ORGANIZED—LARCENOUS

Definition Frauds arising out of organized conspiracies whose corporate objective is crime. The conspiracies may or may not involve or include employees or business contacts of the victim company.

The frauds are simple and unconcealed because:

(a) the loss will not be recognized or, if recognized, the thief cannot be identified, or
(b) concealment is not possible because the thief does not have access to an available concealment course, or
(c) the victim condones the theft.

Examples

Australian gang fleeces bank

Australian crooks who have operated a 100-strong shoplifting gang in Britain for nearly ten years have turned to bank robbery. In a few months they have 'shoplifted' £100 000 in cash and foreign currency and traveller's cheques from banks and travel agencies in the centre of London.

The robbers are believed to have been trained in the new techniques at the gang's school in Sydney.

The gang distracts the attention of the staff, either by complaining loudly about the service or by fighting each other or acting drunk. Once a member relieved himself against a bank wall.

While this is going on another member of the gang sneaks in and grabs the loot. They also follow postmen and pick up registered mail after it is delivered.

The victim's attention was diverted from what was purely a larcenous act. The distraction did not amount to a misrepresentation.

Gems gang paid £10 000 to cleaner

Robbers paid £10 000 to the cleaner employed at a Hatton Garden diamond firm for information that led to the theft of £5000 in cash and £291 451 worth of precious stones an Old Bailey jury was told yesterday.

Engineer arrested by FBI

A disclosure by a member of the board of a glass manufacturing company led to the arrest in the US of a motor engineer. The engineer is alleged to have signed a £1 000 000 agreement to supply information about the glass company's process used under licence by a car manufacturing company. He was arrested in Washington by agents of the FBI.

Most successful cases of industrial espionage fall into this category. Note the following points.

1. They are organized. The theft of information may be at the request of a competitor or other external source. This person or organization would not normally have access to the victim's information. Access is obtained by a subverted employee/business contact or through a professional spy. On the other hand, the theft may be arranged by an employee, who then has to find a purchaser for the information.
2. They are usually unconcealed. Concealment is rarely necessary since the theft of intangible information seldom comes to light.

Secrets of laser beam tubes stolen

A case of industrial espionage involving laser beam equipment used in tanks, top secret establishments and hospitals was revealed at the Crown Court. It concerned the loss of plans developed over two years by one of only two companies producing lasers in the UK.

A man was convicted of stealing papers, plans, price lists, circuit diagrams and brochures belonging to the subject company between January 1969 and May 1973. He was given a nine-month suspended prison sentence. He had been an employee of the subject company.

The theft called for organization and was larcenous (without concealment).

£30 000 whisky haul

Two masked men stole a lorry containing whisky valued at £30 000. Fifteen days earlier another lorry containing whisky valued at £36 000 was stolen from a yard after the driver had been kidnapped.

Typical of larcenous acts by organized gangs. Concealment of the 'high-impact' loss was not possible.

Characteristics of frauds in category E1

- Frauds in this category are invariably preplanned and directed at unrecorded assets (industrial espionage) or high-value, easily disposable consumer goods.
- They often involve collusion with an employee of the victim company or rely on inside information (this is particularly true in cases of cargo hijacking).

- Disposal of the stolen goods is often arranged before the act of theft.
- Such frauds are usually short term (although their duration may be extended by the selection of different victims).
- Usually the frauds are large scale.
- The thieves are exposed to detection in all phases of the fraud (from the planning through to the disposal of the stolen goods). There is seldom any audit trail after the event.

CATEGORY E2   EXTERNAL—ORGANIZED—MISREPRESENTATIVE

Definition   Frauds arising out of organized conspiracies whose corporate objective is crime. The conspiracies may or may not involve or include employees or business contacts of the victim company.

The frauds involve misrepresentation of a physical, personal or commercial reality before, during or after a larcenous theft, to assist in or to conceal its commission. Without concealment the loss and the guilt of the thief may be obvious.

Examples

£9000 trick of missing empties

An empties fiddle caused a loss of more than £9000 to a soft drink manufacturer, an Old Bailey judge was told yesterday. The sum represented credit paid to Mr X for non-existent returns of bottles and crates to the company's depot. Six lorry drivers and mates employed by the company and Mr X pleaded guilty to the charges and were each sentenced to nine months' imprisonment, suspended for two years. The judge remarked that this was a swindle on a fairly wide scale which needed the cooperation of drivers and their mates.

Prosecuting counsel said that £9064 was credited to Mr X by the soft drinks firm in a period of four years. At certain times of the day there was no physical check at the soft drinks yard on empty bottles and crates returned. The drivers and mates took advantage of this.

The fraud was achieved by the misrepresentation of a physical reality: the quantity of empties returned was inflated. The fraud may have been further assisted by accounts manipulation.

Swindle in fake watches

Crime syndicates are making millions of pounds by selling counterfeit Swiss watches. They are affecting the economics of the Swiss watch industry.

Delegates to the Interpol conference at Frankfurt have been asked to intensify police and customs activities to break up the syndicate. A report compiled by Interpol headquarters said that hundreds or thousands of the fake watches are being transported around the world.

The gangs obtain cheap watch movements, make their own cases and straps, and mark the parts with the inscriptions used by the Swiss watchmakers. The watches, described as unreliable, cost only about £1 to £2.50, but are being sold in shops and on the streets at from £20 to £40.

This is the iceberg tip of an enormous problem. Usually the counterfeit watches are smuggled into the country while the counterfeiters themselves remain outside the jurisdiction of British courts.

Characteristics of frauds in category E2

- The misrepresentation usually involves a physical reality and is directed at assisting and is contiguous with the theft act.
- The misrepresentation may be directed at the victim company, resulting in the loss of a tangible asset, or at a third party, when the loss may be tangible or intangible.
- The frauds may be long or short term but are usually costly to the victim.
- They may or may not include people employed by the victim company.
- The thieves are most exposed during the theft act or while the misrepresentation is being made.

Other frauds in category E2

- counterfeit products
- forgery (misrepresentation of a physical reality)

CATEGORY E3 EXTERNAL—ORGANIZED—MANIPULATIVE

Definition Frauds arising out of organized conspiracies whose corporate objective is crime. The conspiracies may or may not involve or include employees or business contacts of the victim company.

The frauds involve manipulation of accounting records before, during or after a larcenous or misrepresentative theft, to assist in or conceal its commission. Without concealment the loss and the guilt of the thief may be obvious.

Example

Mafia used computer in £1m plot

A Mafia-linked plot to tap municipal treasuries throughout America of millions of dollars by manipulation of a city computer system may have been nipped in the bud by a swoop on an embezzlement ring in Los Angeles. Acting on a tip from Congressional investigators, agents arrested two men and are seeking three others over a plan to defraud the Los Angeles Treasury of £2 million with municipal cheques to phoney corporate accounts, laundered through domestic and foreign banks. Investigators say they have not yet determined precisely how the plan was to be worked. But it apparently involved the juggling of accounts in the Los Angeles City administrative offices and the payment of cheques by the city's computer to bogus corporations. It is being assumed that someone within the city government had been cooperating in the scheme.

Agents for the Senate Permanent Sub-Committee on Investigations say they have information that similar schemes involving the same suspects are being planned for other big cities in the US.

The concealment course—manipulation—was undoubtedly obtained through a dishonest or coerced employee of the municipal authority.

Characteristics of frauds in category E3

- These frauds are invariably large and spectacular, usually short term, and tend to stem from internal frauds ('muscled in' by organized gangs).
- They usually involve employees of the victim company who, through greed or coercion, become parties to the conspiracy.
- Manipulation is normally intended to assist in the commission of the crime; concealment of the loss is often a secondary consideration since—from the organized criminal's point of view—an internal contact is expendable.
- The manipulated records are those to which the internal contact has access.
- The impact of the loss is often obvious in the early stages in non-financial, managerial or statistical records.
- The thief is most exposed to detection in the concealment stage or when stolen goods are converted into cash.

CATEGORY CDE4 EXTERNAL EXTORSIVE

Definition Frauds committed essentially by sources external to the victim company (although they may involve employees and business contacts) and which use force, coercion or blackmail as a means to theft achievement or concealment. The frauds may or may not be concealed.

Examples

CID probe affairs of dustmen in protection racket

Dustmen alleged to be running a protection racket worth thousands of pounds in London's Chelsea and Kensington areas are being investigated by the CID.

Businessmen claimed that some dustmen were demanding money from them before they would make extra collections. Others complained that they had been threatened with violence unless they paid up. One man said he had already paid about £1000.

Others said that dustmen allegedly involved in the racket had threatened to scatter refuse in and around their premises, and pointed out that if they did so it would be 'bad for business'.

Carbon paper frauds made £120 000 profit

A five-year-long carbon paper fraud which netted £120 000 in pure profit was described at the Old Bailey when ten men admitted charges of plotting to defraud by deception. One company was invoiced for enough carbon paper to last 3000 years said the prosecuting counsel. The carbon paper was bought in job lots at £1 a thousand sheets or through suppliers at £3.50 and then resold at £40 a thousand sheets. Company buyers known as 'dupes' were bribed with champagne, cigarettes or cash and threatened with exposure to their employers once they succumbed to the stationery salesmen.

One dupe swamped with unwanted carbon paper smuggled hundreds of sheets from his office at night under his raincoat and burnt it in an incinerator so his employers would not find out how much he had accepted.

£70 000 blackmail demand sent to Coca Cola firm

A £70 000 blackmail plot to put a poisonous weedkiller into two bottles of Coca Cola and distribute them with normal supplies throughout Britain was described in court recently. The blackmail demand had been sent to the vice-president of the Coca Cola Corporation in Britain.

Two charged with strychnine in the Smash potato plot

Two men had a wicked and vicious plan to blackmail Cadbury Schweppes for £80 000 by releasing some of the firm's products on to the market treated with lethal doses of poison, it was alleged at the Crown Court yesterday. But they were arrested as they made their fourth attempt to collect a suitcase which they thought contained money.

It was alleged that the men sent the firm an envelope containing enough strychnine to kill 100 people and a note saying that the poison had been put in 6000 packets of Cadbury's Smash— the instant mash potato—5000 lb of chocs and 10 gross of drinks. It would be impossible to check the introduction of poisons into some of the products because of their large range and wide distribution.

£1 million demand to stop bombs in Disneyland

A man who threatened to set off seven bombs in Disneyland, the giant amusement park in Anaheim, California, and at Disney World in Orlando, Florida, unless he was paid a ransom of £1 300 000 was arrested as he picked up a box which he believed contained half the money.

Ex-soldier jailed for threatening to blow up Harrods

A former parachute regiment colour sergeant was sentenced to four years' imprisonment at the Old Bailey yesterday for trying to obtain £30 000 from Harrods by making bomb threats on two occasions.

Tenders corruption may have cost Britain £29 million

A judge described how bullying and bribing, leading to disclosures of secret documents to a foreign company's representative, may have cost Britain a £29 million contract. The court was told that the case involved tenders by several companies for a £200 million contract. The accused were an employee of the British consulting company and a Frenchman. The Briton, it was said, had unwillingly, but for money, handed over documents giving details of the British tenders. He had been bullied by the Frenchman into doing something he did not want to do.

'Daughter kidnap' hoaxer gets £12 000

A London bank manager handed over £12 000 after being hoaxed into believing that his 15-year-old daughter had been kidnapped. But the girl was safe and well, taking extra tuition at her school. Immediately the manager received the call he telephoned his daughter's school and was told that she was on a refreshment break and no one knew where she was.

The manager took the money to a phone booth a mile away from the bank. He then returned to his office and called the police.

This case either involved someone closely connected with the daughter or good preplanning by organized criminals. The call was timed to coincide with the girl's absence from her classes.

Three directors feared links with gang

Three company directors told the police they were scared of a property dealer because of his connection with a London gang.

The frightened directors supplied false invoices for use in a grant application to a government sponsored body, said the prosecuting counsel. The three directors are among ten accused of an alleged conspiracy to defraud a government department.

Characteristics of frauds in category CDE4

- The application of force or blackmail may overcome the normal constraints on theft opportunities and concealment courses.
- Threats from external sources may be directed towards the proprietors of the victim company when:
  - the frauds are essentially short term;
  - they are invariably illegal;
  - the losses are overt and obvious.
- When a threat is directed towards an employee of the victim company or another business contact:
  - the loss may be hidden from the victim company, depending on the concealment course available to the subject of the extortion;
  - the fraud may be long or short term;
  - the demands are invariably illegal.
- In all cases the thief is exposed to risk of detection if the subject of the extortion calls for assistance before the fraud comes to a natural end.

High risk areas of fraud

Because many, if not most, frauds are not reported to the police or publicized, it is difficult to identify high risk areas with precision. However, personal experience of more than 20 years suggests that the league table of the most common frauds are as follows:

Fraud committed by	Owners or shareholders in an existing company
Against	Potential investors or an acquiring company
Type	Window dressing: false representations
Mechanics	The accounts or operations of the prospect to be acquired are doctored to make it appear more attractive than it truly is. The most common method is inflation of stocks and debtors' balances or the suppression of liabilities. Often accounts are window dressed by transactions with related parties
Average loss per case	£5 million plus
Fraud committed by	Employees in discretionary positions such as buyers, sales managers, investment advisers, etc., in collusion with customers and suppliers
Against	Employer
Type	Bribery
Mechanics	Bribes are paid by third parties for favourable treatment. The corrupt payments are either hidden in the books of the payer, disguised as 'agents'

	fees', etc., made from associated companies of the payer or paid in cash from off-book funds
Average loss per case	Bribery extends across a wide range, but the average loss per case is estimated at over £300 000 in direct and consequential costs
Fraud committed by	Employees or organized criminals
Against	Users of electronic funds transfer systems: usually banks
Type	EFTS or wire transfer frauds
Mechanics	One-time frauds. Apparently genuine instructions are given for the transfer of funds by electronic means. They are often authenticated by 'test keys'. The funds are usually laundered through a number of banks before being converted to cash. Frequently the transfer instructions will be given immediately before a national holiday in the sending but not the receiving country: this gives the criminals extra time to convert funds and escape
Average loss per case	Over £1 million
Fraud committed by	Employees
Against	Employer
Type	Conflict of interest
Mechanics	These are similar to cases of bribery but are often rationalized by the perpetrator as justified. Examples include theft of sales leads diverted by the salesman to a company in which he has an undisclosed interest: moonlighting by computer programmers: misuse of company resources for a private interest, etc.
Average loss per case	Not estimable
Fraud committed by	Employees, often in collusion with suppliers
Against	Employers
Type	Inflation of purchases
Mechanics	Purchase values are inflated. Overpayments are converted through the account of the supplier and shared with the employee
Average loss per case	£100 000 plus
Fraud committed by	Third parties, organized criminals and opportunists

Against	Brand leaders
Type	Counterfeit products
Mechanics	Branded products are counterfeited and 'passed off' through normal marketing channels. They are often of poor quality and have an enormous effect on the victim's reputation and genuine business
Average loss per case	Unlimited

Fraud committed by	Organized criminals
Against	Major corporations
Type	Extortion
Mechanics	The criminals threaten to poison products (usually food or drugs) supplied by the victim unless a ransom payment is made
Average loss per case	Difficult to estimate the consequential effect of publicity, etc. In one case, total losses exceeded £2 million

Fraud committed by	Employees in collusion with customers (salesman, accounts department, etc.)
Against	Employer
Type	Sales suppression
Mechanics	Accounts and control equipment are manipulated so that customers, with whom the employee is in collusion, are not invoiced for goods or granted fictitious credits
Average loss per case	£50 000 plus

Fraud committed by	Competitors
Against	Copyright and patent owners: particularly of computer software
Type	Pirating
Mechanics	Dishonest competitors or licensees make unauthorized copies of the victims' products and sell them as genuine
Average loss per case	In computer software, over £1 million

Fraud committed by	Competitors (home or overseas)
Against	Market leaders
Type	Industrial espionage
Mechanics	Usually through subverted employees of the victim, systematic search of the victim's trash for sensitive papers or by electronic bugging
Average loss per case	Unlimited

Fraud committed by	Employees (such as loan officers) who are authorized to advance funds to third parties
Against	Usually banks and finance houses
Type	Fictitious loan advances
Mechanics	Advances are made in return for bribes, to companies in which the employee has a concealed interest or in response to blackmail or other threats
Average loss per case	Virtually unlimited

Fraud committed by	Organized criminals
Against	Investors
Type	Investment and franchising frauds
Mechanics	Investors are tempted to invest in fictitious commodity transactions, franchising schemes, unlisted securities, false certificate, etc.
Average loss per case	£10 000

Fraud committed by	Drivers of delivery vehicles
Against	Employers and customers
Type	Short delivery
Mechanics	Often by clever misrepresentation, drivers short deliver goods to commercial customers. They are often converted to cash by sales to genuine (but dishonest) customers of the victim company
Average loss per case	On average £5000 per driver per year

Fraud committed by	Employees (investment/pension department) and foreign exchange
Against	Employer
Type	Diversions and coat tailing
Mechanics	Private and concealed trading in securities, commodities or foreign exchange in which favourable transactions are routed to the employee and unfavourable ones to the employer. Also misuse of company funds to move a market in favour of an employee's private interest
Average loss per case	Impossible to quantify

Fraud committed by	Employees (branch managers and accounts department)
Against	Employer
Type	Lapping

Mechanics	Entries are lapped through accounts of suppliers and customers to conceal cash or asset thefts
Average loss per case	£2000

Fraud committed by	Employees (mail room and cash accounting)
Against	Employer
Type	Theft of incoming cash and external conversion of incoming cheques
Mechanics	Suppression
Average loss per case	Usually short term and low value (i.e., less than £50 000)

Fraud committed by	Employees
Against	Employers
Type	Travelling expenses
Mechanics	Travelling and hotel bills are inflated, airline tickets switched for a cheaper class, false entertaining claims
Average loss per case	Usually less than £1000 per annum but an institutionalized method of fraud

Fraud committed by	Workers
Against	Employers
Type	Theft of materials
Mechanics	Unconcealed removal of company assets and tools
Average loss per case	Institutionalized

Fraud committed by	Employees (accounting office)
Against	Employers
Type	Manipulation of adjustments, etc.
Mechanics	Various, depending on opportunity
Average loss per case	£10 000

Obviously each organization faces different risks, depending to a large extent on the quality of its employees and controls. The following chapters set out the background and working methodology through which risks can· be identified, detected and prevented.

Conclusions

To sum up, the available data suggests that corporate fraud results from a combination of motivational and situational factors in which the critical point is the presence of an opportunity. Further, a criminal will only exploit an opportunity when he perceives a low chance of detection. Common sense

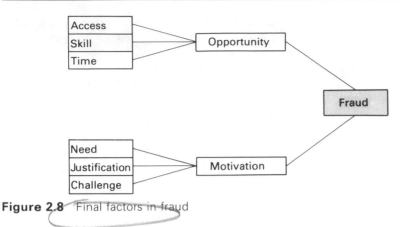

Figure 2.8 Final factors in fraud

suggests that there is no opportunity when immediate detection is obviously inevitable. The connection is as shown in Figure 2.8.

Fraud is often predictable both in its direction and extent and depends on the effect of controls and internal management climate of the organizations concerned. Companies can be divided into four types (as shown on Table 2.5).

Table 2.5 Categories of fraud exposures

Motivation governed by:	Opportunities governed by:	
	Good controls	Poor controls
Clear management style and personnel practices	TYPE 1 Fraud unlikely	TYPE 2 Fraud possible
Weak or dishonest management, poor personnel practices	TYPE 3 Fraud probable	TYPE 4 Fraud inevitable

It follows that if motivation for dishonesty can be denied, the chances of crime are reduced; if opportunities can be limited and detection made a strong possibility, most frauds will be prevented.

Current practice, unfortunately, falls short of these ideals and there are too many Type 4 victims and far too many criminals motivated to exploit them. However, the position is far from hopeless and effective controls can be introduced in even the most exposed company. All it requires is a little care and awareness.

3. Records and essentials of computer processing

Rule 3: Debits, like cars, are best kept on the same side of the track

This chapter examines the fundamentals of accounting and computer controls which frauds have to overcome to succeed.

Accounting records

Accounts are designed to show the net worth and profitability of a business, to comply with tax and other statutory requirements and to provide management with the information needed for day-to-day judgements.

FINAL ACCOUNTS

Net worth—the excess of assets over liabilities—is summarized at the end of each financial period on a balance sheet, which also shows the owner's equity or share capital under the following formula:

Current assets ⎫   Current liabilities
plus   ⎬ equals   Long-term liabilities
Fixed and intangible assets ⎭   Owner's equity

Some assets can be converted easily into cash should it be necessary to do so—these are called current or 'quick'—while others may be slow, fixed or intangible depending on how long they take to turn to cash. Liabilities may be current, long term or permanent.

The second important statement of a business, usually prepared annually, is the profit and loss account. It shows how the business has performed and calculates profitability after making provision for such things as bad debts and for replacing fixed assets when they wear out (depreciation).

Balance sheets and profit and loss accounts may be prepared for a branch of business (possibly on an informal basis), for a company as a whole, or consolidated for a group of companies.

Figure 3.1 shows the way in which final accounts are prepared, starting from source documents on the left-hand side. Of particular importance is the value attached to inventory (B).

A major fraud may have an impact on the victim's final accounts and on one or more of the ratios used to measure business performance (see Table 3.1).

Measurements of performance from final accounts

Entries on final accounts are often extracted to calculate the following items (see also Figure 3.1).

Current assets to current liabilities

This compares the current assets of a business with its current liabilities. This—sometimes called a current ratio—is intended to show whether or not a company can meet its liabilities. Current assets include cash and easily realizable securities and stock; current liabilities include all debts and outstanding short-term payments.

$$\text{Current ratio} = \frac{\text{Current assets}}{\text{Current liabilities}}$$

Generally speaking, the larger the ratio the safer the business is considered to be.

Quick ratio

A second ratio frequently used is the comparison of liquid assets and current liabilities, called the quick ratio. This gives the managers of the company or investors a better idea of its ability to cover short-term debts (liquidity) because stocks—which are not normally quickly convertible at their book value—are excluded from the calculation

$$\text{Quick ratio} = \frac{\text{Current assets } \textit{minus} \text{ stocks}}{\text{Short-term liabilities}}$$

Certain frauds, described later, will cause a reduction of both the current and quick ratios.

Average collection period

This ratio, which indicates the credit control and collection practices of a business, is calculated by the formula:

$$\text{Average collection period} = \frac{\text{Debtors' balances} \times 365}{\text{Annual credit sales}}$$

It is often a worthless exercise to set down optimum collection periods for a business-to-business comparison. An important and more useful measure is to compare figures year to year in the same company.

As a general rule, in a well run business, average collection periods should be no more than one-third greater than net terms. For example, where net terms are set for 30 days, the average collection period should not exceed 40 days.

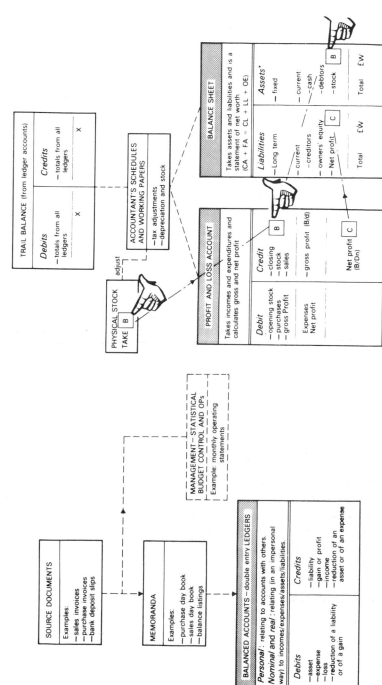

Figure 3.1 Preparation of final accounts

Where frauds are concealed by fraudulent postings to debtors' accounts, or where cash sales are suppressed, the average collection period may rise dramatically.

Ratio of turnover to inventory

This ratio may be applied to total sales and total inventories and is a measure of the adequacy of stocks.

$$\text{Turnover} = \frac{\text{Cost of sales}}{\text{Inventory}} \quad \text{or} \quad \frac{\text{Sales}}{\text{Inventory}}$$

Retailers of perishable goods normally have a stock turnover of around 28 times per year, while manufacturers of steel sheets may turn over stocks no more than once a year.

Frauds concealed by an inflation of inventory or suppression of sales may distort stock turnover calculations—by reducing year-to-year or branch-to-branch comparisons.

Ratio of cash sales to credit sales

This is another useful ratio mainly for historical comparisons with the same business. If, for example, Branch A of a multiple grocery chain has a ratio of cash to credit of $1:5$ while the remainder of the branches have a ratio of $1:3$, suppression of cash sales at Branch A may be a possibility. The ratio may also suggest that Branch A is the victim of a credit fraud, and such a distortion, coupled with an extended average collection period, should be sufficient grounds for conducting a more detailed investigation of debtors' balances.

Ratio of net profit to sales

This is an absolute ratio which may be sufficiently distorted to lead to the first suspicions of fraud. The ratio will naturally vary from business to business. Historical comparisons within the same business are useful yardsticks and may detect frauds where concealment is terminated in an expense account or where sales are suppressed. Serious profit variations between branches should also be cause for concern.

Dependency of ratios

Although only six ratios have been mentioned, there are many others that are frequently used in measuring the performance of businesses. Table 3.2 summarizes 15 of these under the cross-matrix of numerators and divisors. Thus, ratio 1 is obtained by dividing current assets (numerator) by current liabilities (divisor); ratio 10 by dividing fixed assets (numerator) by tangible net worth (divisor) and so on. Where a high ratio is regarded as being a more favourable indicator to the health of a business, its reference number is shown in brackets and where a lower ratio is considered more favourable it is marked with an asterisk.

The interdependence of the ratios is perhaps their greatest weakness, since merely by inflating inventories or suppressing current liabilities, the apparent health of a business can be improved, either to deceive outside investors or to conceal internal fraud.

Ratios can also be improved without resorting to fraud. For example, if

	£	
Current assets	= 30 000	Current ratio = 1.5
Current liabilities	= 20 000	

the current ratio of 1.5 may not enable the company to obtain finance, merely because it is lower than the accepted yardstick of 2.

However, if the company pays off £10 000 of its liabilities, the figures become

	£	
Current assets	= 20 000	Current ratio = 2.0
Current liabilities	= 10 000	

giving a 'satisfactory' ratio of 2.

It is always necessary to take care in using ratios because there are ways—both fraudulent and non-fraudulent—of 'improving' them (see Table 3.2).

Table 3.1 Financial ratios

	NUMERATOR									
DIVISOR	Current assets	Net profits	Net sales	Fixed assets	Current liabilities	Total liabilities	Inventory	Funded debt	Debtors	Cash sales
Current liabilities	(1)									
Net sales		(5)								
Tangible net worth (TNW)		(6)	(8)	10	11*	12*				
Net working capital (NWC)		(7)	(9)				13*	15*		
Inventory			(3)		14*					
Credit sales									2*	4

Table 3.2 Methods of improving financial ratios

| Name of ratio | Ratios and normal performance yardsticks | | Fraudulently Improved |
	Ratio no.	Yardstick	
Current ratio	1	2 times	Higher
Collection period	2	Net terms + $\frac{1}{3}$	Lower
Net sales; inventory	3	Industry average	Higher
Cash; credit sales	4	Company average	– – – – –
Net sales: profits	5	Company average	Higher
Net profit; TNW	6	Company average	Higher
Net profit; NWC	7	Industry average (× 1.25 times)	} Higher
Net sales: TNW	8	Industry average (× 1.25 times)	} Higher
Net sales: NWC	9	Industry average	Higher
Fixed assets: TNW	10	Industry average	– – – – –
Current debt: TNW	11	Less than 75%	Lower
Total debt: TNW	12	Less than 100%	Lower
Inventory; NWC	13	Industry average	Lower
Current debt; inventory	14	Industry average	Lower
Funded debt; NWC	15	Less than 100%	Lower

DAY-TO-DAY RECORDS

To get to the position where a business can prepare its balance sheet and profit and loss account accurate records must be kept on a day-to-day basis.

The records may be kept by an old lady sitting in the corner of an office or they may be processed by computer. Either way there are recognized accounting principles that will, or at least should, apply to both.

First there are what may be called source documents. These are sales invoices, orders, dispatch notes, purchase orders, etc., which are the first basic record of a transaction or the movement of an asset. They are usually completed by a person who has most direct responsibility for the asset or first-hand knowledge of the transaction involved.

Source documents will be summarized on some form of listing such as sales or purchase day books; these are often referred to as memoranda or journals. Entries are transferred from these into double entry accounts.

DOUBLE ENTRY ACCOUNTS

Double entry accounts are the cornerstone of most formal systems and are based on the principle that when one account benefits, another concedes an equivalent amount. For example, when a customer pays his bill his personal account is credited—because it has given something—while the cash account is debited—because it has gained.

Thus, it is the fundamental rule of double entry accounts that for every debit entry there must be a corresponding credit entry, and vice versa. Each double entry is between accounts in the same set of books; one account gives or yields something and is credited and another receives something and is debited. The sum of all debits should equal the sum of credits.

Therefore:

A debit entry represents

- the creation or addition to an asset an expense or a loss
- the reduction of a liability or a gain

A credit entry represents

- the creation of or addition to a liability, a gain, a profit or an income
- the reduction of an asset or an expense

An excess of debits over credits, called a debit balance represents

- *an asset* (if it represents cash or something that can be converted into cash)
- *an expense* (if the balance is not convertible) or *a loss*

A credit balance (i.e., an excess of credits over debits) represents

- *a liability*
- *a gain or profit*

Within each double entry system there are different types of accounts. First, there are personal accounts which relate to other entities (suppliers, customers, agents and so on). Personal accounts show the history of the business relationship and whether the account holder owes or is owed money.

Nominal accounts relate to assets, liabilities, expenses and incomes, summarized in an impersonal way. Such things as advertising, freight, wages, sales and purchases are shown on accounts in the nominal ledger. Real accounts are usually included in the nominal ledger and relate to physical assets: real accounts always have a related physical inventory.

There is a further group of accounts which fall technically into the double entry system; these are called suspense accounts. They are used to hold debits and credits, which for one reason or another cannot be posted immediately to their proper personal, nominal or real accounts, or which are of such a transitory nature that formal posting would not be worth while or necessary.

The number and value of entries in suspense accounts will depend upon the business concerned and on how well managed it is. Entries will change from day to day as queries are cleared up. But as soon as one unresolved entry is posted, another may arise. The difficulty of reconciling suspense accounts makes them useful to thieves. Transfers in and out of suspense accounts are usually made by journal vouchers, adjustments requests, similar source documents or inputs through a computer terminal.

Vouchers are normally controlled—numerically—and are authorized by a responsible accounting employee. This, at least, is the theory. In practice, vouchers can be used fraudulently to:

- transfer entries between personal, real or nominal accounts
- transfer entries to and from suspense accounts
- write off bad debts and depreciation allowances

and to make a variety of other adjustments, often without adequate control; journals and vouchers can be dangerous.

Finally, control accounts summarize and check on the accuracy of individual postings to ledgers. Their structure and extent will vary, but they are usually very important in computer systems and often replace reconciliations of balances on individual accounts. If control account totals agree, the assumption is made that subsidiary personal and nominal accounts must also be correct; this can be a dangerous assumption.

Structure of nominal ledgers and budgets

Most organizations formalize the structure of their ledgers and have established procedures for opening new and closing old accounts. Frequently nominal and real accounts will be indexed on a chart of accounts which is linked to cost and profit centres for budgetary and management accounting purposes.

Source documents or computer input will be endorsed with the appropriate account code and from this, nominal and personal ledgers will be updated. Individual departments and branches may also have separate codes for budgeting and control purposes.

There are four important principles from a fraud prevention point of view:

- the opening of new accounts in all ledgers should be closely controlled;
- accounts in the nominal ledger should be divided into the smallest units possible, so that even small frauds have an obvious impact;
- budgetary and management accounts should be integrated as closely as possible with the nominal ledger; they should be consistently coded;
- responsibilities for cost and profit centres should be clearly assigned; deviations should be reported on an exception basis to senior management.

The object should be to monitor income and expenditure as closely as possible and to minimize the number of loosely controlled accounts, particularly in the nominal ledger in which consequential debits can be concealed.

Closing off nominal and other accounts

At the end of each financial period, all accounts in the double entry system are listed on a trial balance. The profit and loss account absorbs all income and expense items. The balance sheet, which is a snapshot of the net worth of the business, takes balances from asset and liability accounts.

Accounts closed to profit and loss start at zero in the next financial period, while those transferred to the balance sheet—after adjustment—are written back into the appropriate ledger for the next period.

IMPACT OF FRAUD ON FINAL ACCOUNTS

Theoretically, when an asset is stolen its related account should be credited and the thief's personal account debited. However, the essence of fraud is that the thief should not have to pay, thus he has to ensure that the theoretical debit to his personal account is concealed. The primary purpose of account manipulations is to conceal the debit that arises as a consequence of theft.

The accounts in which consequential debits are finally posted will determine whether a fraud results in a reduction in profit or an overstatement of net worth, or both. Consider the following examples:

> A cashier in Company A is engaged in fraud. He has access to cash sales invoices and to cash. He steals cash and conceals the fraud by destroying the appropriate sales invoice. The result of the manipulation is:
>
> — a reduction in the cash held (asset)
> — a suppression of sales (income)

Suppression of sales income affects profit and theft of cash reduces net worth. Because the fraud results in reduced profit, the victim effectively gains a tax allowance on the amount stolen. When concealment is made to an income or expense account, because of tax implications, £1 stolen may mean a loss of only 50p.

> If, on the other hand, the cashier has access to personal ledgers, he may conceal a cash shortage by properly recording sales and by falsely posting consequential debits to accounts of customers. The result of the manipulation is:
>
> — a reduction in the cash held
> — inflation of debtors' balances

The manipulation does not affect turnover, therefore, profits on gross sales figures are assumed at a higher rate than they truly are and there are no tax benefits. The impact of the fraud is in an asset account and is hidden in the balance sheet.

It can be seen from these examples that frauds concealed in asset or liability accounts are vulnerable and dangerous (see also Table 3.3).

Table 3.3 Effects of fraud concealment

Income or expenses	*Frauds concealed in* *Assets or liabilities*
Affect profits and net worth	Do not affect profits
Closed to profit and loss	Hidden on the balance sheet
Victim should notice reduced profitability	Victim may not detect inflated assets or suppressed liabilities
Reduced tax liabilities	No tax set-off
	Often result in collapse of victim company

Those cases of fraud which have resulted in the collapse of the victim company have invariably been concealed in asset or liability accounts.

STOCK RECORDS

The way in which a company maintains records of its inventory has a significant affect on fraud. The values entered into double entry accounts are insufficient to control stocks on a day-to-day basis and detailed working records will be required. These may be computer controlled or kept manually but in all cases should show opening and closing stocks, receipts and deliveries.

Working stock records are usually maintained by people who also have control of the corresponding physical assets and this breaks the accounting principle of separation of duties.

At frequent, but random, times, the holding of particular stock lines may be checked and as a result adjustments to book stocks may be necessary. These should be closely monitored and consolidated into management accounts. Extreme care should also be taken over damaged goods written out of stock.

TRANSPORTATION AND OTHER RECORDS

Informal records, such as routing sheets, drivers' logs and contract notes seldom form part of a company's formal accounting system, yet they may be invaluable for the detection and investigation of fraud.

Wherever possible all source documents relating to the delivery or receipt of assets should be stored after use in a place to which the normal custodians do not have access.

STATISTICAL RECORDS

Double entry or balanced books are seldom sufficiently detailed to enable a commercial manager to keep up to date and to plan ahead. Computers provide the means for other forms of management and statistical records including the following.

Sales reports summarized:

- by sales representative area against targets
- by branch or region against targets or last year's figures
- by customers against target or previous year's figures
- by type of goods against target or previous performance

Purchase statistics summarized:

- by supplier
- by type of goods
- by purchase contract number
- by department or branch
- by cost centre

The source of information used for statistical and management reports may or may not be the same as is used for preparing balanced books. Often statistical information is compiled from the front or source end of an accounting system and may not be corrected by subsequent formal adjustments. Wherever possible—from a fraud detection and prevention aspect—statistical records should reflect *exactly* the same information as that used in double entry accounts.

The impact of fraud on statistical records is often overlooked by the thief— and even when considered, may be beyond his control. While consequential debits may be concealed by manipulation of accounts or misrepresentations, symptoms may remain obvious in statistical records, in one of the following ways:

- in absolute terms, as a distortion of reasonableness, for example, distortion of profits, expenses, incomes and sales volumes;
- in historical trends, for example, variations in performance from one year to another;
- in comparative or proportional patterns, for example, distortion in branch-to-branch performance.

Statistical reports are often invaluable in both the detection and investigation of fraud as demonstrated in the following example.

X is a manufacturer of high class audio/radio equipment which is guaranteed for 12 months. Marketing is through a chain of wholesalers and retail shops and mail order customers.

A clerk working for X—in collusion with the proprietors of P Limited—interfered with the processing of dispatch notes, with the result that P was not invoiced for various bulk consignments of new goods and spare parts. The fraud was therefore concealed by the negative manipulation of sales documents. Stocks were loosely controlled and no obvious account/inventory discrepancy occurred.

However, the final retail customers of P Limited (generally members of the public), returned their guarantee cards to X for registration. In a particular year the cards returned by P's customers compared with its purchases from X were as below.

Guarantee cards returned to X		Goods invoiced by X to P	
Model A 1790	30	Model A 1790	5
Model Z 2333	250	Model Z 2333	70
Model 2667	700	Model 2667	100
Model 3339	190	Model 3339	3

The symptoms of fraud seem obvious. They were noticed by X Limited, who, however, assumed that P had built up and was disposing of old stock and that this fact accounted for an apparent excess of sales over purchases.

Had X taken its investigation one step further and compared serial numbers it would have discovered the fraud earlier. When the case was finally resolved it was found that P Limited had defrauded of over £57 000.

CORRESPONDENCE, PERSONAL TRAVELLING EXPENSES AND TELEPHONE BILLING RECORDS

These can be vitally important in an investigation in providing corroboration or entries in formal records and to enable witnesses to reconstruct the sequence of events. Travelling expense claims and supporting vouchers should be retained under secure arrangements for at least three years.

INFORMAL AND PERSONAL RECORDS

Thieves almost invariably retain private records of their dishonesty. Whether or not these help a thief rationalize that he is only 'borrowing' is a question for the criminal psychologist. What is clear in practice is that records such as rough notes, bank paying in and betting slips or credit card vouchers relating directly to fraud can be found in the thief's possession. Uncovering these can be a major step in any investigation.

Computer processing

Computers do not change accounting principles nor the concealment of fraud. They merely support an environment of security or insecurity in which accounts can be manipulated.

It is difficult to generalize on computer operations; there are so many different types of hardware, operating software and programs that the combinations are limitless. Different manufacturers use different terms for the same components or processes.

While accepting these limitations, this section presents an overview of those aspects of computing which are considered to have the greatest bearing on fraud.

BASIC OPERATIONS

Computer hardware components, such as the central processing unit (CPU), peripherals, such as terminals or disk drives, are of little use by themselves.

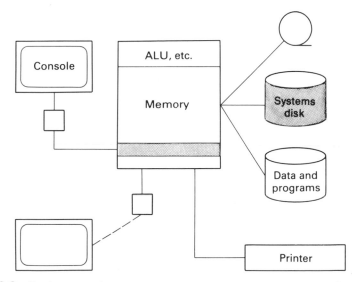

Figure 3.2   Basic computer components

Components are connected by a high speed communications channel, sometimes called a bus or a highway and are driven by software usually referred to as the operating system (see Figure 3.2).

OPERATING SYSTEMS

Operating systems control the ways in which the various components interact with each other and for special functions such as the interpretation or compilation of programs, teleprocessing and for data base management. Security is largely dependent on features incorporated into operating software.

The version of the operating system supplied by the vendor has to be configured to match the specification of the hardware concerned: configuration will take account of the numbers and types of terminals connected, offline storage units, etc., and is much like fine tuning a car engine to suit the needs of the driver. Configuration usually allows the user to select different security options and to set the level of detail that will be recorded on activity journals or console logs.

Operating systems are usually held on a disk connected directly to the central processing unit. Operators with access to the systems console load or bootstrap the operating system (or parts of it) into main memory. From this initial program load, the system is live and tasks can be performed.

Operating systems are frequently improved by the vendors and new versions are produced as updates (slight modifications) or upgrades (usually significant changes). Many users have their own systems programmers who maintain and amend operating systems to fit the needs of users or to optimize performance.

Some computer vendors insist on having diagnostic lines connected into users' machines so that performance can be monitored without the need for visits by technicians. Sometimes changes will be made to operating system through diagnostic lines and this presents a hazard; particularly if data files and application programs are running at the time.

Various utilities support the functions provided by operating systems. These include facilities for editing, copying files for back-up purposes or controlling program and file libraries, etc. Some are extremely dangerous since they can be used to overcome access controls, browse through and edit restricted libraries and make changes to data held in main memory or on disk often without leaving any trail.

Operating systems normally support two levels of processing, sometimes referred to as supervisory and user state. The supervisory mode grants high level privileges to facilities: including free access to all files and programs held on the system. In the user mode privileges are normally limited to discrete files and programs.

Programs running in the user state will require facilities (such as input or output) normally restricted to the supervisory level. The operating system recognizes these requests and if they are authorized will execute them on behalf of the user.

The methods in which operating systems grant supervisory privileges to user programs vary quite considerably and it is not necessary to mention them here, except to say that control over supervisory routines and user access to them is crucially important.

The operating system keeps track of where data and instructions are physically located on disk or main memory through a series of registers which, like the physical location of data, are transparent to most users.

Security is enforced on the assumption that users cannot access a physical address unless aided by the central processing unit which checks authority and logs activity. This is not a correct assumption and software utilities enable a skilled user to trace and alter data and instructions at their physical address without control. This is obviously a serious risk.

APPLICATION PROGRAMS

Computer systems perform tasks, such as processing accounts payable through application programs. Task orientated application software may be developed by a user or bought in as a packaged product. Programs are usually written in a high level language such as Cobol or PL1. Each computer language has its own set of commands or reserved words which are recognized by the computer. Programs written in high level languages are usually referred to as source versions and they are entered into a computer via an input device such as a keyboard or card reader.

A module in the operating system interprets the instructions in the source program and prepares a version in machine code which the computer can understand. The machine code program is usually referred to as the object version (see Figure 3.3).

There are two ways in which source programs are converted into object or machine code. In smaller machines they are processed by a module in the

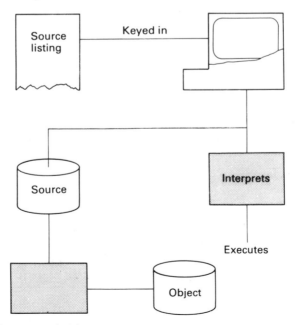

Figure 3.3 Source and object programs

operating system called an interpreter. This takes one line of the source program, converts it to machine code and then executes it. It then takes the next line, interprets and executes it and continues with the cycle until processing is complete.

In larger machines source code is converted through a compiler which produces a complete object version which is held in the production library and executes without further interpretation.

Machines which convert source programs through line after line interpretation are usually slower and far less secure than those using compilers.

In some computer installations tight control is applied over all compilations and software automatically assigns version numbers to both source and production programs, supposedly ensuring that no unauthorized compilations have taken place. Clearly, any fraudulent alteration to a program has to be effective at the production or object rather than the source level and, if properly applied, control over compilations can improve security.

Programs, whether compiled or interpreted contain instructions which are executed in a strict sequence to perform specific tasks. The operating system keeps track of each program step and provides the interface to data files, input, output and main memory. It also handles requests for supervisory level privileges.

The strict sequential processing of instructions will often be overridden by conditional jumps. For example discount allowed on a sales invoice may depend on its total value as follows:

Gross value of invoice   £100:   discount 2 per cent
Gross value of invoice   £101–200: discount 5 per cent

The program will branch depending on the condition encountered (i.e., the gross value) as shown in Table 3.4.

Table 3.4 Typical conditional statements

Program line	Instruction
100	Calculate gross value
110	If gross value more than 101 goto 130
120	Discount = 2% of gross
130	Discount = 5% of gross
140	Calculate net value (GV − discount)
150	etc.

Conditional jumps can be placed anywhere in a program and their form is usually far more complex than in the example set out in Table 3.4. They are also at the heart of frauds involving unauthorized program patches, discussed in depth in Chapter 7.

Bought in or packaged programs—such as software for processing the nominal ledger—are usually cheaper to install than those developed in-house. The user purchases an object version on disk or tape and sets of instruction manuals: users will seldom be provided with a source listing. Maintenance of the program will be undertaken by the vendor, usually in the form of updates.

It may, therefore, appear that bought-in packages are less exposed to fraudulent alteration than those developed by a user and to an extent this is true. However, software vendors usually try to design their products so that they have universal appeal and are easily adaptable to the features required by individual users.

This flexibility is incorporated into object programs in the form of options or transaction codes, but these may not be shown in the customized manuals supplied to users. For example in one popular accounts receivable package there is the option to make postings to an internal '999' account. Sales classified under this code are written out of inventory, but not charged to customers. If the user does not require this feature, the software remains unchanged although the section in the manual is removed. It would be possible for a well informed user to gain by entering the 999 code against sales to customers with whom he is in collusion. The printout for the 999 account could be destroyed. Security of packaged products is often illusory.

DATA FILES AND DATA BASES

Users may set up their own data files for each application (such as accounts payable) or all corporate information may be shared, in whole or in part, by all users on one or more data base.

Data bases are becoming more common since they provide major benefits including consistency of information across applications and processing speed. They can present serious problems of access control (which users are entitled to access which fields) and accountability for changes to data.

Clearly files held on line on a disk are more exposed to unauthorized access than those held on tape, which have to be loaded by operators prior to processing. However, the structure of data files and the media on which they are held makes little difference to the methods of account manipulation: it merely affects the 'way in'.

Magnetic impulses, representing data, are written on to tape and disk and are located by the central processing unit through a system of registers, indexes or directories. Password restriction usually applies only to the directories. It is sometimes possible to crack security with utility software which is able to trace and read data at a physical level and without access to protected directories.

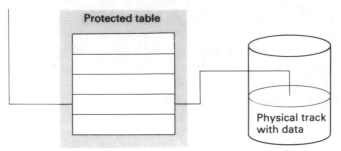

Figure 3.4 Methods of data protection

Deletion of data normally takes place by removal of its directory entry. This can be compared to removing the index from a book rather than deleting paragraphs of text. This fact can be important in fraud investigations: data may be suppressed from accounting records and deleted from computer files yet still remain in image form at an unindexed address on tape or disk. This is a point worth considering in the investigation of computer fraud (see Figure 3.4).

TERMINALS AND REMOTE ACCESS

The number, location and type of terminals connected to a computer system have a significant impact on exposures to fraud.

Terminals may be individually connected, linked through a local area network or by dial-up facilities. Terminal users may be granted access without restriction, on presentation of a password or through some form of hardware identifier in a terminal.

Dial-up facilities can result in major security problems. Essentially, one or more telephone numbers are connected to the computer or a communications controller.

Remote users dial the number and are connected to the computer through a modem which converts the analogue signals on the telephone lines to digital format (see Figure 3.5).

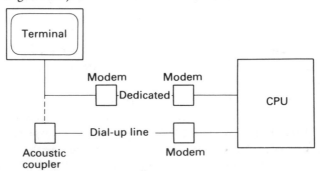

Figure 3.5 Communication methods

The opportunities for unauthorized access are obvious and to a large extent security depends on keeping the telephone numbers and associated passwords secret.

PASSWORDS

Most systems have a 'security manager's password' which is similar to a master key and has no limits on access to files and facilities. The person designated 'security manager' is able—through the operating system or file security utilities—to delegate privileges to other users. Manufacturers sensibly argue the principle of 'least privilege' which states that users should be granted the lowest possible access rights, consistent with their job requirements. Operating systems and file security packages should establish and enforce these controls.

Passwords, once allocated, may be changed by users, by the security manager or automatically by the system. However, systems that rely exclusively on password security are doomed to failure:

- people choose passwords which are easy to guess (such as the names of their husbands or wives or popular figures such as Batman, Robin, etc.);
- passwords are often written down on terminals or in manuals;
- passwords are changed too infrequently;
- in systems which require passwords to be changed, it is not uncommon to find repetitive patterns of use. For example in one supposedly high security installation which required passwords to be changed every two weeks, the senior manager rotated between two passwords–Hugh or Hughgo: his first name was Hugh!;
- users frequently fail to change standard passwords and file names allocated by equipment suppliers.

Perhaps more importantly, users may be totally unable to reconstruct which user had which passwords at a given time. Thus if fraud is detected it may not be possible to prove responsibility to the satisfaction of a court. The clear lesson is that password security is vitally important.

QUEUING, SPOOLING AND PRINTING

Not all components of a computer operate at the same speed: printers are slow and rather than delay all operations, data is buffered on disk or tape while awaiting printout.

For example, after all processing a totalled and balanced file of sales invoices may be dumped to a disk until the printers become free.

Similarly, in banking systems, payment instructions may be dumped to disk waiting transmission to correspondent banks.

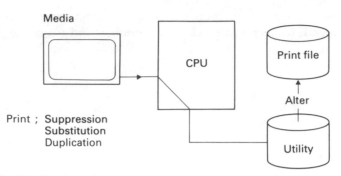

Figure 3.6 Falsification of output

These practices can be extremely dangerous if edit utilities are available. These could be used to change or delete data from the buffer, without distorting balanced files of approved transactions (see Figure 3.6).

SYSTEMS CONSOLE AND JOURNALLING

Multi-user computers will have at least one console or supervisory terminal. This will be used for initial program load and other supervisory tasks. Access to the console automatically grants high level privileges and for this reason passwords should be carefully assigned.

Operators are responsible for loading tapes and disks, for maintaining source and production libraries (often a separate function) preparing back-up and for responding to requests from users generally. They are clearly in a privileged position.

Activity on the computer may be logged or journalled: its form and extent will depend on the operating system and how it was configured. Generally micro computers and many minis have no or very limited facilities for journalling. After the event it may be impossible to trace who accessed files or even made changes to programs.

On larger machines journals will usually be retained on a disk, on a console printer or on both. These may be essential in proving responsibility for fraud or abuse and to trace the cause of errors. Too often, however, journal records are easy to destroy either by removal of paper from the printer, giving a disable command to the operating system or by deleting incriminating entries from the disk.

The console or supervisory terminal on most computers has a standard keyboard, printer and screen. On very old and on some very advanced mini computers there is an additional facility for operator intervention through the front panel of the central processing unit itself.

The front panel may have a series of toggle switches which can be either on or off and which represent binary notation. They have two display registers: one for the address in main memory or for peripherals connected to the bus and another for data. Thus operators can change data or instructions in any known address by manipulation of the toggle switches. These operations do not print out on the console log. In fact instructions through the front panel can disable the log, take the console printer offline or make other high level supervisory commands without leaving a trace. They are dangerous.

JOB ACCOUNTING

In most computer applications the amount of time taken on the central processing unit is monitored as the basis for charging user departments (or customers in a computer bureau) for the resources used. For example, if in a given period a company department has the benefit of 12 hours of computer processing, it is charged on the basis of that figure—possibly with some adjustment for the amount of operator time necessary and for the number of files used or produced.

In many companies 'customer billing' is one of the most important jobs; it is often the most accurate. Processing and billing records are useful in fraud detection and may indicate that files have been accessed without authority or that computer time or resources have been misused.

MACHINE FAILURES

Hardware failures are becoming less common but their impact can be substantial and the methods of recovery vary from one machine to another. Check points are usually incorporated into operating systems or application programs which enable processing to restart from an agreed point.

Crashes may result in sensitive data or passwords being released to unauthorized users. Repeated but unexplained failures may be an indication of abuse or attempted unauthorized access. Most machines are vulnerable during the initial program load and crashes can be deliberately induced as a means of breaching security.

CORRECTION OF ERRORS AND ADJUSTMENTS

In even the best run systems, errors will occur: proof listings may be out of balance, customers may claim their accounts are incorrect or processing may halt prematurely. In any of these cases corrections may have to be made quickly to data files and sometimes to programs. Often referred to as 'fast and dirty' fixes they are at best risky and at worst an open invitation to fraud.

Software utilities can be used to change files and programs directly, without the need to pass through the compiler or input or output controls. It is possible to enter one-sided transactions, to pass credit entries without a corresponding debit in such a way that control totals appear to be in agreement. Thus the method of controlling adjustments and correcting errors is crucially important in preventing fraud.

BACK-UP MEDIA AND PROGRAMS

Many computer installations ensure that data and programs are duplicated in an off site store for use in an emergency. However, without care these arrangements can lead to other exposures.

Firstly, it is important to ensure that responsibilities for prime and back-up media are properly separated: one person should never have access to both because it introduces unacceptable risks of theft, extortion or damage.

Secondly, it is quite possible for a person to remove a back-up program and amend it at a bureau with lines of fraudulent code in the knowledge that it will be loaded next time the system crashes.

Conclusions

To thieves, controls and accounting records are at worst an enemy and at best a necessary inconvenience. Even professional embezzlers would prefer to be able to steal assets without having to resort to manipulating accounts.

The interaction between formal controls and criminal behaviour creates patterns which thieves, no matter how skilled, cannot overcome completely.

Chapter 7 explains where and how these symptoms of fraud can be found.

4. Elements of fraud: theft act and conversion

Rule 4:   Unexplained wealth, excused by the rich aunt, rich wife, family money and football pools win story, remains unexplained

Fraud elements

It is important to remember one absolutely basic fact about fraud, thieves steal assets. The manipulation of records or other forms of concealment are necessary evils, rather than being ends in themselves.

A central feature of all frauds is the theft act: this is the stage in which a physical asset or financial interest is obtained by a thief. A theft act may be a one-time event or repeated as part of a systematic fraud: it may or may not be concealed.

Most white collar and nearly all computer frauds have three elements (see Table 4.1).

Table 4.1   Elements of fraud

1 *Theft act*	2 *Concealment*	3 *Conversion*
Purpose: Obtains possession	Hides loss Achieves opportunity for gain Shields responsibility Provides a plausible excuse	Converts benefit to a form the thief would prefer to possess
Types: Concealed or unconcealed	Manipulation of accounts Misrepresentation of a physical, personal or commercial fact	Cheques False credits Goods

Often these elements are closely connected much like links in a chain. They may occur in any sequence: for example manipulation of records may take place before or after its related theft act. Conversion may be arranged before the theft act or before or after a false credit has been manipulated.

Whatever the timing might be, each element exposes a thief and his accomplices to the risk of detection: it is simply a question of knowing where and what to look for.

This chapter examines two of the elements: theft acts and conversions. Chapter 5 deals in depth with the different forms of concealment.

Theft acts

A theft act can be defined as an element in one-time or systematic frauds in which the thief *obtains possession* of the asset or interest he desires. It is an event which has physical and behavioural symptoms; it takes place in the real world rather than in computer systems or accounting; it inevitably results in a debit to the victim's net worth.

Theft acts can be divided into two types: those which are unconcealed and those which are achieved or hidden by manipulation of accounts or misrepresentation of realities.

UNCONCEALED THEFT ACTS

Thefts remain unconcealed for a number of reasons:

– the loss will not be detected and concealment is not necessary;
– the victim condones the crime;
– the perpetrators have no means of or need for concealing the loss;
– the perpetrator plans to commit a one-time fraud and escape.

Each of these and lessons that can be learned from them will be examined.

Losses not detected

As stated in Chapter 3, theft of a physical asset results in an account/inventory discrepancy which can only be rectified if the asset or an equivalent value is replaced.

Unconcealed thefts are possible, if not invited, when inventories are not closely controlled. There are three main aspects of inventory control:

– receipts or deliveries inwards
– warehousing
– deliveries outwards

and in each one, opportunities for unconcealed thefts arise.

Companies are often exposed to short delivery by suppliers or their drivers. This is particularly true of material which is difficult to check, such as bulk liquids. Short delivery is a common if not institutionalized method of fraud.

There are many items of value which are not included on inventories or valued as assets: few companies have control over sensitive business information, such as product formulae, marketing and investment plans, customer and prospect lists. Theft of these 'assets' results in no obvious loss and is seldom detected. Small tools and equipment, often of high value, stationery and photocopying are all difficult to control and easy to steal without concealment.

Possibly the most valuable uncontrolled asset of any company is the paid time of its employees and moonlighting and inflation of hours worked is seldom considered dishonest by the perpetrator. The losses can be enormous as the following example shows:

> A Limited employed more than 200 drivers for its delivery trucks. The union had agreed with the company that drivers would be paid on the basis of scheduled hours, rather than the actual hours at work. The distance to each customer was used as the basis for calculating the scheduled hours. Each day drivers would be allocated a number of deliveries and their scheduled hours would be calculated: overtime would be paid where more than 8 scheduled hours were worked in any day. The agreement also allowed for drivers to work and finish: thus if they were able to complete their scheduled work in half the time allotted, they could return their trucks to the depot and go home early.

> At the end of the first year of operation, pay rates and scheduled hours came up for renegotiation and management was able to argue that schedules were overgenerous and it was pointed out that there were many occasions when drivers had reported back to the factory in less than half of the scheduled hours allocated.

> The union had to make concessions but gave the unofficial instructions to its members that any driver who returned to the depot earlier than the scheduled hours allowed would be subject to censure. It was suggested that drivers should 'lose' any spare time in cafés or pubs.

> This obviously could not apply to the night shift for few cafés were open, but the system seemed to work generally in the drivers' favour because the following year the union was able to negotiate even more generous scheduled times based on the hours that drivers were actually away from the factory. These times were taken from the drivers' log sheets and from a record of entry and exit times maintained by the security guards.

> However, management's suspicions were aroused and observation was kept on the plant at night. It was seen that drivers who returned and went home at, say, 2.00 a.m. were entered in the security guard's record with return times of 6.30 a.m. or later. Eventually the police were informed, further observations were kept and 50 drivers admitted bribing the security guard to record return times later than they truly were.

Based on this observation the company calculated that it had overpaid its drivers more than £100 000 in one year.

Similar abuses take place in white collar areas: who checks that highly paid programmers are coding company systems rather than working during office hours on moonlight jobs? Who checks that sales representatives and service engineers are not using time paid for by their employer for personal or conflicting interests?

Companies should identify all of their 'assets' and ensure that controls are sufficient to minimize the risk of unconcealed thefts.

Condoned losses

The idea that small frauds should be allowed as an encouragement to employees was discussed and hopefully dismissed as mindless in Chapter 1. Nevertheless some victims are prepared to tolerate losses, possibly in the belief that practices are ingrained, unchangeable or in their own interest to continue. The following example illustrates the problem:

X Limited is a high street retailer with hundreds of outlets throughout the UK. Stocks were issued and charged out to shops at retail value.

Managers were required to submit daily and weekly returns which showed opening stocks, receipts, sales and cash banked all at retail prices. Shortages, which were easy to identify, were the responsibility of the managers.

However, during their training courses, managers were told, albeit unofficially, that they could cover shortages by increasing the retail prices of selected goods. The practice of marking goods on display at greater than the proper prices was known to and condoned by senior management.

A shop manager's house was burgled and he reported the theft of his television and video to the police: he did not mention that £38 000 in pound notes had also been taken. As the result of other enquiries the burglar was caught and the majority of the cash recovered. The manager was interviewed and admitted that the cash was the result of overpricing and that he was holding it on the company's behalf against losses that might occur in the future.

The company refused to prosecute and did not even trouble to conduct an audit at the store. It did, however, suggest that the manager should deposit the cash in the company's account!

Even on supposedly small scales, condoned crime creates an environment in which employees can rationalize major dishonesty: it is the start of a slippery slope.

No means of or need for concealing the loss

The person who most needs to conceal a fraud is the person whose guilt would otherwise be obvious. Usually the person accountable for an asset automatically has access to a means of concealment. Accountability for an asset usually provides an opportunity for concealing its loss. Opportunist thieves, on the other hand, have no accountability and if they are able to contrive access and remove an asset there is little likelihood that they will be traced. The following example is typical:

> L Limited is a major clearing bank. At 4.00 p.m. a person walked in off the street and stole £4000 which a cashier had left on the counter while 'cashing up'. He was never traced. The bank manager told the press 'There is nothing basically wrong with our security, someone merely forgot to shut the door'.

One-time fraud

Smash and grab frauds usually remain unconcealed: they succeed either because the thief believes he can remain anonymous or rely on a fast escape as a means of avoiding apprehension. The following example is typical.

> The case involved a large engineering firm in the Middle East, where foreign contract personnel were required to lodge their passports with their company as a deterrent to fraud.
>
> The personnel department held the passports of all foreign contract employees, one of whom was an English foreman. One of his duties was to distribute the weekly wages, in cash, to sections of the workforce. One day he simply vanished with the payroll, amounting to some $300 000. The belief was that he could not get far without his passport and would soon be apprehended. It was then discovered that not only was his passport missing, but so was his entire personal file. It was subsequently established that he had stolen these, with comparative ease, from the personnel department shortly before taking the money.
>
> The agency in the UK that had recruited him was contacted, to obtain information about his background and likely whereabouts. It transpired that he had responded to a newspaper advertisement and that no reference had been asked for, or offered. He was a man with no past!
>
> The recruiting agency's attitude was that 'foreign companies want personnel for these contracts yesterday. Taking and checking references takes time and costs money. The companies don't want it done.'

Opportunist frauds can normally be prevented by effective physical security, by good access control and by insisting that the correct identities of people in positions of trust are known.

CONCEALED THEFT ACTS

Most thefts are supported or achieved by the manipulation of records or misrepresentation of physical, personal or commercial realities. These are discussed in the next chapter.

However, even in the most complex computer frauds, the theft act may be straightforward and easily detectable. They are also the most simple to prove to a jury.

Conversion

Conversion, which is an element in most frauds, can be divided into three categories:

– conversion of cheques
– conversion of false accounting credits
– conversion of stolen goods

and in each there are some common and predictable patterns.

CHEQUE CONVERSIONS

Both incoming and outgoing cheques are vulnerable to fraud, although opportunities vary much in line with the differential of opportunity theory. There are three major variations:

– cheques converted by opportunists
– cheques converted by a person with access to the accounts of the drawer (disbursements)
– cheques converted by a person with access to the accounts of the payee (incoming cheques)

which should be considered. The differences can be illustrated by considering the fraudulent conversion of a cheque drawn by Company X and payable to Company Y which falls into the hands of an opportunist.

An external or opportunist criminal

The following conversion opportunities are available:

1. He may cash the cheque at a bank, using some form of pretext.
2. He may endorse the cheque (as Y) and deposit it in a bank or building society account over which he has control.
3. He may use the cheque, posing as an employee of X or Y to 'buy' a banker's cheque or more easily negotiable payment.
4. He may call on Y, posing as an employee of X, and collect goods to the value of the cheque.
5. He may open an account in the name of Y and deposit the cheque.

6. He may negotiate the cheque with a third party.
7. He may alter the name of the payee.
8. He may establish contact with an employee of X or Y and share in the proceeds of internal conversion.

All of these methods carry considerable risk for the thief, but when the loss comes to notice, his identity and responsibility may not be traceable.

Conversion of a disbursement cheque

If the cheque falls into the hands of a dishonest employee of X, the opportunities for conversion are extended (see Figure 4.1).

1. He may use any of the methods listed above, exploiting his position to confuse or delay recognition of the loss.
2. He may substitute the cheque among X's bank deposits, if necessary giving the explanation to the bank cashier that it is his company's policy to deposit spoiled cheques for internal control purposes. The thief can then use this false credit to conceal the theft of cash.
3. He may report that the cheque has been lost and obtain a duplicate: both cheques can be sent to Y and the incoming refund converted.
4. He may open the cheque, using company stamps and stationery.

The thief has the added advantage of being able to recover and destroy incriminating cheques after cancellation and return by the bank. He may be able to preplan the fraud to ensure that the name of the payee entered on the cheque assists the conversion. The following case illustrates this point:

> Mr F worked for a major international company and he noticed that because of limited capacity in the company's computer system, the data

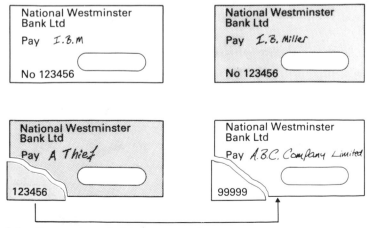

Figure 4.1 Conversion of disbursement cheques

field used to print the name of payees on disbursement cheques was often abbreviated. Cheques for one supplier whose name was International Manufacturing Consolidated Enterprises Company Limited were always prepared showing the name IMCECOL. F opened a building society account in the name of Ian Michael Cecol and deposited cheques due to the supplier into it.

There have been hundreds of cases of similar types of conversion which demonstrate that abbreviated names of genuine payees can be exploited with ease.

Conversion of incoming cheques (see Figure 4.2)

National Westminster Bank Ltd

Pay *A.B.C. Company Limited*

£4,500 00

123456

- Endorse
- Credit account of an accomplice
- Substitute for personal cheque in a lower amount (e.g., after discount)
- Substitute in place of stolen cash
- Inter-account lapping

Figure 4.2   Conversion of incoming cheques

A dishonest employee of Y may convert the cheque as follows:

1. He may use any of the methods available to the opportunist.
2. He may deposit the cheque unrecorded in the personal ledger for X and use the resulting false credit to conceal the theft of cash. He may apply the credit to the account of an accomplice and share the benefits with him.
3. He may deposit the cheque unrecorded in the cash book and ledger and use it to cover the withdrawal of an equivalent amount in cash.

Conversion of incoming cheques can be extremely difficult to detect, particularly when part of a systematic 'roll over' or 'lapping' fraud. They are often totally outside the accounts of the victim.

CONVERSION OF FALSE ACCOUNTING CREDITS

For the purposes of this section, the assumption is made that a false credit rests in the account of X Limited, a normal legitimate supplier of the thief's employer. Theoretically the account would be:

Account with X Limited	
'By fraud false credits'	£300

The thief may convert this credit as follows.

Issue a disbursement cheque

A disbursement cheque—ostensibly payable to X—can be prepared by the thief and converted in any of the ways mentioned in the previous section.

Collect goods

A false set of sales documents can be prepared (value £300, invoiced to X) to cover the collection of goods by accomplice. Alternatively the credit can be applied to the account of a customer: the thief sharing in the resulting benefit.

Account transfer

The credit may be transferred to an account in which he has an interest. From this account the credit can be converted by the issue of a disbursement cheque or a delivery of goods.

Refund from X Limited

The thief may contact X and ask for a refund of the £300. X's incoming cheque can be converted without further manipulation.

Conversion of false accounting credits is the life blood of computer frauds.

CONVERSION OF STOLEN GOODS

The last type is the conversion of stolen goods into cash: it is an extremely dangerous element for a thief because he may have to extend the circle of risk to include a receiver.

There are two possibilities:

— conversion through an innocent receiver
— conversion through a dishonest third party

each of which has risks and benefits for both the thief and the receiver.

Conversion through an innocent receiver (see Figure 4.3)

It is possible that a thief can establish an apparently legitimate front to cover the sale of stolen goods. The following case is a classic example.

> At Pan American Airways transit warehouse in New York a supervisor was able to steal navigation systems and on-board computers for Boeing

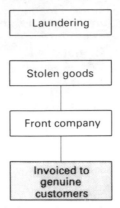

Figure 4.3   Methods of laundering stolen goods

747 aircraft. The devices in question are about the size of a small desk drawer.

He is alleged to have stolen a total of seven computers valued at $3 million and disposed of them through a front company he set up— Aviation Services and Supply. The thefts were discovered when one of the units stolen by the supervisor and sold through Aviation Services was returned to the manufacturer for repair.

This case says little for the victim's system of inventory control; that $3 million worth of equipment can go missing without notice is not a desirable position. But it is possible that the supervisor was able to write the equipment off inventory records, possibly on the basis that it had been used in the repair of the aircraft fleet. The second lesson is the ease of conversion and the fact that entirely reputable and innocent buyers became customers. Presumably he was able to undercut legitimate suppliers of the equipment.

Conversion through a dishonest third party

This is the most common method for converting stolen goods into cash and on a commercial scale usually involves maximum collusion (see Chapter 1). When thieves find a willing receiver, it is usually much like bees around a honey pot.

Sometimes reputable companies, with dishonest employees, will receive stolen goods.

F Limited is a distributor of luxury products with branches throughout Europe. A manager of a major supermarket owned by F let it be known that he would be interested in buying stolen goods for cash from the company's truck drivers. Drivers were sometimes able to obtain surplus goods either by stealing them from the central warehouse or by short delivering to other customers. The manager would keep a close record of his 'personal stocks', which would be placed on display racks for sale alongside genuine merchandise. At the end of each accounting period he would remove his 'personal takings'.

It is more common to find that the receiver is a small trader, usually at the bottom end of the market concerned. In all cases, however, conversion of stolen goods is a risky practice for thieves and often leaves a predictable impact.

> A clerk working for an airline had the job of preparing customs documentation, warehousing invoices and delivery notes. Working in collusion with a dishonest customer of his employer, the clerk prepared delivery notes for goods not intended for his accomplice. The accomplice would collect these or have them delivered to his premises. The clerk would then destroy all copies of the dispatch notes. When the genuine consignors complained, responsibility for the loss was impossible to establish.

Contrast this with the case of a lorry driver who short delivers customer X and sells the stolen goods to Y—his receiver. He is at risk from the moment he fails to deliver his full consignment; he may be questioned *en route* to or from Y's premises. Y has no documentation to cover the receipt and is similarly at risk.

In the last example, the thieves could significantly reduce the risk if Y began to order goods from the thief's employer, preferably on the same day and on the same truck as deliveries to X or other customers that the dishonest truck driver can short deliver. This arrangement reduces the risk of detection—the driver has a legitimate reason for being at Y's premises and can claim that the excess goods were left on board his truck by accident. In short, he is able to put forward a plausible excuse.

Customer Y has legitimate 'cover' for the stolen goods once they are included among his other stock. He can claim that he purchased all his stock legitimately and can produce purchase invoices in support. Provided his detected stock does not exceed the total of the legitimate invoices, he is safe.

This style of conversion—involving sales of stolen goods to regular customers of the victim—gives both an internal thief and his receiver additional protection during the theft act and conversion phases. They are able to give a plausible excuse for their dishonesty. When internal thieves dispose of stolen goods to independent receivers they are more exposed.

Because of these obvious disadvantages, it is not uncommon for receivers of stolen property to establish business connections with the thieves' employers. However, looked at more deeply, the obvious advantages of a business connection, described above, may be outweighed by serious disadvantages that neither the thief nor the dishonest employee takes into account: the impact of the *conversion* of stolen goods in the statistical records of the victim company.

Thieving Leyland workers shock

Disturbing evidence has come to light of a vast racket in stolen car parts at British Leyland—the company that is being rescued at a cost to the taxpayer of £1400 million. 'The stuff knocked off by workers must have cost the company millions of pounds', the manager of a service station in Oxford told *Sunday People* reporters . . . enquiries at other garages in the Oxford area confirmed that an extensive range of spare parts . . . are on regular offer from workers at the Cowley plant. Things like alternators, spark plugs, hub caps and light fittings are offered at a fraction of their proper price. . . . A maintenance worker said 'I have worked there for 25 years and some of the blokes will take anything that moves'. Another worker said that it was virtually impossible to steal from the pressed steel plant because of the size of the parts but added, 'You'd be dumbfounded at the gear that gets past security; it's a joke'.

If stolen parts had been disposed of to regular contracted customers of the car firm, then presumably a large-scale fraud would have an impact—either historical, proportional, or absolute—on the victim's statistical or marketing records.

In some industries the impact arising from the sale of stolen goods to regular customers of the victim is glaringly obvious in statistical records, not only in the case of larcenous or manipulative frauds.

An international manufacturer and distributor of razor blades had different price levels in each of the European countries. The highest European prices were more than 30 per cent below those charged for identical products in the American market, the home of the parent company.

Prior to the EEC treaty, European customers agreed, as part of their contract, that they would not ship products to the USA. The company found that blades were appearing in discount shops in America, priced at such levels that diversion by European customers was suspected.

In Europe, men preferred single edge blades; Americans preferred double edged or continuous strip blades.

The company's statistics showed the general distribution of sales between the various types of blades:

	% Single edge	Total sales % Double edge	% Strip
Europe	80	10	10
USA	15	72	13

With the exceptions noted below, European customers' trading patterns showed deviations from the normal of no greater than plus or minus 5 per cent.

The cheap blades offered in America were of the double edged variety. Analysis of European sales statistics indicated two customers whose distribution patterns were significantly out of line: double edged blades accounted for over 50 per cent of their purchases.

The customers were interviewed and admitted that they had diverted large quantities of double edged blades to America. They were warned to stop their practice but no civil or criminal action was taken against them nor was the estimated loss in American sales realizations, of over $1 million, recovered.

General rules

Some general conclusions can be drawn from these examples.

When the receiver of goods is a customer of the victim

- Theft acts and conversions can be more easily explained; often there is a plausible excuse for dishonesty and for the physical removal and storage of goods.
- Business contact may be established between the receiver and the victim to lay the ground work for a plausible explanation.
- Detection or interception during a delivery of stolen goods to a 'receiver' often fails to prove guilty knowledge—there is a plausible excuse.
- Records of legitimate sales to the receiver/customer may show the impact of theft and conversion:
  - absolute ratios and volumes (e.g., sales reductions)
  - historical trends and ratios (e.g., reductions year to year)
  - proportional trends and ratios (e.g., grades or type)
  - reasonableness factors (e.g., intervals between sales)
  - cancelled legitimate orders (because of full stocks of stolen goods).

When the receiver is independent of the victim

- The internal thief and the receiver are exposed to detection at the time goods are delivered, or at the time of theft.
- The receiver may not have legitimate 'cover' for stocks of stolen goods.
- Stolen goods on display may be detected by the victim's sales representatives.

- Returned guarantee cards, customer claims or other ancillary records and events may disclose the fraud.
- Sales and statistical records kept by the victim will not normally highlight evidence of conversion.

Therefore, in cases where the receiver of stolen goods is also a legitimate customer of the company from whom they have been stolen, evidence of conversion may remain in that company's statistical records. The analysis of such records—both manually and via the computer—is described later (see Chapter 7).

OTHER SYMPTOMS OF CONVERSION AND THEFT

The personal behavioural patterns of thieves and receivers often provide additional pointers for the investigator.

Glossy lifestyle based on £450 000 fiddle, says QC

Five company directors lived the lifestyle as depicted in glossy magazines with Rolls-Royces, magnificent suits, several houses and expensive foreign travel, a court was told yesterday. 'Where did the money come from?' 'The answer is . . . it came without their permission from the coffers of X bank', said Mr C.R., prosecuting. He said that during an 18-month period the directors 'cross fired' cheques totalling £41 million. The cars run by the directors were magnificent; they included Rolls-Royces, Cadillacs, Jensens, Mercedes and Alpha Romeos.

There is a strange feature common to most criminals: their inability to use the spoils of crime in a modest, reasonable or prudent way. Thieves are usually big spenders, live beyond their incomes and draw attention to themselves. These are standard behavioural symptoms of fraud conversion.

It is unnecessary to dwell too long on these behavioural symptoms associated with fraud, since they are usually obvious. But, on the other hand, companies are always reluctant to suspect the worst of a £5000 p.a. clerk driving to work in a Rolls. The 'football pools', 'rich aunt' explanations are all too readily accepted, when an hour or two spent on research would establish cause for concern, further investigation and ultimately detection.

Unexplained employee, customer or supplier wealth is a symptom of fraud and should never be ignored or lightly dismissed as legitimate.

The obvious signs of fraud conversion are just a small part of the whole host of symptoms that follow in the wake of fraud. Symptoms in physical forms, personal behaviour and accounting records are often equally obvious. Their detection and recognition are explained in Chapters 6 and 7.

5. Elements of fraud: concealment

Rule 5: When in doubt, follow the asset

Concealment plays a vital role in many corporate frauds and it is a fruitful element for investigators or auditors to explore since its traces are often permanent and predictable.

Concealment is of two types:

Manipulation	*Misrepresentation*
– falsification of accounts	– falsification of physical, personal or commercial realities

either of which can be used to achieve a theft or to hide its commission.

This chapter examines the concealment of systematic frauds in detail and demonstrates how its impact is often non-variable.

Manipulation

When an asset is stolen a debit arises in the double entry accounts concerned, which can only be replaced if the asset or an equivalent is returned. Thus, the first object of manipulation is to hide or disguise consequential debits that result from fraud by:

– creating false credits to counterbalance them;
– transferring them into loosely controlled accounts where their impact will not be noticed.

When this prime objective cannot be achieved or where a thief is particularly cautious, he may take steps to avoid blame or to provide a plausible excuse if challenged. The interrelations of these concealment possibilities is shown in Figure 5.1.

PRIMARY MANIPULATION

Debits arise as a consequence of theft:

– they are created in the account of the asset stolen at the time of the theft;
– they cannot be removed unless the asset or its equivalent is returned;

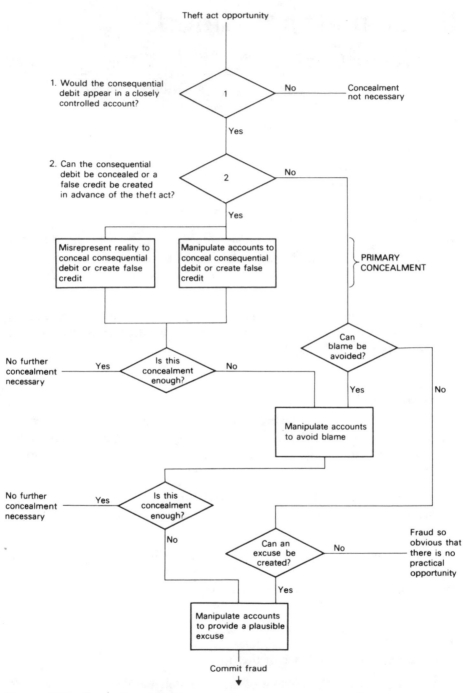

Figure 5.1 Concealment logic

- they are transferable between accounts;
- they are divisible;
- they may be combined with consequential debits arising from other thefts or with genuine debits;
- they may be deducted from or set against false or genuine credits;
- they may change their form from recorded to unrecorded and back again.

Consequential debits may be concealed by negative means, when they are not posted, or positively when a false credit is created to counterbalance them.

False accounting credits may be created to counterbalance a consequential debit:

- prior to the theft act
- concurrent with the theft act
- after the theft act

In the last two instances credits are usually generated to achieve theft, but in the last instance to conceal it. False credits may have factual bases or they may be completely fictitious.

It follows that suppression of consequential debits or creation of false credits is possible in many areas of a company's business. They have the following impact.

1. Consequential debits in accounts closed to the balance sheet affect net worth as an overstated asset or understated liability, and are potentially extremely serious. They can accumulate from year to year and their eventual disclosure may have disastrous consequences on the victim concerned.
2. Debits in accounts closed to profit and loss result in a reduction in the year's profits. Their impact is normally measurable within the year.

Opportunities for concealment are governed by the availability of loosely controlled accounts in which consequential debits may be hidden. These will vary from company to company depending to a large extent on the way its nominal ledger is structured. Also some personal accounts can be classified as loosely controlled, particularly when a criminal takes steps to discredit the accounting system by inducing deliberate errors or by rolling over or lapping entries between accounts. There are loosely controlled accounts in all accounting systems.

Figures 5.2, 5.3, 5.4, 5.5, and 5.7 show how false credits can be created and consequential debits suppressed in:

- purchase records—tangibles (Figure 5.2)
- purchase records—intangibles and services (Figure 5.3)
- payment records—disbursements (Figure 5.4)

– sales records (Figure 5.5)
– receipts—receivables (Figure 5.7)

The figures are not intended to represent complete or necessarily efficient accounting systems, nor are the methods of manipulation described the only possibilities. They are meant to show the general impacts of manipulations and to point up some of the vulnerable points at which manipulative frauds occur.

Manipulative frauds involving purchases of goods

The vast majority of frauds involving purchases are committed by or with the collusion of the victim company's employees (internal or organized frauds) and involve the production of false entries or the inflation of genuine items.

Figure 5.2 shows a possible accounting system for controlling and recording the purchase of tangible goods, stocks and assets.

The objective of manipulation is the creation of a false credit in the personal account of a supplier (H) either by inflating the value of a genuine purchase, by creating a completely false one, by diverting a debit from or credit to such an account and by transferring the consequential debit to a loosely controlled real account (G). These manipulations will ensure that:

– a credit in a personal account (H) is available for conversion or for concealment of an existing consequential debit;
– a consequential debit rests in a loosely controlled real account (G).

The first usual step is that the thief or an accomplice has to select or establish a personal account in the victim's purchase ledger (H) in which false credits can be generated and through which conversion can take place. The account may be that of a genuine supplier or it may be totally fictitious.

If the thief chooses to establish a dummy supplier's account he will need to ensure that its address is under his control—often the 'drop address' will be that of a relative, a friend, a mail forwarding company, bank or lawyer's office or a post office box. He also has to consider what level of detail will be shown on the false purchase invoices, particularly the telephone number, tax registration and company incorporation references.

Once a suitable drop address and an account based on it has been established, primary manipulation is possible at any of the stages shown on Figure 5.2.

Stage A: Purchase orders

Most cases of bribery of buyers or purchasing agents (kickbacks) are usually fully and apparently properly documented from the original purchase order (A) through to settlement. Often the consequential debit is incorporated into

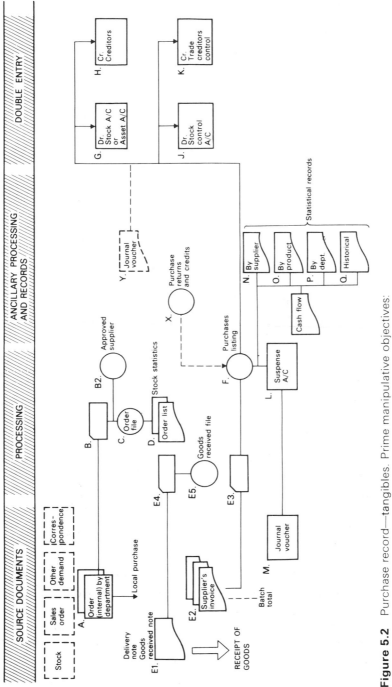

Figure 5.2 Purchase record—tangibles. Prime manipulative objectives:

— inflate an expense to create a false credit in account H
— transfer the consequential debit to a loosely controlled account G

an inflated stock or purchase value and is difficult to detect. This is particularly true when, for example, the cost of a major construction project is inflated to cover bribes paid to purchasing agents.

Although official accounting records including purchase orders appear to expose corrupt purchasing agents to minimal risks of detection, the circumstances surrounding the award of a contract often provide the first suspicion of fraud.

Many companies insist that all contract work and purchases over a certain limit go out for competitive bidding. More often than not, a specified number of companies must be invited to submit tenders before a contract is awarded. Provided the corrupt purchase agent complies with this rule, little attention is paid to the actual number of tenders received or to the unsuccessful bidders. That is to say, the rules usually specify that a certain number of tenders must be invited; they do not usually insist on the number of tenders actually received or that vendors must be independent.

It is therefore possible for a corrupt purchasing agent—wishing to pass business to a supplier with whom he is in collusion—to select and send invitations to tender to fictitious companies, to subsidiaries of the corrupt supplier, or to genuine suppliers who do not undertake the particular type of work. Thus, the specified number of tenders can be complied with without endangering the corrupt or favoured supplier's monopoly.

Another dangerous situation arises when companies rely on architects or surveyors to arrange quotations for contract work. Although the majority of practitioners in both professions are honest, there are always exceptions; it is also possible that an employee of the architect or surveyor might have been corrupted by a contractor and attempt to direct further business to his accomplice. The case below illustrates these dangers.

> The chief civil engineer employed on a major construction site died suddenly before the project had been completed. His wife was asked to call at the office to collect his personal belongings. While emptying his desk she found a bank account—not in her husband's name—with over $1 million on deposit. An investigation followed and it was established that the husband had awarded contracts to supplier X and had been paid a 10 per cent override on all of X's charges. The commission had been padded into X's billings to the construction company.
>
> The engineer had been required to send invitations to tender to four contractors prior to any work being awarded. The investigation established that only three companies—including X—had submitted bids. The two other companies were subsidiaries of X and had been incorporated for the sole purpose of 'rigging' bids.

Certain purchases are more open to corrupt practices than others; the most vulnerable are discussed later (see pages 203–205, also 373–374). Bribes may be paid to cause an employee or agent of the victim company to:

- accept lower standards of work or goods than those specified;
- accept higher prices, 'on cost' adjustments or overruns to budgets;
- accept tender revisions after a contract has been awarded.

Bribery and corruption is a major cause of corporate loss since invariably commission payments—or whatever they are euphemistically called—are covered by inflating the bill to the customer.

Reliable estimates suggest that for every $1 paid as a bribe the victim organization will probably lose between $500 and $1000 in unwanted or substandard goods, lost profits or lost opportunities.

Corruption, like all frauds, leaves a recognizable documentary impact:

- high numbers of 'emergency contracts' which are not put out to tender;
- frequently allowed overruns to initial budgets;
- a high incidence of order splitting to avoid the need to obtain competitive tenders or board level approval;
- a high incidence of repair charges or warrantee claims associated with a particular supplier.

Besides corruption, there are many manipulative frauds which depend on false purchase orders as a preliminary step to fraud.

A most common fraud which centres on stage A is 'order splitting'; dividing large orders into two or more parts to bypass a corrupt employee's authority levels.

> Company C's purchasing policy insisted that all purchases over £100 were dealt with by the head office central purchasing department. A manager of one of C's branches—who had been bribed by a local supplier—placed orders with that supplier in regular amounts below the £100 limit. Thus, where goods ordered were priced at £500, the manager would complete six or more small purchase orders and was paid a 'commission' on them. Had the orders been placed centrally, the local supplier would not have been successful.

Another type of fraud whose manipulative element begins at stage A is the passing through the company accounts of personal expenses and bills for other enterprises in which an employee has an undisclosed interest.

> X was an employee of Y Limited. Immediately before his retirement he placed orders on Y's stationery for goods required by him in the consultancy business he proposed to establish. The goods were delivered to X's home, but paid for by Y Limited.

Stage E: Goods received notes

The physical delivery and receipt of goods is usually open to fraud and goods may be short delivered with or without collusion of the victim's employees. Once a delivery note (E1) has been signed further concealment may not be necessary. Although a stock difference may arise, it is usually so vague as to avoid blame being directed towards the thief, since similar stock shortages can occur for a whole number of other reasons.

However, unless short delivery frauds are concealed, their extent and duration should be limited. Without internal collusion they are essentially opportunist.

Stages E–F: Open files of purchase orders

A signed purchase invoice (E2) reconciled with an open purchase file (C) is as valuable as a blank cheque. At this stage a number of manipulative frauds are possible.

- An invoice (E2) may be pushed through the accounting system more than once, thereby creating a credit in a personal account (H) and a consequential debit in a stock account (G).
- The invoice value (E2) may be fraudulently increased after authorization, either on the face of the document itself or by manipulation of computer input (E3). If the thief is able to intercept outgoing cheques, the supplier, whose invoices are used may be completely genuine and oblivious to the fact that his name is being misused:
- Invoice summaries (F) may be falsely totalled, either manually or on an adding machine or computer, as follows:
  - During a particular day or accounting period a number of invoices have been received from supplier X with whom an employee is in collusion.
    Invoices received from X Limited

No. 1001	Amount	£200
1002		300
1003		700
1008		100
1009		200

These are listed on an adding machine as:

£200
300
700
100
200   At this stage the adding machine tape is wound through the machine and the criminal adds two further figures:

£500
600   He then winds back the tape and prints the total.

Total   £2600

The invoices and the adding machine tape are stapled together and the £2600 posted to the personal account (H) of the supplier. A false credit of £1100 is thereby created.

The case above is a simple example, but the same principle can be applied to more sophisticated frauds and in less easily identifiable amounts.

Normally purchase invoices should be validated against an open purchases file (C) before being authorized. If there is no cross-reference between open purchase orders (or goods received files E5) and authorized purchase invoices, the possibilities of fraud are increased.

Other manipulations

The system also exposed the following frauds:

- A quantity of goods may be returned to a supplier and the resulting credit note and incoming cheque converted externally.
- Discounts may not be taken, i.e., the gross amounts of invoices (E2) may be posted to the creditors' accounts (H), thereby building up a false credit. Conversion may be by any of the standard methods.
- Journal vouchers (Y) may be fraudulently compiled to alter, divert or duplicate input data after authorization for apparently legitimate (e.g., VAT adjustments) or fictitious reasons. False credits may be built into a supplier's account in which the thief has an interest. Such credits might arise by transfer from suspense accounts (L) or from other suppliers' accounts.
- Ancillary costs, e.g., freight, customs duty, foreign exchange charges associated with real purchases may be inflated.
- Exceptions to the system may be exploited. For example:
  - *contra* accounts with suppliers who are also customers may be fraudulently adjusted;
  - petty cash or local purchases may be deducted directly from sales income or cash floats.

Purchasing fraud symptoms and loosely controlled accounts

Manipulation of the type described will result in a difference between physical assets and their related accounts. If stocks are closely controlled, secondary manipulation may be necessary.

Some accounts are better—from a thief's point of view—than others in concealing consequential debits arising from the manipulation of purchases:

- high activity, multiple supplier stock accounts whose related inventories are difficult to quantify or value or which are beyond the day-to-day control of the victim (remote stores, overseas stocks, etc.);
- working stocks and materials inventories;
- accounts which are excluded from a basic control system, for example:
  - 'on-consignment' stocks
  - on-hire or leased stocks
  - maintenance and repair accounts (especially those not posted to closely controlled cost centre)
  - 'messy', troublesome or dirty inventory accounts (e.g., waste material, scrap, rejects, etc.).

The most favoured accounts in which to create false credits and through which conversion takes place include:

- accounts in which the thief has an interest;
- fictitious and dummy front companies;
- accounts with criminal accomplices, when the thief can share in real values fraudulently obtained;
- accounts with legitimate suppliers whose controls are weak;
- accounts with genuine suppliers whose refund cheques can be converted (basically those which do not produce monthly statements).

Even though consequential debits and false credits may be adequately concealed in the formal books, evidence of fraud may be obvious in statistical or management records (N–Q).
Purchasing statistics may reveal:

- absolute increase in volumes or values of purchases;
- distortion in yearly trends as between different types of goods;
- regular purchases from a supplier, consistently below the central purchasing limits.

Product statistics may reveal:

- distortion in purchase volumes when compared with previous trends or manufacturing formulae.

Management reports may reveal:

- inconsistent trends in fixed or variable costs
- distortion of historical trends
- budget discrepancies

Notwithstanding the dangers of detection inherent in all cases of positive manipulation, purchasing frauds are commonplace and usually involve substantial amounts.

Manipulative frauds involving intangible services and expenses

Figure 5.3 represents an accounting system for recording purchases of intangible services and expenses which have no related real inventories. They are obviously excellent accounts to conceal consequential debits, since account/inventory discrepancies do not arise.

The aim of manipulation is to create a credit in a personal account (H) while at the same time ensuring that the consequential debit is posted to a loosely controlled nominal account (G).

Manipulation can be achieved in all the ways described in the previous section and it is not necessary to repeat them here. It is sufficient to note the following points:

– frauds involving the inflation of intangible expenses are a major fraud area;
– they normally involve internal collusion;
– they are achieved by positive rather than negative manipulation and leave detectable audit trails.

Where expenses are written back to discrete cost centres, inflations are more likely to be noticed.

A prudent thief will pick the nominal account in which fraud is concealed with care and will ensure that:

– fictitious costs are confused in statistical or budgetary records;
– the costs are posted to large departments whose costs are difficult to control and monitor:
– the fictitious cost falls into an expense category whose budget is seldom exhausted within the financial period concerned.

In all purchase manipulations, it is essential that a fraudulent credit is created in the account of a genuine or fictitious supplier: conversion is then straightforward.

Manipulative fraud involving disbursements

False credits may be created through a disbursement system such as that shown on Figure 5.4 in which payments are authorized from:

– balances outstanding on creditors' accounts;
– cash purchase invoices;
– payroll, pension, commission, personal expenses and similar records.

The object of manipulation is to conceal a consequential debit in a creditor's

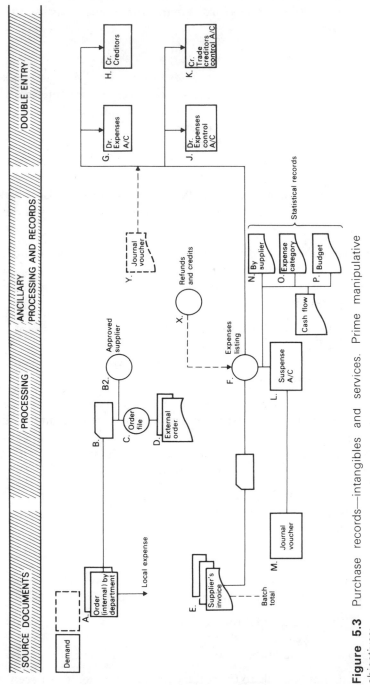

Figure 5.3 Purchase records—intangibles and services. Prime manipulative objectives:

– inflate an expense account to create a false credit in account H
– transfer the consequential debit to a loosely controlled account G

personal account (H) or in a nominal heading. This objective is usually achieved by prior manipulation of purchase records, although it is also possible by creating false disbursements not recorded on the bank statement, or under-recording incoming cash or bank deposits.

These manoeuvres have the effect of inflating the cash inventory (hard cash or the bank balance) over that recorded in the ledgers. These unrecorded excesses may be converted by withholding incoming payments, or by the issue of a disbursement cheque to the thief, or by any other of the methods of conversion discussed in Chapter 4.

Manipulation is possible at the following stages.

Stage A: Payment request

Disbursement cheques may be prepared—based on payment requests—for a higher amount than is due to a creditor. For example, when a credit balance of £2000 rests in a supplier's account and a discount of £200 is receivable, a disbursement cheque may be prepared for £2000. The thief then has three main courses open to him.

1. He may contact the supplier, asking for the £200 to be refunded and deposit the amount, unrecorded in the ledger, thus creating a false credit. Alternatively he may simply convert the incoming payment.
2. Alternatively, the thief may draw a cheque for £1800 payable to the supplier and a further cheque for £200 payable to himself or to an accomplice.
3. He may convert the cheque for £2000 and replace it with a personal cheque, drawn to the supplier for £1800.

Stages B and C: Computer input

Computer input (B) may be manipulated to divert a debit from an account in which a thief has an interest to another account. This typically takes place in lapping frauds.

Also at stage C, a dishonest commercial advantage may be obtained by making payments before their due date. If, for example, it is a company's policy to pay suppliers two months after invoice date, an internal thief may seek personal reward if he agrees to place a certain supplier's invoices on the payment file earlier than justified. The supplier gains through prompt payment, the employee through a kickback and the victim loses the advantage of the company's cash planning.

Stage G: Bank statements

Bank statements, because they are invariably accepted as accurate, are an excellent aid to a thief in creating false credits. The potential fraudulent uses of bank statements are discussed later.

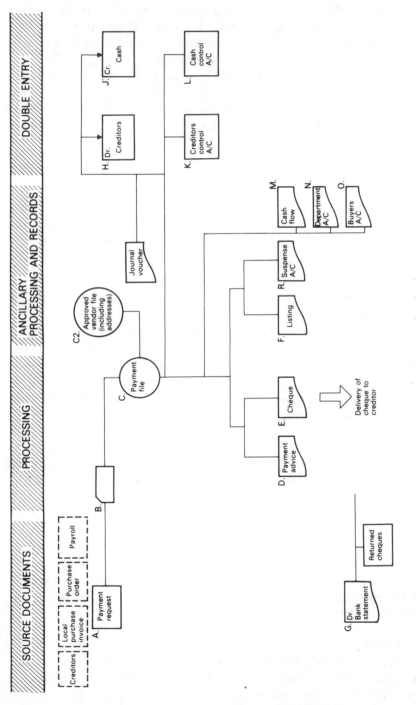

Figure 5.4 Payment record—disbursements. Prime manipulative objectives:

- create a false credit in the cash account J
- conceal a debit in the credit account H

Exception to the control system

The system described in Figure 5.4 shows mainstream processing, but in real life there are exceptions, extraordinary transactions which are handled separately. These are frequently open to manipulation and include:

- payments drawn to cash
- overseas payments, particularly wire transfers
- cashier's or banker's cheques
- payments to agents and commission agents
- deposits, advances and on account payments

Disbursement fraud symptoms

Disbursement frauds are usually traceable from their impact on the nominal ledger, from payment instructions and cancelled cheques. Detection of these is discussed in Chapter 7.

Manipulative frauds in accounts receivable: Sales

Sales revenue is highly exposed to fraud; manipulation is usually by negative means involving the destruction of documents or suppression of accounting entries.

Figure 5.5 (on page 120) shows a typical system for processing sales and accounts receivable. The object of manipulation is the creation of a false credit in the account of a debtor (L) by:

- suppression of sales debits (i.e., an unrecorded credit)
- diversion of credits from other accounts

which will be converted either by the release of goods or through a refund cheque.

Stages A–G: Sales orders and dispatch notes

Normally documents shown in stages A to G are essential to obtain release of goods from the victim's custody and are, therefore, usually safe from negative manipulation. However, dispatch notes, stock transfer requests and similar source documents may be subject to alteration or destruction after a theft has been achieved.

There are exceptions to this general rule. For example, an order (A) or input data (B) may be altered prior to the theft act to show the name of X when the goods are to be collected from the victim by Y. In such manipulations, an apparently valid dispatch note (G) is available against which the goods will be released. The manipulation results in a debit being posted to the account of X rather than Y. Such frauds are usually short term.

Long firm or credit frauds are usually concealed from the sales order stage.

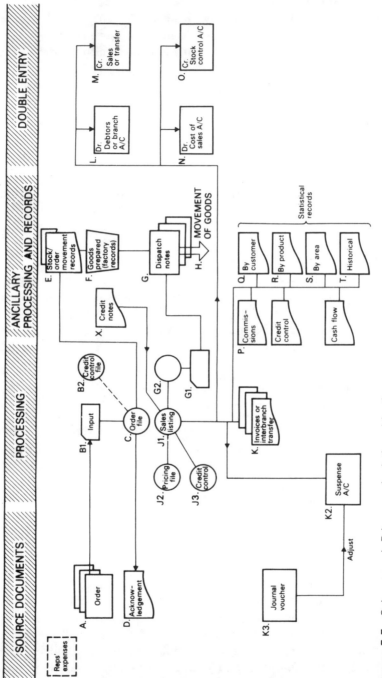

Figure 5.5 Sales record. Prime manipulative objectives:
– create a false credit in a debtor's account L
– suppress or conceal a consequential debit in the sales account M

The term 'long firm' refers to frauds committed by organized criminals who operate as follows:

- they set up or take over apparently legitimate front companies;
- the companies order goods on credit. In the early days supplies are paid for promptly to establish confidence and a good credit rating;
- the size of orders is increased and debts are built up with as many suppliers as possible;
- the goods are sold for cash and at prices below cost;
- finally, the criminals disappear, leaving enormous debts, no recoverable stock and few, if any, clues as to their true identity.

The frauds are essentially misrepresentation and should be detected at an early stage if the intended victims exercise good credit control.

Stage G: Dispatch notes

At this point, release of the victim's goods has been authorized by a dispatch note (G). If the accounting copies of these documents can be destroyed, no debit will be posted to the customer's personal ledger (L). Cash sales are usually suppressed by negative manipulations; the resulting consequential debit (to stock or cost of goods sold) may or may not be obvious, depending on how closely the accounts/inventories are controlled.

At stage G1, where dispatch information is converted into computer form, false data may be introduced. Names may be substituted (customer X for Y) or, more dangerously, a sale made to customer X may be billed to a branch or remote warehouse of the victim company, or the debit rejected into a suspense or bad debt account (K2) from which further manipulations may be made.

In manual systems, the top copy of dispatch notes—used as a loading authority or a gate pass—can be made out in higher quantities or for greater values than the copies used for accounting purposes. Dispatch notes may also be reused to support larcenous thefts.

Stage J: Pricing file and credit control

At this stage, accounting copy dispatch notes (G) are priced from information kept on the master pricing file (J2). False credits can be created or debits suppressed by altering transaction data or master file information (see Figure 5.6).

Correct transaction	× Correct master file information	= Correct book-keeping entry
False transaction	× Master file information	= False book-keeping entry
Transaction	× False master file information	= False book-keeping entry

Figure 5.6 Manipulation of master file and transaction data

Transaction data may be manipulated by:

- altering quantities
- backdating dates of delivery to avoid price increases
- altering customer names (X for Y)

after the goods have been released by the victim company.

Master files may be manipulated as follows:
- altering the rebate levels allowable to a particular customer
- altering credit limits
- failing to incorporate price increases into the file generally or against a particular customer
- altering quantity rebates, transport or freight costs (f.o.b. to c.i.f.)

> For example, assume that customer X is genuinely given the benefit of maximum discounts. Shipments made to Y—with whom an employee is in collusion—can be input into the system as if they were for X and priced accordingly. The debit resulting in X's account can be reposted to Y's by journal voucher as though it were a genuine mistake. Source documents can be corrected. Y has thus gained the advantage of receiving a discounted price to which he is not entitled.

In many companies, alteration of master files is a simple matter. When general price changes are made, it is often left to a representative to authorize price increase to special customers as the following example shows:

> Company C is a wholesaler of radio equipment, dealing through representatives with UK and overseas retailers. Some of these retailers, because of their size and the volume of their business, were termed special customers and were controlled by sales managers rather than sales representatives. The special customers received certain price advantages and credit terms and were not necessarily subject to the same price fluctuations as the smaller customers.
>
> For this reason, when C made price changes, the master file entries for special customers were not automatically raised and it was left to sales managers to advise what proportion of any price increase should be passed on. C raised its prices by 23 per cent; the master pricing file for all regular customers was uplifted by this amount. Some sales managers uplifted the prices to special customers by the same amount; others, because of business considerations, recommended lower amounts, ranging from 10 to 20 per cent.
>
> They submitted data input forms to their head office and new prices were incorporated into the master files. However, one sales manager approached a special customer who agreed to pay a 5 per cent kickback in

cash if their prices were not increased. No one in C's head office noticed this and the company lost over £50 000. By the time the mistake came to light, the customer had gone into liquidation.

The priced transaction file (J1) is used for preparing statistical records (Q, R, S and T), sales ledger posting (L and M) and invoices (K). Manipulation may result in debit entries being rejected into a suspense account (K2) instead of being posted to a debtor's account (L). There are two main possibilities.

Balances can remain in the suspense account until year end when the following occurs:

- debit balances which have not been properly posted become due for payment. Favoured customers have received a financial advantage through extended credit;
- credit control systems (J3), because of the underdebiting to the proper accounts, may be bypassed (e.g., further credit granted to long firm or other thieves).

Balances can be further manipulated from the suspense accounts, by journal voucher:

- they may be posted to bad debts;
- they may be posted into loosely controlled personal accounts;
- they may be used in lapping frauds.

In all cases, suspense accounts are a fruitful area for fraudulent manipulation.

Stage K3: Journal vouchers

Journal adjustments can be made to carry out a variety of frauds, from inter-account transfers, pricing alterations, credits and returns. In most systems they are extremely vulnerable.

Stage P: Commission

Commission supposedly due to agents or sales representatives may be fraudulently increased—with or without collusion—and converted through any of the methods described in Chapter 4.

Stage X: Credit notes

False credit notes (X) can be created and passed to customers supposedly for:

- goods returned
- price concessions
- samples
- spoiled or substandard goods
- container deposits

In the same way, discounts may be fraudulently increased so that a false credit is created in a debtor's account (L).

Sales fraud symptoms

Although manipulative frauds involving sales can be complex, the overriding objective is suppression by negative manipulation often with the following impact.

Factory and manufacturing records (E–F) may reveal:

- stock shortages
- movement of goods not invoiced
- missing or out of sequence source documents
- shipping charges not supported by sales invoices
- work records not supported by a sales charge

Miscellaneous records may reveal:

- salesman's travelling and commission records not supported by sales
- low conversion rate of sales leads
- inconsistent interbranch transfers or stock holdings in remote warehouses

Statistical records (Q–T) may reveal historical, proportional, absolute or other distortions in sales patterns:

- by customer account reference
- by salesman's area
- by branch
- by product

The best accounts—from a thief's point of view—to post or hold consequential debits arising in sales accounting are:

- loosely controlled personal or inventory accounts
- overseas customers
- government departments
- bad debt accounts (either with collusion or by retrospective adjustments)
- loosely controlled internal transfer accounts
- accounts that record exceptions to the basic control system
- suspense accounts (temporary concealment)

The credibility of closely controlled personal accounts (of suppliers and customers) can be deliberately destroyed; particularly when subject to frequent errors and adjustments.

Manipulative frauds involving receipts

Receipts are mainly exposed to fraudulent conversion:

- theft of incoming cash;
- conversion of incoming cheques (recorded in the cash book but unrecorded or falsely recorded as to origin in the sales ledger) or replaced by personal cheques in a lower amount;

but they can also be exploited in the manipulation element of fraud.

Figure 5.7 (on page 126) shows a system of recording incoming payments. The object of manipulation is to conceal consequential debits in a debtor's account (F).

False credits generated in the receivables system depend upon the creation of a cash surplus (either hard cash or in the bank account) over and above that recorded in the ledger and/or cash book. The surplus may simply be removed, transferred to another account, used to conceal an existing debit or converted in any of the ways discussed in Chapter 4.

For most practical purposes the manipulation of receivables depends upon the availability of incoming funds which are inadequately controlled. These may be:

- unconventional or unexpected income, such as sales of scrap or raw materials, advance payments, bad debt dividends received, supplier refunds;
- payments fom loosely controlled debtors' accounts;
- refunds manipulated by a thief through accounts payable;
- on-account payments, deposits, refunds.

The main manipulation possibilities are as shown below.

Stage A: Paying in slip

The thief can choose one of the following courses:

- He may deposit a cheque in the victim's bank account, posting a false credit to the account of an accomplice. The consequential debit (as an unrecorded credit) is created in the loosely controlled account from which the receipt originated.
- He may deposit the proper amount of cheques received in the bank account while debiting the cash book with a lower amount (i.e., a false credit to cash). For example, when a cheque for £700 is received and deposited in the bank account, the following entries can be made:

Debit   Cash   £500   (unrecorded credit of £200)
Credit Debtor X   £700
Debit   Discount £200

An unrecorded credit of £200 rests in the cash account, while the consequential debit is charged to discounts allowed, and will be written off

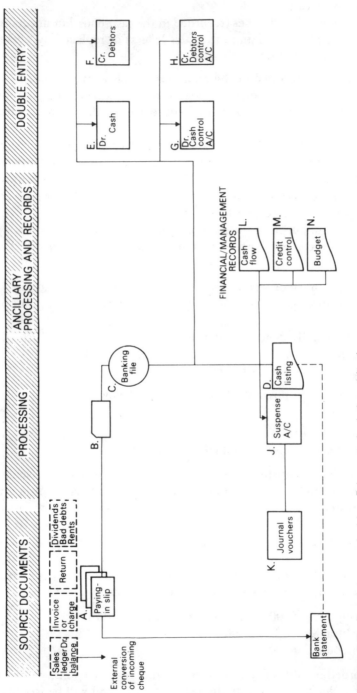

Figure 5.7 Receipts—receivables. Prime manipulative objectives:

- create a false credit in the debtor's account F
- conceal the consequential debit in a debtor's account F
- or variations

against profits at the end of the financial period. Incoming cash to the value of £200 can be stolen without further concealment.

These manipulations are similar to those used for the fraudulent conversion of incoming cheques but with one fundamental difference. Where a thief converts an incoming cheque by endorsing it and paying it in to an account over which he has control, it will not bear the stamp of the victim's banker: it is an external conversion. Cheques used to create fraudulent credits (and internal conversions) are paid into the victim's bank account, although they will not be properly recorded in the sales ledger.

Internal conversions and manipulations are usually simple to detect: the same is seldom true for external conversion of incoming cheques simply because their impact is completely outside the victim's control.

Stage B: Data input

Computer input may be manipulated. For example, a cheque received from X can be credited to the account of Y or to suspense. Balances can be rolled over as in a conventional lapping fraud.

Stage K: Journal vouchers

Journal vouchers may also be used to carry out fraudulent inter-account transfers (i.e., between ledgers (F)) but again the overriding consideration is the availability of a loosely controlled account (usually of a debtor) in which to conceal the consequential debits.

A useful account is the victim's own; in some cases it is possible for a thief to pay in disbursement cheques drawn by the victim with normal bank deposits, as the following example demonstrates:

> B was a cashier employed by C, a small retailer. B had control of purchase invoices and bank deposits. This division in duties was deliberate. C believed that it would eliminate any risk of fraud. B submitted purchase invoices to his manager for approval and C prepared disbursement cheques on the strength of them. Once or twice a month B would resubmit invoices and obtain duplicate disbursement cheques. B would include these with normal bank deposits and, when first questioned by the bank cashier, explained that it was company policy to pay in 'spoiled cheques' for internal control purposes. This simple scheme built up credits in the cash account which B converted to his own benefit.

Receipt fraud symptoms

At the heart of internal conversion of receipts is the deposit of cheques wrongly recorded in the cash book and ledgers as to their nature and origin.

Once the cheques have been deposited they are returned to the payers and are then outside the victim's domain.

However, symptoms of fraud include:

– incorrect or inconsistent number of items on paying in slips when compared against the cash book and ledgers
– missing or photocopied paying in slips
– unstamped paying in slips
– file copies of paying in slips not bearing a bank stamp
– alterations on paying in slips
– differences between cash book entries and items recorded on paying in slips

Methods for detecting frauds involving incoming funds are discussed in Chapter 7, page 209.

Manipulative frauds involving miscellaneous accounts

Most of the common methods of manipulative frauds have been discussed in the previous sections. There are, however, two other important areas: bank accounts and exceptions.

Manipulation involving bank accounts

Although seldom used as a primary means of manipulation, bank accounts, because of their assumed reliability, are useful to thieves.

Bank accounts may be forged—this is particularly easy if the proprietors of a business are prepared to accept photocopied statements or, worse still, no statements at all!

Also genuine errors on bank statements can be exploited by an internal thief. For example:

On a certain day the bank made an error in Company X's statement and immediately rectified it with a *contra* entry.

The statement showed:
Dr £2710.58
Cr   £2710.58

but contained no further explanation. A thief working for X:

1. prepared false deposit slips for:
   £1200.38—Jones ⎱
   £1510.20—Smith ⎰ Total £2710.58
2. sent copies through for posting in the cash book and ledger (for Jones and Smith);
3. prepared a number of false purchase invoices totalling £2710.58, using photocopies of old records;
4. backed up the false invoices with photocopied disbursement cheques;

    5. filed the purchase invoices and cheques in their proper places;
    6. called on Smith and Jones and collected a half share in the fictitious
       credits to their accounts.

There are a number of variations on this type of fraud, limited only by the imagination of the thief and his access to records. Their advantage from the thief's point of view is the extra credibility that an apparently correct bank statement adds to the deception.

Cheques may be 'cross-fired' between bank accounts to conceal fraud. The *modus operandi* is the existence of two accounts (these may be bank accounts, creditors'/debtors', stock accounts, or taxation accounts) in which debits on one account are not posted until after the counterpart credits have been applied to the other. For example:

> Company X and Company Y are members of the same group and controlled by common directorships. Both companies are registered for sales tax (VAT) purposes; one company having to submit its three-monthly returns for the periods April/June, July/September, October/December and January/March and the other on a later 'stagger' terminating in quarters ending July, October, January and April. The system used for collecting VAT by the Customs and Excise Department is such that, when purchases are made, any tax included in the purchase price is credited against the purchaser's returns, based on quarterly sales. Thus, if a company buys £10 000 worth of goods in a quarter, VAT of say £800 included in that amount is set against the tax payable.
>
> Purchase invoices can be cross-fired between the two companies so that false credits of tax are established.
>
> Company X put through a false sale to Y of say 30K in April and Y uses the input tax to claim a credit from the Customs and Excise in its return due in April. Company X does not have to account for its sales tax until 30 June. Towards the end of June, Company Y falsifies an invoice to X for say 50K, X in its June return has to account for its original false sale of 30K to Y, but can now offset the greater tax credit arising from Y's false invoice for 50K.
>
> This cycle can continue, almost indefinitely, with fictitious invoices and credit notes being cross-fired between two or more associated companies. When the fraud has spiralled to a large amount the company (either X or Y) which happens to be holding responsibility for the tax can be put into liquidation to avoid payment altogether.

A similar method is used for cross-firing between bank accounts—the credit appearing in account X being used for two or three days while clearance takes place in Y's account. Then the process is reversed.

Exceptions

Exceptions can arise from the nature of a particular transaction or they can occur when certain aspects of the business are changing. When, for example, a company begins to change from a manual accounting system to computer processing it is not unusual for a certain amount of confusion to arise. Confusion is life blood to criminals; fraud symptoms can be concealed among system failures and errors.

Another favourite exception for thieves occurs at the end of the financial year or during takeover negotiations, when books are being finalized and the urgency to complete the business makes for carelessness. Extreme work pressure can introduce mistakes that thieves can exploit. Exceptions to established systems or procedures are invariably vulnerable to fraud.

Points on primary manipulation

Most of the manipulations described in this chapter require free access to at least some of the victim's records and therefore involve employees of the victim company and fall within categories A3, B3 and C3 shown in Chapter 2. Although a major aim of manipulation is to avoid detection, it has repercussions and side effects that a thief cannot entirely control or predict. In many cases, therefore, the criminal has to take steps to avoid blame should his first line of defence fail and a loss come to light. This can be termed secondary concealment.

SECONDARY CONCEALMENT: AVOIDANCE OF BLAME

Normally the best way for a thief to avoid blame is to conceal the loss by primary manipulation. A loss may remain exposed for a number of reasons. Possibly the thief has no access to a suitable concealment course, or the loss is so large that it just cannot be concealed. This is often true of one-time frauds.

Unless he relies on extortion or misrepresentation as a means of avoiding detection, or false identification as a means of avoiding apprehension, it may be necessary for a thief to take steps to prevent blame pointing at him. Even where a thief has been able to conceal a loss, he may still wish to take additional precautions.

The avoidance of blame is a strange phenomenon. Internal thieves rarely blame their own colleagues in a face-to-face confrontation or name them directly. They are often prepared to cover their own guilt by pointing blame towards a group of people but seldom towards a named colleague.

The situation is quite different where professional criminals are involved. They are usually prepared to blame others, with little or no regard for their status, friendship or innocence. They will frequently produce perjured evidence to support their case in the knowledge that if detected the penalties would be no greater than if convicted for the original offence, and there is always the chance that their false explanations will be accepted.

These points have a direct bearing on blame avoidance and in interviewing people suspected of fraud. Although internal criminals might have the means of diverting blame to an innocent colleague, they will seldom use it. Even under suspicion, during interrogation, the guilty employee (unless he is a professional criminal) will seldom blame another employee he knows to be innocent.

Against this background, some general points can be made on blame avoidance.

Blame avoidance by internal criminals

Manipulations designed to avoid blame are usually restricted to source and informal documents. Possible methods include:

- falsified correspondence appearing to give the thief permission for what otherwise would obviously be a dishonest act;
- falsified receipts and invoices obtained from third parties justifying the thief's possession of stolen goods (cover invoices);
- IOUs and other informal and uncorroborated documents designed to make an otherwise overt criminal act seem innocent;
- deliberately confused records or broken equipment so that 'error' may be claimed;
- destruction of correspondence or source documents to avoid accountability for a loss;
- falsified signatures and entries on receipts or work records, etc., either to establish the thief's supposed innocence or to support an alibi.

Avoidance of blame by negative means—missing or destroyed documents—is more satisfactory from a thief's viewpoint. A document that has been falsified is always open to disproof. A missing document leaves no evidence, but may adequately divert blame or provide a non-criminal excuse.

Blame avoidance by external criminals

Since the means of primary concealment is not always available to external criminals—because records are outside their domain—they often rely more heavily on manipulation to avoid blame or to provide a plausible excuse for dishonesty. Possible methods include:

- falsified documents, obtained from third parties, intended to cover the possession of stolen goods;
- deliberately confused records so that error may be claimed;
- fictitious documents directing blame towards an employee of the victim company or another innocent party.

External criminals are often prepared to go to enormous lengths to forge and falsify correspondence and their own internal records.

Another type of manipulation closely associated with the avoidance of blame is that contrived to provide a plausible excuse for dishonesty.

PLAUSIBLE EXCUSES

It is possible that criminologists have underestimated the value to thieves of a course of concealment that simply provides them with a plausible excuse for fraud.

Internal criminals generally wish to conceal fraud to:

- escape punishment
- avoid the social stigma attached to detection and criminal prosecution
- avoid making restitution

Total concealment of a loss, coupled with efforts to avoid blame, is likely to satisfy all three requirements—while satisfaction of the first two may be sufficient for most white collar criminals.

Before a criminal can be convicted it is necessary to establish that he acted with guilty intent. 'Guilty knowledge' is an essential ingredient of most criminal offences.

Thus, all a thief may need to do to avoid prosecution is to establish—to a reasonable level of doubt—that he acted without criminal intent. If he can satisfy his manager, an investigator, the police or a court that his action was not intentionally dishonest he may be safe.

Thus where a thief is unable to conceal a loss or avoid blame, he may still believe that fraud is worth the risk if he can provide a plausible, non-criminal excuse if challenged.

It follows that control systems should be such that the criminal is prevented from giving an innocent explanation for criminal conduct. Systems should commit him irrevocably at the earliest stage to a criminal action incapable of innocent excuse.

CONCLUSION ON MANIPULATIONS

Manipulated records are often obvious. When consequential debits in balanced books are suppressed, equally revealing symptoms may be glaringly obvious in statistical or other records. When source documents are manipulated, side impacts in balanced books or statistical records may leave the fraud exposed. Detecting manipulations depends on five things:

- finding the true reason for deviations from procedures;
- knowing where to look and what to look for;
- following through initial suspicions and not being distracted by plausible excuses;

- tracing transactions recorded in formal books to source documents, correspondence, real inventories and business performance;
- testing critical points for positive or negative manipulations.

Properly designed accounting systems can limit the ability of thieves to conceal losses, avoid blame and provide acceptable excuses for dishonesty. The overriding objective, from a fraud prevention point of view, is to structure controls so that:

- fraud results in an obvious account/inventory discrepancy or in a distortion of a closely controlled expense/income account;
- a thief is forced to record his dishonesty (the potential for negative concealments should be removed);
- the thief is committed to an inexcusable course of conduct at the earliest stage of a fraudulent transaction;
- the thief's identity and accountability are clear.

Fraud defences and detection procedures are discussed in detail in Chapters 8, 9 and 11. The second element of concealment is misrepresentation.

Misrepresentation

Misrepresentation is the real world equivalent of manipulation and is a member of the concealment family. Whereas manipulation is concerned with the falsification of accounts, misrepresentation relates to deception involving physical, personal or commercial realities. Misrepresentation may be at the same time as, before or after a theft act. It may be used as a means of achieving a theft or as a way of concealing it.

Just as the thief's position governs his access to records so—to a large extent—it determines the situations, circumstances and facts he may misrepresent.

A thief's ability to misrepresent:

- a physical reality varies directly with his contact with the victim;
- a personal reality varies inversely with his knowledge of the victim;
- a commercial reality varies directly with the gullibility and greed of the victim.

Misrepresentations can be examined under the headings shown above.

MISREPRESENTATION OF PHYSICAL REALITIES

These misrepresentations may be employed to conceal a loss or to achieve a gain and fall into one of two categories:

- inflation of inventories
- interference with control and measuring equipment

Inflation of inventories

In many cases suspicion is first aroused by disclosure of an account/inventory discrepancy which can be concealed by:

- manipulating an account to agree with the lower value of the inventory;
- misrepresenting the inventory by inflating its value to agree with an unaltered account.

Physical inventories can be made to appear to agree with their related accounts by inflating quantity, price or value. The prevention and detection of such frauds is discussed in Chapters 8, 9 and 11.

Interference with control equipment

The second kind of physcial misrepresentation involves interference with measuring or control equipment, such as weighbridges, scales, flow meters and cash tills on which many companies rely to measure their stock, sales, purchases and cash takings.

The variety of equipment used for control purposes is so great that it is not possible to deal with all of it in detail but it normally consists of:

SENSOR	CONTROL	OUTPUT
(input)	(logic)	(printer)

Figure 5.8 summarizes the most usual methods of interference with control equipment for fraudulent purposes.

Possibly the two most common and easy methods of defeating control equipment are (a) to break it (which makes control impossible) or (b) to introduce false and discrediting errors.

In most cases unit counters and accumulators are vulnerable to interference. These are normally mechanical or electrical counters, like those on a car speedometer. The unit counter equates to the resettable 'trip' register and the accumulator is the equivalent of the total distance recorder. If the drive or linkage from the measurement sensor can be broken or disconnected, the unit counter will under-record. Similarly, the accumulator—which is normally geared from the unit counter—will not display the true total.

Alternatively, both the unit counter and the accumulator may be wound back to display lower totals or wound forward to give higher totals, depending on the purpose of the interference. It is also possible to wind a counter forward to achieve a lower total. For example, on a six digit register or counter the true total is 010440, and the thief wishes to reduce to 010200 to conceal or achieve fraud. He may wind the figures forward (perhaps using an electric

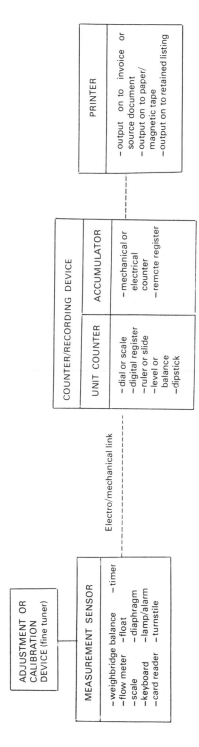

ADJUSTMENT OR CALIBRATION DEVICE (fine tuner)

MEASUREMENT SENSOR
- weighbridge balance
- flow meter
- scale
- keyboard
- card reader
- timer
- float
- diaphragm
- lamp/alarm
- turnstile

Electro/mechanical link

COUNTER/RECORDING DEVICE

UNIT COUNTER	ACCUMULATOR
– dial or scale – digital register – ruler or slide – level or balance – dipstick	– mechanical or electrical counter – remote register

PRINTER
- output on to invoice or source document
- output on to paper/magnetic tape
- output on to retained listing

METHODS OF INTERFERENCE

MEASUREMENT SENSOR AND ADJUSTER	ELECTRO/MECHANICAL LINK	COUNTING AND RECORDING DEVICES	LINK	PRINTER
– under- or over-calibration using the adjustment device – misrepresentation of a physical inventory/fact – operation at rates outside the normal performance accuracy of the sensor – sensor bypassed, turned off or discredited by induced errors – false input – failure to reset before use – BREAKAGE	– breaking the link between the sensor and counter – application of excess torque to drive, gearing or link – introduction of magnetic influence, fusing or power surges – BREAKAGE	– breaking drive connection – separating drive/levers/gears – blocking rotation of digital registers – substitution – recalibrating – deliberate misreading – failure to reset/false resetting – winding back or forward or winding through the capacity of the register – induced errors to destroy the credibility of the machine – machine turned 'off' or bypassed – BREAKAGE	– as previous	– printer turned off – cardboard between printing face and paper to prevent print – destruction of printed record – duplication of printed record (reuse of old records) – substitution – erased printout – BREAKAGE

Figure 5.8 Control equipment schematic and interference methods

drill attached to the gearing mechanism) through the total capacity of the register and then stop short of the true figure as follows:

Starting true figure	010440
wind forward	010441
	2
	010500
	999999 (capacity of register)
	000000 (resets to zero)
	000001 (wound forward)
	010200 (finish)

By using this method a thief is able to under-record even on machinery which the manufacturers claim cannot be wound back.

Machine interference usually takes place for one of the following purposes:

1. To inflate purchase, for example:

   - weighbridge interference, including under-recording tare weights of delivery trucks and over-recording gross weights;
   - flow meter interference (for liquid products) including failure to reset machinery to zero before a new delivery commences.

2. To inflate stock, for example:

   - weighbridge manipulations;
   - inflation of tank dips for liquid products;
   - misreading of temperatures (affecting the conversion from bulk to standard gallons);
   - misreading metric/imperial converters.

3. To suppress sales, for example:

   - weighbridge interference, including over-recording the tare weights on collection trucks and under-recording gross weights on deliveries;
   - interference with liquid flow meters to under-record product delivered;
   - interference with cash tills;
   - interference with ticket printers, including the reuse of old tickets.

Given a basically insecure measuring machine, the victim company has two options open—three, if you count deciding to do nothing. The first is to build in further physical barriers or supervision, so that interference becomes more difficult.

In the oil industry, where flow meters are vulnerable, some companies have built elaborate cages around sensitive machinery in the hope that unlawful access can be prevented.

The second choice is to identify vulnerable machinery and to concentrate defences on detection of interference. Security seals fall into this category. They do not physically prevent fraud, but they give an early warning—when broken or missing—that machinery may have been compromised.

The choice between preventing crime by physical means or by deterring potential criminals by making detection more certain is examined in more detail in Chapter 10.

MISREPRESENTATION OF PERSONAL REALITIES

Examples of personal misrepresentation can be seen in the newspapers almost every day: people claiming to be gas repair men and then running off with a householder's cash; companies claiming to be legitimate branches of honest enterprises and then conducting massive credit frauds. Confidence tricks, scams and a whole host of other frauds rely on a misrepresentation to separate the victim from the assets a thief seeks. Frequently a victim is chosen because of his own greed and gullibility.

The conversion of stolen cheques, misuse of credit cards and most other frauds involving misrepresentation of personal realities have one thing in common; sooner or later the victim will realize that he has been defrauded. Thus these frauds are usually one time or short term.

Although frauds involving personal misrepresentations are interesting and often amusing (except for the victim) it is unnecessary to spend a great deal of time discussing them in this text.

They are detectable during the theft act, provided the victim is alert to the possibilities and carries out proper checks into the identity, background and intentions of those with whom he plans to do business.

MISREPRESENTATION OF COMMERCIAL REALITIES

The complexity of commerce gives criminals the opportunity of sophisticated commercial misrepresentations to achieve theft, to avoid blame, or in some cases to conceal a loss. All classes of criminals—internal, external and organized—have the chance to misrepresent a commercial reality, provided the victim is gullible enough. The following case is typical:

> The disappearance in bizarre circumstances in the past two weeks of 20 people from small coastal communities in Oregon was being investigated amid reports of an imaginative fraud scheme involving a 'flying saucer' and hints of mass murder.
>
> Sheriff's officers at Newport said that the 20 individuals had vanished without trace after being told to give away all their possessions and children so that they could be transported in a flying saucer to a better life.

The commercial realities most often falsified are:

- creditworthiness of a potential customer;
- the origin, specification or manufacturers of goods offered for sale (passing-off offences);
- the independence of a supplier or customer (involving conflicts of interests and bribery);
- the profitability of a proposed business venture (to encourage investors);
- franchise, pyramid and sales schemes;
- commodity investment schemes;
- loan sharking;
- injury and insurance claims (these may also involve personal or physical representations);
- window dressing: this can apply to external frauds (to mislead potential investors) as well as to internal cases (to mislead senior management). The methods most commonly used include:
  - inflation of debtors and inventories,
  - suppression of liabilities,
  - intercompany transactions.

In most circumstances misrepresentation can be prevented or detected if the potential victim simply checks all the material facts before parting with his funds.

CONCLUSIONS ON MISREPRESENTATIONS

Misrepresentation is an important link in the chain that makes up fraud, another element in which a thief is open to detection. Whereas manipulations arise and are detectable in an accounting context, misrepresentations are most exposed at or before an act of theft. They can be detected—at least in most cases—if the victim carries out basic checks into the identity of the thief, into his commercial intentions, or into the accuracy of stock and integrity of his control machinery.

Unlike manipulations, misrepresentations leave few symptoms after the event other than an overt loss. Controls should be designed, wherever possible, to introduce an audit trail into the misrepresentative element of fraud. Banks which have introduced cameras or finger print identifiers at their cash points have been able to reduce frauds committed through personal misrepresentation simply because the criminals realize that an audit trail exists through which they can be identified.

The rule is when prevention is impossible, detection should be made inevitable.

6. Computer related fraud

Rule 6: A fail safe program will destroy others

Background

Much has been written and said about computer fraud, mostly by people whose chastity has never been threatened by exposure to real-life criminals or actual investigations. This is not to say that academic research does not have its place but a great deal of available material is at best misleading and at worst deliberately so. We have been flooded with reports which foretell enormous frauds, zapping of programs, salamis, trojan horses and timebombs. A whole vocabulary of buzz words has been built up which further confuses what is admittedly a complex subject.

Countermeasures to defend against chilling, although speculative, risks have ranged from electromagnetic shielding of computer centres down to hundreds of audit and security techniques that in some instances defy description or understanding—even by their authors. Complex and costly solutions to problems of doubtful authenticity abound.

In practice many recommended controls, although technically stimulating, are practically useless, built as they are on nebulous assessments of risks, inaccurate data and often a total misunderstanding as to the psychology of criminal, dishonest or violent behaviour.

It is no wonder that senior managers are often confused over the action that should be taken to protect their computer systems! It is also no wonder that, in the confusion, organizations either remain unnecessarily exposed or overprotected against risks that don't exist.

Loss producing incidents can occur in any aspects of business: markets can collapse, customers may default, products may be surpassed by those of competitors or key employees defect to the opposition. These events, if not predictable, are at least known about and can be controlled by good business management. Managers face commercial risks every day and are able to deal with them. They have direct personal experience on which to make reasoned judgements. *Good managers are risk takers but in computing whoever saw the calculations that went with the 'calculated risk'?*

Computer related risks are difficult to deal with: they are usually outside the direct personal experience of senior managers and it is all too easy to overlook glaring exposures with the statement 'it can never happen to us'. It is also easy to panic or over-react. Achieving the correct balance between actual risks and sensible controls is seldom easy.

In far too many cases, organizations which pride themselves on their commercial judgement, reach conclusions on computer security or, worse still, abdicate responsibilities in blind faith, on inadequate information and in the hope that problems will go away. The timebomb of irrelevant security ticks away.

This chapter does not pretend to give all of the answers. It does try to set out some principles which arise in practice, illustrates them by case studies and attempts to set a foundation for evaluating fraud risks in individual computer systems (see Figure 6.1).

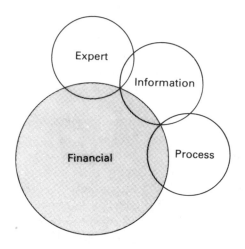

Figure 6.1   Computer systems types

A misunderstood problem

The nature and extent of computer fraud is often confused by a combination of the following attitudes.

DEFINITION OF COMPUTER FRAUD

People have grave difficulty in defining what is meant by computer fraud: some argue that everything except the most technical manipulation should be excluded. Much like Hans Christian Andersen's fairy tale of the king's new suit, the answer is simple. Computer manufacturers have claimed every conceivable benefit from the introduction of their equipment: faster processing, lower costs, increased management control and staff savings. These are usually true and well justified. But if all of the positive benefits are claimed, then all of the adverse consequences must be accepted. Thus this chapter is based on the view that any financial dishonesty that takes place in a computer environment is a computer fraud.

FEAR OF THE UNKNOWN

Human nature and haphazard intuition are unreliable stepping stones to logical decisions. Why is it, for example, that people worry about being killed by a bomb, or in an air crash when at the same time they refuse to wear safety belts, they drink and drive, smoke and do a whole variety of things that are equally as fatal and which have a far greater probability of occurrence?

Instincts can lead us to worry about things we don't understand, while overlooking or accepting more significant and probable risks whose dangers are self-evident.

Some companies seem to accept losses from pilfering, embezzlement, espionage, theft, conflicts of interest, unfair competition, marketing and consumer frauds without concern. Allowances for such losses are often built into the costings of products. The very same companies that tolerate gross wastage in manual operations take exception to being defrauded by computer, over-react and install defences which are not necessary.

WHEN IN DOUBT: PANIC

If the theory about fear of the unknown is a true explanation for the panicky reaction to computer fraud, then it may be that pressures from senior managers for security against risks they don't understand cause subordinates to put in defences they don't understand or don't believe necessary.

How often do companies really analyse the risks to which they are exposed whether computer related or not, and decide on comprehensive loss control policies, strategies and tactics? For example less than 5 per cent of British companies have any policy on security and loss control; less than 10 per cent have actually made a determined effort to evaluate their risks.

If panic governs security, it is bound to fail; if computer security is taken as an isolated subject and other parts of a company's operation left unattended and exposed, what sort of security is that? Computer security should be part of an overall risk management and loss control programme: it is not a stand alone problem.

DRACULA IN CHARGE OF THE BLOODBANK AND VESTED INTERESTS

Irrelevant security can also result from putting the wrong people in the driving seat. When computer security is delegated to technicians problems of bias are almost bound to arise.

The first bias is that 'it can't happen to us' or that 'my system is safe'. There is an old rule which applies here 'Never ask a barber if you need a haircut'. Technicians often have a vested interest: it is like asking Dracula to advise on the security of the bloodbank.

It is perhaps no more than justice that people who believe it can never happen put themselves on offer as precisely the soft targets that criminals choose to exploit.

A more common fault, evident in organizations that do try to take security seriously, is a bias towards over-complication and irrelevance to the real world. What experience of crime, criminals and villainy in business can a young programmer or systems analyst be expected to have? It is quite unrealistic to believe that the hard facts of corporate life, major slices of which are ridden with corruption and dishonesty, can be known to and be defended against by an honest man who has never ventured outside the data processing environment.

Companies can be swayed into a course of confused complexity, defending against potential frauds that exist only in the mind of the technocrat, while overlooking more mundane, more likely but costly risks simply because they are not intellectually stimulating or capable of technical description as computer frauds.

Without proper direction, technicians may identify only those fraud possibilities they themselves could commit. But common sense suggests that the more technical a fraud possibility, the fewer people there are available to commit it. *Probabilities of fraud vary inversely with the technical skill necessary to pull them off.*

In computer crime and corporate fraud the greatest losses occur through obvious opportunities, available to people with a low level of criminal skill and against victims who believed it could never happen to them.

A recent study (Table 6.1) conducted for the *Computer Fraud and Security Bulletin* illustrated a lack of awareness of security risks.

Table 6.1   Attitudes to security risks

Question/statement	Directors	Managers	Technical staff
Our computer security is not inadequate	60%	45%	10%
We do not believe there are any risks because:			
– controls are in place	60%	45%	5%
– we have never lost before and there is no reason to suppose the future will be any different	10%	20%	20%
– people can be trusted	10%	30%	80%

The results are interesting because they illustrate the differing views of senior management and computer technicians. Clearly, managers thought security was better than it truly was. Technicians appeared to have blind faith in the idea that people (i.e., they) can be trusted: the facts prove that the contrary is often the case.

WATCH THE MACHINE: FORGET THE MAN AND HIS MOTIVATION

The fourth reason for failures in computer security may be an extension of the second one. If responsibilities are abdicated to people who don't understand the risks, how can their employers expect to get sensible defences? The idea that fraud can be prevented with layer upon layer of restrictions, access controls and before-the-event measures is quite wrong. Preventive defences may do nothing but restrict honest people, while allowing criminals and their associates a free run.

There are four elements necessary prior to the commission of fraud:

- Opportunity
- Low chance of detection
- Rationalization
- Justification

and an effective system of defence should attack or counter each one. This is particularly true of computer security; too often little attention is given to controlling the personnel, accounting and other aspects which form the environment in which technical problems and abuses occur. The rule sometimes seems to be to control the machine but to forget the man!

CONCENTRATION AND BOTTLENECKS

While the vertical integration of companies and concentration of resources into large centralized units have produced many efficiencies, they have also resulted in new and greater security exposures. We can see, perhaps too late, the adverse consequences of putting all of a company's eggs into one basket. Concentrated units, or 'bottlenecks', present themselves as ideal targets for terrorism, sabotage, subversion, strikes, protests, sit-ins, disruption, natural and accidental catastrophies.

Corporate life is totally dependent on computers for its survival; data centres are the ultimate bottleneck. Deprived of these resources for even a short period, society would collapse or at least would find life intolerable.

Even today, the security implications of concentration are being overlooked; electronic mail, corporate electronic funds transfer systems, data bases and local area networks are stacking even more eggs in the same basket, ready for the final grand omelette.

The starting point

Practical experience of investigating many cases of fraud and abuse shows that computers are more likely to change the nature of risks rather than to increase them in the geometrical proportions some experts suggest.

These changes have been brought about through a number of factors:

1. Density and transparency of information held in computers.
2. Concentration of assets and capital cost.
3. Absence of human intervention and accountability.
4. Invisibility of file contents.
5. Remote access to stored information.
6. Fragile operating environments.
7. Reliance on the honesty of a young, new breed of technocrats.

But risks vary from one computer system to another and arise from a combination of factors unique to the organization concerned. It is axiomatic that controls should be commensurate with risks (see Figure 6.2), thus the logical starting point is to understand the nature of risks.

Figure 6.2   Risks and controls

The nature of risks in computer systems

All security risks can be divided into two elements: first is *probability* or how often an event is likely to occur. The second is *criticality*, which is the cost with each occurrence. In computer systems, probability usually varies inversely with criticality. That is to say that the most likely risks are usually of low cost: conversely, risks of low probability are often catastrophic.

Elements of probability and criticality can be shown in a matrix as shown in Table 6.2.

Risks can also be divided into two categories: those whose impact is obvious (called *overt risks*) and those which may not be obvious or which may be deliberately concealed (called *covert risks*). They may also be subdivided according to their cause: *accidental*; *natural*; *deliberate* (see Table 6.3).

Usually, overt incidents result in insurance claims or public disclosure and other users can obtain a good idea of their probability and criticality from published figures and reports.

Table 6.2 Probability and criticality of risks

		Probability		
		High		Low
C				Terrorism
R				Major fraud
I	High	Fraud		Strikes
T			Sabotage	
I				
C				
A			Subversion	
L		Privacy		
I	Low	Faults		Errors
T		Errors		Minor floods
Y			Accidents	

Table 6.3 Examples of risks in computer systems

	Overt	Covert
Accident	Fire	
	Errors	Errors
Natural	Flood	Leakage
	Storm	Static
Deliberate	Strikes	Fraud
	Theft	Subversion
	Sabotage	Espionage

Covert risks seldom receive the same level of publicity: perhaps they are passed off as accidents or the victim may choose not to publicize the fact that he has been defrauded. It is reckoned that 85 per cent of discovered fraud cases are not prosecuted. Thus published reports on the incidence of computer crime are of little value in assessing covert risks in individual systems.

DIVISIONS IN COVERT RISKS

This chapter focuses on deliberate and covert risks of fraud which fall into two basic divisions.

One-time smash and grab frauds

In most systems there are possibilities for criminals to gain from a one-time smash, grab and run. They are usually the most difficult to counter and, fortunately, the least common. The following case is typical of the type:

> A consultant employed by an American bank managed to discover the 'secret' EFTS codes required to make overseas wire transfer payments. In fact the secret code was pinned to the wall in the operations centre. He then transferred over 10 million dollars to an account in Switzerland from which he purchased diamonds.
>
> He smuggled these into the USA and was caught when he poured them into an ashtray in a restaurant. The person to whom he boasted about his success, reported him to the FBI. At this point, the bank did not even know that the funds were missing!

Smash and grab frauds rely on fast escape by the perpetrator and absence of an audit trail. Few victims are as lucky as the American bank in getting their money back.

Systematic frauds

Systematic frauds are the most common and the most costly but, as in manual systems, their impact is usually predictable. There are three distinct elements:

Way in	*Manipulation method*	*Conversion*
Access	Concealment	

Mainstream methods of fraud

Mainstream computer frauds are governed by the differential of opportunity theory and to a large extent depend on the access a criminal has, or is able to contrive, to achieve a financial benefit. Frauds can therefore be examined in two stages: access and manipulation method.

ACCESS OR WAY IN

Access to systems, accounts and computer resources may be abused within a thief's authority level or it may be contrived.

	Way in or method	
Fraud committed	Internal fraud	External fraud
Within access authorized	Breach of trust	
Access contrived	Skill or inadequate security	

Breaches of trust

Opportunities available to existing employees and others who require access privileges to perform their jobs cannot be totally eliminated. But the dividing line between honest and dishonest behaviour is often a matter of motivation which to a large extent is determined by ethical climate and standards within the organization concerned. It is vital that employees in positions of trust understand what is expected of them, what they can and cannot do and realize that penalties will be enforced if they transgress. Frequently data processing employees overstep the line simply because they don't know that there is a line.

However, in many cases determined and previously convicted criminals deliberately infiltrate the victim organization by applying for and obtaining employment. They succeed because the victim fails to make adequate checks into the background of job candidates.

Thus a number of frauds are totally preventable if the victim exercises care and checks thoroughly into the background of all job candidates *before* granting them access to sensitive operations.

Access through skill

Historically, the majority of computer frauds have been committed by people who have broken the trust placed in them or have deliberately sought employment to obtain the necessary access.

But recently there has been an explosion in frauds committed by people who have extended their access privileges or contrived ways in to computer systems. The reasons for this change are not too difficult to discover:

- computer networks and dial-up facilities have been easy for outsiders to discover and penetrate;
- companies have attempted to protect their systems by passwords and account codes: these have not been securely handled;
- dedicated keyboards have been replaced by all purpose intelligent terminals which, through channel selection, can access all nodes on a network;
- high level privileges have been granted to too many users: the 'need to go' principle has been overlooked;
- at universities, students are encouraged to crack systems' security: often the 'hacker' or freak is admired.

External and unauthorized access by skilled systems' breakers is likely to become more important in the future and it is worth while to examine the ways they can break in and exploit security weaknesses.

Access to most systems is granted providing the correct communications connection is made, the right account or user name selected and the correct password entered.

Dial port and network access

Finding the dial port number of a computer system is usually a simple task: one major bank is known to publish them in its internal directory: students at polytechnics are known to swap numbers and hacking techniques much like stamp collectors. They may use considerable skill as the following example shows:

The University of Alberta's $9 million Amdahl computer system was used by about 5000 clients including 3500 students, local hospitals, businesses and government departments. Every user was allocated an access code or password against which the charges for computer resources were made and accumulated into monthly bills. Only commercial users had to pay their bills although the students' records of usage were examined against university projects and budgets. Towards the end of 1977, a student, Christensen, discovered a method of diverting costs (which should have been charged against his access code) to other users.

The university staff knew about the method used by Christensen but did nothing about it because a planned new computer would soon have closed the gap. However, the improvement took longer than expected and Christensen's method of access (named the 'green code') got into general circulation and was being used by as many as 3000 different people. Because of this gross misuse, the university decided to install a tracking device to trap and log the password of anyone trying to use the 'green code'. Within ten days 20 people were caught, including Christensen. They were all told to stop using the method: to ensure this Christensen and his friend McLaughlin were withdrawn as users and their passwords were invalidated.

For the following six months the systems were back to normal, crashing once per week on average, but things went beyond a joke when the computer began to break down at least once per day. Experts decided that the breakdowns were attributable to malicious users and detailed examinations were made of the systems resources and usage log.

Late one August evening, two of the experts went to look at the computerized log but could not get access to it. A little later, a 'user' accessed files of the registration clerk! This was a very serious breach for whoever was playing with the system had obtained access to the core, identification codes, passwords and commands for every piece of information in the computer banks.

This misuse was then followed by a systems 'crash' and even the librarian could not get access to his own computerized files.

Technologists were called in, but each time they tried to access a file a mysterious command blocked the request. Finally one word appeared on the technician's screen: 'Tilt'. This, as players of pin ball machines will know, is a special word and not one normally associated with computers. The university considered drastic measures and finally set a trap which would catch the password and the name of any program being executed at the time of a system crash.

While all of this checking was going on, the system crashed again and the technicians found that a program named 'Q3H3' had been executing. However, the user, whoever he was, had access to the master console and was able to discover what the technicians (who were watching him) were doing, and could make his escape before they were able to trace him.

However, when program 'Q3H3' was called again, the technicians were able to make the necessary trace and they found the source of the trouble—Christensen—sitting at a terminal in the university's geology department and in the process of 'toe-holding' yet again. The student explained that he was simply 'challenging' security: he claimed to have no financial motivation.

In more sophisticated systems or to tap into data lines it might be necessary to use a datascope or similar device to unravel transmission speeds and protocols. Breaking in to a communications line is not difficult (see Figure 6.3).

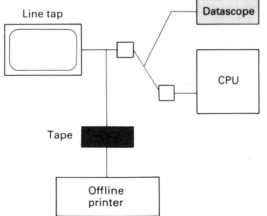

Figure 6.3 Methods of line tapping

File names

Far too many users do not change the file names allocated when their systems are delivered. Files called SYSTEM, SYSMAN, SALESIN, CUSTMR are almost guaranteed to exist on systems supplied by one particular manufacturer, not because the systems are inherently insecure but simply because users are too lazy or too unconcerned to change them. If an unauthorized user can gain access to just one file he might then be able to 'toe hold' to higher levels. This is a typical example.

> Low level users of a computer system wrote a games program into one of their files and told the computer operator that he was welcome to use it in any free moment. The operator would *set host* or access this games file through the systems console which had the highest privilege levels. Unbeknown to him, the users had written a small routine in the games program which, when called by the systems console, dumped all privileged passwords into their file. They then used them to access protected information.

Passwords

Passwords are inherently insecure and can quite frequently be guessed.

> In one system, passwords were often the same as the file or account name: thus the password for the file EXPRO was Expro. Any person who knew the name of a file or better still had access to the directory could type in 'File Name' followed by 'File Name' and would then have unrestricted access.

Frequently used passwords such as Batman, Robin, Flash and the first names of users open the way to systems penetration. Passwords written alongside terminals, on desk pads or identification cards, make it all too simple for the fraudsman who has no authority, to contrive access. When he does and succeeds, there is seldom any trail to pin down his identity. Password breaking can have staggering consequences:

> Problems at National CSS, the $100 million data processing subsidiary of Dun and Bradstreet, sent disturbing ripples across the hitherto undisturbed pond of America's $26 billion a year timesharing industry. Public and user confidence has been threatened, and experienced data processors appear to be running for cover. Statements to the effect that no timesharing system is secure, that NCSS is no worse and probably better than most, and 'the only safe computer is a dead computer' have featured in the popular press.
>
> The disarray arises from the compromise of the NCSS password directory. Password directories are a traditional target for computer tamperers—'hackers' and 'freakers'—simply because they hold all of the keys to the facilities they are intended to protect. A senior executive of NCSS pointed out that trying to make users comply with password security is like trying to get members of the public to wear safety belts—

sometimes they will, sometimes they won't, but mostly they don't give a damn.

NCSS was taken over by Dun and Bradstreet in 1979. Its base is in Wilton, Connecticut, where it has three mainframes. It has another large installation in California. These processors are linked by an elaborate data network servicing the requirements of approximately 8000 timesharing customers.

A major user of NCSS is Dun and Bradstreet itself. The system maintains the D and B data base 'Dunsvue', which holds the credit ratings of many American and international companies.

The problems came to light almost by accident. A man called Larry Smith, a former systems employee of NCSS, left the company with some of his colleagues to set up a company called the Guild, which operated from a base in Richmond, Connecticut. The company began quite successfully, and managed to persuade a number of NCSS's clients to transfer their business to the Guild—among them Media Metrics Inc., a small advertising firm from California. Then the partners in the Guild split up and Smith formed another venture which was named Hanson and Smith, this too was based in Connecticut.

In October 1981, Smith was an entitled user of the NCSS service and he was angered to find that someone had been misusing his password and charging unauthorized jobs to it. He was angered still further when he discovered that where the RAMIS billing system used by NCSS should have logged his usage details, there was instead recorded a number of rude four letter words. He phoned NCSS to complain.

At about the same time as Smith's phone call to NCSS, an employee of Media Metrics was rummaging through the company's files, held on the Guild computer, to try to find some more storage space. In dumping out what data was held on file he found that Media Metrics' system was holding a computer copy of NCSS's password file. He told his boss, who in turn advised the Guild and NCSS. NCSS had no idea that the system had been compromised, but acted quickly once the problem was brought to its attention. Lawyers representing NCSS reported their suspicions to the FBI, but then became withdrawn and uncooperative when the FBI could not guarantee that the case could be handled quietly.

One source stated that cooperating with NCSS 'was like drawing teeth', although the level of support did, apparently, increase after the FBI had threatened senior executives with Grand Jury subpoenas.

NCSS put out a general broadcast to all of its users, stating, in what some clients considered to be a curt and uninformative letter, 'It has come to our attention that a former employee may have obtained information which could potentially compromise systems access security.

Although a breach of customers' security is unlikely, in line with our *total* commitment to maintain *absolute* security, we strongly urge that you immediately change all passwords by which you access the National CSS system.'

Terminal simulation programs

In some cases, higher levels of skill are used. In a 1979 edition of the *Computer Fraud and Security Bulletin*, a case was reported as follows:

A programmer wrote an 'invisible' program to interface between the terminal and operating system. The program would set up the normal screen display prior to logging on. However, it was linked to the terminal simulation program rather than directly into the operating system.

Users, seeing the normal screen layout, would enter their user code and password which would be captured by the program and recorded in a file. Log on would fail so the user would try again. This time, being connected to the real operating system, he would gain access. The programmer would then examine his files and extract the users' passwords.

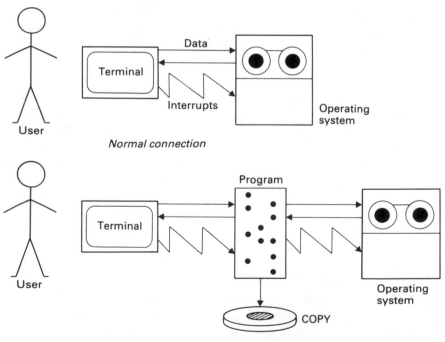

Figure 6.4 Terminal simulation programs

Since this report first appeared, Network Security Management Limited has discovered a number of terminal simulation programs: the last one being at a major credit card company where the program was used to capture passwords to an important online customer accounting system (see Figure 6.4).

Operating systems weaknesses

Some operating systems have weaknesses which allow passwords and security controls generally to be broken. For example:

> The IBM System/38 was launched in 1981. The unusual design of an integrated hardware/software/data base package promised a much higher level of security than earlier systems where users could freely access and modify files.
>
> On the System/38 the dividing lines between the three components are not readily discernible to the user because the operating software is delivered in microcode already integrated with the hardware. This means the internal workings of the machine are virtually inaccessible to the user. This may not be such an advantage when the system goes wrong, but it is a positive benefit as far as security is concerned.

Security control is achieved at two levels:

1. The system level which is controlled by the security officer who creates and maintains a profile for each authorized user of the system. The security officer should be the only person who can control the security procedures and who has full authority across the system.
2. The user level consists of authorized programs, files, data and systems resources such as printers and terminals. When a user signs on to the system, his profile is checked so that he can access only those resources to which he is entitled.

A user who creates an object such as a program becomes its owner and either he/she or the security officer can authorize other users to have access to it. Some commonly used programs are available for public use, but the security officer can restrict any program by removing its public authority status.

However, a loophole occurs when objects are being copied on to the system from a back-up diskette. In some installations, the operator is allowed to copy using the RESTORE function.

A contract programmer wanted to develop a method which allowed him to obtain users' passwords in a protected machine.

His method consisted of creating a program under the security officer's profile but which had public authority. The contract programmer used a System/38 at a timesharing bureau where security was not strict.

The programmer wrote the following program which he called 'Key'.

```
PGM
CALL QCL
END PGM
```

He then compiled and copied it on to a diskette together with a number of programs on which he had been working for the victim organization. He then took the diskette along to the user site where the operator copied all of the program on to the system.

The key program was automatically allocated the systems manager's profile or machine, thus allowing the protected password file to be read.

Card access system

Systems that permit access based on physical identifiers such as magnetically encoded cards are also vulnerable to penetration:

Atlantic Richfield Oil Company (ARCO) owned and operated a bulk fuel distribution depot at Vinfield just outside Los Angeles. Its turnover of 60 million gallons of petroleum products per month is drawn by its own fleet of tankers to supply tied ARCO service stations as well as serving smaller oil distribution companies and hauliers.

Both its own drivers and drivers employed by its independent customers were issued with small encoded plastic cards which identified authorized employees to the ARCO computer. The cards, when entered into appropriate readers, allowed product to be loaded into road tankers for delivery throughout the Los Angeles area.

After loading, the computer captured details of the product concerned and, in the case of the independent hauliers, debited their account with the cash equivalent of the products loaded.

The problem arose because a group of criminals were able to produce forged copies of ARCO loading/identification cards. Police raided the home of Gordon Clemmence, an ex-ARCO service station manager, and tanker driver, Joel Smith, and removed machines for making forged cards, hundreds of blank cards and some forged cards ready for use.

This raid followed complaints from some of ARCO's customers who claimed that they had been charged with products not loaded by them. Thrifty Oil Company was debited with $194 000 relating to 19 loads of gasoline which it claimed it had never ordered or received. The loss came to light when Thrifty's management examined its statement with

ARCO. The initial thought was that the debits were simply computer errors, but further research indicated fraud rather than mistake.

The problem got so bad that a number of wholesalers formed a vigilante group to review security.

Journal records and console log suppression

In some cases, access to a system may be bludgeoned in the sense that the perpetrator will overtly ignore or force his way through security controls in the knowledge that he can suppress all traces of his responsibility from systems journals and console logs.

Methods of suppressing these records obviously vary from one machine to another and may be as simple as removing paper from the console printer to software patches to the operating system.

On many systems it is possible to disable journals through toggle switches on the front panel of the central processing unit (see Figure 6.5) or to access, read or change data at its physical address.

Deliberately induced errors

It may also be possible for a criminal to discredit controls to such an extent that obvious symptoms of fraud or illegal access are overlooked as yet further errors. For example, if supposedly erroneous access control software denies access to genuine users it may be deactivated; in the process unauthorized users may then gain entry without detection.

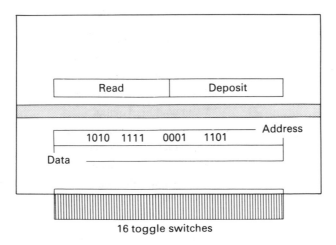

Figure 6.5 Front panel operations

Conclusions on ways in

The governing factor in most computer frauds is access; either contrived by skill or through a breach of trust. If unauthorized users can be controlled many risks are eliminated. It is an unfortunate fact that the most simple way to penetrate security is for the criminal to join the target company as an employee: companies seldom check thoroughly into the backgrounds of people to whom the security of their vital data processing resources is entrusted.

Having gained access, there are a number of manipulation possibilities that are discussed in the following section.

MAINSTREAM MANIPULATION METHODS

Although access or ways in will vary and frauds may be one time or systematic, manipulation has common patterns. These can be summarized, according to the differential of opportunity theory, as shown in Figure 6.6.

Each one of these methods can be used to reach the standard position in which a false accounting credit is free or ready for conversion or to conceal an existing consequential debit. The accounting objectives of computer fraud are simply to arrive at the position shown in Figure 6.7.

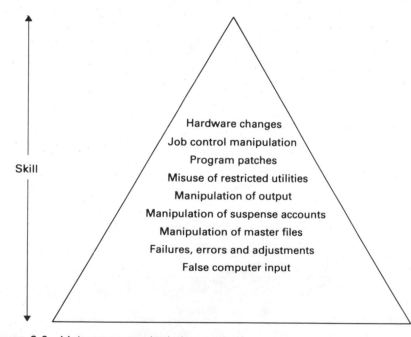

Skill

Hardware changes
Job control manipulation
Program patches
Misuse of restricted utilities
Manipulation of output
Manipulation of suspense accounts
Manipulation of master files
Failures, errors and adjustments
False computer input

Figure 6.6   Mainstream manipulation methods

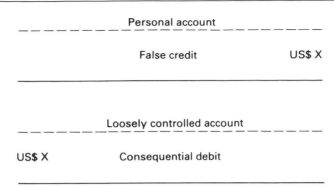

Figure 6.7   Positive and negative manipulation

Falsification of input

The vast majority (62 per cent) of known cases of computer fraud in US government systems involved the falsification of data prior to or during its introduction into a computer. Input can be looked upon as being of two basic kinds: the first is transaction data (see Table 6.4) and the second transaction entry codes (see Table 6.6 on page 167).

Falsification of transaction data

Falsification can be positive when additional data is inserted, such as the inflation of purchase transactions or sales credits, or negative when information such as sales data or purchase returns are suppressed.

Table 6.4   Positive and negative manipulation

	Type of manipulation	
System	*Positive*	*Negative*
Sales		√
Sales credit notes	√	
Purchases	√	
Purchase returns		√
Disbursements	√	√
Receivables		√
Payroll	√	√

When the falsification takes place prior to input, it follows that control totals are established with the frauds already inbuilt. Input and output balances will appear to agree and the accuracy of the accounts may be assumed.

This can be a very dangerous assumption. It is quite possible for control totals to be out of agreement with their subsidiary ledgers and accounts. For example, trade debtors' balances may not be supported by the totals of customers' accounts.

The following cases are typical of frauds involving the manipulation of computer input:

> A female clerk working for an area health authority was responsible for processing the payroll and personal expenses of National Health doctors. Salaries were paid monthly and the doctors could have their travelling and other expenses paid by cheque with their salaries or they could be paid by a separate cheque (sometimes manually prepared and sometimes computerized). The woman received claims from doctors and invariably processed their expenses with their monthly salary cheques. She would then reintroduce the expense claims into the system and obtain a second cheque for just the expense element.
>
> The doctors, having been paid their expenses with their salaries, were satisfied and the woman simply converted the second cheques by withdrawing cash from local banks and, allegedly, from the county treasurer's office.

The fraud called for limited computing knowledge. The false credits were built into the personal payroll and expense accounts of doctors and the consequential debits concealed in the nominal account for travelling expenses. Besides these financial impacts, the fraud distorted budgetary and statistical records.

A second case involving the manipulation of input was committed at the head office of a timber company:

> A senior buyer of the company created three false supplier (trade creditor) accounts using names he had dreamed up and addresses of his girlfriends as their registered offices.
>
> He had stationery printed and then typed invoices to his employer for supplies of nuts and bolts, advertising materials and stationery. He mailed the invoices to his employer and then signed them, stating that the expenses had been incurred and that the goods had been received. The false invoice values were fed into the company's accounting system and in due course the cheques were paid. They were cashed through bank accounts which the dishonest buyer had opened specially for the purpose.

The false accounting credits were accumulated in the dummy creditors' accounts: the consequential debits were posted to loosely controlled manufacturing and expense accounts, where their impact was not noticed. The fraud, amounting to over £90 000 was detected on a routine check by the local Customs and Excise officer, who was verifying the company's tax return.

These cases were committed by *positive manipulation*: the creation of false documents or false accounting entries. It is possible to commit fraud by the destruction of a record or the omission of an accounting entry. This is termed negative manipulation:

> X Limited is the British affiliate of a major American perfumery and toiletry company which distributes a large range of preparations for men and women through independent retailers.
>
> X's accounts were, and are still, maintained on an IBM mainframe computer.
>
> The sales/accounting, order entry, stock records and manufacturing orders were run on an integrated basis; much of it online and real time. When customers placed orders, details were entered through one of many terminals in the sales accounting office.
>
> The customer's order would be packed and dispatch notes prepared. In due course the delivery would be scheduled and the goods dispatched on one of the company's vehicles.
>
> The customer would sign for receipt of goods, on one copy of the computer produced dispatch note/invoice. His account would be debited automatically at the time the dispatch notes were first prepared. Nominal and stock accounts would be entered from the same basic data.
>
> One thing that should be obvious about the system is that it is rigid. The sales manager expressed concern over the delays in processing orders from market traders. He explained that these stallholders would attend markets during the day and would not have access to a telephone.
>
> Most orders from market traders were received after 4.00 p.m. and could not be delivered until the following day. He said the company was losing business because of this and proposed a system for processing urgent orders. A new system was agreed.
>
> When a customer required goods faster than they could be prepared and released through the computer system, the sales manager was authorized to write out a dispatch note, take it to the warehouse and have the goods delivered almost straight away. The customer would sign the handwritten dispatch note. One copy would be brought back and fed into the computer for invoicing and to update stock and customer records.
>
> The sales manager called on a number of cash customers and said that he had been authorized by the British managing director to offer them selected lines of the company's products at 'knock down rates'. The sales manager explained that the American parent company was being

'difficult' over advertising budgets and that the British board had decided to start up a separate fund (without the American parent's permission).

The sales manager said, if the customers agreed to his proposal, they would receive a letter from the managing director authorizing the transactions and the general terms of trade. A number of customers agreed.

In due course they received a letter, purporting to have been signed by the British managing director, thanking them for their business and telling them that their cheques should be made payable to the company's solicitors who were to maintain the advertising account.

The letter also stated that the sales manager could only be contacted after 4.00 p.m. and that orders must be telephoned to him personally. For many months, the customers ordered vast quantities of goods (well over £500 000 worth), which were delivered on dispatch notes written out by the sales manager. The customers' cheques were paid to the solicitors named in the managing director's letter.

Then the bubble burst. The sales manager was working a fraud unbeknown to his managing director. The solicitor named was his own and the funds converted to his own use. He had told the solicitor that he had bought redundant goods from his employer and was selling them off on his own account. He told the solicitor that he did not want to pay the money into his own bank account for 'tax reasons'. The managing director's letter was forged. When customers phoned in with their orders the sales manager would write out a dispatch note, but after the goods had been delivered and paid for he would destroy all copies. They would never be input into the computer.

This fraud resulted in the following obvious impacts:

- vast stock losses
- missing delivery notes
- a dramatic drop off in regular orders placed by the customers involved in the fraud (a classic symptom)

and succeeded because of an exception to what otherwise seems a good system. This, so often, is the case. The manipulation was negative and the conversion was achieved through an innocent third party.

Adjustments and input to correct errors are also vulnerable to manipulation. The following case is typical of its kind:

X is a major and reputable oil company. Virtually all of its accounting and stock control routines were run on IBM mainframe with many remote terminals. Each of the company's regional offices had remote job

entry terminals for batch processing and visual display units for online
file enquiry and master file updating.

The majority of the oil company's customers were filling stations and
other large bulk petroleum buyers. Turnover ran into thousands of
millions of pounds. Orders from these customers would be keyed in
prior to and as authority for delivery. Thus suppression of sales invoices
was extremely unlikely. The basic system had been analysed from a
fraud prevention point of view and was considered sound.

Most service stations were operated by tenants—people who leased
the premises which the oil company owned. Tenants entered into
contracts with the oil company to buy only its products; they were
allowed a margin between their buying prices and the prices they
charged customers. From these gross margins they deducted costs and
were usually left with a fair profit.

The remaining service stations were run by dealers. These were
people who owned the premises and equipment themselves. They paid
no rent to the oil company but merely entered into a contract to buy
products at a scheduled price. Dealers could fix their own sales prices.
Thus there was flexibility built into the oil company's accounting system
to distinguish between tenants' and dealers' operations. The pricing and
billing structure was fundamentally different, but was well documented.

However, from time to time, tenants would have insufficient profits to
carry on in business; some might be declared bankrupt or retire and the
service station, owned by the oil company, would become vacant. It
could take weeks or months to find a new tenant. This position was
clearly unsatisfactory to the oil company; having made a large capital
investment in buying and fitting out a service station, it would expect to
receive income from it. The systems designers had assumed that it would
be a simple matter to find new tenants but, in fact, this was seldom the
case. Thus, a third type of operation became necessary—that of
'temporary management'. Under this arrangement, the local regional
office would try to find a person who would be prepared to manage the
empty service station for a period sufficient to find a new permanent
tenant. These temporary managers—although not officially oil company
employees—would be paid a salary, but would have no share in the
profits of the business they operated.

When the sales accounting system had been designed, the systems
analysts had not fully considered what would happen if a tenant failed in
business. Would the temporary operation be given an account number as
a tenant or as a dealer? How would costs be charged? What profit and
cost centres would the temporary operation be controlled through? How
would payments made by the temporary manager be credited to his

account? What accounts would the temporary manager be required to keep? Some of these questions were answered, but not all. Temporary operations were an exception to the rule.

The accounting manuals for operations by dealers and tenants were straightforward but for temporary management a senior clerk in the appropriate regional office had to design his own system, hoping that what he did would not conflict with the computerized accounting. It was the senior clerk's responsibility to find temporary managers. He could place an advertisement in a local paper and offer the job to any applicant, whether qualified or not, of his personal choosing. There was another problem with this arrangement; permanent employees of the company were normally checked for suitability and honesty, but nothing had been written about pre-employment checking for temporary managers. This was a serious omission.

The senior clerk in one region—let us call him Percy Jones—was a long service employee with the oil company and, although fairly junior in rank, had the reputation for hard work and was considered a loyal company employee. If there was a complaint about him, it was that he was disorganized. Jones was given the job of developing the system for the management of vacant service stations in his region and for the selection and control of temporary managers. A simplified version of the accounting system he developed is shown in Figure 6.8.

Deliveries of petrol worth, say, £2000 would be made to the station, charged on an invoice and debited to the monthly statement. The manager would sell some of that stock (to motorists) for say £2000 and with oil and other sales would have a gross revenue of £3000. This would be shown on the record of service station sales. He would deduct his operation costs (£1500) and deposit the balance of £3000 in the bank to the credit of the oil company's account. This, too, would be shown on the monthly statement.

Over the period of temporary operation, a small credit balance should have accumulated on the monthly statement, and this would be transferred to profit and loss by a journal voucher. If thefts took place at the service station, the net amount banked would be below that expected and the monthly statement might show a debit balance. Journal entries would write out balances to profit and loss. Thus, journal vouchers could be used to transfer profits or to write off losses.

As far as Jones was concerned, the most important work was that in respect of which someone—usually his boss—shouted at him the most. In November of the year concerned, the tenancy of two service stations owned by the oil company became vacant and the sales manager for the area asked Jones to find temporary managers to run them. Jones,

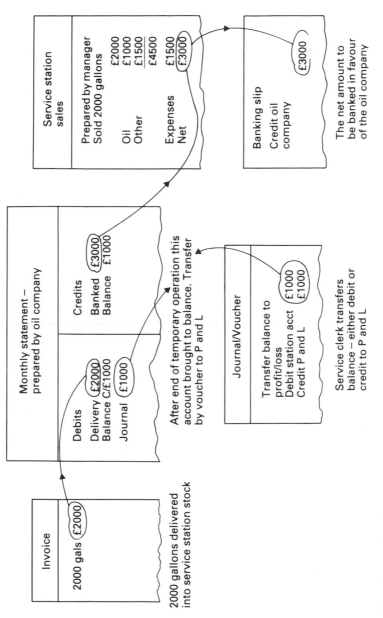

Invoice

2000 gals £2000

2000 gallons delivered into service station stock

Monthly statement – prepared by oil company

Debits

Delivery £2000
Balance C/£1000
Journal £1000

Credits

Banked £3000
Balance £1000

After end of temporary operation this account brought to balance. Transfer by voucher to P and L

Journal/Voucher

Transfer balance to profit/loss
Debit station acct £1000
Credit P and L £1000

Service clerk transfers balance – either debit or credit to P and L

Service station sales

Prepared by manager
Sold 2000 gallons

	£2000
	£1000
Oil	£1500
Other	£4500
Expenses	£1500
Net	£3000

Banking slip

Credit oil company

£3000

The net amount to be banked in favour of the oil company

Figure 6.8 Accounting flow chart

possibly in panic and because he knew of no one else suitable, recommended a man called James Rogers to manage both service stations. Rogers, at that time, was also acting as temporary manager of two other vacant service stations.

Unbeknown to Jones, Mr Rogers had other business interests. He ran a small finance company, which was in serious financial difficulties, and he was involved in other shaky ventures. There were some clear conflicts of interest.

Jones agreed that Rogers should receive a salary of £100 per week for each service station. Thus for £400 per week Rogers agreed to take on work which should have required four or five men. His motives were never questioned. Rogers, without authority, appointed sub-managers at three of the four service stations, and he agreed to pay each of them a weekly wage of £75. Had the senior management of the oil company known what was going on, it is unlikely that the arrangement would have been allowed to continue. But to senior management, temporary operations were a pain in the neck and Jones seemed to be in control. He never complained. From time to time the regional manager was asked to sign journal vouchers and other pieces of paper which appeared to be genuine.

Allowance was made for Jones's confused method of working. He would see the regional manager and ask him, say, to sign a voucher writing off £1000. Jones would explain that there was an error somewhere in the monthly statement which he had not had time to identify. He complained that he was being pressed by head office to finish the monthly accounts and that the adjustments would be self-correcting. 'It will all come right in the end', he would say.

To add to the problem, journal vouchers, when submitted by Jones to his regional manager, were signed and then returned to him for inputting into the computer. Again a fundamental rule was broken—never return documents after authorization to the person responsible for their preparation. These weaknesses were not noticed and Jones's department was never audited.

In December, head office questioned a series of journal vouchers which had been input into computerized accounting by Jones. At one of the service stations there was a large deficit, and without discussion, Jones opened a new customer account number and prepared vouchers to cover the debit on the old monthly statement (see Table 6.5).

Thus the old monthly statement for the temporary manager, Rogers, received credits to the value of £9048, and the newly opened account started off in fine form with a credit balance. The debits for these transfers went into large head office accounts relating to

Table 6.5 Adjustment vouchers

Date	Journal no.	Amount	Reason
	184	Cr. 3688	Agency fees in excess of income
	185	Cr. 235	Product leakage
Credits	186	Cr. 2870	Sales promotion
to	192	Cr. 800	Special sales support
monthly	193	Cr. 211	Damage to vehicles
statement	194	Cr. 1244	Loss on operation

operations by dealers and tenants. The losses were hidden, or so Jones thought.

Jones when questioned said the amounts of the vouchers were 'arbitrary'. When asked to check further, Jones then discovered that on the returns submitted by Rogers there were short bankings, amounting to £4800. He identified this difference by comparing the 'net' amounts on the record of service station sales with copies of the bank deposit slips. Rogers had actually banked £4800 less than he had claimed to have done.

Jones was interviewed at length and maintained that all of the other service stations operated by Rogers were satisfactory. He said he had prepared adjustment vouchers at some of these other service stations, but he was perfectly satisfied that they were correct and related to genuine operating losses. However, on further examination by auditors, it was found that more than £7000 had been written out of the accounts of the other service stations, on fictitious journal vouchers.

A full analysis of the service station books revealed that losses had occurred for the following reasons:

Station 1—loss of £4375

	£
− inflation of wages and expenses	1000
− short bankings	3000
− suppression of credit account receipts and car workshop income	375

These losses caused the monthly statements to show a debit balance of £4300. Jones wrote off this loss by putting through the following journal vouchers:

Leakage of gasoline	187
Promotional costs	437

Sales promotion (price rebate)	2125
Wages	2100
Promotional material	350
Additional fees	400

These credits, when passed through the computer, were set against the debit balance of £4300. The resulting credit of £1300 was then transferred to a newly opened monthly statement for Rogers's use.

Jones and Rogers, with others, appeared before the Crown Court on a series of charges under the Theft Act 1968. After a long trial, Jones was found not guilty and Rogers guilty and sentenced to three years' imprisonment. The basis of Jones's defence was that he was rushed and did not think—there was no guilty intention on his part and he was sorry for the trouble he had caused his employer. His explanation was accepted.

Symptoms of frauds involving false transaction input

- may involve the creation of false data, or the destruction of genuine input;
- usually show up as stock losses;
- do not distort input/output or processing controls;
- are the most simple and probable method of computer fraud;
- are usually concealed in loosely controlled expense and income accounts:

  - manufacturing stocks
  - stationery, printing and office services
  - plant maintenance, servicing and repairs
  - suspense, adjustment and transit accounts;

- conversion usually takes place through accounts of debtors or creditors by the release of goods or outwards payment.

These frauds usually involve low levels of skill: they are the most common.

Falsification of transaction entry codes

Transaction entry codes are used on interactive systems and in batch processing to identify to a computer the different nature of transactions and their different accounting requirements. For example, a sales processing system might have the following codes:

    001 Cash sale
    002 Credit sale
    003 Replacement free of charge
    005 Credit (faulty goods)
    006 Inter-company transfer

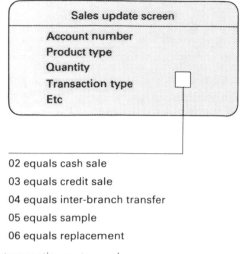

02 equals cash sale

03 equals credit sale

04 equals inter-branch transfer

05 equals sample

06 equals replacement

Figure 6.9   False transaction entry codes

Each one of these codes, input with transaction data, will carry a different accounting connotation (see Table 6.6 and Figure 6.9).

Table 6.6   Accounting consequences of transaction entry codes

	Debit	Credit
Code 001	Cash	Cash sales
Code 002	Debtors (personal)	Sales
Code 003	Replacement	Debtors
Code 006	Receiving branch	Dispatching branch

These are obviously simple examples, but they exist in many, if not most, computer applications. They can be fraudulently exploited unless care is taken. For example:

> A clerk working in a discount radio and TV wholesale company entered transaction codes as free replacement issues for what should have been full price third party sales. The clerk, in collusion with a customer of the company, milked over £10000.

Here the false credit (through un–posted debits) was built up in the personal account of the customer with whom the clerk was in collusion. The consequential debits were posted to the 'replacement account'. Conversion of the credits was achieved by the issue of free goods to the dishonest customer.

Particularly dangerous are bought-in packages such as those used to run general and nominal ledgers. Often the manuals for each customer will be tailored to suit his needs but the executable software will not be changed. Manuals may not refer to the unwanted codes, screen menus or options.

A small company bought a general ledger package. The software was said to check all purchase invoices to prevent double payments.

A file of all paid invoices was maintained and all new invoices checked by reference to:

— the name of the supplier
— the invoice number and date
— the amount

A terminal operator, who had used the package at a previous employers, knew that the software had facilities to consolidate and prepare group accounts. He knew that on the consolidated version, the double payment check called also for a company code number to be entered. For example company code 1 was the group account, code 2 for the manufacturing division, code 3 for sales department, etc. The software would recognize these divisions and would prepare accounts for each division as well as for the group. Double payment checks were separate for each company.

He entered purchase invoices more than once by prefixing them with the unused division code. The additional credits to suppliers' accounts were not picked up by the system nor noticed by management. He then transferred the credits into dummy vendor accounts through which they were converted.

Symptoms of frauds involving transaction entry codes:

— seldom result in stock loses;
— do not affect control totals;
— have a direct impact on exceptional nominal headings such as: free issues, trade samples, inter-company transfers;
— are a simple, easy and open method of fraud, which when discovered can be explained as accidental errors by all parties concerned.

The prudent user will check precisely what codes are embedded in software. Particular care should be taken over bought-in packages and over codes which adjust stocks without a corresponding debit to the account of a third party.

Communications

Communication channels have vital security implications; not least of which is their vulnerability to tapping, leakage of information and to the possibilities of remote and unauthorized access.

Communication networks have featured in financial frauds but their role has been to convey false input to its financial end point rather than being a method of fraud in its own account. Dial-up facilities have been misused to give a thief access to a computer so that he can then manipulate it.

International Business Week reporters disclosed just how easy it is to tap into data lines. They say that with readily available parts, including small microphone, AM/FM radio, a $2000 modem and a Texas Instruments printer, any would-be tapper can start up in business.

The *modus operandi* is simple:

1. Search for the victims' data/telephone lines within the building.
2. Tune the microphone and the radio to the same frequency.
3. Listen to the transmissions on the lines (picked up by the mike and played on the radio) for a high pitched whine typical of computer transmissions.
4. Record the transmitted 'high whine' on cassette.
5. Play the recording through the modem/printer to reproduce details of the messages.

Communications lines are particularly vulnerable at junction boxes and frame points. They are also extremely vulnerable at main distribution frames and switching centres maintained by telephone companies.

Failures, errors and poor adjustments

It is axiomatic that fraud is more likely (and less difficult to conceal and perpetrate) in poorly controlled and inefficient systems. When the management of a company cannot rely on its computer output, even the most blatant symptoms of fraud can be overlooked.

A Limited is a major multinational company. Raw materials were bought from large (and reputable) companies. Some suppliers were UK based and some overseas: some were affiliates of A and some were independent. Management of the company believed that transactions with third parties were most important and they were controlled. But inter-company/inter-affiliate transactions were not thought vulnerable and at the quarterly management meetings everyone found it difficult to reconcile the state of play between the various affiliated accounts.

No one really bothered about vast discrepancies. Affiliate A would be unable to reconcile its indebtedness to affiliates B and C. B and C would have had different balances arising from the same and simple transactions. The view was that since these transaction were 'in the same family' everything would come right in the end. On account payments were made between the affiliate and associated companies; some were regular but were unplanned and, as it turned out, many were fraudulent.

Mr G, who worked for the English affiliate of A Limited as assistant to the financial director, joined the company in the mid-1970s. The fact that he claimed totally false qualifications and had served a term of imprisonment for fraud never came to light.

G was given a job of maintaining the accounts of affiliate and third party suppliers.

He would prepare cheque requisitions for the director's signature. These were debited to the appropriate account by computer. G simply issued duplicate cheques payable to say Golla AB (a Swedish affiliate) and opened up an account with a local bank in the name of 'Mr A B Golla'. The cheques were deposited and the funds used for his own benefit. He stole over £3 000 000 by this method.

The fraud was discovered by the bank. A cheque drawn by 'Mr Golla', payable to Mr G put the account into overdraft. The bank checked, saw that the referee for opening the account was none other than the beneficiary of this large cheque G and phoned A Limited. From that point the investigation commenced.

This fraud was simple and exploited an obvious gap in controls. Concealment relied on irreconcilable debtor/creditor balances. The fraud continued through one financial year end and would have escaped again had it not been for an alert bank cashier.

Computer mistakes can be capitalized on by third parties, as the following American case shows.

'We had no way of knowing what was going on because it balanced out on the computer' said an employee of the United Bank of California (UBC), USA, after what appears to have been a simple input error allowed a client to disappear with $927 288 to the good. It is a statement worth framing in every accountant's office.

The trouble began in June 1978 when a real estate agent client of UBC gave the bank instructions to transfer $927 288 from one account to another. A bank employee apparently made a mistake in keying in the account number and, instead of the transfer going through as intended, the credit was passed to a small private customer whose balance stood at 55c.

The funds were withdrawn and laundered through a number of banks before disappearing without hope of recovery.

What is remarkable is that it took two weeks for the error to be discovered. Even more remarkable is that this sort of problem had arisen before and that checks were not built into the system.

Symptoms of errors exploited for fraud
- Usually the symptoms are obvious but are overlooked among the multitude of genuine errors.
- Errors may be deliberately introduced to discredit the system as a prelude to fraud.

Errors usually present an obvious gap through which frauds can escape. Every effort should be made to provide systems with high levels of accuracy and reliability and with the minimum of exceptions.

Manipulation of master files

The manipulation of master files may be positive or negative. False entries of value per unit, sales or purchase credit limits, discount rates, or price zones can be placed into a master file so that when transaction data is processed it results in a false credit to a personal account and a consequential debit concealed in a loosely controlled account.

Typically master files will be established in the areas shown in Table 6.7 (on page 172). Manipulation of standing data in master files can result in fraud.

> The manager of a large chemical company used master file amendment forms to give a discount normally allowable for inter-group transfers to a third party customer. Delivery notes were processed through the system and prices at 60 per cent of the true value. The manager obtained his benefit in cash from the customer.

Here, the false credit was built into the account of the customer (through an under-recorded debit). The consequential debits were posted to an account 'Discounts on Inter-Group Transfers'. The management of the company paid little attention to this account, believing that is was of low risk.

In interactive systems, a master file might be amended only momentarily while a transaction is being fraudulently processed. After processing, the correct information can be reinstated.

Symptoms of frauds involving the manipulation of master files
- They seldom show as stock losses.
- They usually affect pricing or other fixed data against which transactions are processed:
  - sales/price zones/schedules
  - wholesaler, retailer, export price adjustments
  - special discount, rebate, quantity discounts, etc.
  - purchase contract prices, adjustments, bonus rates
  - credit control.

Table 6.7 Typical master files

Type of master file and usual contents	Alteration possible by
Payroll master	
− employee name and payroll number	− local managers
− salary rates	− data input clerks
− commission bonus or overtime payments	− secretaries
− income tax codes and other deductions	
Customer master	
− customer name/account number	− data input clerks
− cash or credit terms	− sales representatives
− credit limits	− sales managers
− credit extension terms	− sales support staff and secretaries
Pricing master	
− customer name/account number	− data input clerks
− basic price lists	− sales representatives
− rebate levels discount rates	− sales managers
− quantity discounts	− support staff and secretaries
Supplier's master (approved vendors)	
− supplier's name address and account number	− data input clerks
− trading terms	− purchasing department
− goods codes	
Stock master	
− goods code	− data input clerks
− stock write-off and adjustments	− warehouse staff
− reorder levels	− purchasing department
− loss tolerances	− sales department
− manufacturing formulae	− research laboratory

− They are an easy means of fraud without distorting control totals and balances.

There have been very few reported cases in which master files have been deliberately tampered with. This is an amazing position in view of their ease of manipulation and the lack of an audit trail once the fraud has been committed. Master file amendments should be closely controlled.

Suspense account manipulation

In most systems, in whatever mode they run, there are some transactions which, for one reason or another, will be posted into a suspense account.

These are part of the formal double entry book-keeping system. Typically, companies will have a cash suspense account. This will be used to hold credits which cannot be traced to a debtor's account: perhaps because there was insufficient identification on the incoming payment voucher.

Suspense accounts are vulnerable, since they are often left to one person to resolve and fraud can be concealed outside the normal transaction balancing.

Wells Fargo has 380 branches spread throughout the USA: it is the eleventh largest bank, employs 100 auditors and rightly prides itself on rapid growth and good customer service.

L. Ben Lewis was the operations officer, at Beverly Drive, California. In his early forties, Lewis had served with the bank for eleven years, a number of them in its central data processing department. He was regarded as a good employee, although there were clearly things about his personal and private business life of which his employers knew nothing.

Wells Fargo did not know that Lewis had taken an interest in Mohammad Ali Professional Sports Inc. Apparently the bank did not have a clearly defined conflict of interest policy (this is a common failing in far too many companies), nor did it require key executives to provide regular net worth statements to the auditors.

Mohammad Ali Professional Sports Inc. (MAPS) was a promoter of professional boxing and other events, to which Mohammad Ali lent his name without any day-to-day involvement. The chairman, Harold J. Smith was a flamboyant personality who splashed money about in vast amounts. On one occasion he is said to have given Larry Holmes, for a time the heavyweight champion of the world, $500 000 stuffed in a pillow case as an inducement to accept a fighting engagement. The president of MAPS was Sammy Marshall, a former Wells Fargo employee.

MAPS had at least 13 separate bank accounts at two of Wells Fargo's branches at Beverly Hills and Santa Monica. When MAPS cashed a cheque at a branch other than the one at which it had an account, the transactions would be credited to the branch's cash account and debited from the branch settlement account (BSA). The voucher would be input into the bank's central computer and processed so that ultimately the charge would be made to the MAPS account on which the cheque was drawn (Figure 6.10, page 174).

The bank obviously recognized that a simple fraud could be operated by any bank employee (through his own account or in collusion with a customer) who was prepared to hand out cash and delay or defer the posting of the voucher to the branch settlement account. An automatic

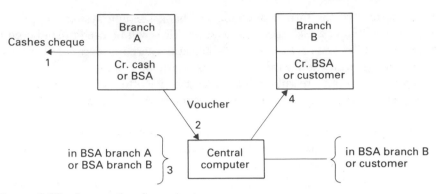

Figure 6.10 Accounting flow chart

system was therefore set up that would produce red flag reports of any item in a branch settlement account which had not been cleared within five days. These reports were reviewed by senior bank officers and invariably followed up. A second automatic check based on the value of each transaction hitting the branch settlement account was also put in place and an automatic report generated of all items of over $1 million dollars.

Lewis's dishonesty began in 1977 when he noticed a chink in Wells Fargo's armour. The mechanics of the fraud were horribly simple:

- a cheque for $100 000 dollars would be drawn on a MAPS account;
- it would be posted to the branch settlement account;
- before the five-day red flag report was produced MAPS would draw another cheque (for say $400 000) and this would be posted to the branch settlement account;
- Lewis would then generate a credit to the branch settlement account showing that the previous $100 000 was cleared and in so doing he would avoid the report of the first transaction going to the management.

Thus every five days, he would need to generate more vouchers, the new debits to the branch settlement account being big enough to free cash to the MAPS personnel while still repaying the previous balance before five days had elapsed.

It was thus a straightforward lapping, or teeming and lading, fraud with the balance outstanding being rolled over into ever increasing amounts of debt. In 1980 the dimension of the fraud increased and in the last quarter alone more than $12 million was skimmed off the branch settlement account. At this point in time Lewis was having to put through 25 separate vouchers (each less than the warning level of $1 million) every five days. His manipulation took him five minutes to complete. Then Lewis made a fundamental mistake and sent one of the fraudulent vouchers to the wrong branch. Managers already suspected that all was not well and this error naturally stimulated their interest even further.

On 23 January 1981, Lewis was summoned to the bank's conference room where he was confronted by senior Wells Fargo managers. He admitted to a number of false entries in the branch settlement account and to other misdeeds.

Symptoms of frauds involving suspense accounts
- They involve regular adjustments.
- Personal accounts receive the benefits of unposted debits or fraudulent credits.
- Credit amounts may be divorced and concealed from their initiating entries.

The prudent user should ensure that suspense accounts are closely controlled.

Manipulation of output
Computer output may be duplicated, suppressed or altered as a means to the concealment or achievement of fraud.

One case, in the USA, involved an operator who pushed the 'print' key 39 times when his own payroll cheque was being processed. Then—demonstrating an amazing lack of imagination—presented them to his own bank for payment all at the same time!

A cleverer fraud occurred at the Flagler Dog Track, Miami.

The dog track accepted bets from punters on a totalizer system. Punters would place money (on what they thought was to be the winning dog) at a number of ticket machines spread around the course. They would be given a computer produced ticket showing the race and the dog on which their money had been placed. The ticket machines were linked to two computers which, for continuity and back-up reasons, were run together. Thus if one machine failed, the other would continue to process.

The 'odds' on each dog were calculated by the computers on a pool system. Thus if there had been $10 000 placed on the race and the winning dog had 100 tickets issued against it, each of the ticket holders would collect $100. These 'odds' were displayed on a large illuminated board which was connected to and updated by the computer as the bets were being placed.

If one of the machine operators tried to issue an additional winning ticket, after the race had been run, the fraud would have been obvious and the genuine winners would have soon complained (there would have been 101 to share out the money instead of 100).

Two things detracted from security. The first was that in the computer room there was a ticket printing machine for test purposes. The second problem was that punters would place combination bets. They could, for example, anticipate 1st, 2nd and 3rd winners in a race and gain in multiples of the combined odds. These were called 'trifecta bets'.

Because there were so many possible combinations, these odds could not be displayed on the illuminated board. Thus the punters could never calculate what the odds were or what their winnings should be.

The fraud run by the computer operators was both simple and rewarding.

Both computers would be live. Bets would be taken through the ticket machines and the odds for straight winners calculated and displayed.

Odds for combinations would be calculated but retained in computer memory for printout immediately after the race.

When the race was run and the winners known, the operators would destroy the printout of the prime computer and through their own ticket machine print a number of winning combination bets. The odds would be calculated on the back-up machine and the operators would substitute this then have one of their associates produce the forged tickets to collect the winnings.

Despite the advances in technology, printers and tape drives are still the slowest devices in computing. Often data is placed in a queue for printing or spooling. The data held back may be on a disk, tape or in memory. All accounting processes will have been completed and balances struck. If these files can be accessed (for example by systems software) data can be altered, added to or deleted without distorting control totals and balances.

In one recent case invoice details were held on a buffer file prior to printing and updating debtors' ledger accounts. At this point the stock accounts had been credited. A programmer using a simple edit program deleted items from the file with the result that invoices were not produced and certain customers' accounts under-debited. The fraud amounted to more than £500 000.

In some instances this procedure was also used to conceal simple thefts from the warehouse. In these cases dummy customer orders would be entered into the system, processed so that stocks would be 'downdated' and then deleted prior to printing. The customers concerned knew nothing of the frauds.

The level of skill necessary to commit frauds on output can vary considerably:

> In a UK oil depot a supervisor, who could by no means be described as an academic giant, found that loads of petrol could be stolen merely by placing a piece of thick card between the printing head and paper on the line printer.
> The result was that loads which had been delivered were not recorded.

Computer output is usually taken for granted. Systems should ensure output is accurate, timely and complete.

Restricted utilities

Restricted utilities are powerful software tools, used by programmers to fix faulty systems, correct file balances and generally assist in housekeeping operations. They are the little 'tools of the trade' which are present on most systems.

Restricted utilities will vary from one manufacturer to another. On IBM, DITTO and SUPERZAP are the most powerful: on DEC systems, PATCH and SOS EDITOR have equivalent powers.

Such utilities enable a skilled person to access disks and memory at the physical level: he can delete or add items at will and even more dangerously erase all evidence of their use (see Figure 6.11).

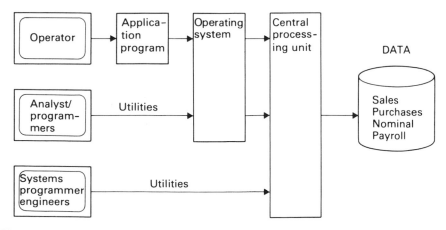

Figure 6.11 Restricted utilities

Symptoms of frauds involving restricted utilities
- Usually none: the installation looks secure!
- The obvious symptom to watch for is the presence of any restricted utilities on a system. In one case, where management insisted that utilities should be held offline and mounted under control, a programmer borrowed a copy of an edit program from another site and loaded it on to his employer's computer system. He took the precaution of giving the program an innocuous name.

Manufacturers are slowly waking up to the dangers of utility software and many have put out recommendations on how it should be controlled. It may be a case of closing the stable door after the horse has bolted!

Program patches

Programs can be rigged with patches which divert transaction data into a fraudulent routine. In plain language, a patch might state:

- Is the transaction for John Smith's account?
- If not, then process normally.
- Else (the fraud routine)
    halve the debit and post to Smith's account
    use the correct amount to post control totals.
- Process next transaction.

The routine will give Smith's account the benefit of a false credit (by way of half of the true debit); the control totals will appear correct, but the debtors' control account will not be supported by the outstanding balances in the personal accounts of debtors.

Conversion, so far as John Smith is concerned, is automatic, since he pays just half price for his goods. The benefit to the internal programmer/thief can be obtained in cash.

It is conceivable that after the program has been run a few times, the dishonest programmer can change it, possibly during routine maintenance, correct it and withdraw the unauthorized routine. The audit trail then becomes cold (see Figure 6.12).

The hub of all programming frauds is a trigger, or conditional jump, which diverts transaction data from a genuine routine into a fraulent one. In the example, the trigger is John Smith's account number.

The following case shows that high levels of skill and almost unrestricted access are necessary to patch programs.

In Shreveport, USA, Michael Murray, a 30-year-old ex-employee of Digital Electronic Services Inc., perpetrated an alleged fraud involving US $100 000. Murray, and the firm that employed him, had been

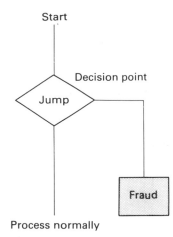

Figure 6.12 Program patches

engaged by the National Bonded Money Order Company to program its
Datapoint Corporation 550 mini computer. Digital developed most of
the software for the company's money order processing system and also
provided some packages off the shelf.

The software development work seemed to go very well but, as usual,
some residual bugs had not been cleared up at the time the system went
fully operational. Apparently, unhappy at Digital Electronic Services
Inc., Murray went to work directly for National Bonded. His job with
his new employer was to clear up the bugs in the system.

It seems that Murray cleared up the problems extremely well but in
addition reprogrammed the system so that money orders which had been
made payable to fictitious people and cashed by him were suppressed
from the printouts. Over 1000 money orders were ignored by the system
after the cheques had been returned.

The fraud came to light in April 1981 when it appears there were large
paper losses in National Bonded's money order system. The District
Attorney's office, under Robert Gillespie, was called in. However, before
much of the valuable evidence could be secured, there was a mysterious
robbery and many printouts and supporting documents were stolen.
Murray was interviewed by the DA and admitted to using National
Bonded's funds to pay off his credit cards, to speculate on the gaming
tables and to invest in a private company in a data communication field.
Murray later assisted police in recovering much of the evidence which
had been stolen from National Bonded's premises.

An unauthorized, fraudulent routine may be introduced in many parts of a
program.

Validation stage

- to reject valid data
- to accept invalid data
- to bypass control balances
- to divert Dr/Cr between accounts without affecting control totals

Processing stage

- diversion between accounts
- round down/up accumulations
- master file referral
- positive manipulations
- suppression or rejection
- control balance suppression
- false proof listing
- plausible excuse manipulations
- adjustment to processed files

Output

- print suppression
- print duplication

Systems accounting files

- to suppress records of use
- to avoid computer charges

To achieve a program fraud a thief may need as a minimum:

1. Knowledge that a program exists and what it does.
2. Access to program and systems documentation; source listings, object code and/or executable files.
3. Time and skill necessary to design and introduce the patch without:

   - leaving a trail in the documentation
   - being detected in the process
   - the facility for full testing
   - budget allocation
   - test and additional files being noticed
   - spot checks
   - interest by other programmers
   - no new complications or system crashes caused by the patch.

4. Preparation of amended documentation.
5. Removal of old documentation.

6. New compilations.
7. New library listings.
8. Unnoticed CPU time to test, compile and run.
9. No disclosure by co-conspirators.
10. Loosely controlled accounts in which to conceal the fraud.
11. Accessible accounts in which to convert the fraud.
12. Unnoticed concealment and conversion in user departments.
13. Intimate knowledge of the 'side impacts' of the fraud in budgetary and statistical records.

In most companies such levels of skill seldom have to be deployed to achieve a fraudulent financial gain!

Symptoms of frauds involving program patches
– They involve relatively high technical skills.
– They can result in no obvious symptoms, particularly when the patch leaves correct control totals. For example, a patch can result in this position:

	(£)
Debits to customer A	1000
Debits to customer B	1000
Debits to customer C	5000
(halved from 10 000 by a fraudulent patch)	
CONTROL TOTAL	12 000

– The trigger that causes a program to jump into a fraudulent routine is unlikely to be detected by test packs, ITF or other conventional means of auditing. (See page 400 et seq.)
– After exploitation, the program may destroy or may be corrected during routine maintenance, thus removing any audit trails.

A more simple (but very effective) method of patching a program would involve manipulation of job control instructions.

Job control manipulation

Job controls (or procedures) direct the process of a computer application; they tell the computer which program to execute, which data to read and do the work which, in old systems, was performed manually by the operator.

JCL is a high level language which interfaces with the operating system of the computer.

Most organizations try to prevent programmers making changes to

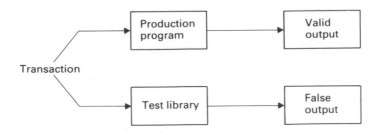

Figure 6.13   Fraud through JCL statements

executable programs or load modules. All program changes are carried out in a test library (which may be uncontrolled) and when checked and approved, are transferred under control to production.

It is possible that patches could be inserted in a program in a test library and procedure or JCL instructions given to run this program rather than the tested and correct production version (see Figure 6.13). The output from the patched test program would appear genuine.

Hardware changes

Hardware may be altered, reprogrammed or substituted as a means to fraud. The following case illustrates the risk of this type of manipulation:

> The Argent Corporation which ran four casinos in Las Vegas— 'Stardust', 'Freemont', 'Hacienda' and 'Marina' came under investigation by the Nevada Gambling Commission for an alleged fraud.
>
> At least $7 million in US quarters, weighing 150 tons, allegedly disappeared, in an 18-month period.
>
> The Commission believed that coins taken from the casino's fruit machines were skimmed off through a sophisticated fraud based on a computerized weighing machine. A further $3.5 million was paid out to supposed gamblers, without a shred of documentation, and further millions had been lost as a result of kickbacks and 'soft counts' in winnings at the gambling tables.
>
> Meters in the machines were rigged to register a payout one-third greater than actual. When the contents of the cash drawers were emptied out, they were put into a Toledo model 8130 electronic weighing machine, manufactured by the Reliance Electric Co.
>
> However, one of the engineers, who designed the Toledo, had in the meantime been recruited by Argent and it was alleged that he altered the circuitry so that it underweighed all cash boxes by an amount sufficient to hide the extra.

A computer analysis put the odds of the casinos actually having to make the payouts they claimed to have done at one chance in 3 875 000 000 000 000 000 000 000 000 000 000 000 000 000 000 000.

Frauds involving changes to hardware are uncommon and usually extremely difficult to detect. Because of rampant thefts of software, many vendors are supplying their products on chips rather than on floppy disks, which are much more difficult to copy. This change will make operating systems, particularly, more transparent to users (they will be unable to make changes) but on the other hand substitution of chips with built-in program patches will be almost impossible to detect. We can expect more frauds of this type in the future.

Other methods of fraud in computer systems

The previous section described mainstream or conventional methods of computer fraud. There are other risks.

EXTORTION AND SABOTAGE

Because of their importance and the dependence the users have on their continued availability, computers are likely targets for extortion and sabotage, which may or may not be financially motivated.

> According to *Computerworld* a computer operator employee inserted a metal object causing a short circuit in a disk drive file 56 times in two years; $500 000 was spent attempting to correct the problem. As a last resort sabotage was suspected and a TV monitor used to catch the suspect. He is quoted as saying his reason was an overpowering urge to shut the computer down.

Ancillary services, such as air conditioning, power supplies, fire detectors and extinguishers, are also prime targets for violence and sabotage, and are often inadequately protected.

Systems sabotage can also be achieved by the deliberate introduction of error routines so that processing is interrupted or compromised, possibly to the extent where customers and business associates lose faith in the victim company and the accounts it produces.

Programs can be deliberately sabotaged to produce inferior goods, overrun minimum stock holdings or arranged in other ways to destroy the ability of the victim to trade. Corporate planning programs and financial forecasts can be manipulated to cause disruption to a business:

> Recently a local council urged constituents to cut out all unnecessary use of electricity, gas, water and public services and utilities. The program

was backed up with letters addressed, by computer, to all householders. The television programme *That's Life* reported the fact that one constituent had received 14 copies of the computer produced letter, while another constituent had received 10 copies—each letter bearing a normal rate postage stamp. Whether these letters were sent as a result of a mistake or a sabotaged program is a matter for conjecture; the damage to the council's reputation, however, was abundantly clear.

In computing, the potential for damage and disruption is almost limitless.

PRIVACY INFRINGEMENTS

Another area of security risk arises from privacy requirements. Privacy may be defined as an individual's right to restrict the dissemination of personal details, or characteristics, and from a security standpoint it is the counterpart of trade secrets protection.

Perhaps the greatest risk to privacy is carelessness and error, accidental disclosures rather than deliberate and planned violations.

However, it is possible that privacy requirements could be used in extorsive crimes or to sabotage the reputation of the victim company or government department.

For example, a thief working for the victim might deliberately program the release of private information involving an accomplice, so that the accomplice can enter into a civil suit for damages. Private information might also be deliberately released to cause embarrassment to the victim.

THEFT OF RESOURCES

Theft of computer time and resources, often brought about by conflicting interests of employees in key positions, can involve substantial losses as the following example shows:

When Frank Lewis applied for a job as a programmer with CHB Foods Inc. of Los Angeles he said nothing about his private software business, named Arid Computer Company. He said nothing about his partner in Arid, Kathy Benedict, nor his intention to carry out private work in company time and using company resources. Had CHB known the true position it is unlikely that Lewis would have been engaged, but, it appears, no one asked the right questions and he was not going to volunteer the information.

Lewis was a good programmer, and his work for his food wholesaling employer was more than acceptable. Work pressures built up and he recommended to CHB that they recruit Kathy Benedict. His advice was accepted and the two worked closely together, sometimes to the exclusion of other programmers in their team.

Frequently they would exclude their colleagues from the machine room when they were testing programs and this led to friction, comment and finally suspicion.

The suspicions were well founded and investigations showed that Lewis and Benedict were spending up to 50 per cent of their time on work for one of their employer's competitors—Certified Foods Inc.— which had engaged Arid as consultants to advise on program development.

Lewis and Benedict were charged with the theft of computer time and were dismissed from their jobs.

The case is a classic in many respects:

- Possible conflicting interests were not disclosed at the time of recruitment.
  The conflict was not disclosed by the persons concerned.
- The misuse of time and resources can be 'rationalized' as acceptable. In one recent UK case a programmer who had stolen copies of his employer's software to support his private business asked 'What's the problem? It didn't harm them: I did a good day's work and what I do with my private time is my own business.'
- Costs of conflicting interests can be high, both in wasted production time and, as in this case, in additional labour costs. For example it is doubtful that Ms Benedict's services would have been required had Lewis devoted his attentions, full time, to the work of his employer.

Frequently employees will allow their personal interests to conflict with those of their employer for relatively small rewards.

Sandvik UK, a West Midlands company which manufactures saws and other tools, is totally computer dependent. In 1979, it relied on Burroughs hardware, but had begun the gradual transfer of data to an IBM system. The computer was used to process the company's payroll, stock control records, invoices and orders.

Early in 1979, senior management and security staff at the Halesowen, Birmingham plant began to think they had a well educated ghost on their hands. Suddenly the number of computer malfunctions, normally two a year, soared to an unacceptable level.

At first most of the malfunctions could be traced to failures in environmental equipment. Smoke detector circuits would fail causing air conditioning units to close down, odd switches in the room ventilation system would be mysteriously switched off, the humidifiers were interfered with. All these happenings had a similar effect: the computer crashed.

The resulting chaos was catastrophic for the company; salaries could be paid only with the help of other computer users in the area, the company fell behind with invoicing and deliveries and the overtime bill spiralled as computer staff struggled to keep abreast of the work. Yet there was worse to come. Suddenly the 'poltergeist' switched its attention from the environmental equipment to the computer itself. Between June and September 1979, malfunction followed malfunction. Burroughs' engineers investigated each failure and in September 1979 they reported to the management of Sandvik that the problems were caused by:

'1. High average voltage supply (surges or "spikes");
 2. Hot spots in the computer room;
 3. The humidity balance in the room.'

Sandvik was not convinced, but by this time it was desperately in need of a solution and suspected that the system had been deliberately sabotaged. The company began to look closely at the overtime bills of those people who were responsible for 'tidying up' after each disaster. Eventually the firm's security manager, Mr E. Dukes, voiced his suspicions to the local police.

The police had a considerable workload at that time, but they were able to loan the company sophisticated TV surveillance equipment, with fish-eye lenses, which was installed in the ceiling of the computer room. Security personnel used this equipment to monitor those shifts with large overtime bills. It was not long before their effort was rewarded, and they filmed a terminal operator removing panels from the machine and inserting a screwdriver.

The next morning they confronted the operator, Paul Brierley, and he quickly confessed to sabotaging the computer. Burroughs' engineers found that printed circuits within the machine had been lightly scratched causing short circuits and other malfunctions.

The police were called, and Brierley admitted that he had damaged his company's equipment to ensure that he would be able to increase his take home pay with overtime. He was charged with two offences of obtaining a pecuniary advantage by deception. When he appeared before local magistrates in October 1980 he asked for a further 18 similar offences to be taken into consideration. The court heard that Brierley had been living beyond his means and had relied on overtime to meet his debts. He was placed on probation for 12 months and ordered to pay £1687 compensation for overtime claimed.

Conclusion

The differential of opportunity theory is relevant to computer fraud and governs both the way in and the method of manipulation. As the cases show the range of fraud possibilities is very wide but the opportunities for conversion can be limited without collusion. Conversion is a dangerous stage for all criminals and computer fraud is no exception. It usually leaves easily detectable traces.

The detection, investigation and prevention of computer fraud are discussed in the following chapters.

7. Detection techniques

Rule 7:   *You can hear a lot by just listening*
Ruke 7a: *You can see a lot by just looking*
Rule 7.b: *People will believe anything providing it is overheard or seen through the crack in a door*

Detection can be defined as the uncovering of fraud symptoms in circumstances where no prior suspicion exists. This chapter explains a number of techniques which have succeeded in uncovering frauds to a value of at least $100 000 000 over the past few years.

The purpose and benefits of fraud detection

Every person has the right to protect his property, his income, his safety and security. Corporate bodies have an obligation to shareholders and to their employees for such things as safety, welfare and, of course, protection of assets. To what extent security is inexorably tied up with profitability is a matter for debate, but common sense suggests that when a company is operating efficiently the two are inseparable. It is easier to lose profits than to make them. Companies which are performing badly—for whatever reason, including being defrauded—are unlikely to be in the best position to cater for the long-term welfare of their staff and interests of their shareholders.

Thus the first objective of detection is to assist in the creation of a healthy and profitable corporate environment by preventing fraudulent losses.

Secondly, detection should lead to investigation and the recovery of lost funds; either from the perpetrators, receivers, third parties or insurance carriers. These possibilities are discussed in Chapter 8.

The techniques outlined in this chapter are based on the overriding belief that a company has the obligation to protect its assets. That this obligation should be discharged honestly and fairly goes without question. The techniques will not entrap an innocent person nor should they embarrass him or invade his privacy. They will, however, cause serious problems for a thief and may result in difficult management decisions. These points must be understood from the outset; the techniques work and should be handled with care.

Some techniques detect the symptoms of theft, others manipulation and misrepresentation and others concealment.

The techniques are described under the following headings:

- Critical point auditing
- Job sensitivity analysis
- Vulnerability charts
- Invigilation and created checks
- Observation
- Undercover investigations and informants
- Business intelligence
- Spot checking
- Criminal targeting

Basic rules

There are some rules that apply to fraud detection generally.

1. Never overlook the obvious. People who are not experienced in fraud investigations may think that its workings are so complex that they would never have the ability to detect it. This belief would be quite wrong. The majority of frauds exploit glaring gaps in a system of control and leave obvious symptoms. Aspiring fraud detectors should remain alert, recognize fraud symptoms for what they are, and when they do appear, follow them through, never being satisfied with the first excuse or explanation that comes along. The following report illustrates this rule.

£66 724 fraud revealed by 24p discrepancy

Dining car workers on trains running between Kings Cross and the North and Scotland defrauded British Rail of £66 724 in one year, an Old Bailey judge was told. The fraud came to light by chance when a 'gimlet eyed' control clerk discovered a discrepancy of 24p on a receipt tendered for £300. Prosecuting counsel said the fraud was a cunning and persistent one. Many dining car attendants perfectly innocently paid over money collected from passengers to one or other of the nine accused, thinking it would be handed in at a central point. Instead it was pocketed and receipts were forged.

2. Look for deviations—never seek the most complex solution. Inexperienced investigators often look for complex explanations for possible fraud symptoms. The correct approach is to start by examining the most obvious solution. If necessary, eliminate it and go on to the next most simple answer.
3. Always concentrate on the weakest, most simple, point in a fraud. Most frauds have three elements; theft act, concealment and conversion. In some the theft act will be difficult to identify and in others it will be

straightforward and simple. In some frauds it may be the conversion element that is difficult, in others concealment.

The fraud detector should always consider each of the elements and try to identify the one in which the most overt symptoms will appear. He should then concentrate on that element.

When suspected fraud appears unduly complex—the rule is to 'follow the asset'. By establishing where cash or stocks ended up and then working backwards, complex concealments may be unravelled.

4. If accounts have been manipulated or records destroyed, the person whose guilt would otherwise have been the most obvious should be treated as the prime suspect.

5. If, after an investigation of all available facts, guilt appears to point towards a particular person, the chances are he is the responsible party. This is another common-sense rule. The detector should always examine a case closely and objectively and, having done so, may be able to see the probable method of theft and will suspect someone as the guilty party. The chances are, at this stage, that the person so identified is responsible even though it is usual to find he is a trusted and highly regarded employee!

6. Fraud detection and prevention is not a once-off exercise but rather a routine aspect of business. The techniques outlined in this chapter are not things that a company needs to consider only once. Some can be applied in a routine way—computer produced surveillance reports, for example, can be used to monitor day-to-day and month-to-month business. Vulnerability charts and other analyses need updating to take account of changes in business practices and risks. Fraud detection— like all loss prevention plans—should be a continuing management function.

7. It is not necessary to detect all frauds at any one time. The main objective of fraud detection is prevention. A deterrent is established with each case detected and investigated. It is not necessary to seek the impossible of stamping out all fraud at a stroke.

8. To detect fraud, resources must be allocated specifically to that task. Fraud detection cannot be achieved as a 'spin off' from conventional auditing. To detect fraud, resources must be specifically assigned.

9. Detecting fraud is hard work. When the reader gets further into this chapter he might well be inclined to throw up his hands in horror at the amount of work necessary to detect fraud. He would be right in assuming that fraud detection is hard work. Often long and difficult hours are spent and sometimes wasted, since not all enquiries will produce results.

Once fraud has been detected and the initial symptoms identified, the work proper—the investigation—still has to begin. This, too, can be tedious and time consuming, but the effort is usually worth while.

10. The reason why fraud escapes detection is usually because nobody is made accountable for the task. The idea that fraud will be detected by auditors or police is usually mistaken. An auditor is a watchdog, not a bloodhound; the police investigate fraud, they seldom detect it. They act or respond to reported crime and if the symptoms of fraud are not picked up by the victim there is nothing for the police to respond to.

Responsibilities|for|fraud\detection, prevention and security should be clearly assigned.

Detection techniques should be viewed against the background of these rules.

Critical or key point auditing

Most commercial organizations have vulnerable points and operations in which fraud is most likely to occur. When these vulnerable or critical points are exploited, impacts occur in predictable and often non-variable ways. Fraud succeeds because these impacts are hidden among thousands of regular transactions.

The major symptoms of fraud include:

- stock losses
- inflation of expenses and assets
- suppression of sales and liabilities
- deviations from normal procedures
- missing documents
- broken control machinery
- distortion of historical or proportional trends

Critical point auditing is a technique which, through the examination of accounts and records, the symptoms of manipulations and conversions can be identified; it is a filter.

The outcome of a critical point audit is a list of fraud symptoms or possibly fraudulent items from which detailed investigations may be made.

Within the general heading of critical point auditing there are two prime examination methods; analysis of trends and specific tests. These are described later.

PROBLEMS ARISING FROM THE USE OF THE TECHNIQUE

Since critical point audits can be carried out discreetly, they have a major attraction of being able to avoid employee relations problems, while at the same time being highly effective.

The disadvantages are the time it can take to carry out an audit and the faith required of the people concerned that their efforts will produce results. If these problems can be overcome, the technique is almost certain to succeed in detecting at least some frauds:

> A European company looked upon its American counterpart and associate with disbelief. At management meetings, the American company revealed that it had detected a whole string of frauds and that sizeable cash recoveries had been made. For two or three years the American company reported its efforts to stamp out losses and finally, fed up with derogatory comments, offered to send its investigator to Europe to examine vulnerabilities in its associated company. The investigator spent a week in the European company and, using a computer run of sales credits (recorded in customers' statistical records), compiled a list of fraud symptoms. The list was laughed at as being meaningless, even though some customers had received credits for goods of types and quantitites that had never been invoiced to them. The investigator picked what he thought was the smallest fraud on the list and investigated it, using conventional methods. The result was a loss, from uninvoiced sales, of over £100 000.

The point from this example is a fundamental one and that is a reluctance to accept that techniques could be effective and worth the effort. Once this barrier has been overcome the chances of success are very high.

PROBABILITY OF DETECTION

The probability that fraud symptoms will be detected as a result of a critical point audit is higher than pure percentages. Driven on by greed and forced to manipulate records or engage in other falsification, a thief leaves many trails. The probability of detecting these symptoms depends on three factors.

- the size of the company and the number of transactions, accounts and records (both fraudulent and non-fraudulent) that are available for examinations (the total sample);
- the number of the items examined from the total sample;
- the number of fraudulent items.

For the reason explained earlier, a company is unlikely to have been cheated by one thief only once. The chances are that a number of thieves both external and internal will have been at work, all pushing their frauds to the maximum extent possible. The number of fraudulent items is usually high.

Bearing this fact in mind, the probability of detecting fraud can be estimated with reasonable accuracy.

If the letter F is taken to be the probability of detecting one recognizable fraud symptom and A is the probability of detecting no fraud symptoms then, since absolute certainty is taken as 1,

F = 1 − A

This idea of looking at the failure as well as the success rate is important as the following example shows:

> When there are 8 white balls and 2 black balls in a bucket and tests are to be made for the presence of black balls by drawing 3 balls at random, the probability of drawing out at least 1 black ball is greater than pure percentage chance.
>
> There are in fact 120 possible combinations of 3 balls and 56 combinations of white balls which would fail to satisfy the test. The failure rate is therefore 56/120 or 7/15. The success rate (the chance of picking out at least 1 black ball) is 1 − 7/15 or 8/15 = 0.533: a 53 per cent chance of success, with a 33 per cent test.

Much of an accountant's normal checking is done on monthly and other totals rather than on an item basis. This may, in fact, reduce the probability of detecting fraud if the thief concentrates his dishonesty in one, two or three months and behaves properly for the rest of the year. For example:

> There are 1000 transactions a month and just 6 false items. If the check is made on 3000 items (i.e., 25 per cent of the yearly total of 12 000) the probabilities of detection are as follows:
>
> Chances 0.91 if there is one false item in each of 6 months
> 0.84 if the items are in 5 months
> 0.75 if the items are in 4 months
> 0.62 if the items are in 3 months
> 0.45 if the items are in 2 months
> 0.25 if the items are in 1 month

Thus, in critical point audits, checks are made on items and not on monthly blocks or total. There is a substantial drift in the economy of effort towards the lower percentage of item checking as the number of false items increases, as shown in Table 7.1.

When the sample is itself refined by the use of specific tests on the most vulnerable areas, the probability of success is extremely high.

PLANNING FOR THE AUDIT

Since any audit will involve considerable effort it should be carefully preplanned.

Table 7.1 Probability of detection

Test %	Probability	Economy
10	0.19	0.09
20	0.36	0.16
30	0.51	0.21
40	0.64	0.24
50	0.75	0.25
60	0.84	0.24
70	0.91	0.21
80	0.96	0.16
90	0.99	0.09
100	1.00	—

Staff selection

The staff selected to carry out the work should not be regular employees in the area under review. The reasons for this belief are as follows:

- Regular employees are more likely to let subjective judgements creep into the analysis and accept explanations where they should not be accepted. This is particularly true of 'plausible excuse' concealments.
- To obtain the maximum benefit from the exercise it should be carried out with surprise and objectivity. Although some tests may be conducted covertly the best results will be obtained if overt examinations are made and direct questions asked. This may introduce an element of confrontation between the audit team and employees and sour relationships after the review has been completed.

Ideally the audit team should consist of people who understand the culture of the company, who are trained and if possible professional accountants or investigators. At least two people should be assigned to the work.

The second important piece of preplanning is deciding the extent of the audit.

The extent of the audit (the audit unit)

It is unwise to take too large a unit of a business to examine in the first instance. Although critical point audits may include all departments of a company, they should, wherever possible, be broken down into self-contained sections and tackled one at a time.

In companies that have a number of small branches each one should be audited separately, although the maximum use should be made of consolidated and interrelated records for trend analysis. The third preplanning consideration is the period that the audit is meant to cover.

Period of the audit

Although it is usually best to audit current records there are difficulties that may arise. When current records are used, normal business operations may be hindered and fraudulent transactions may not have been finalized.

If there is no real or direct suspicion of fraud, and the staff within the area under review have not changed significantly, it may be preferable to examine records up to 12 months past. This approach has a number of advantages:

- it allows normal business operations to go unhindered;
- all documents (particularly paid cheques) will have been cleared and filed;
- transactions will have been posted from suspense accounts;
- statistical records will have been produced and adjusted.

Using old records has a number of disadvantages:

- the audit may not detect 'live' frauds;
- the audit will not detect frauds currently awaiting concealment;
- real inventories cannot be compared with their book-keeping equivalents.

There are, however, many tests on current records that can be conducted on a routine basis without disrupting operations; the period selected must, in the final analysis, be decided on a case-by-case basis.

METHOD OF APPROACH

Critical point audits can be used in any organization but the more accurate and comprehensive its records the more effective the technique will be in weeding out symptoms of fraud.

When accounts are mentioned on a computer, specific tests can be made using audit software either on a one-time basis or to provide regular reports of exceptions and deviations. However, the majority of tests are relevant to both computerized and manual systems. The techniques are arranged in the following order:

1. Historical, proportional and inter-company analysis
2. Specific tests

1. Historical, proportional and inter-company analysis

These tests concentrate on examining the reasonableness of entries in accounts and involve comparison in performance between similar branches of a multiple organization and analysis of historical trends.

The filter is based on:

- final accounts
- trial balances
- bugetary records

with relevant figures being extracted and analysed.

The tests are essentially subjective, comparing costs and incomes (variable, fixed and semi-variable) within the business itself or on a year-to-year basis.

Historical comparisons are useful in two ways. First, to pick up the symptoms of internal manipulative and misrepresentative frauds and, second, to detect symptoms of conversions in customers' and suppliers' accounts.

The impact of fraud on historical ratios and absolute performance is a useful point to examine further. A thief cannot guarantee regularity to his criminal behaviour. He may be determined and persistent but, if supervision at work suddenly increases or if new security controls or accounting procedures are introduced, he may have no opportunity to steal. It may take him time and effort to create new opportunities.

This erratic nature of opportunities leads to inconsistency and an erratic impact on records and accounts. These patterns are detectable through analyses of the type shown on Figure 7.1.

Anchor information is composed of facts and accounts which are the least likely to have been fraudulently manipulated and which, given an indication of the true earning potential of the company, should be entered at the top of the analysis sheet.

In Figure 7.1 capital employed has been taken as one anchor and fixed assets as another. Both are set as 100 per cent in year 1. Lower down, accounts which vary as a result of sales (either directly or indirectly) are shown, as well as variable costs and incomes.

Across the figure chart—in yearly columns—are entered the amounts that relate to each heading listed in column 1 and percentages related to the base year (year 1). The object is to identify unusual trends or distortions in year to year figures and between related accounts.

Suppose, for example, the pattern shown in Table 7.2 emerged.

Table 7.2 Impact of fraud on trends (figures in percentages)

	Year 1	Year 2	Years 3	Year 4	Year 5
Sales	100	120	130	130	140
Sales tax	100	110	120	100	110
Debtors	100	105	100	170	210

Attention should be paid to the debtors' balances and to check that frauds had not been concealed by posting consequential debits to customers' accounts. Alternatively, the obvious increases in debtors' balances might indicate that the company has become the victim of a long firm or bankruptcy fraud.

All distortions and deviations from the norm should be followed through.

ACCOUNT HEADING (taken from trial balance, final accounts or departmental budgets, etc.)		AMOUNT ENTERED IN ACCOUNTS						
		YEAR 1		YEAR 2		YEAR 7		REMARKS
Details (examples only)	Ref.	Amount	%	Amount	%	Amount	%	
CAPITAL EMPLOYED			100					
FIXED ASSETS			100					
–property –plant and machinery –furniture –office equipment –hand tools –etc.								
CURRENT ASSETS								

–cash
–deposits
–inventory (working stocks)
  –type 1 (e.g., work in
    progress)
  –type 2
  –type 3 (etc.)
–marketable securities
–and as listed on trial balance								

INTANGIBLE ASSETS								
–copyrights –designs and development –expenses –exploration expenses –franchises –goodwill –licences –patents and patterns –and as listed on trial –balance								
INCOME								
–sales (broken by type/dep't) –discounts received –and as listed on trial balance								
DEBTORS AND BAD DEBTS								
EXPENSES								
–purchases (by type/dep't) –discounts allowed –and as listed on trial balance								
CREDITORS'								

RATIOS
  = current and quick
  = collection period
  = turnover/inventory
  = cash/credit sales
  = net profit/sales
  = return on assets
    employed
  = depreciation/assets
    (and as shown in
    Chapter 3)								

Figure 7.1 An analysis working sheet

Along the bottom of Figure 7.1, financial and inter-company ratios can be calculated. Comparison of performance with similar companies can be used as a means of identifying the impact of continuing frauds that fail to distort historical trends.

Where a similar company cannot be found, an alternative is to take average performances for a particular trade. Often figures can be obtained from a trade association or government departments.

Figure 7.1 can also be used for comparing the performance of and detecting fraud in branches within a multiple organization. In this case a chart is prepared for each branch (using budget or other figures). Distortions caused by consequential debits—or impacts in statistical records—will stand out against the average. More detailed investigations can then be carried out at the branches in question.

In very large companies, where accounts are consolidated, analysis may not be effective. In these cases other detection techniques may be used.

2. Specific tests

The specific tests described below focus on high risk areas of fraud as follows:

- Purchases
- Disbursement cheques
- Sales and marketing
- Incoming cheques
- Stock, assets and inventories
- Payroll and personnel
- Statistical records
- General accounting
- Control machinery
- Transportation
- Mail references

All or some of these tests may be used on a random basis or may be programmed to produce exception reports.

Purchases

Purchase frauds normally involve inflation of invoiced amounts or suppression of debits and returns. The key fact in all purchase frauds is the availability of a false credit in the personal account of a supplier: to be converted by the issue of a cheque, to cover the short delivery of stolen goods or to recover the costs of a bribe.

Frequently criminals can achieve this key position by posting direct entries in the ledger but are unable to support them by source documents, such as goods inwards records or correspondence. Thus verification should trace credit entries from the purchase ledger to corroborating evidence.

The personal accounts used to hold and convert false credits will be selected by a criminal with care. The options are:

- a completely false account over which he has control
- an account of an accomplice
- the account of a genuine supplier

Thus the first critical audit test is to verify the existence and bona fides of suppliers. The audit tests are written as direct instructions to avoid ambiguity.

Entity verification

Test 1   Compare all addresses and telephone numbers recorded for employees (including next of kin) with master file addresses for suppliers.

Purpose   This test detects cases where employees set up fictitious suppliers using their own addresses, or the address of a relative to receive false disbursement cheques and correspondence.

Test 2   Extract details of the past employers of key employees. Check the names of past employers against the current suppliers' master file.

Purpose   Often employees will falsify invoices using stationery from a past employer. The credits can be converted with an accomplice still working for the ex-employer or by any of the other ways discussed in Chapter 5.

Test 3   Extract details of companies asking for references on ex-employees (i.e., their new employers). Check these names against the current suppliers' master file.

Purpose   This is the reverse of test 2 and detects cases of collusive fraud involving ex- and current employees.

Test 4   Examine suppliers' master files for accommodation addresses, PO boxes and common addresses for supposedly unrelated suppliers. Details of office service companies which offer mail forwarding services can usually be found in classified telephone directories.

Purpose   To detect front companies and 'mail drops' which are often used to support purchase frauds.

Test 5   Print out from cheque production programs details of all suppliers whose names are printed out in abbreviated form (e.g., IBM, ICL).

Purpose   A common method of fraud depends on the generation of false credits in the account of a reputable supplier by reusing (with some alterations) purchase invoices already paid. The credit can be lapped from the account or converted by any of the standard methods. Where cheques are produced with the payee's name

abbreviated, they can be converted directly by simple alteration; for example from I.B.M. to I.B. Masters. This test
identifies vulnerable accounts.

Follow up

Examine a selection of cancelled disbursement cheques. Look
for:

- alteration of payees' names and dates;
- endorsements to third parties;
- inconsistent bank cancellation stamps;
- uncancelled cheques;
- missing cheques;
- torn or recornered cheques (i.e., where the serial number
  has been torn off);
- photocopied cheques.

Test 6   Select a number of competitive tenders submitted to the
company (for such things as construction projects, printing,
office cleaning, security) and check company registration files,
correspondence, telephone numbers. Look for common links
(directors, lawyers, office addresses, etc.).

Purpose   This test is intended to identify 'bid rigging' and sub-
contracting among connected companies.

Invoice verification

False invoices often bear obvious symptoms of fraud.

Test 1   Examine batches of paid purchase invoices. Put those that have
any of the following characteristics to one side for detailed
investigation:

- bearing an accommodation or post office box number as
  the only address;
- showing no telephone number;
- not an original copy (i.e., photo or carbon copy);
- unfolded (i.e., indicating they did not arrive in the post);
- goods described only by a computer code number;
- bearing alterations, especially increases in amounts;
- for high risk goods such as carbon paper, directories, typewriter ribbons, which are often used as a cover for extorsive
  frauds;
- out of sequence numbering.

Follow up

Carry out detailed verification of goods inwards records, correspondence, etc.

Ledger verifications

Standard audits should trace credits from the purchase ledger to supporting source documentation. The following tests are effective in identifying conflicts of interests and bribery of purchasing agents.

Test 1   Look for accounts opened after the appointment of individual buyers and authorized signatories. Analyse these as shown in Table 7.3.

Table 7.3   Relationship of accounts to buyers

Supplier	Date of first invoice from supplier	Invoices approved by	Employment commenced
ABC	12.4.1978	J. C. Clement	1.3.1978
DEF	1.1.1976	J. C. Clement	
GHI	12.2.1953	J. C. Clement	
XYZ	1.1.1976	J. P. James	12.9.1976

Purpose   Often buyers will introduce suppliers with whom they have worked before (and possibly been bribed) to their new employers. Although the majority of cases will be innocent, there are some worthy of detailed investigation. In this case the connection between ABC and Mr Clement should be examined.

Test 2   Compare the current year and past year's purchase ledger and look for:

- ceased accounts;
- new accounts;
- unusual trends in the volume passing through an account;
- credits passed through accounts other than for goods received and debits other than cash.

Purpose   Fraud distorts normal patterns and criminals can seldom guarantee consistency of performance. Examine changes carefully.

Test 3   Examine the authority levels of employees to place orders and sign purchase invoices. For example the office manager might be allowed to approve invoices to a value of £500, the department manager to £1000, etc. Analyse purchase invoices against individual authorities as shown in Table 7.4.

Table 7.4   Impact of order and invoice splitting

Signatory	Authority limit	Distribution of payments signed as % of authority limit			
		0/50	51/75	76/90	91/100
Smith	1000	10	10	20	60
Jones	1000	5	10	60	25
Parker	5000	8	10	70	12

The example in Table 7.4 shows that 60 per cent of the invoices approved by Smith are within 10 per cent of his authority limit, i.e., between £910 and 1000 this would be worthy of further investigation.

Purpose   Many cases of corruption are supported by order and invoice splitting. Thus an employee with an authority limit of say £1000 will place orders with favoured suppliers above this amount. They will be invoiced and approved by splitting the charges: usually in amounts just below the level the dishonest employee is allowed to approve, i.e., in the example just below £1000. Charts of the kind shown (Table 7.4) will often disclose these frauds.

Test 4   Check for suppressed purchase returns.
           Examine

— customer complaints for faulty goods (passed back to the original supplier and for which credit is due);
— goods outwards and postal records;
— warehouse records;
— laboratory and test records;
— correspondence.

Ensure that appropriate refunds for substandard goods returned to the company and passed back to its suppliers have been received.

Purpose   Purchase returns can be suppressed and the incoming cheques converted by the thief.

Test 5   Select a number of credits in the purchase ledger and trace them to invoices, correspondence and goods inwards records:

  – look for altered records and entries or out of sequence source documents;
  – look for (and suspect) missing records.

Purpose   To succeed, criminals must ensure that a credit is posted to personal account through which conversion can be made: he may not be able to falsify source documents.

Test 6   Check on credit cards issued by the company.
Check fuel consumption records for all company vehicles and look for patterns in the use of credit and agency cards by drivers when they are working away from their home base:

  – regular use of the same filling station in a distant town suggests collusion with forecourt employees;
  – reuse of the same credit card on the same day at the same filling station indicates fraud.

Purpose   Inflated and fictitious fuel purchases are an institutionalized method of fraud which operates as follows: the credit card voucher will be made out for more fuel than was put into the tank (say 50 gallons instead of 20). This allows the filling station attendant to remove cash to the value of the inflated amount (in the example 30 gallons) which he shares with the driver. In one case, so great was the inflation that the victim company's trucks were consuming 2 gallons to the mile!

Test 7   Test for the bribery and corruption of buyers.
Select a small number of contracts handled by the purchasing or contracts department, particularly where the supplier has no published price list, where charges are on a cost plus basis or where the contractor's charges are supported by third party invoices (i.e., sub-contractors) Look for:

  – costs above the industry norm;
  – goods supplied outside the contractor's normal line of business;
  – contracts awarded without competitive bids;
  – substandard goods;
  – 'overruns' and emergency extensions to the basic contract sum;

– contract prices just below a central or board level authority
limit;
– supporting charges incapable of verification;
– unrealistic physical conditions (i.e., the total capacity or turn
round times of trucks);
– the contractor is not listed in the telephone directory;
– and check premium rates allowed for say Sunday working,
working in wet weather, above a certain height from the
ground, etc.

Purpose   The object is to look for cases where inflated charges have been
approved and paid. Invariably this involves a kickback to a
company employee.

Follow up

When selection of possibly suspicious contracts and contractors
has been made, further action should be taken along the
following lines:

– check the ownership of the contracting companies concerned
and of all their associates;
– check the ownership of other companies which made unsuccessful bids for the contract(s);
– examine correspondence and agreements carefully for both
successful and unsuccessful contractors. Look for similar
typing styles, and signatures. Extract terms and conditions
which allow the contractor to charge premium rates or
overruns as shown in Table 7.5

Table 7.5 Reasons for premium payments

Clause permiting premium rates overruns	Value per month (£)	Method of control
Sunday working	3000	Timeclock and supervisory checks
Wet working	2000	Supervisor's report
Premium quality ballast	10 000	Invoice

High value items should be selected for further investigation and corroboration. Frequently it will be found that low level company employees have enormous discretion (with opportunities for personal gain) in approving additional charges under a contract.

Disbursement cheques

Test 1 A random sample of cancelled disbursement cheques should be carefully examined. Look for:

- endorsements to third parties:
- cheques paid through building society accounts;
- cheques missing from a series;
- altered cheques (particularly date, amount, payee) (see Figure 7.2, where cheque numbers arc substituted);
- uncancelled cheques;
- incorrect endorsements;
- abbreviated payee names;

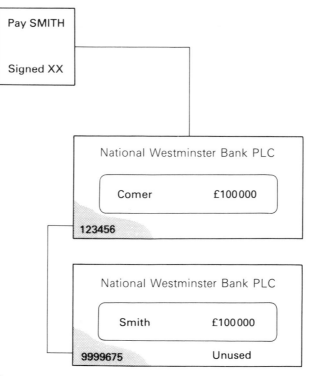

Figure 7.2 Doctored cancelled cheques

– cheques drawn in favour of a bank (these can be used to buy
negotiable bankers' drafts);
– photocopied cheques;
– recornered, renumbered cheques;
– endorsements of local banks for distant suppliers.

Purpose   These tests will detect many cases of conversion. All discrepancies should be traced to source documents.

Follow up

Cancelled disbursement cheques may be routinely monitored
for symptoms of conversion. The name and address of each
payee's bank can be held on computer file: when cheques are
returned from the bank, details of the account through which
they were paid can be input and compared with the standing
data. Exceptions can be listed out.

Sales and marketing

Manipulation of sales usually involves suppression, the object being to gain
possession of goods without the relevant personal account being debited.
Being the opposite of purchases, normal verification should flow from source
documents, making sure they have been posted to the appropriate ledger.

Test 1   Print out from master files and sales ledgers details of:

– customers with the lowest prices or highest discounts;
– customers with no master pricing information (their invoices
will be rejected for manual processing);
– customers whose master file entry has a fixed price flag;
– current sales versus last year's sales (to detect unusual
trends);
– balances in excess of credit limits;
– collection periods greater than X months;
– high ratio of credits other than from the cash book posted to
the account;
– journal vouchers transferring debit items from the account.

Purpose   This test should disclose cases in which master files, journal
vouchers and suspense accounts have been manipulated.

Test 2   Analyse files of sales orders, dispatch notes, warehouse records
and invoices and compare the usage and serial numbers of these
against formal sales invoices.

Purpose   To identify invoice suppression.

Test 3

Purpose

Examine sales invoice files (computer tapes or printouts) and summarize, in customer order, cancellations and sales credits. Also examine the alteration of customers' names on delivery notes and invoices to detect lapping frauds and manipulation of discount rates or credit terms. This is a critical test. Cancelled orders and credit notes are often a sign of internal manipulative fraud, where input has been suppressed after the goods have been delivered. They are also a signal of conversion, when receivers are also customers of the victim company.

Test 4

Purpose

Examine all goods issued free, to other branches of the company, to remote warehouses for storage, advertising and promotion purposes or generally leaving company premises without a third party account being debited. All companies have a system for the free issue of goods, although they will claim they do not. There is an obvious danger that such systems can be exploited.

Test 5

Check and verify all unusual incomes. Most companies receive income from unusual sources, such as insurance refunds, bad debt dividends, royalties, advance payments, etc., all of which are difficult to control and which may not be reflected as outstanding in ledgers. Look for the source of these incomes including:

– sales of unwanted fixed assets
– sales of waste paper (also consider confidentiality issues)
– advance fees and rental income
– specially handled sales
– cash sales and sales to staff
– inter-branch transfers
– refunds
– bad debt dividends
– advance payments and deposits
– sales of broken or substandard products

and verify their completeness by mail reference or personal visits.

Test 6

Test that there is no second (an off-record) sales invoicing system by making test purchases and looking for informal sales records such as

- challenge note books
- photocopied blank invoices
- uninvoiced delivery notes

Purpose   The easiest way of suppressing sales is to have a completely off-record system which is not included in the formal accounts of the victim company. In one supermarket, the manager bought an additional cash till unbeknown to his head office. All income from that till was for his personal account. Auditors never noticed that there were eight cash out points rather than seven!

In a furniture warehouse, the manager had a separate set of sales invoices printed. He issued these to staff and told them they were for use ater 2.00 p.m. each Saturday. He explained that he had to close the formal books at this time to make sure they balanced and that the 'special series' would be carried forward to the following week. Management at head office became conditioned to low sales at the store on Saturday afternoons, they reasoned that the adjacent football stadium deterred customers: in fact the opposite was true.

Test 7   Examine sales ledgers and credit notes for regular adjustments favouring particular customers. Trace a number of items to goods inwards or warehouse records and correspondence.

Purpose   The creation of false sales credits is a common method of fraud, which to succeed must be passed into the sales ledgers but the thieves may not be able to create false source documents. Regular credits to the account of one customer (when they are out of proportion with the business as whole) should be treated with suspicion.

Test 8   Examine correspondence files: look into and follow up complaints from customers of errors in invoices and statements submitted to them. Trace these through to orders, delivery notes and sales ledger: look for lapped or rolled over entries.

Purpose   Customer complaints are often the first sign of lapping frauds.

Test 9   Special checks for unfair competition.
Manufacturers of branded products are plagued with counterfeiters and pirates:

- examine quality control and guarantee records for indications that pirate goods have been returned to the victim;

- check carton and container supplier's sales to third parties and sales of rejects and scrap (these can be used to package pirate copies);
- examine the company's international and customer price lists (as well as discount terms) and check what diversions (parallel trading) are possible. The Treaty of Rome may restrict the action that can be taken, but experience suggests that cross-border traders also deal in counterfeit products;
- examine customers' sales statistics to detect unusual buying trends, indicating that they could be receivers or diverters.
- monitor mail room operations for theft and diversion (to an employee's personal business) of incoming replies to advertisements and sales promotions;
- 'seed' mailing lists with dummy customers: if the list is stolen and misused this fact should become obvious when the dummy customer receives mail shots.

Purpose   To detect marketing parallel trading and counterfeiting frauds.

Incoming cheques

Incoming cheques can be converted inside the victim organization or externally: external conversions are difficult to identify except by mail references on external visits. In either case incoming cheques are vulnerable to fraud.

Test 1   Obtain a selection of original paying in slips from the bank, compare these with duplicate copies and look for:

- differences between the amount of cash and the amount of cheques deposited;
- differences in the dates of deposit;
- omitted names of payees abbreviated or different names.

Purpose   To detect suppressed or manipulated incoming items.

Test 2   Examine copy paying in slips and verify those which:

- omit to show details of individual credits (in totals only);
- omit to show the division between cash and cheques;
- omit to show payee names (or which show initials only);
- are photocopies;
- bear no bank stamp or signature;
- bear alterations;
- bear dates inconsistent with the posting of credits in the sales ledger.

Efforts should also be made to detect missing paying in slips, although since most companies fail to prenumber them, this can be difficult.

Purpose   To detect the symptoms of lapping and internal conversion.

Test 3   Extract a selection of cash payments from the sales ledger and trace them to paying in slips and cash books. Look for differences in dates, payee names, and number of individual credits.

Purpose   In lapping frauds credits from one customer will be applied to the account of another to conceal previous thefts. The pattern is often as shown in Table 7.6.

Table 7.6   Signs of lapping frauds

Payment received from		Applied to the account of	
	£		£
Smith	1000	Smith	1000
Jones	2000	Jones	1000
Parker	3100	Parker	1100
		Arnold	3000
Total	6100		6100

Thus the paying in slips will show three items, while the sales ledger has four. This type of discrepancy can be picked up by computer analysis or by manual extraction.

Stock, assets and inventories
Control over physical assets and working inventories has a significant effect on a company's exposure to fraud and can be subject to sales suppression, purchase inflation and unconcealed thefts. Annual stocktakings are particularly vulnerable.

Test 1   Examine detailed inventory files, select and print out:

  – products (description, volume, value) which have the longest turnover periods on the basis that fictitious stocks never get sold;
  – product lines currently in stock but not on the inventory for previous years;

- product lines, held in stock in previous years, but not available currently;
- all adjustments to book stock as a result of annual and other physical stock checks, summarized by product type and location;
- details of all assets with a nil value (fully depreciated) on the assets register for the previous year, not currently listed.

Purpose To detect stock thefts and the concealment of frauds in inventory values.

Test 2 Examine the schedules for the previous year's annual stocktake:

- examine each line and consider the reasonableness of the alleged holdings in relation to turnover and the storage space available for the recorded inventory;
- examine the work records of company drivers at the time of the annual stocktaking (often stocks will be moved from warehouse to warehouse and double counted);
- examine purchase invoices from independent transport contractors during the stocktaking period to detect movements of stock between warehouses;
- examine clocking in and overtime records for warehouse employees and drivers during the stocktaking period;
- examine working schedules for alterations, duplications and changes to values;
- verify goods in transit (in and out) at the time of stocktaking;
- examine purchase orders and correspondence files for goods held on consignment or sale or return at the time of the stocktaking;
- check consistency of temperature adjustments for all bulk liquid stocks;
- verify the bona fides of purchase and sales credit notes immediately before/after an annual stocktaking.

Test 3 Examine accounts relating to odd assets such as:

- packaging and containers (pallets)
- hired goods
- sales promotion and prize schemes
- printing and stationery
- canteen food
- plant on hire

and trace a selection of items to purchase records and inventory listings.

Purpose   Often control over unconventional stocks permits unconcealed thefts. This test checks the obvious areas.

Payroll and personnel

In practice, large payroll frauds are uncommon and are certainly not a mainstream method. However, undertake the following tests.

Test 1   Select and print out:

- new employees joining in the year: trace a selection of these to personnel files, telephone directories and voters' registers;
- payments for casual labour, summarized in department or branch order;
- pensioners over 80 years old: verify existence from voters' register or telephone records.

Purpose   These verifications should detect 'straw men': people included on payroll files who do not exist.

Test 2   Examine payroll master files and print out:

- adjustments (gross pay and tax) over x per cent
- salaries greater than £x
- increases greater than x per cent
- income tax versus total salaries

Purpose   In many computerized payroll systems adjustments can be entered to improve the pay of a dishonest employee or his colleagues. These tests should detect the more simple manipulations.

Test 3   Examine personnel files and print out details of:

- employees who do not take holidays
- the holiday addresses of employees

Purpose   Standard accounting textbooks warn that criminals rarely take holidays, in case their dishonesty is discovered in their absence. Practical experience shows this is rarely true: criminals usually take extremely expensive holidays. The only criminals who cannot afford to take absences from work are those involved in lapping frauds: other, more sensible, criminals can be much more flexible.

It is interesting to note when a number of employees all show the same address for their vacation. Often the reason is free accommodation provided by a supplier. This form of payoff has been detected by this simple test.

Analysis of statistical records

Statistical records may contain interesting patterns of manipulation and conversion. They are worthy of close attention:

Test 1   Select and print out:

Sales statistics:
- Details of customers whose volumes of purchases have declined against the normal trend and particularly when cancelled orders and returned goods are the supposed reason. This could indicate that they are receiving stolen goods from other sources.
- Examine customers' records and compare volumes and proportions of goods bought against credit notes, goods returned and end customer complaints. Receivers find it almost impossible to purchase stolen goods in the proportions dictated by the marketplace. For example a printout (see Table 7.7) might show that customer DEF has apparently sold more of products 456 and 999 to his end customers (who returned the guarantee cards to the wholesaler) than he bought from the wholesaler.

Table 7.7   Impact of frauds on statistical records

Product number	Sales and (guarantee cards) returned to the wholesaler by end buyers of the wholesaler's customers				
	Retailer				
	ABC	DEF	GHI	JKL	MNO
123	20(5)	80(62)	15(3)	40(2)	100(6)
456	100(30)	5(6)	8(1)	30(4)	50(9)
999	30(8)	1(15)	9(2)	10(3)	20(6)

- In multiple branch operations, check the ratio of cash to credit sales. Low ratios suggest suppression of cash sales or lapping of debits through customers' accounts.

- Similarly examine the ratios of bad debts to sales and bad debt recoveries. Inconsistent ratios suggest suppression of sales (concealed in bad debt accounts) or conversion of incoming bad debt dividends.
- Examine the ratio of successful to unsuccessful calls made by sales representatives, service engineers, etc. Low ratios indicate inefficiency or conflicts of interest, to which the employer's orders and service work is diverted.

Purchases:

- Analyse the expense budgets of each cost centre and print out details of all expense items which

  - distort normal patterns in the company: check to the underlying authority, correspondence and source documents;
  - were below 50 per cent of budget at the start of the third quarter and over 90 per cent at year end.

Purpose   Frequently criminals will choose accounts for the suppression of consequential debits which they know will not overrun their budget at year end. The simple method is to delay manipulation until the third quarter and to choose account headings which are likely to be in surprise. This test detects such manipulation.

General accounting

Test 1   Identify transaction entry codes in all systems and print out details of those which:

- adjust stock with no debit to a personal account;
- write off goods, debts or stock;
- give special pricing or fixed prices to customers;
- allow the free issue of products;
- relate to free offers, promotional samples or incentive schemes;
- adjust final accounts and formal entries.

Purpose   In practice, transaction entry codes are vulnerable to fraud. This test should identify the most dangerous suspect items that should be carefully checked.

Test 2   Examine the chart of accounts in the nominal ledger and identify those headings which are unlikely to be closely controlled:

- large or global corporate accounts over which no single department has control:

- office furniture repair
- computer development costs
- general maintenance
- office cleaning
- scrap disposal
- advertising
- expense accounts for items not included in manufacturing costing systems:
  - nuts, bolts, washers, screws, wire
  - stationery and printing
  - sales and promotional printing
- accounts held by domineering departments or managers, who resent interference;
- black money and corporate slush funds, overseas agents' commission accounts. These are ideal accounts for a criminal to exploit simply because he knows the victim is unlikely to prosecute.

Purpose   Postings to loosely controlled nominal accounts should be checked back to source documents.

Test 3   Search for consequential debits held in suspense at year end.
      Consequential debits can be held in suspense, either in their year of creation or as items carried forward to the next accounting period.

- Examine items uncleared at the close of the last financial year:
  - incoming and outgoing cheques
  - goods in transit
  - on consignment stocks
  - sales invoices and dispatch notes
  - unposted purchase credits
  - cash suspense account

and check that they have been correctly posted into the appropriate double entry accounts.

Test 4   Identify all suspense accounts and verify a selection of postings:

- check the bona fides of personal accounts which receive the benefit of credits transferred from suspense;
- check accounts whose debit entries are often transferred to suspense;

       – examine journal vouchers for sequence integrity and for alteration after they have been approved.

Purpose   To detect manipulative frauds in which debits and credits are washed through suspense accounts.

Test 5   Test for inter-account transfers (lapping).
      Where control accounts are maintained, tests can be made on the possibility of inter-account lapping, which is usually inconsistent with source documents. The following analysis can be conducted manually or by computer:

      – select an alphabetical group of personal accounts, in the sales ledger (say F to L) for a given financial period (say one month);
      – list and total all debit and credit entries posted to these accounts;
      – extract similar listings (for the alphabetical group F to L) from the cash book, invoices or sales day book;
      – compare

Debits from source	Debits from ledger
16 998.53	16 998.53
Credits from source	Credits from ledger
15 965.22	22 778.73

      The credit figures in this example indicate that items have been lapped or incorrectly posted to one or more accounts in the sample (F to L). Further investigation should establish the accounts involved and the reasons for the discrepancy.

Control machinery

Interference with control machinery is a common method of misrepresentative frauds.

Test 1   Identity vulnerable control machinery (weighbridges, meters, scales, thermometers, etc.) used by the company to control inventories of goods in or out:

      – examine the precise nature of use and the consequences if interfered with;
      – catalogue methods of interference;
      – examine past cases of interferences and breakdowns for patterns (time, shift, etc.);

– examine repair and service records (check for patterns);
– inspect machinery (look for physical interference).

Purpose   These tests should indicate whether a control machine can be and has been interferred with. The normal method of follow up is to keep covert observation on the equipment concerned.

Transportation

Transport costs are a significant element in the profit or loss of most companies: they are often open to rampant abuse and fraud.

Test 1   Identify the company's suppliers of new vehicles, maintenance and services. Examine:

– competitive tenders and verify cost justification of existing suppliers of new vehicles;
– a number of purchase invoices for tyres and verify that the appropriate quality and quantity have been received.

Purpose   Tyres for large articulated vehicles are expensive and attractive for thieves. Often defects are reported on virtually new tyres, replacements bought but never fitted. Employees of the supplier thus build up excess stocks which are sold for cash. This test should detect the obvious cases.

Test 2   Check the miles per gallon performance of company vehicles.

Purpose   This test should detect short deliveries of bulk fuel as well as agency credit card frauds: both of which are almost institutionalized methods.

Test 3   Examine the routing sheets of the company's delivery drivers: these preplan loads and routes for a given day and should be allocated on a random basis. However, look for:

– amendment to loads, drivers and customers: often dishonest drivers will switch routes to give themselves better opportunities for fraud. They may bribe the routing supervisor or other colleagues to arrange their loads so that their first customer is one who can be short delivered and their second a receiver;
– drivers who are regularly scheduled with partly loaded trucks: the spare capacity can be used to transport stolen goods.

Purpose   These tests have proved effective in detecting many frauds by delivery truck drivers. Other methods are discussed later.

Mail references

Mail references to suppliers and customers have a useful part to play in the detection of fraud and in following up possible symptoms. To give the greatest chance of success, mail references should call for replies to be sent other than to the company's main place of business (where they might be intercepted and suppressed) and should be based on unresolved areas arising from the critical point tests. Selection guidelines are set out in Table 7.8.

Job sensitivity analysis

Every job in every organization has varying opportunities for fraud, depending on such factors as access, skills and the time available to plan and execute. This technique is based on the simple question: 'if a thief worked in this job, what could he do?' It is a simple analysis of fraud risks viewed through the eyes of a potential thief.

METHOD OF APPROACH

The starting point is to identify all job positions, in the company or department under review from:

organization charts
individual job description
accounting manuals and forms
authority schedules

and to prepare analysis sheets for each one, including full- and part-time employees, contract staff such as cleaners, security guards, drivers and programmers.

Summary sheets should be prepared to show the precise specifications of each job noting the difference between approved access to accounts, inventories computer systems and access which could be contrived. For example a sales order clerk may not have approval to access purchase records, but if he shares office space with a member of purchasing department, it would be unrealistic to assume that he could not read, falsify or remove these records. The difference between approved authority and informal access is usually significant.

Factors which should be considered in the analysis are given below.

Reporting level

Generally the more senior the employee, the greater his discretion to operate outside normal controls for his own benefit or for the benefit of third parties with whom he is in collusion.

Table 7.8 Mail references

Suppliers

Accounts with no back-up papers — ledger postings not supported by basic documents

Accounts supported by irregular documents
- odd or unusual invoice printing
- no phone number, address, registered office or VAT number shown
- photocopied documents
- altered documents
- unfolded documents
- once-off large transactions
- incorrect extensions
- incorrect adding machine summaries

Accounts with irregular trading patterns
- distorted reasonableness, proportional or historical ratios
- high prices or low discount rates
- omission of purchase credit notes (detected from quality control and other factory records)
- descriptions of goods shown only by code numbers

New and closed accounts — particularly with unusual trading patterns

Accounts with possible manipulations of paid cheques
- missing disbursement cheques
- odd endorsements on cheques
- photocopied disbursement cheques

Customers

Accounts with low prices, high credit limits — particularly when credits other than cash regularly appear

Accounts with inconsistent back-up documents
- dispatch notes, etc., not supported by sales invoices
- sales credits not supported by correspondence
- high frequency of cancelled invoices/orders

Bad debt accounts
- dividend received
- postings to account after insolvency identified

Odd transactions — scrap and raw materials sales

Possible credit frauds — extended credit or collection periods

New and closed A/C — particularly with unusual trading patterns

Accounts with unusual trading patterns — distorted reasonableness, proportional or historical ratios

Level of day-to-day supervision

It is usually easier for a thief to operate when his manager is stretched by other responsibilities. Ironically the easiest people to deceive are those who are the busiest or who frequently travel away from their office, particularly on long alcoholic lunches.

Also the level of technical control which management exercises should be considered. The dangerous positions are where subordinates have greater skills than their manager or where the manager is from an entirely different professional background. For example:

Manager
(accountant)

Employee 1	Employee 2	Employee 3	Employee 4
(accountant)	(accountant)	(accountant)	(commodity trader and investments)

In this structure, the manager clearly has less task control over employee 4 and under most circumstances will have to take much of what he does on trust. Further, the employee may believe that, being outside the profession of his manager and colleagues, his chances of promotion are limited. This is a typical position in which Durkheim's theory of 'anomie' applies.

Place of work

An employee's normal place of work also has an affect on his ability to commit fraud: firstly because it determines the records, etc., to which he has access and, secondly, because it influences his ability to behave dishonestly without being seen or overheard by colleagues. Practical experience suggests the following ratings:

High risk
- Branches remote from head office (particularly overseas).
- Single occupancy offices or private work area (this may also apply after normal working hours when other employees have gone home).
- Travelling employees with no fixed base (including transport drivers).
- Work areas shared by one other person.
- Open work areas.

Lower risk
Clearly there will be exceptions, but the absence of external surveillance by colleagues has a bearing on the opportunities of fraud.

Skill and qualifications

The skill to identify and commit fraud is obviously an important consideration: often 'over-qualified' employees identify opportunities others do not suspect. They may also rationalize dishonesty for personal gain as justified in view of the poor way they perceive themselves to have been treated by their employer.

Personal characteristics

The personal characteristics of employees should be considered. Danger symptoms include:

– unexplained wealth
– high cash spending (drinking, slow horses, fast cars and even faster women!)
– disgruntled over lack of promotion or resentful
– selfish
– disregard for instructions and procedures
– overly self-important

Although there are exceptions, these indicators should never be ignored, particularly the first one. The 'rich aunt' story is usually untrue!

Approved authority levels

Most companies set down the authority delegated to employees both on their job descriptions and in authority manuals. These should be noted carefully. Special dangers arise where an employee is able to exercise discretion in favour of third parties (suppliers, customers, etc.) on his own authority.

Deviations

Consider all deviations or exceptions to procedures allowed in the position under review. The reasons for all exceptions and the authority for them should be carefully checked.

General tasks and access to records

Although controls establishing separations between the duties of employees are recommended, they are of limited value in practice. Employees are seldom denied access to any records or any part of their employers' premises: computer centres are perhaps the only exceptions. Whether authorized or contrived, the following activities should be considered:

High risk
– Authorizes electronic funds transfer payments
– Controls the investment of funds or foreign exchange
– Approves advances to third parties
– Approves contacts with third parties
– Reconciles bank statements
– Manages nominal ledger entries and adjustment

- Approves purchase orders
- Approves sales prices and discounts for customers
- Authorizes disbursement cheques
- Handles bank deposits
- Controls sensitive business information
- Manages account of third parties
- Writes off bad debts
- Controls physical inventories

Low risk
Special consideration should be given to 'one-time' fraud opportunities and the nominal account in which the symptoms of fraud can be concealed.

Brainstorming

The factors for each job should be considered from the position of a would-be thief and precise specifications of his fraud opportunities written down. Ideally this analysis should be conducted by a group of trusted employees, with different skills and should include:

- assets at risk
- method of theft
- method of concealment: positive or negative
- accounts in which losses might arise
- method of conversion
- maximum possible loss

for both one-time and systematic frauds. Each member of the team should complete working sheets independently. These should be brainstormed and final versions produced for each job.

Follow up

The analysis points up high risk jobs and the methods of possible fraud. Detailed tests should be made to determine whether the opportunities have been exploited.

Vulnerability charts

Fraud can occur only when there is an opportunity. Generally speaking, the greater or more easy the opportunity, the more often it is likely to have been exploited.

A vulnerability may be defined as the opportunity for an act unfavourable to the victim to occur without detection.

A vulnerability chart is shown in Figure 7.3. It is simply a schedule of risks arranged in order of probability.

BRANCH OR UNIT ....

DATE PREPARED ....

BY ....

ASSETS AND INTERESTS AT RISK			THEFT OPPORTUNITIES ARE AVAILABLE TO			MOVEMENT IS POSSIBLE BY		CONTROLS	MANAGEMENT	CONCEALMENT IS POSSIBLE BY		CONVERSION OUTLETS		TOTAL POINTS
Description	Value or turnover	PTS	Names or job positions	No. of people	PTS	Names or job titles	PTS	PTS	PTS	Names or job titles	PTS	Names	PTS	
1	2a	2b	3	4	5	6	7	8	9	10	11	12	13	14

Figure 7.3 Vulnerability chart

Charts are useful in the following circumstances:

- As an analysis of corporate fraud risks—possibly on a once-off basis, though preferably reviewed at least once every year.
- When organized criminals are believed to be operating in an industry or against a company and the methods of fraud are not known. In this case they point out the most likely method of theft and identify the company employees most likely to be involved.
- When conversion symptoms are revealed (for example, when the victim's goods are being sold cheaply) but the method of theft is not known. In this case they identify possible thieves, concealment courses and conversion outlets.

Vulnerability charts therefore involve:

- identification of assets at risk
- identification of potential thieves
- possible methods of fraud
- effectiveness of controls
- possible concealment courses
- the possibilities for conversion

These are referred to as *vulnerability elements*.

To be able to assess vulnerabilities it is essential to have detailed information about the company, branch or department concerned. The first step in preparing a vulnerability chart is to collect this information.

The following paragraphs set out the steps that are necessary for assessing fraud vulnerabilities at one operating location or in one unit. A chart of a company's fraud vulnerabilities would be represented by the sum of the charts for its individual units.

Each chart should be set out along the lines shown in Figure 7.3 and sufficient space should be left to make additional notes.

Some method of ranking vulnerabilities is necessary: the rationale is that the greatest vulnerability is the one most likely to be exploited.

It is important that the system of ranking is not to too cumbersome. The charts are meant to be a useful guide to fraud risks. They will not be mathematically precise and to try to make them so would be misleading and a waste of time.

A method of ranking which has proved useful and practical is first to allocate points to the various elements, set out on the body of the chart, on a scale of 0 to 10. Second, allocate 0 points to elements heavily in favour of fraud, on a scale rising to 10 points for elements that are heavily weighted against fraud. Where an element does not apply to the particular asset, 5 points are added to the total as a neutral entry. At the end of the exercise, all points are totalled. The lowest total indicates the assets which are most vulnerable, as well as the most likely methods of fraud.

When the quantification has been made, the company has the choice of carrying out a detailed investigation of the potential high loss areas or of introducing preventive controls.

Charts can be completed as explained below.

COLUMNS 1 AND 2a

These should show full details of the assets at risk within the branch or department concerned and should give special attention to unconventional, unrecorded and intangible assets and losses that could arise from unfair competitive activity and espionage (i.e., giving rise to no account/inventory discrepancy).

The maximum value of the assets at risk—or annual turnover—should also be shown, as this will give a measure of criticality. The maximum tolerable loss figure should also be noted in column 2a. This is simply the size of the loss that the company would accept as normal. For example, in some oil companies losses of 0.5 per cent at retail service stations are tolerated. When losses are acceptable it follows that thieves can operate—keeping losses below the tolerable level—without having to resort to complex concealments.

Obviously the accuracy and completeness of columns 1 and 2 determine the overall utility of a chart. If assets at risk are missed from these columns then the chart may fail. Appropriate managers should be consulted and, if necessary, employees' advice sought. It is sometimes possible to 'brainstorm' vulnerability charts and to involve a group of experienced and trusted employees in the compilation. This approach is particularly useful in identifying computer risks.

COLUMN 2b

In attempting to measure vulnerabilities, due regard must be paid to the attractiveness of assets. The manufacturers of toys and, say, perfumes face threats different from the manufacturers of metal sheets. In the former case the assets are generally attractive and removable while in the latter they may be more difficult to steal and dispose of.

Small, high value assets are attractive to most internal thieves and to external receivers who may be able to dispose of them for cash. Large assets usually have a restricted illegal market.

A points allocation, depending on the attractiveness of assets at risk, should be entered in column 2b.

The allocation should be along the following lines:

Cash and equivalents	0	Highly vulnerable
Secret business information	0	
High value, low bulk items	1	
Normal products of the victim company	2	
Stocks, raw materials	2	
Plant and machinery (small size)	3	
Fixed assets (large)	4/7	
Buildings	10	Barely vulnerable

The allocations shown above may be increased or decreased depending on the requirements and judgements of the company concerned. They should, however, be an accurate reflection of the *relative* attractiveness of the assets at risk.

COLUMNS 3 AND 4

These columns try to identify the people who have, or who can contrive the opportunity to steal the assets in columns 1 and 2.

Under this heading would be included people who have normal working access and people who by manipulation of documents can have the assets or interests delivered through the normal commercial process into their possession.

Thus, the list may include operations and management employees, business contacts, opportunists and so on. The total number of people and their job positions should be shown in columns 3 and 4. If the numbers in an access or opportunity position are small then names instead of job titles could be shown in column 3.

This part of the chart requires care and attention to detail. The identification of possible thieves is a difficult and sometimes distasteful task, but if fraud is to be detected such steps must be taken. The analysis should be conducted under the headings of:

Internal criminals
A management employees
B operations employees

External criminals
C business contacts
D opportunist
E organized

So far as headings D and E are concerned, the local police or trade association may be able to assist in identifying criminal conspiracies and local opportunists. Headings A, B and C are within a company's knowledge.

Internal criminals

Most managers form conclusions about the reliability of employees. Such opinions are, of course, subjective and may be based on personality differences. However, the knowledge of a local manager can be useful in developing a vulnerability chart.

Those employees whom the manager considers unreliable should be noted and particular care given to the assets and fraud opportunities that come in their domain. Extra attention should be given for one of two reasons. First, if an employee is unreliable or careless he is less likely to detect or control frauds committed on the company by third parties. Second, if he is dishonest, the chances are that when given an opportunity he will exploit it himself.

Signs that might indicate employee unreliability or dishonesty include:

- interests in other competitive businesses
- friends or relations engaged in competitive businesses
- gambling, drug use, or alcoholism
- poor time keeping, frequent absence for spurious reasons
- close social or personal relationships with suppliers, contractors and customers, particularly when they are thought to be unreliable
- excess financial commitments
- lack of company loyalty

Business competitors

The standing of business competitors at home and overseas can have a direct bearing on the risks of industrial espionage and on the possibility of unfair competitive activity—passing-off and the like. These should be considered.

COLUMN 5

This column should measure the reliability of the people and companies who have an opportunity to steal the assets listed in column 1. A low number of points should be allocated where there are some people or companies who are clearly unreliable or dishonest.

But when opportunities are restricted to a small group of people, all of whom are considered trustworthy, a high points allocation would be appropriate.

COLUMNS 6 AND 7

One of the basic ingredients of opportunities was the ability to separate the asset or interest from its owner. Columns 6 and 7 take account of this fact and attempt to measure the ease of transportation or movement of each asset listed in columns 1 and 2.

Column 6 may show the names of the people concerned or it may simply show their job positions. An attempt should be made to relate the people or groups shown in this column with those shown in column 3. When names or groups are included in both columns, less collusion is needed to achieve theft. When, on the other hand, no names or groups are the same, collusion may be necessary to steal or move the asset or interest.

It is important to bear in mind that, although some people who have the opportunity to steal may not have a direct means of removal, they may be in a position to achieve movement without collusion. For example, the warehouseman (who has access to an asset and therefore an opportunity to steal it) may be able, without collusion, to make out a false delivery note that would cause someone who has the means of transportation to move the asset innocently. This sort of position should be noted in column 6 and the points total in column 7 completed accordingly.

COLUMN 8

This column reflects on a points basis the efficiency of controls over each asset listed in columns 1 and 2. A low points total should be allocated where theft is possible without concealment. Similarly, low points should be allocated where concealment is possible by negative means; by the removal or destruction of a record as opposed to the creation of a false one. On the other hand, if controls are good and thefts cause an account/inventory discrepancy to appear in a closely controlled real account and concealment is difficult, then a high points allocation may be appropriate.

In trying to assess the efficiency of controls, special attention should be paid to exceptions to normal procedures. If the listing of assets in column 1 has been completed properly then exceptions should appear and their controls can be measured.

This is a good point to mention again some of the exceptions that often provide fraud opportunities:

- non-standard sales, such as scrap materials, by-products, raw materials, rejects
- specially handled shipments—inter-branch transfers and other goods movements, both in and out, that do not result in a billing to a third party
- rental and special incomes
- cash sales (where they are exceptions), including sales to staff
- bad debts, 'write-offs', and dividends receivable
- gift, promotion schemes and sales incentives
- credit cards
- local cash purchases
- purchases and sales credits
- inter-account transfers and journal vouchers
- purchases below central limits

COLUMN 9

Fraud is unlikely to occur when management is efficient and enquiring. When expenses and costs are written back into a unit budget that is controlled by a 'figures orientated' manager the chances for successful fraud are that much less.

In the same way, when sales are written back to small profit centres the chances of suppressed incomes are probably low.

If the manager is constantly on the golf course or at the bar, weak or generally incompetent, then the risks of fraud are high—first, because more junior employees can justify their dishonesty by saying to themselves that it is no more than the manager is doing or deserves and, second, because the manager would be unlikely to spot the symptoms of frauds committed by others.

Column 9 therefore measures the efficiency of management control over the unit. Where control is poor, a low points allocation should be made. If management appears to be efficient (and perhaps had detected previous frauds) then a high points entry should reflect this position.

COLUMNS 10 AND 11

The availability of a cogent concealment course is a necessary ingredient of most large-scale or extended frauds. In these columns should be entered details of the names or job groups of people who have the means of concealing the theft of assets listed in columns 1 and 2.

Where the names or groupings are different from those shown in columns 3 and 6 then, without collusion, manipulative frauds may not be possible. Although there is nothing particularly difficult or unusual about collusion, fraud risks are less when collusion is essential. This is particularly true when collusion is necessary at different levels in the management structure or between management and operations workers. Where large-scale conspiracy is the only way to achieve or conceal a theft, then a higher number of points should be entered in column 11 than would be shown in a case where one employee or one group has access to the asset (column 1), to a means of removal (column 6), and to a concealment course (column 10).

In looking at the concealment possibilities it is also useful to consider what effects the concealment—particularly the manipulation of financial records—will have on other company accounts. A separate note should be made of such side effects.

COLUMNS 12 AND 13

The points entered in column 13 will reflect the reliability of business competitors and the availability of receivers in the trade in question. When previous experience indicates that stolen company goods have appeared in cash markets, account should be taken of the fact in a relatively low points allocation in column 13.

Where the only possible buyers of a particular stolen asset would be a government department then a high allocation of points would be appropriate. Overseas markets and export conversions should not be ignored in this analysis. Very often trade associations are able to assist in identifying less reputable traders. The company itself, from its own financial and statistical records, should be able to establish which business associates are in serious financial difficulty and who may therefore be tempted to buy stolen goods.

Experience shows that, besides the organized crime syndicates, the firms most likely to be in the market for stolen goods are:

- essentially cash traders at the lower end of the market concerned
- single owner/operator businesses
- businesses with a history of previous failures, bankruptcy and liquidations
- businesses whose proprietors have been previously convicted for fraud or other dishonesty
- high turnover businesses which consistently place small orders (i.e., poor cash flow)
- itinerant traders
- businesses currently in financial trouble

These factors should be used in assessing the likelihood of outlets for stolen goods. On a parallel line, the conversion possibilities for stolen business intelligence should be assessed and appropriate points entered in column 13.

COLUMN 14

Column 14 will show the total points accumulated against each of the assets or interests at risk. The lowest points total (allowing for all neutral entries) will indicate the highest fraud vulnerabilities.

Column 2 will show the criticality of the risk. From this point the company may choose to carry out more detailed investigations—using one of the techniques mentioned later—or it may decide to institute defensive controls or merely to be more alert to identify high risk areas of operation.

EXAMPLE OF THE USE OF A VULNERABILITY CHART

Vulnerability charts merely direct attention towards particular risk areas; normally they do not produce evidence of fraud by themselves. However there are exceptions as in the following case:

A perfumery company had reasons to believe that sensitive product and marketing information was finding its way into the hands of an overseas competitor. Rival products were hitting the market within weeks of the victim promoting a new line. A private detective was instructed to make investigations but was unable to produce conclusive proof of espionage. He did confirm that the rival's products bore remarkable similarities to the victim's.

The victim company decided to look carefully through its operation to try to establish where its information was most exposed and how it could be stolen, believing, quite correctly, that its security systems were generally good.

The analysis (essentially a vulnerability chart) established that sensitive information was most exposed when it was sent to the company's advertising agents so that packaging could be designed and promotion arranged. This, however, was a purely relative assessment and the victim had no other reason for believing that the leak might be occurring in this direction.

The victim—in the form of its two directors—designed and compiled a fictitious but revolutionary new product which unbeknown to all other employees of the company they sent to the advertising agency. Within weeks an employee of the victim company approached one of the directors and asked if he could be shown the file on the new product because he was concerned with registering the name and trade mark. Not surprisingly, he was questioned closely and subsequently admitted that he and his wife, who worked for the advertising agency, had been selling business information to a competitor. His wife had mentioned the fictitious new product to her husband who, being a keen employee, disclosed an interest that trapped him. Few frauds are revealed this easily, and other techniques have to be considered.

Invigilation and created checks

In most dictionaries the word 'invigilate' refers to the close supervision of candidates during examinations, so that they do not crib or cheat. In the commercial context, the word has a similar meaning: 'to impose such temporary controls on a business or part of a business that during the period of supervision fraud is virtually impossible'. In short, the creation of a controlled, fraud-free environment.

Opportunity is a necessary condition if fraud is to occur. When temporary controls are made so strict that opportunities do not arise, or frauds result in immediate detection, a fraud-free profile can be established. It is then a simple matter to look back at historical losses and patterns and determine which were fraudulent and which were genuine. The following case illustrates this point.

An oil installation was experiencing stock losses of 0.23 per cent of turnover; which at that time was not particularly unusual. However, the manager suspected that fraud was taking place but was not sure how or when. Observation and other investigations failed to produce evidence.

For a 30-day period the installation was saturated with security guards on the pretext that a warning of a terrorist attack had been received. Every movement of goods both in and out was checked. All documents were verified. During the period of the invigilation losses ceased.

After the invigilation had been called off, records kept at the plant were examined for absolute, proportional and reasonableness changes during the invigilation period. It was noted that two service stations— which prior to the exercise had bought on average only 2000 gallons of petrol a week—suddenly doubled their orders and during the 30 days had received more than 19 000 gallons each. It was further discovered that a shift foreman who in 23 years' service had taken no sick leave was away from work for 19 of the 30 days.

Two or three months were allowed to elapse and covert observation was kept on the service stations, whose orders by this time has reverted to 2000 gallons per week (for various geographical reasons, observation of the installation was almost impossible).

Using night vision equipment and cameras, unrecorded deliveries to the service stations were detected. The owners were interviewed and their books examined. They were subsequently charged with fraud extending back for two years and involving 62 000 gallons of product. The shift foreman was not involved. Enquiries suggested that he was a loyal and trustworthy servant. His absence had been genuinely caused by the serious illness of his wife.

Although recovery was not made from the service stations' operators, the termination of the fraud brought a direct saving to the oil company. Further, the dishonest staff working at the terminal—some of whom were not caught or dismissed—were impressed by management's skill in weeding out a fraud that they had believed foolpoof. How much of this impression carried forward and stopped further frauds, and for how long, is conjecture, but no doubt it did have some effect.

Invigilations designed to detect or measure the impact of fraud and to establish genuine operating losses can be used in the following circumstances:

- when stock losses (account/inventory discrepancies) arise and it is not clear whether they are caused through fraud, inefficiency or poor plant and equipment
- when collusive or organized crime is suspected
- when the size of the loss exceeds the anticipated cost of the invigilation

METHOD OF OPERATION AND PROBLEM AREAS

Invigilations can be carried out in any business and at any time: they are, however, expensive and rely on the selection of reliable and experienced staff for their effectiveness. Using vulnerability charts as a guide, it is possible to establish points within an operation which are critical to fraud opportunities. A logic tree can be prepared for the business as a whole, or for a particular unit, showing what conditions *must* exist for fraud to be possible.

Such conditions might include:

— availability of vulnerable stocks
— poor controls over the receipt and loading of goods
— poor or weak controls over accounting records
— poor controls over exceptional transactions or unconventional assets
— poor or weak supervision, generally or at specific times
— reliance on inaccurate control or measuring equipment

Clearly, if all weak points were to be controlled by double banking security guards or auditors, business would soon grind to a halt and staff relations become intolerable. Therefore the first rule of invigilations is to concentrate on the physical movement of goods, the real assets that are essential to most frauds. Bearing this point in mind, an invigilation can be planned along the following lines.

1. Obtain management's agreement to the exercise.
2. Determine the precise objectives—whether the invigilation is intended to detect past and existing frauds or to set a Plimsoll line of non-fraudulent losses for future reference.
3. Restrict the exercise to a discrete and self-contained area of the business— for example, a branch of a multiple company or operating department of a large industrial complex. Too much ambition in the size of an invigilation will prove costly and possibly ineffective.
4. Decide on the precise nature of increased temporary controls that are necessary to remove fraud opportunities and determine the level and depth of temporary controls and how they will be exploited.
5. Analyse past records to establish the operating profile for the unit under review:

    — normal losses
    — number and nature of transactions per day
    — number and type of exceptional transactions
    — number of vehicle movements in and out
    — number of staff, visitors, etc.

The analysis should centre on critical points and should be sufficient to set against a similar exercise after the invigilation has taken place. That is, it

Table 7.9 Examples of invigilation impacts

Differences in operation noted during the invigilation period		Fraud possibilities prior to invigilation period
Physical and operational	Documentary and behavioural	
Reduction in total stock losses	– increase in the number and amount of cash sales invoices or increased ratio between cash and credit sales	– suppression of cash sales by negative manipulation of source documents
	– increase in sales with no change in the ratio between cash and credit sales	– suppression of sales, possibly at management level
	– increase in sales with higher ratio of credit sales to cash sales	– suppression of credit sales—possibly to a regular customer/accomplice
	– increase in sales to a particular customer or group of customers	– suppression of sales involving manipulation of accounts of the customer(s) concerned or sales of stolen goods to the customers whose business has increased
	– opening of new customers' accounts, closing of existing accounts	– conversion of goods involving the accounts concerned
	– cancelled customer orders reinstated or change in cancellation patterns	– indicative of conversions involving the customers concerned
	– reduction in the number or value of purchases	– inflation of purchases and/or expenses by a person who does not have access to a concealment course
	– unusual delays in receipt of goods from a regular supplier	– inflation of purchases and possibly bribery of company's purchasing agent
No change in loss patterns	*sales increase* – numbers of invoices – values – types of goods – particular customers	– manipulative frauds involving management employees and the suppression of sales and clearance of account/inventory discrepancies
	decrease in purchases – numbers of invoices – types of goods – particular suppliers	– manipulative frauds at management level, involving inflation of purchases and clearance of account inventory discrepancies

Table 7.9—*Continued*

Differences in operation noted during the invigilation period		Fraud possibilities prior to invigilation period
Physical and operational	*Documentary and behavioural*	
Inconsistent changes in normal loss patterns (e.g., the same in some lines of goods and up or down in others)		– product switching—selling or receiving low value goods as high. Probably manipulative management frauds
	– changes in customer buying patterns or in the types of goods bought	– manipulative frauds involving product switching or price rigging
	– cancelled orders by customers who normally purchase goods of the type whose loss patterns have changed	– manipulative frauds and conversions involving the customers concerned
Reduction in control machinery failures: seals broken, etc.		– misrepresentative frauds involving operations employees (machinery interference)
Change in loaders'/drivers' work patterns, times of arrival at work, etc.		– larcenous frauds involving operations employees
	– reduction in payroll	– payroll padding fraud

should be able to detect changes in business patterns during the fraud-free operation.

6. Check all physical stocks and then deploy invigilators at the points determined at step 4. Make sure all goods movements are recorded on the appropriate company documentation.
7. Retain the temporary controls through the whole of business hours for at least 14 days, and longer if possible.
8. Check the results of the invigilation, particularly

   – stock losses
   – operating patterns different from those recorded at 5

9. Analyse the results (see Table 7.9) and decide on follow-up action—e.g., further analysis of documents, interviews, or other investigation methods.

Table 7.9 is not intended to cover every possible result of an invigilation. Other impacts will arise, depending on the nature of the business in the company unit concerned. These impacts can be identified by closely comparing operations and losses before the invigilation with the fraud-free profile established during it.

Although accounting functions may be controlled during an invigilation it is unlikely that total suppression of manipulative opportunities and concealment courses will have taken place.

A sub-technique of invigilation which is designed specifically to detect account manipulations as well as some operations frauds is that of created or induced error checks. The technique is based on the concept that, given an opportunity that is perceived to have no risk, the criminal will exploit it. Thus, during a period of invigilation—when controls on physical movements are high—apparent errors and fraud opportunities can be introduced into the business system. The way in which they are dealt with can be monitored to detect concealment courses that a thief has previously used.

The areas selected for this type of check should be picked with care. They should not entrap an innocent party and they should be compatible with the invigilation of physical situations.

It may appear paradoxical to try to tempt people into fraud when controls are at their highest but, with further explanation, the rationale may become clear.

First, thieves, particularly if they have been successful for a long time, may become arrogant enough to believe they are too clever to get caught. Bearing in mind that an internal thief has broken the natural trust that should link him and the company, then it is not unreasonable to believe that with the broken trust comes contempt for the company and for its management. The internal thief may see the invigilation as a challenge which, coupled with his arrogance and contempt, may lead him into taking risks that an honest person would regard as foolish.

Second, thieves live up to their income—that is, up to both their genuine pay and their dishonest gain from fraud. Deprived or under the threat of deprivation, the thief will exploit a risky opportunity for purely financial reasons.

Finally, the thief may have sufficient intelligence to realize that, if he suddenly stops his fraud during the period of the invigilation, symptoms will become obvious. He may have no option but to continue. In practice, therefore, embezzlers will often try to exploit fraud opportunities even when controls are at their highest.

Created checks can be put into any part of the system but, to avoid arousing the thief's suspicions, they should be introduced discreetly and preferably by a trusted employee or business contact, rather than by auditors, security or senior management.

A number of different induced errors may be considered.

Errors involving goods

- Deliberately overloaded delivery vehicles may be used to detect thefts and conversions by drivers/warehouse staff.
- Deliberately overloaded 'goods in' vehicles may be used to check on the honesty of receiving clerks, warehousemen and suppliers' drivers.
- Induced—*and obvious*—errors may be introduced into control machinery: weighbridges, cash tills, etc., as a check on internal manipulative frauds.

Note   Because of the possible cost to the company such checks should be short term.

Errors involving income

- Bad debt dividends, supplier refunds or other unusual income may be created to test for cheque conversions/lapping frauds.
- Created incoming cash cheques may be used to test for suppression and conversion.
- Created credit notes from suppliers may be used to test for manipulative frauds.
- Created returns by customers may be used to check accuracy of ledger posting.
- Removal of cash sales documents may be used to check for theft of cash (i.e., created cash overages).
- Created overpayments to suppliers may be used to test normal controls.

Errors involving disbursements and purchases

- Created invoice errors (after authorization) may be used to test for manipulative frauds.
- Created purchase returns may be used to check for suppression and manipulation of ledger postings.

Errors involving awards of contracts, bribery and competitive activity

- Contrived bribe offers for the award of contracts may be used to test the honesty of purchasing agents.
- Offers of competitive supplies to contracted customers may be used to test their reliability.
- Contrived offers of competitive agencies to sales representatives may be used to test their reliability.

Errors involving company bank accounts

Created checks can also be made through the company's bankers. In view of the fraud possibilities involving bank accounts (see Chapter 5) the bank could be asked to:

- make deliberate and self-cancelling *contra* entries on statements
- duplicate charges for overseas drafts
- duplicate account charges

Obviously, care has to be taken in making such checks and the bank should be indemnified in writing against loss.

Created checks are often effective and can expose the mechanics of past and often large-scale frauds providing the results are carefully followed up. The regular thief who accepts a created fraud opportunity is likely to conceal it in the same way as he had concealed frauds initiated entirely by him; he is likely to use the same method of conversion and the same receiver.

By monitoring created checks, significant leads are given to detecting previous frauds. However, only in exceptional circumstances should a company consider prosecuting for fraud when the evidence is restricted to that arising from a deliberately induced error or created check.

Created checks can in certain circumstances amount to entrapment and their admissibility as evidence may be in doubt. They are, however, legitimate leads and should be looked upon as such, not stretched into offences in their own right.

PREVENTIVE INVIGILATIONS

Invigilations can also be used in a preventive way. It is surprising how often criminals become honest when they believe they are being watched. Those of us who have spotted the police car in the rear view mirror will know the feeling: speed is reduced and good driving habits that have been ignored suddenly reappear.

In the criminal mind an unidentified man lurking behind the bushes or peering into the factory yard is automatically taken to be a police officer. The car that follows the dishonest driver is suspected to be 'tail'.

If it is fair to say that when criminals believe they are being watched they behave honestly, then it also seems possible for a company to capitalize on this fact. Perhaps the day will come when—purely as a defensive mechanism—managers of competing companies will agree that twice a week they will make a clumsy attempt to follow a competitor's delivery vehicle or to be seen looking into his yard with binoculars, simply to create the impression in criminal minds that the police are on their trail.

This unconventional approach to fraud prevention may be more useful than some of the other more scientific methods. No guarantee can be made as to its effectiveness because practical experience is limited. It would seem, however, that to be successful, basic principles should be observed.

- The person carrying out the 'observation' should be unknown to the suspected criminals.
- He should be reasonably obvious and should make sure that he is seen.
- He should be seen making notes.
- He should not be traceable to a car that in turn is traceable to him. He should assume that the criminals will check out the registration of the car he uses.
- He should be prepared with a 'story', should he be challenged by an employee or associate of the subject company. The explanation should not be too plausible; it should leave the lingering doubt that he is not being frank.
- He should be reasonably regular with his observations and should concentrate them around the time when the maximum number of people will see him.
- He should never try to enter company premises.
- If challenged by the police, he should tell the truth and explain the purpose of his action.

It can be taken as a certainty that criminals working within an organization which is subject to this type of exercise will be put on their guard and may be deterred. It would be foolhardy to claim that they would be permanently put off but, if, as a result of the *ad hoc* and blundered surveillance, they forgo one fraud opportunity, the exercise will have been worth while.

Similar techniques can be applied in the management crime sphere: techniques that suggest to an internal—although unidentified—thief that he is under suspicion will introduce an element of uncertainty that discourages fraud.

One advantage of these checks is that they discriminate favourably between honest and dishonest people. Criminals are most likely to notice the casual observer or the following vehicle: innocent people with nothing to hide will not have the same defensive mechanism and will not be alarmed.

Observation

Strictly speaking, observation of criminal behaviour is an investigative as well as a detection technique. It is, however, logical to discuss the subject in this chapter, as it can be a prime method of detecting frauds in their theft act and conversion elements.

Theft acts, conversion and misrepresentations involving personal, commercial and physical realities are most usually manifested in physical ways. They are detectable by observing physical behaviour and performance and then comparing what happened to what is recorded.

METHODS AND PROBLEMS

Observation intended to detect fraud should be covert. The observer should watch and record on paper, film or magnetic tape physical facts, acts and movements which could form part of a fraud.

Observation—simply watching, looking and gathering evidence—is in compliance with all western laws and does not breach privacy standards.

This compliance with the law does not, of course, imply general acceptance of the technique and it is not unknown for work problems to arise from the disclosure that surveillance has taken place.

To ensure that surveillance remains a closely guarded secret high professional standards must be maintained.

Observations can be divided into

- surveillance using the human skills
- surveillance using mechanical means

and may be further subdivided into

- static or fixed point observations
- mobile observations (tailing)

Dealing with the last item first, mobile observation calls for the observer to follow the suspected criminal on foot or in a vehicle. Although the rewards can be high—for example, a thief can be followed to identify a 'receiver'—the chance of failure for an amateur is equally high. A thief can be forewarned and what otherwise might have been a good and rewarding detection can be frustrated. For this reason 'tailing' should not be attempted by anyone but a professional investigator.

It is important for the untrained person to work within his limitations and to be guided by the overriding rule that if an observation stands a chance of alerting a thief it should not be attempted. It is far better to lose a tail or to miss evidence—without alerting the criminal—than it is to press too hard.

Against this background, surveillance of moving targets is outside the scope of this text.

On the other hand, static observation from a fixed position, using either the human eye or ear or mechanical means, is a skill that can be learned and can bring profitable results provided the observer exercises care and common sense, absolute accuracy and fairness.

The first problem for the would-be observer is to locate—with precision—the scene that should be observed. This scene may have been identified from one of the other techniques or information may have been received suggesting that fraudulent activity is to take place, at a given location. The scene may be a factory yard, an office or other commercial or industrial premises belonging to a receiver or other suspects.

The second problem is to anticipate the action most likely to occur at the scene. Will, for example, company trucks be seen making deliveries where they should not be or will machinery be interfered with? Will the action be something that can be observed at a distance or can evidence be obtained only at close range?

Clearly, the chances of observing an unauthorized delivery of stolen carpet rolls to a receiver who is not a legitimate customer of the victim are greater than the chance of gaining acceptable evidence of sales of stolen jewellery delivered to a receiver who is also a genuine customer. In the first case the rolls can be counted as they are being delivered and photographs obtained. In the second case the precision of the observation must be that much greater, for who will be able to see that the thief took five diamond rings out of a box instead of four?

This point is fundamental to any observation: the most likely action and the size of the goods involved (if any) must be allowed for and the chances of a successful observation accurately assessed.

Very often the observer has a choice of scenes and, if he finds one element of a fraud difficult to observe, then he should consider whether other elements of the same fraud give a higher chance of success. If observation of the scene of the theft act is unduly difficult, a more satisfactory answer may be to concentrate on the scene of the conversion.

When action in the scene is likely to be complex or difficult to monitor, the observer should back up his personal view with a video tape recording or film. This precaution gives him a chance to corroborate his first-hand evidence and also allows a court or company management the chance of satisfying themselves as to the truth of the facts and acts in issue.

Once the scene to be observed has been identified and the activity anticipated, consideration should be given to other factors.

Scene illumination

The lighting of the scene can be critical. Sunlight should not glare directly into the observer's eyes: first, because it reduces his own range of vision and, second, because it increases his exposure to detection. The observation point should be selected so that the sun is behind the observer or in a neutral position at the time when criminal activity is expected to occur at the scene.

Another consideration on illumination is whether or not there will be sufficient light to carry out the observation. To add further illumination to the scene itself (assuming it is on company premises) is likely to alert or deter the criminals. Therefore, from a detection point of view, the observer must consider some assistance to his own viewing potential. An efficient way of doing this is with night vision equipment: either ultraviolet active devices—which bathe the scene in ultraviolet, invisible light—or passive ones which intensify natural light.

Traffic flows

Another important consideration in selecting the observation point for an outdoor scene is traffic flow. A good position can be spoilt by parked traffic or peak hour build-up.

The static observation position should be selected after the scene has been examined at the most likely time observation will be successful (e.g., during business hours, weekends or at night).

In the situation shown in Figure 7.4, where delivery to a receiver, X, is suspected, the most likely route for the thief's vehicle is from A to B. An observation point at C will not give a clear view of the loading ramp of the vehicle or the receiver's doors, because the vehicle itself will block the line of sight. A more suitable observation point (if one can be found) would be at point D or E.

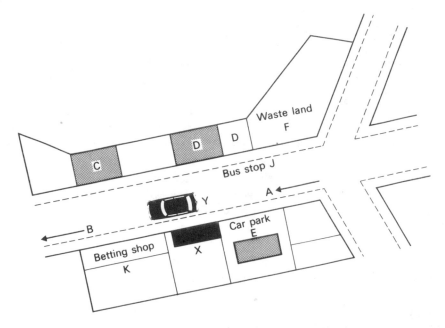

Fixed point (static) points at D or E. From an observation vehicle at E (in car park) or F. Casual observation from bus stop (J) or betting shop (K). Thief's delivery vehicle shown as Y

Figure 7.4 Selection of the observation point

Selection of the observation position

When preliminary reconnaissance of the scene has taken place the likely requirements and position of the observation point can be determined.

The overriding criteria are:

- the position should give a clear view of the crime scene at the time when criminal activity is anticipated;
- its use should not expose the observer to the chance of detection;
- the observer should be able to use the post for prolonged periods without being disturbed;
- the point should not be suspected by the criminals.

These criteria will determine whether fixed premises can be used or whether a vehicle or temporary means of surveillance is the only possibility.

Observation from a building

If a suitable point can be found in a building owned by the victim company then—with the qualifying points mentioned later—obtaining access should not be a problem.

If, however, the only suitable premises are owned by third parties a decision has to be made: should those third parties be asked for their assistance in allowing the use of their premises? Much will depend on the stature of and relationship with the companies or persons which own the premises selected. If they are business competitors or totally unconnected third parties, the risks of an overt request to use their premises may be too high. If, on the other hand, there are reasons to believe that the owners would be sympathetic to the victim's cause, an open and honest request, preferably at board or senior management level, should be made.

Assuming that permission to use a suitable room has been obtained, the observer's problems are not over. He needs a method of entry and exit that will not cause suspicion. The observer should think of a plausible reason for visiting the premises. If this is impossible, the observer may have to get into position before employees arrive and leave after they have left, keeping himself locked in during the working day, or night.

The interior of the room should be darker than the outside scene. This may be achieved by purely natural means or boxes or curtains may be rearranged internally to give this effect.

Observation from a vehicle

When a suitable room cannot be found, the best alternative is a vehicle: either a van, lorry, car or caravan. The scene and the type of activity normally in it will determine the type of vehicle that would not arouse suspicion. A

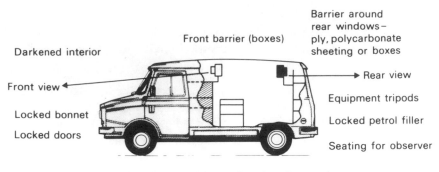

Barrier around
rear windows –
ply, polycarbonate
sheeting or boxes

Front barrier (boxes)

Darkened interior

→ Rear view

Front view ◄

Equipment tripods

Locked bonnet

Locked petrol filler

Locked doors

Seating for observer

No exterior markings and 'neutral' registration number

Figure 7.5 Observation van

commercial van can be temporarily adapted as an observation post, bearing in mind the following points (see Figure 7.5).

1. It should give the maximum possible vision to the observer, through the back and front windows and through any side vents.
2. The partition between the cab and the goods compartment should be obscured with a barrier consisting of stacked boxes, tubes or rolls of cloth, carpet or wire arranged so that the observer can see out but so that no one can see him. The goods used for the barrier should not be theft-attractive.
3. The back windows should be obscured with boxes, or one-way polycarbonate sheeting.
4. The inside of the vehicle should be darker than the outside scene. It should be impossible for an outsider to see through the length of the vehicle.
5. The vehicle should carry a portable, battery powered hair drier to clear condensation from the inside of windows and toilet facilities.
6. The doors and petrol filler cap should be fitted with good quality locks.
7. The registration of the vehicle should not be traceable to the victim company (or to a private investigator).

Two people are usually required to conduct an observation from a vehicle. The observer should be hidden inside the vehicle before it arrives at the observation scene. The driver should park, lock up and leave. He should return at a prearranged time, or when summoned by radio.

While at the scene, the observer should not smoke or jump about inside the vehicle. Nothing is more likely to alert criminals and alarm the public than an 'empty' van with cigarette smoke billowing out of the vents or rocking backwards and forwards on its springs!

Short-term surveillance

It is possible to conduct a short-term observation using a private car if the following procedure is adopted.

1. The car should be parked as close as possible to the scene of the anticipated crime.
2. The observer should try to give the appearance that he or she is waiting for the driver of the car to return—he may sit in a passenger or rear seat. Children, dogs, domestic articles and shopping will assist in giving the observer's vehicle a routine appearance.
3. A tyre may be let down or other breakdown contrived to give an apparently genuine reason for waiting in the desired position. This may be essential when the observer's car has to park in a no-waiting area.
4. Binoculars and other observation equipment cannot normally be used from a private car, simply because their use would undoubtedly alert the criminals.

Observation may also be conducted by 'walk-pasts' from open positions, with the observer using bus stops, shops, etc., as a reason for being at the scene.

The observer, whether in a building, parked van or private car, should have a prepared explanation if he is challenged. A simple ploy, that should not alert the criminals, is to use market research, road traffic or other surveys as a reason for his presence. This sort of explanation should be backed up with survey forms or other corroborating material.

When, because of the scene and its position, such an explanation would be unacceptable, the observer should suggest that he is in fact watching a target different to the one actually under surveillance. If he is watching premises A, he should know sufficient about adjacent premises at B, to give a plausible explanation if challenged by people from A.

Mechanical surveillance

In some situations it is impossible for the observer to get close enough to the scene to allow him to identify the actions taking place with sufficient clarity. Thefts of small items from enclosed premises are almost impossible to observe from a distance.

In some cases, it is possible to assist the observer by providing mechanical or electronic detection devices.

Bleepers and trip devices

These are designed to give a remote indication when goods are moved or other predetermined action (e.g., desk drawers are unlocked) takes place. When thefts from offices are suspected, the observer may stay away from the scene and instead alarm calculators or other equipment that is attractive to thieves. When these are moved the alarm directs the observer to the scene and to detection of the thief in the act.

An alternative is to fix magnetic labels inside theft-attractive items. The sensing device can be located at the exit to the building and will give off an alarm when goods in which magnetic labels have been inserted are removed.

Other detection aids

Where thefts are taking place from a specific room or internal area a hard wired microphone may be used to give audible indication when unauthorized entry has taken place. Alternatively, closed circuit television cameras or time phased, fixed frame cameras can be positioned so that a photograph of the thief in the act of theft is obtained.

OBSERVATION EQUIPMENT AND RECORDS

The observer may need equipment to prove the accuracy of his observation and to obtain evidence for follow-up purposes.

Camera

A reflex camera with a choice of lenses up to 300 mm is ideal. Zoom lenses, operating between 80 mm and 300 mm, are good general purpose surveillance aids. The camera should have an integral or automatic light meter and focusing device. A wide selection of filters is also useful, as is an automatic motor so that rapid sequence shots can be taken.

The camera should be loaded with colour film. Light levels should be carefully taken and corrected as the observation progresses.

Clock or wrist watch

The accuracy of the observation will depend on a detailed record of movements in the scene and the times such movements occurred. A reliable clock or watch is essential.

Binoculars

A good pair of binoculars (8×40 or 10×40) is useful in most observations. Within the observation room or vehicle a fixed or temporary mounting should be available so that the burden of holding up heavy photographic equipment or binoculars is avoided.

Communications

The observer should be provided with a means of communications so that, if necessary, he can summon help. When the observation point is in a building a normal telephone line—provided access to it can be obtained without arousing suspicion—would be suitable. When observation is to take place from a vehicle, radio transmitters/receivers may be hired. The *driver* of the observation vehicle should remain within radio distance of the scene under surveillance.

This arrangement will allow the driver to act as a corroborating witness should the observer summon him when important action is taking place in the scene.

Observation record

A detailed observation record should be kept showing:

- date and day of observation
- name of observer
- name of driver/corroborating witness
- position from which observation was made (observation point)
- distance from the scene
- time observation began/finished
- time each photograph from was shot (cross-referenced to frame and film number)

The record should be written up as each event (even an innocent one) is seen and should be initialled by the person making it.

Films—if required for evidential purposes—should be developed and printed under the control of the observer. When this cannot be done the chain of evidence—from the purchase of the new film through to the finished prints—should be recorded so that formal statements to show that the films have not been tampered with can be taken. The negatives should be carefully preserved and should not be cut, separated or touched up. Films should be run continuously: that is to say, all the frames should be used and even those that do not produce a satisfactory print should be retained in their series.

Verifying the observation record

The observation record can be used as a check on recorded information and accounts. At the end of the surveillance the record should be transcribed into a form in which it can be compared with recorded commercial information—invoices, accounts, etc.

The general approach is to list out, down one side of a schedule, the action which has been observed and, down the other side, the recorded information (the information in the victim's records and accounts).

Differences between observed and recorded information should be examined carefully.

It is a bad practice to write in the original record after the observation has finished. The dates and times that entries were made in the record may be critical if the case gets to court. To have to admit that some entries were made as the events occurred, and that others were made at undetermined times may be confusing and may destroy the integrity of the record as a whole. The rule is to keep the observation record as a contemporaneous and original note.

Where the observed action differs from information recorded in the books of the company (for example, when driver A's records showed him delivering to Smith and yet he was observed making a delivery to Jones) then probably prima facie evidence of fraud has been obtained.

At this stage the observation record and relevant documents should—if it is company policy to do so—be handed over to the police. Where it is the company's wish to deal with the matter internally, the observation record and photographs can be used for disciplinary or defensive action.

Undercover investigations and informants

The detection techniques previously outlined can be conducted in a routine fashion and are effective in revealing symptoms of most corporate frauds. When criminal conspiracies are at work, using extortion and force, undercover investigations may succeed where other techniques would fail. And when vulnerability charts or invigilations have pointed up areas of concern, the only way to advance general suspicion to the point of positive proof may be by the use of an undercover investigator or agent.

The object of undercover investigation is to gain, by covert means, information and leads that can be used and proved in a conventional open investigation.

Companies in the UK have appeared reluctant to use undercover agents—perhaps because management believes that such methods are not 'playing the game'. A point which should have been made patently clear by now is that fraud is anything but a game. When a company believes itself to be the victim of organized collusive fraud, it is foolish to ignore any legal and ethical means of redress.

Undercover investigations can provide the means of countering large-scale collusive crimes. When properly controlled, they are legally and morally acceptable. Their object is not to entrap honest people but to weed out committed criminal conspiracies.

Company policy will determine whether an undercover investigation is to take place but this is the time to mention some of the disadvantages.

First, if badly conducted, the investigation is bound to come to the notice of the criminals. This puts the agent at risk of personal attack and it may expose the company to labour relations problems. Second, if the agent—perhaps to enhance his own performance—resorts to illegal or unethical methods then he and the company are at risk: they may be exposed to civil action for damages and criticism in the courts.

The easiest error for an agent to make is to contravene the rules covering *agents provocateurs*. Although case and statute law varies from country to country there are some international principles:

- The agent may invite another person to commit a crime. If that other person declines, he must not be pursued or asked again. One refusal to participate in crime should be taken as final.
- The agent must not put pressure on an innocent person to commit an act he would not otherwise commit.

The third problem with undercover investigations is that the investigation may be stopped without sufficient evidence coming to light. This situation is most likely to arise when company management expects results too fast. It is therefore essential that any undercover investigation is handled with extreme care. Further, an undercover investigation carried out as a 'fishing expedition' is doomed to failure. The agent, operating in an information vacuum, is unable to achieve the results he hopes for and pushes harder; management, anticipating positive results, becomes more impatient. A combination of these factors puts the whole scheme in jeopardy.

Against this background undercover investigations are recommended only when the following circumstances obtain:

- Large-scale collusive crime is considered likely.
- Conventional methods of investigation are likely to fail.
- The investigation can be controlled.
- The investigation is carried out in strict compliance with the law and morality of the company and country concerned.
- Facilities exist for following up—by conventional investigative means—information developed by the undercover agent.
- The investigation can be restricted to its prime purpose.
- The investigation can remain a boardroom secret.
- The agent is allowed to take all necessary time and is guaranteed that he will not be called to give evidence in court.
- The police are informed as soon as admissible evidence is obtained.

A company wishing to conduct an undercover investigation into the heart of a criminal conspiracy *on its own premises* has essentially three sources available to it.

First, it can call upon the police who, under certain circumstances, may be prepared to allow an officer to act as an undercover agent. Second, the company may try to convert an existing employee or business contact into an informant. Finally, a private investigator may be employed.

For all practical purposes, the second alternative should be ruled out. The existing employee may disclose his purpose through lack of skill or experience. An untrained person is also unlikely to have the ability to penetrate an organized group. He has the personal danger to contend with and the risk, after the case is concluded, of being branded as an informant or management stooge.

In many countries police are too committed to public and violent crime to become involved in speculative investigations in the commercial sphere. Often the only viable choice is the employment of a private investigator.

There are some investigations which a company itself can organize without calling for professional assistance. For this reason, undercover investigations will be discussed in more depth.

ROLES OF UNDERCOVER INVESTIGATORS

Evidence of fraud can be detected in the theft act, concealment or conversion stages. Conventional use of undercover agents is at or in the theft act, that is at the heart of the conspiracy.

In the commercial domain it is often more profitable and more simple to use an undercover agent to detect and gain evidence of conversion, and then to work back by conventional means to evidence of theft, manipulation and misrepresentation.

Undercover agents can be used as potential receivers or suppliers in the conversion element of commercial frauds.

Agent as potential receiver

If large-scale internal theft is suspected the victim company may be able to convince an existing and honest customer to act as a buyer or receiver 'to put the message out' that he is interested in buying stolen or tax free goods.

This approach must, of course, be carefully and properly conducted to ensure that it does not entrap or tempt otherwise innocent people into crime. But with this condition taken care of, undercover agents acting in such a capacity have a good chance of detecting fraud.

> Detectives in New York set up a 'thieves' market' in a decoy store near police headquarters and acting as fences recovered more than £1 million worth of stolen property for about £30 000. Seventy-nine people who sold them stolen goods were arrested and another 150 are being sought. The chief of detectives said business was so brisk that the burglars, robbers, shoplifters and pickpockets and other thieves who were lured had to be told to come back the next day . . .
>
> A similar operation was set up in Washington by police and FBI agents resulting in the arrest of 108 thieves and dishonest government employees.

Agent as potential supplier

An undercover agent may assume the counterpart role to that described above and may approach suspected receivers to see if they are interested in buying ostensibly stolen goods.

A positive reply may lead to evidence of previous fraud, as in the case below.

> A company which manufactured and distributed, through wholesalers and retailers, perfumery and toiletries believed that large quantities of its products were being stolen and sold to cash traders, some of whom were legitimate customers of the company.
>
> A trusted company driver—who in the course of six months was rotated so that he made deliveries to *all* customers—and a sales representative—who was similarly briefed to visit likely receivers (who were not at that time customers of the company)—compiled a list of eight companies which indicated they would be prepared to buy stolen goods. Three of the customers in their discussions with the driver explained that they had previously bought stolen goods from his colleagues.
>
> These customers were kept under observation and in due course they and a number of the company's drivers were arrested, charged and convicted of fraud.

Thus, in the commercial environment an undercover investigator can assume one of three fundamental roles:

- as the hub of a criminal conspiracy
- as a potential receiver
- as a potential supplier

In all three roles there are some basic rules that should be followed.

GETTING THE INVESTIGATOR TO WORK

Getting the investigator into a position where he can operate in a way that does not cause immediate suspicion is a difficult task. It must be remembered that, if an organized group is at work, its members will be careful and will not readily accept an outsider unless they have overwhelming reasons for believing that he is on 'their side'. Selection of the investigator and the role he is to play is the first essential. It would be foolhardy to expect that a 60-year-old agent could easily infiltrate a group of young drug addicts. However, it is not necessary for the agent to convince or gain the confidence of all the members of a group. The confidence of one conspirator is usually sufficient to break a case.

Depending on the particular circumstances, the best place to introduce the investigator should be determined, according to the following factors:

- the age group and sex of the members of the suspected conspiracy
- their area of operation (factory, warehouse, transport, research, or external premises)
- their jobs, skills and interests (particularly leisure interests) of the suspects
- their status within, or relationship with, the victim company
- their home addresses and family interests
- the nature of the suspected fraud:
  - the place of suspected theft acts
  - the method of concealment
  - the place and method of conversion
  - other factors (including the dates and times of the alleged thefts)

Wherever possible, the agent should work away from the victim company's premises.

There may be cases, however, where the only solution is to take the investigator on to the victim's payroll, as a colleague of the suspected thieves. When this position arises the following precautions should be taken:

- The agent should be provided with an acceptable profile. His claimed background and job experience should not be capable of disproof.
- The agent should be provided with a flat or lodging near to the place of work, an appropriate vehicle and clothes.
- He should be given off-site training in the role he is expected to fill.

Before the investigator is taken on, one of the people involved in the suspected conspiracy may be transferred or enrolled for an off-site training course of at least three months' duration.

The agent may be taken on as a 'temporary' and serve an overlap period of duty with the man he is intended to replace. During this time he may do one of two things. Either he should show no suspicion but try to put himself in a position where regular employees feel they have a 'hold' over him: he can ask one of the conspirators to clock him in or he may get caught in some other minor infringement of company rules (he should not break the law). Alternatively, he can be nosey and tell the conspirators that he 'wants in', but to do this successfully he will need to have detected some evidence of fraud.

If the weak point in the conspiracy is off the company's main premises, so much the better. When the agent can be established as a possible receiver of stolen goods, the creation of a credible identity becomes that much more simple. He might be put in as the manager of a shop or a branch of the company, or other likely outlet for stolen goods. Often companies that are not directly connected with the victim will help if the problem is explained to them.

Reports and contact between the agent and the victim company should be kept to a minimum. It is a dangerous practice to have the agent submit regular reports—sooner or later one is bound to go astray. On the other hand, the agent should keep accurate notes for his own use and should establish contact with a director of the victim company when significant developments are anticipated. This information should then be used to obtain evidence that can, if necessary, be produced in court without fear of disclosing the source of the information.

In practice this may call for a second investigator who follows up leads and covers events disclosed by the undercover agent.

COMPANY INFORMANTS

A method similar to that of undercover investigation is the development of information sources within a company.

Generally speaking, fellow employees—even when they are honest and trustworthy—are reluctant to inform on dishonest colleagues unless the crime is particularly loathesome.

The best solution is to encourage all staff to be aware of the possibilities of fraud. First, from the preventive point of view, they should realize that if they overstep the line they will be detected and, second, they should be encouraged to report suspicions through the normal channels without need for payment or reward.

CONCLUSIONS ON UNDERCOVER INVESTIGATIONS

In Europe undercover investigations have yet to be used by companies to any great extent. As criminal behaviour becomes more complex and collusion more widespread, new and often hard detection methods become necessary. When an organized gang is at work the chances of full disclosure by conventional means are slim.

A company in this position may have the choice of adopting a hard line approach—such as the employment of an undercover agent—or the acceptance of continuing and possibly incremental fraud.

Undercover investigations, properly handled, are legal and justifiable and, above all, fair. Management has the discretion to call off an investigation if it should appear that innocent people are being entrapped. It also has the choice of reporting the results to the police or of dealing with the case internally.

With this final safety valve and the other checks and balances that management is able to impose on undercover investigations, they are a useful and sometimes irreplaceable detective aid.

The fact that a company has successfully carried out such an exercise soon becomes known in criminal circles and this in itself deters future attempts at fraud. The thought that a customer offering to buy goods is in fact an agent for the victim company, or that the person offering stolen goods for sale is in fact an investigator, breaks up the confidence of criminal groups. It makes them uncertain and may cause them to deflect their attention to a less secure victim.

Business intelligence

All companies have an obligation to their shareholders and employees to take prompt and effective action to meet competition. On a legitimate front, a company's forward plans cannot be expressed meaningfully unless something about the future market climate and competitive intentions is known. Where a company's competitors engage in illegal or unfair acts even more care is necessary.

The term 'business intelligence' normally refers to all legal methods of obtaining information on competitors and competitive intentions. From a fraud detection aspect, the prime objective of business intelligence is to ensure that the company's supplies and sales are not prejudiced by dishonest competitive practices.

For example, it is of interest to a company to know that its competitors are not bribing or coercing third parties—with whom they both conduct business or from whom they both seek approval or the award of contracts. On a lower level, it is of interest to know that a competitor is not obtaining a competitive lead or support by financial frauds on third parties. Income tax or subsidy frauds might allow a competitor to cut its prices and steal a market edge.

The main headings of unfair competititve activity and examples are set out below.

PASSING OFF OR FORGING PRODUCTS

For example:

- analysing products, copying the formulae and offering substitute products for sale at a lower price than the victim's, possibly to the victim's regular customers;
- purchasing rejects or seconds from the victim and reselling them as firsts, possibly buying packaging from the victim's suppliers;
- diverting the victim's products from a low priced market into a high priced market, possibly repacking to suit the market into which diversion is made;
- copying the victim's trade marks, advertising or logos.

PSYCHOLOGICAL SABOTAGE

For example:

- circulating false rumours in the trade and national press or among the victim's workforce or labour unions;
- reporting fictitious but derogatory information to government or debt collection agencies;
- bribing or blackmailing customers or suppliers to make fictitious or inflated complaints to newspapers, television or trade association;
- forming consumer or action groups to lobby public opinion against the victim company.

BLACKMAILING KEY EMPLOYEES OF THE VICTIM

For example:

- to achieve inferior business performance, to disclose trade secrets, to invest in poor, unviable projects.

BLOCKING THE VICTIM COMPANY'S COMMUNICATION CHANNELS AND DISRUPTING WORK

For example:

- making false 'bomb threat' phone calls;
- making false replies to advertisements to tie down the victim's sales force;
- blocking the victim's telephone switchboard by electronic means (on first-party caller systems this is a simple task);
- planting inefficient staff into critical positions in the victim company (for example, a switchboard operator or computer programmer);
- planting militant or disruptive employees on the victim's workforce.

TAKING UNJUSTIFIED LEGAL ACTION AGAINST THE VICTIM

For example:

- causing unfounded complaints to anti-trust or monopolies boards;
- taking out injunctions to prevent the release of new products or advertising campaigns by claiming they infringe copyright or other legislation.

HEADHUNTING

For example:

- suborning key employees of the victim company.

For example:

- auction rigging and insider trading to force up the victim's bids at auctions or on specific contracts;
- market cornering on scarce commodities with the sole intention of harming the victim;
- tax and customs duty evasion by competitors or avoidance of import/export licence requirements or exchange control.

Although some of the examples amount to criminal offences, the majority are no more than 'dirty tricks'. Nonetheless, they are available to dishonest competitors and can cause severe damage to the victim unless they are identified and countered.

A company has essentially two ways of monitoring the honesty of its competitors. First, through its own staff—sales representatives and others who, being exposed to the market, are most likely to pick up information on unfair competitive activity. The second source is trade associations, chambers of trade, and government organizations.

At the heart of any business intelligence system is the setting up of a central point, index or library within the company. In small companies this may be one person who is known to all employees as the person to contact if information on competitors is obtained. This person may be full or part time.

At this central position, genuine commercial and fraud information can be collated, disseminated and actioned. The information that all employees might be asked to report could include:

- competitors' price lists and terms of trade
- samples of goods and consumer reports
- names and addresses of known customers of competitors
- suspected cases of unfair or illegal trading

Reduced to its simplest form— and usually this is all that is required—fraud detection involving the collection of business intelligence is a two-way exchange of information. The first way is alerting all, but especially field staff, to the possibility that some competitors might resort to unfair practices and to ask for employees' cooperation in reporting information to the company's central index or library. The second is the collation of reported information at the central index, for evaluation and dissemination. The circulation of information from the central point may be restricted to other company locations or it may be brought to the attention of trade associations or government departments. Where a competitor is suspected of bribery, corruption, tax or anti-government frauds, the police should be informed.

Spot checking

In this chapter two different roles of spot checking will be examined. First, spot checks to detect fraud in the theft act stage—particularly misrepresentative frauds where a personal, commercial or physical reality is falsified as a means of theft achievement. The second role of spot checks is essentially preventive; we look at the use of spot checks to support a climate of honesty.

USE OF SPOT CHECKS

A spot check may be defined as a special management verification of a particular commercial circumstance or transaction.

Vulnerability charts or management experience may indicate critical points within the business where a surprise check on a transaction or situation may disclose fraud. In the definition of spot check the words 'management act' need emphasis: unless management fully supports the idea of spot checking, serious problems can result.

Whereas spot checks intended for a defensive purpose can be made quietly and sometimes covertly, those intended to detect fraud often involve confrontation and argument. A driver whose vehicle is found with excess goods on board or a shopper stopped in the street is likely to be uncooperative and argumentative. Unless the security guard or the shop assistant who made the checks has management support and has been properly instructed, problems are bound to arise. There is nothing that can destroy the credibility of security more than an absence of management support in the face of problems or threatened legal or industrial action, as the case below shows.

Union bars too-keen thief-catcher

A factory security guard who is too efficient at catching pilferers has been transferred to another job after union leaders threatened a walk-out.

The guard, Mr Stephen Rosengrove, 37, has caught 100 pilferers in six years at Vauxhall Motors, Luton, and the firm estimates he has saved it at least £100 000.

But leaders of the three biggest Vauxhall unions—the Transport Workers, Engineers and Electricians—said they would call 20 000 production workers out on strike unless he was removed.

For these reasons the company's policy on spot checking should be clear and should be written down and given to those people who are asked to carry it out. Management should then support this policy in all situations.

Even when the above provisions have been dealt with, there is always the possibility that militant groups will take exception to the way a particular check has been conducted. This is perhaps part of the cost of fraud prevention and detection, and arises particularly when a company's efforts to stamp out dishonesty are proving effective.

A second important point is the selection of staff to do the job. Although in some circumstances confrontation is almost inevitable, management of the company concerned should do everything in its power to ensure that checks are fair and honest and that the staff conducting them are diplomatic, properly trained and reliable. They should know their rights of search, detention and arrest and should be quite clear on what is admissible evidence and what is not.

SELECTION OF AREAS FOR CHECKING

Checks should be concentrated on the critical areas of fraud. These may be identified from vulnerability charts, previous cases or management experience. Checks will probably be in one of the following categories:

– checks on the movement of goods in and out of company premises or on stocks;
– checks on the completeness of recorded income;
– checks on the accuracy of a material reality.

In the third case the reality may be commercial/personal (when business is contemplated) or physical (as when charges or accounts are based on the accuracy of a machine).

Before discussing the various types of check, we should lay down some general principles.

GENERAL PRINCIPLES

Spot checks should be carried out with the sole intention of detecting fraud symptoms by properly trained staff acting within management authority. Checks should be concentrated on critical points at which the symptoms of fraud are most obvious and in which the criminal's guilt is most clear. That is to say, a point at which he has the least chance of providing a plausible excuse for dishonesty.

If this past point is unclear, then one has only to think of cases of shoplifting where suspects are stopped after they have left the premises concerned. At this point they are committed to a criminal course. Although they may explain that they merely forgot to pay, their explanation is less likely to succeed than if they had been stopped within the shop.

The initial questions asked of the suspected thief should be such that the potential for a plausible excuse at a later date is blocked. For example, the suspected shoplifter might be asked, 'Are you sure you have paid for all of the goods?' or the person who it is suspected has interfered with machinery asked, 'Have you checked that the machine is measuring properly?' These questions should be asked at the earliest possible stage and before the shoplifter's bag is searched or the machine more closely examined. Further questioning should be made in private to protect the rights of both the criminal and the person who has made a genuine mistake.

Checks should be carried out using the element of surprise to the maximum possible extent. Occasionally, after one spot check has been made, the person making it should leave the scene, wait and then return and carry out further checks. It is a mistake to conduct checks on a regular basis. Internal thieves, particularly, will soon recognize a pattern, and steal only when they can anticipate there will be no check.

Checks should be directed at people who—as a result of their connection with the company—have the greatest opportunity to steal. Although care must be taken to avoid victimization, all checks should be designed to give the maximum chance of success. The fact that a thief has been caught soon goes round a shop, factory or office and the deterrent effect is immediate. How long the deterrent lasts is another matter.

When a person or situation is selected for a check, verification should be carried to the point of complete satisfaction. It is better to conduct one or two checks thoroughly than fifty checks badly.

The person carrying out the checks should not be put off by abuse, violence and threats. Criminal responses to questioning are dealt with in Chapter 8 but it is worth pointing out now that aggression and threatened legal action too often allow guilty people to escape.

When a check has proved successful every effort should be made to extend the detection. Often the largest frauds are detected in small ways. When excess goods are found on board a delivery truck, records should be closely examined to determine the method of concealment or intended concealment. When the *modus operandi* has been established for the detected case, records can be examined for past frauds. The current case should be used as a 'lead in' to what might be far larger and more complex schemes.

In the same way, every effort should be made to unravel the intended avenue of conversion. This might be pursued by close questioning of the detected thief, or by assuming that the receiver was to be one of the customers on a detected driver's current route.

The same principle applies to misrepresentative frauds detected by spot checks. When machinery interference is detected or when a pretended personal or commercial reality is revealed as false, the detected symptoms and patterns, concealment courses and intended avenues of conversion should be closely examined.

When a fraud, however small, has just been detected, initiative rests, for once, with the victim, and he should make the best possible use of it.

CHECKS ON THE MOVEMENT OF GOODS

Checks on the movement of bulk goods in and out of commercial premises normally take place at the gatehouse or loading bay. Of frauds involving larcenous removal of goods, possibly the most dangerous are conspiracies among employees of the victim and which include a loader or gatehousekeeper.

Spot checks should therefore be planned to detect collusion. This calls for the management check to be after the normal gatehouse or loading bay controls—after the internal thieves have committed themselves to a course of criminal action. When spot checks are made before the regular controls, an internal checker/thief would escape detection.

This idea of 'checking on the regular checker' can involve physical problems in finding a place to challenge vehicles or check stock. Much will depend on the layout and dimensions of the premises concerned, but usually an area can be found where additional spot checks can be made after the routine or regular controls.

Surprise checks on employees and visitors leaving commercial premises usually have a higher deterrent than detective effect. Although the first one or two people to pass through the check may be caught by surprise, the word will soon spread and the chances of detection will diminish. This is not to say that such checks are not worth while, just that their limitations should be noted. If a vulnerability chart or other information has indicated a risk of larcenous fraud by employees, it is often more efficient from a detection aspect to mark with magnetic or electrical sensors a few of the items which it is believed are being stolen and to place a sensing device at the checking point. Spot checks can then be carried out with a fair degree of success, as in the example described below.

Heathrow gem thief foiled by bleeper

A Heathrow loader was trapped by an electronic device called a 'bleeper'. When he tried to steal a registered parcel of jewels a minute transmitter inside [the package] increased the bleeping signal which was being monitored by security men on radios. The man, one of the first in Britain to be caught through the bleeper, sobbed bitterly when the judge passed an 18-month jail sentence.

Other forms of markers, including invisible dyes, crayons and electromagnetic sensitive tapes and labels can be used to indicate when goods are being stolen. The local police are in a position to offer advice on the subject and the names and addresses of manufacturers. As a general principle any artificial detection aid should conform to the following rules.

- It should be fair and legal to use.
- It should be difficult to detect by a thief and difficult for him to overcome.
- It should give the person monitoring the aid the maximum chance of accurate and prompt detection at the greatest possible distance from the thief.

The distance over which detection is possible is an important factor in the effectiveness of an aid. Ultraviolet crayon can only be detected at very close range and the person who is subjected to a check is left in no doubt that he is under suspicion. Electronic and magnetic devices, on the other hand, can be detected at a distance of 10–12 feet and it is therefore possible to make an overt move only when there is a certainty of success—i.e., following a positive indication on a remote sensor.

Naturally, when detection aids are employed, their description, methods and times of use should be kept a closely guarded secret and the equipment itself should be given a high level of security protection.

CHECKS ON THE COMPLETENESS OF RECORDED INCOME

Spot checks in this category are almost entirely restricted to retail organizations whose major income is in cash.

Test purchasing is one of the common ways of verifying the completeness of cash takings. Experience shows that the most frequent type of sales suppression in retail shops is that where the customer is known to the cashier, who suppresses the sales.

A cashier who suppresses sales has a number of ways of disposing of excess cash. The first and most simple is not to collect the full or proper amount from the person with whom he or she is in collusion. This is the most difficult to detect, unless the customer is challenged outside the premises and a receipt found in a lower amount than the value of goods obtained. Further, unless the customer and the cashier are closely and effectively questioned, the fraud can be passed off as a mistake (a plausible excuse).

The second way in which cash can be removed is 'as it happens'. The cashier simply under-records cash handed over by a customer. When the customer is genuine, then by under-recording the cashier risks immediate detection if the customer complains.

The third possibility is for the cashier to remove cash at the end of the day. By under-recording throughout the day, surplus cash can be built up and removed when the till rolls and cash held are balanced.

The systems used by many retail organizations physically separate the cash from the cashier, so that the cashier totals up recorded sales while an independent person counts the cash. To build up excesses of cash and, more important, to steal them, collusion may be necessary.

Against this background the potential for meaningful spot checks is limited to:

- promiscuous test purchases by undercover investigators who can become accepted by the cashier;
- observation by supervisors on cash tills and on reconciliations of cash and till rolls;
- observation on cash tills by covert closed circuit television;
- challenges on customers leaving the sales area and examination of receipts.

Special checks would be most appropriate when large 'stock losses' appear—most cash/sales suppression frauds result in noticeable account/inventory discrepancies.

CHECKS ON COMMERCIAL AND PERSONAL REALITIES

These checks apply to banks and other organizations whose employees at the point of sale or business are exposed to third-party or external misrepresentations.

Thieves succeed in personal or commercial misrepresentations for one, or sometimes more, of three reasons. First, because the employee is a co-conspirator. Second, because the employee is too busy or does not bother to make a thorough check on the reality (central issue) on whose accuracy the transaction in question depends. The third possibility is when the employee at the point of business is unaware of fraud possibilities.

Spot checking in these circumstances calls for an experienced checker whose time is free to conduct a thorough verification of the central issues at the point of business. A central issue—the fact on whose accuracy a transaction depends—may be the identity of a person presenting a cheque or credit card, his creditworthiness or his intention to carry out some further act.

When it is company policy to make such checks, they should not be rushed. If a person whose bona fides (which are a central issue) are about to be checked tries to pull out of the transaction, any documents he has already handed over should be photocopied and, if he cannot be pursuaded to remain until the checks have been completed, matters should be followed through and resolved in his absence. Attempted fraud should be reported to the police without delay.

When fraud is detected and the thief still remains on company premises, he should be detained while the police are called.

From the brief outline given above, it is clear that people put in to check on commercial and physical realities should be experienced in the particular line of business. Furthermore, they should know what facts are central to the transactions or situations in question and how they can be verified. The telephone numbers of information sources (credit card organizations, banks,

HP companies) should be readily available. The checkers should be taught how to spot false identification papers and forged signatures. They should be instructed in their powers of detention and arrest.

Some of the facts that may be central to a transaction can be checked only by observation or other investigative methods, as in the case below.

> An insurance company decided to employ an investigator and selected a young but retired army officer for the job. On his first day at work he met the president of the company, and was given an office and the keys to a company car. At four o'clock that afternoon, when no job description or work came his way, he enquired about these matters and was told that since he was an investigator he should be able to 'detect' what his job should be.
>
> The following morning he went to the claims department, introduced himself, and asked for a copy of the file on the largest pending personal accident claim. This turned out to be a case involving a man who claimed he had damaged his back and could not walk or work. The amount in suit ran into seven figures.
>
> The investigator drove past the claimant's home and saw a detached bungalow with a raised porch. Sitting in a wheelchair on the porch was a man whom the investigator assumed was the claimant.
>
> The investigator hired a van and kept observation on the bungalow, hoping that he could capture on cine film evidence of the man's mobility (the central issue) and thereby justify a reduction in the claim.
>
> For three or four mornings the investigator saw the newspaper delivery boy arrive and throw the man's newspapers on the porch. The man would come out and, with some difficulty bend down from his wheelchair, and pick up the paper. On the fifth morning the investigator gave the newspaper boy a tip and asked him to throw the newspaper on the front path.
>
> At 8.30 the man came out of his bungalow looked on the porch for his paper and then saw it lying on the path. He looked up and down the road, did not spot the investigator's observation van, then rolled down the blanket covering his legs, dived down the steps, and with great agility picked up the newspaper and returned to his wheelchair. Content that he had not been 'spotted', he started to read.
>
> The man subsequently withdrew his claim and was fortunate to escape prosecution.

Overt spot checks on personal realities can have a high deterrent or preventative effect. Closed circuit television cameras or time phased equipment in banking halls, over the cashier's desk, or in other situations when personal identification is a central issue, have proved effective. A cheque forger, misuser of a credit card or other thief does not wish his true identity to be revealed and the chance—even after a successful crime—that a photograph remains with the victim is in most cases too high a risk for a criminal to contemplate, and he may be deterred.

In the same way, sensitized labels on which finger prints can be taken are a useful deterrent in cases where personal realities can be falsified for criminal gain. The Veriprint Corporation produces sensitive and clean finger print pads (about the same size as a postage stamp) which can be fixed to the back of cheques or credit card vouchers and provide lingering evidence of a thief's true identity.

For some companies, closed circuit cameras and finger print labels may seem a drastic solution. They do, however, have a preventive role to play in high loss areas.

CHECKS ON PHYSICAL REALITIES

Checks in this category cover measuring and control equipment and physical stocks.

Examination of machinery to detect fraudulent interference is a specialist task and is discussed on pages 216–217 on critical point auditing. But there are some general rules covering such checks.

- High value, low bulk stocks should be selected for verification, especially when multiple vendors are involved.
- Particular attention should be paid to unusual stocks and adjustments:
  - at remote warehouses
  - on consignment, sale or return
  - goods returned by customers or awaiting dispatch to suppliers
  - goods waiting for disposal as scrap
- Goods in the course of delivery or receipt should be checked first and marked or segregated to avoid 'double counting'.
- The records relating to the stock should be examined for unauthorized adjustments, alterations and write-offs. The person normally in charge of the stock should be asked to agree the accuracy of the records.
- The results of the check should be written into the normal stock records, signed by the checker and warehouseman.
- All discrepancies—overages or shortages—should be followed up and explanations obtained. It should always be borne in mind that overages may have been deliberately built up to provide the opportunity for theft or to conceal future short deliveries.

In addition to these general points there are particular precautions that should be taken with packaged or bulk liquid stocks.

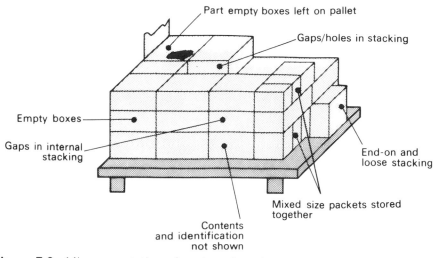

Figure 7.6 Misrepresentation of packaged stocks

Packaged stocks

- A selection of sealed cartons should be opened and the contents checked for quality and quantity. After checking, the cartons should be resealed to deter pilfering.
- Pallets of packet stocks should be carefully checked. Figure 7.6 shows ways of misrepresenting contents and quantities of stacked packages.

Bulk liquid stocks

- Dip sticks should be checked before use to see that
  - they are correct for the tank to be tested
  - the tank calibrations are correct
- Valves between interconnecting tanks should be closed off to prevent transfers, during checking, to suppress shortages.
- Tanks should be tested for the presence of dip sleeves, which can be used to suppress or inflate stocks.
- Vacuum and other gauges should be closely examined before reliance is placed on their readings.
- Water-finding paste should be used to detect stock misrepresentations based upon the suppression of water 'bottoms'.
- Tank calibration tables should be checked with the tank manufacturers or against a standard.
- Specific gravity of valuable liquid stocks (which can be mixed with water or low value liquids) should be checked.

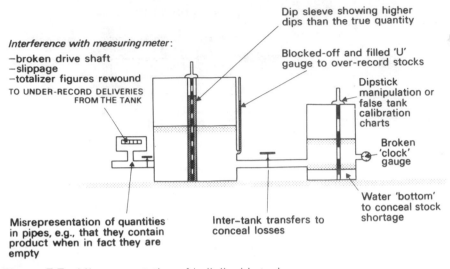

Figure 7.7   Misrepresentation of bulk liquid stocks

Figure 7.7 shows some of the methods of misrepresenting liquid stocks.

Many frauds rely on misrepresentations of stock to conceal otherwise obvious account/inventory discrepancies. Although some stocks are difficult to verify, many frauds are detectable if thorough checks are made. When a company believes itself to be the victim of stock inflations, professional stocktakers should be called in.

SPOT CHECKING THROUGH STAFF ROTATION

Although spot checks are usually best conducted by specially trained staff, a useful and cheap method is the routine job rotation of employees. The practice of rotation is, of course, an accepted preventive accounting technique, but it can also be used for detection purposes, provided management is instructed to follow through queries raised by newly rotated people. See the following example.

Company G introduced a new policy that required all employees to take their full allocation of leave. The manager of the sales office went on holiday and the senior clerk took over. During the manager's absence a number of invoices were rejected from the company's computer processing system and, although the clerk did not know why this happened, he decided that the problem was not urgent and could wait until his boss returned. On his return, the manager cleared the queries. Two years later the sales office manager and three of G's customers were arrested for fraud. Their method had been simple. The master pricing file for sales to the three customers contained a code—entered deliberately by the sales office manager—that rejected computer produced sales invoices for manual pricing. The manager—working manually—priced the invoices at a lower value than was due. Company G lost over £20 000 through this scheme.

The manager thought it too risky to enter computer prices to cover his holiday period and assumed, rightly as things turned out, that his relief would leave the queries for his return.

The lesson? When spot checks are made or staff rotated it is essential that discrepancies of odd events are followed through to the stage of complete satisfaction and are not referred to employees who were previously responsible for the job in question.

CONCLUSIONS ON SPOT CHECKS

Spot checks are a useful detection aid if properly conducted by trained staff. They are not, however, considered to be a prime detection method, except for misrepresentative frauds involving third parties (categories C2, D2 and E2) where the falsification of a reality is contiguous with a theft act.

Criminal targeting

Experience has revealed cases where an employee has been distrusted or suspected of fraud but management has been unable to produce evidence that proves or disproves this suspicion. The presence of successful criminals in a workforce destroys the credibility of security.

Where suspicion is particularly strong and large losses suspected, the people or companies thought responsible can be made the target of in-depth investigation. They may be referred to as 'target criminals'—although, from the outset, concentrated investigation into their activities should be to establish the truth and the case should not be prejudged.

Besides the target criminals that may be identified by a company acting alone, there may be others, operating in a particular trade, whose detection is of general interest. The Tobacco Advisory Board, which was formed by a number of British cigarette manufacturers, has worked successfully to reduce organized crime. By concerted trade action, vehicle hijacking of tobacco goods has fallen significantly. The wines and spirits trade has been equally successful.

So in addition to targets special to a particular company, there may be others that operate against a number of companies within a trade. So far as this second class is concerned, it is vital that enquiries are coordinated. When a number of companies individually pursue one criminal or group of criminals, the results are often disastrous, with one company duplicating or spoiling the investigative work of another.

Target investigations should not be entered into lightly, since they involve time and expense. There may, however, be situations when losses are such, or the criminal environment in a trade so bad, that action must be taken.

The objective of target investigations is to coordinate and concentrate detective resources towards known or suspected criminals and not to relax that objective until the suspicions have been proved or disproved.

The circumstances where a target approach could be used are

— when organized criminals are thought to be operating against a company or industry;
— when internal or competitive crime is eroding business confidence.

METHODS OF INVESTIGATION

Surveillance of an internal criminal's activities both on and off the job is vital in advancing general suspicions to the point of proof. This, as mentioned earlier, calls for professional assistance, unless a static observation point overlooking the scene of theft or conversion can be found.

Undercover investigations may also provide the necessary proof, but in some circumstances—particularly where manipulative fraud is suspected—such methods may be impossible or unsatisfactory. In these cases, created checks may be introduced into the target criminal's domain and controlled fraud opportunities monitored.

Changing the target criminal's job to one which is more easy to monitor is another possibility. Created checks can be introduced into his new position in the certainty that he will seize upon them.

When the target criminal is a business competitor, the action that can be taken will depend on the type of fraud suspected. If it is espionage, false information can be leaked to selected people and the results monitored. The information should be released in such a way that, if the competitor is found to act upon it, his source of information will be clear.

If 'passing-off' offences are suspected, it is perfectly legitimate to arrange for one of the victim company's customers to approach the competitor to record his sales approach and publicity material and to obtain samples for analysis.

In cases where a business contact is suspected of diverting products outside his sales territory, as a means of exploiting his supplier's price structuring, then the victim company (the supplier) has a number of courses available.

First, the goods sold to the suspected company can be marked and the market to which diversion is suspected closely monitored. This approach will involve the victim's representative in the market concerned making test purchases and detailed investigations.

The second approach calls for more preplanning by the victim. All large orders that might be destined for division can be marked during manufacture and containers used that offer the ultimate customer (a retail buyer) the chance of a prize or free offer. For example, razor blade containers might be overprinted with:

> 'Please return this packet after use to (the manufacturer) to receive a free. . . .'

This may involve the victim in additional costs, but it gives him a good chance to monitor ultimate customers and market diversions.

Guarantee cards, included with goods which might be subject to diversion, have a similar use. Their return enables the victim to monitor the ultimate market.

If a dishonest customer wishes to divert goods that bear prize offers or require the return of guarantee cards, he is almost forced to repack, or arrange separate guarantee centres. This will involve additional costs and trouble and may make the fraud unattractive.

CONCLUSIONS ON CRIMINAL TARGETING

The possibilities outlined above are not a comprehensive selection of all methods that can be used against target criminals, although they cover some of the major areas.

Whatever approach is taken—whether by a company acting alone or by a trade association—the objective of proving or disproving suspicions should be pursued with the utmost vigour.

If the police are not involved in the investigation in the first instance, they should be informed as soon as admissible evidence of fraud is obtained and, unless there are exceptional reasons, the case should be prosecuted.

Sooner or later, if a soft line is taken with a target criminal, the fraud will reappear.

8. Investigations

Rule 8:   *When the going gets tough, the tough get careful*
Rule 8a: *The light at the end of the tunnel may be an express train coming your
            way*

Advising some people that they should not rush into fraud investigation is like
telling a 14-year-old boy that he should not smoke. The attractions appear too
great and the drawbacks are not appreciated until too late.

Yet it is vital that the symptoms of fraud are resolved by thorough
investigation. The term 'investigation' is used to describe that stage between
the detection of fraud symptoms and their resolution to the satisfaction of the
victim.

The starting point for an investigation is suspicion of fraud. Figure 8.1
shows an action flow chart for investigations. It is used as a framework for this
chapter.

The chart shows one option: to take no action at all. Although there
may be cases where a company might take no positive action when the
symptoms of fraud are discovered, to decide upon such a course prior to the
facts being investigated is dangerous and unwise. Until suspicions have been
investigated and their truth confirmed or disproved, the company does not
know what problems might lurk below the surface. It does not know what is
being written off or what defensive action might be necessary. When
suspicions concern an employee or business contact there is a two-way
obligation to resolve them; in fairness to the company if true and to the
suspect if untrue. In all cases, therefore, suspicions of fraud should be taken
seriously and should be investigated.

Setting the objectives of an investigation

Immediately after fraud symptoms have come to light, the company or its
professional advisers must make some fundamental decisions unless policy
has already been decided. They must decide what results would be in the best
company interest—whether prosecution of those suspected is desirable or
whether dismissal, civil recovery or some other outcome is preferable.

The fact that fraud symptoms may have been detected should be kept a
closely guarded secret. Discussion should be limited to those people who have
a genuine need to know.

Too often the advantages that a victim has are needlessly thrown away by

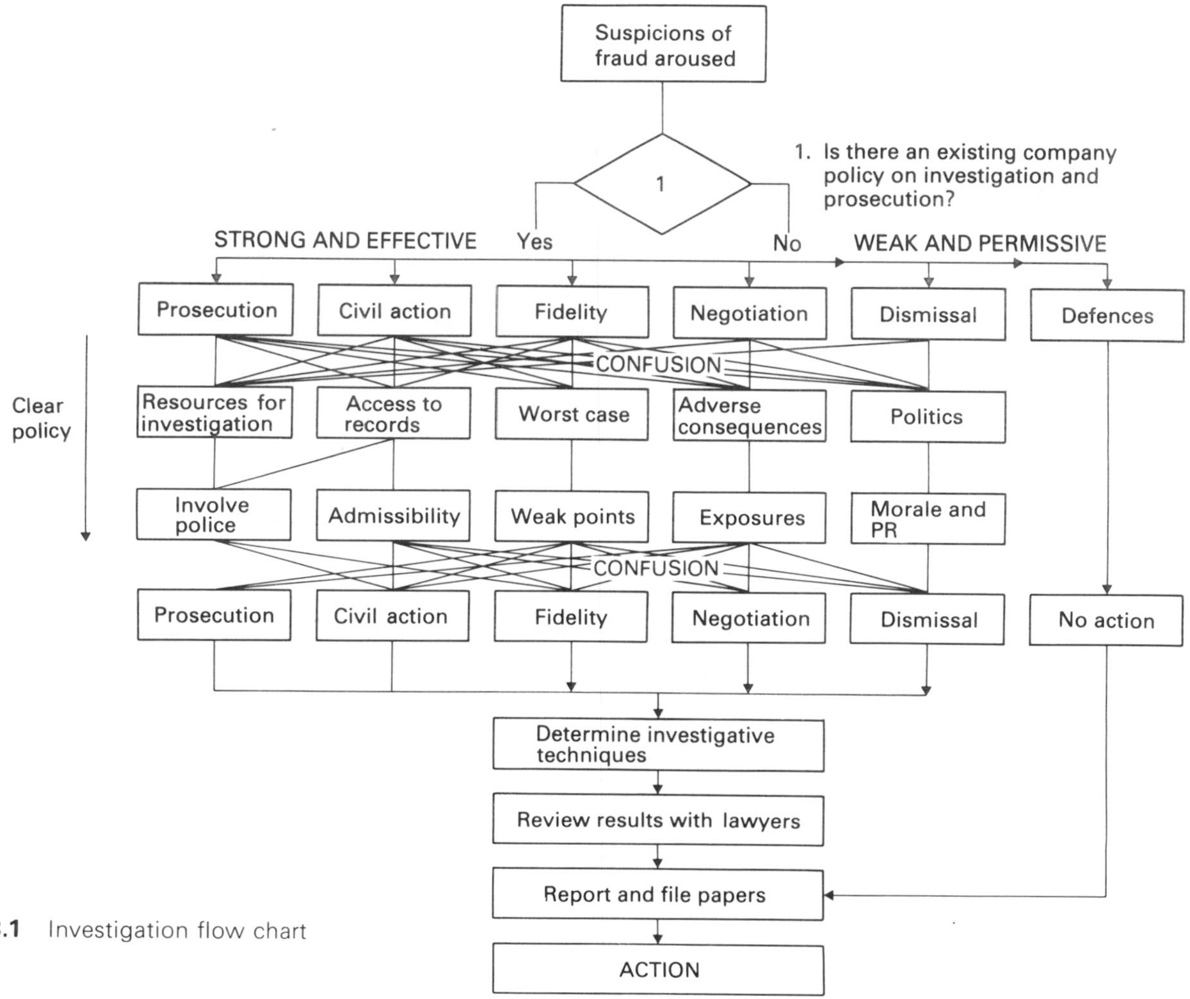

Figure 8.1 Investigation flow chart

careless talk and memos that come to the knowledge of the thieves who are then able to take evasive action. Also, there is always the temptation to try to advance early suspicions a little further—to ask people questions or try to obtain documents that clarify the picture. These unplanned and often unnecessary moves alert criminals and take the initiative from the victim.

What is permissible or judicious action in any given circumstances needs careful consideration, balancing such factors as confidentiality, investigative progress and unnecessary forewarning of the thieves. But generally the fewer people who are told about a pending investigation, the better.

Responsible management should not set out on a course of action when it does not know where it is leading. Too often, when suspicions of fraud are uncovered, the objectives of the investigation are not clear. Senior management may be thinking in terms of prosecution while personnel department thinks merely of dismissal or asking the perpetrator to resign. At best, time and effort that could be better spent elsewhere are wasted. Even more saddening is the situation where a company tries to mount a private prosecution on the basis of a badly conducted investigation.

When the objectives are set and the most desirable outcome of the investigation decided upon, efforts can be concentrated. In fact, the whole investigative process can be eased by an accurate and agreed definition of objectives.

There are three main reasons for conducting investigations:

- to recover funds
- to prevent repetition and deter others
- to clear innocent people

They can be achieved through the objectives shown in Table 8.1.

Table 8.1 Methods of recovering funds

	Recover funds	Prevent reoccurrence
Criminal prosecution		*
Civil litigation	*	*
Negotiation and settlement	*	*
Fidelity insurance	*	
Dismissal		*
Defensive action		*

The advantages and disadvantages of each one, together with factors which should be considered in deciding upon them are discussed below.

PROSECUTION

Many frauds result in criminal prosecution yet this may not seem the best solution. When a company discovers fraud, it is not obliged to make a formal complaint to the police.

In the UK the victim, in exercising his options, must be careful not to contravene the Criminal Law Act 1967. If the victim attempts to extract more from the thief than has been lost he is open to prosecution and a two year prison sentence. The idea is that victims should not be allowed to blackmail perpetrators, nor make a profit from fraud: they are allowed to recover what has been lost and that is all.

The reasons why criminal prosecution should be considered are:

1. It is society's job to decide on the guilt or innocence of people suspected of criminal offences. It could be argued that companies have no right to make society's judgement.
2. It is society's obligation to deter and rehabilitate criminals.
3. Criminal courts can impose punishment—in addition to restitution—and in so doing may deter others from crime.
4. Criminal prosecution may ensure a certainty and consistency of response.
5. The judgement given in a criminal court may be used as the authority for pursuing a civil claim or for enforcing a dismissal notice.
6. Failing to prosecute means that the thief's record remains untarnished, which is unfair to subsequent employers and job applicants with whom he may compete.

Criminal prosecution does not prevent the victim from taking other action; it may dismiss the dishonest employee in addition to prosecuting him, or it may seek civil recovery against the dishonest business contact as well as exposing him before the criminal courts.

The threat of prosecution to white collar and computer criminals is a most effective deterrent although there are some disadvantages.

1. Management-level judgements are placed in the hands of members of the public—juries—who may or may not be qualified to make them.
2. Punishment awarded by the courts is often too lenient and may not serve as a deterrent to others.
3. All the victim's eggs are put in one basket. If prosecution fails, other options—recovery or civil action—may be prejudiced.
4. The elapsed time between detection and conclusion of a criminal prosecution may place the company in a difficult position. It may have to retain employees on paid suspension for up to two years, unable to dismiss them until prosecution is over. It may have to face other indirect losses.

5. Company linen will be washed in public; poor accounting systems may be exposed and the victim may be subject to other criticism and bad publicity.
6. The attention of other thieves may be drawn towards the company and the methods of fraud.
7. Prosecution might be deemed 'malicious' or involve action of unlawful arrest—this, however, is most unlikely.

Thus, there may be disadvantages in prosecuting offenders although they seldom outweigh the benefits in deterring future frauds. The best deterrent is achieved by subjecting detected criminals to maximum harassment: not that it will reform them, but because it will deter others.

For a criminal prosecution to succeed, the police or the company (if it acts as the prosecutor) have to prove with admissible evidence beyond reasonable doubt that the accused person was guilty of the alleged offence.

In fraud cases, this usually means that the company must establish that it has lost or was at the risk of losing something of value. So the first step in criminal proceedings is a statement or schedule of loss. This schedule will have to be supported by first-hand evidence of the facts contained in it. For example, it might be necessary to prove by stock records, sales and purchase invoices that the company has lost $10 000 worth of item X. On the other hand if the thief is found in possession of stolen goods, schedules and loss calculations might not be necessary: the physical evidence may be sufficient proof. Either way, whether by physical evidence (the goods themselves) or documentary evidence (schedules and statements of loss) the victim has to prove that something has been lost, or was under threat of loss.

The next step is to prove that the accused person was responsible for the loss—that he stole the goods or attempted to defraud. If goods are found in his possession and he can offer no explanation, this step may not be too difficult. If he has been seen stealing similar goods, his responsibility may be accepted as beyond reasonable doubt.

The important point, however, is to prove that the accused person acted with intent to defraud. Guilty knowledge may be inferred from the circumstances, from evidence of witnesses or from admissions by the accused person. His admissions may be oral or in writing: they may be made to the company, to the police or to an independent third party.

Evidence of what the suspect said about the fraud, subject to certain rules—Judges' Rules in the UK, the Miranda Ruling in the US—is admissible and valuable evidence in both civil and criminal proceedings; subject to the overriding conditions that the admissions were made voluntarily and are relevant to the facts in issue.

Thus, in most criminal cases of fraud, the prosecution has to prove beyond reasonable doubt:

- a loss or intended loss
- the responsibility for that loss
- the guilty knowledge of the person responsible

The burden of proof can be discharged by:

- physical evidence (the goods themselves)
- documentary evidence
- oral evidence of witnesses who have first-hand knowledge of the facts in issue
- oral evidence of what the accused person has said directly to another person or in his presence

Most evidence is given to a court from the witness box by people who have sworn to tell the truth; documentary and physical evidence (called exhibits) are 'produced' by witnesses. For example, the company's accountant—who has been called as a witness to prove loss—might say: 'I produce a schedule of the amount lost of item X. This schedule was prepared by me from sales invoices, stock records, etc.'

The court might also wish to hear from the people who wrote or have first-hand knowledge of the invoices and stock records on which the accountant based his schedules.

The procedure in British courts is complex and the standards of proof, rightly, extremely high. Before setting the objective of prosecution, the victim should realize just what the procedures are. A summary is given below:

1. A formal complaint is made to the police.
2. The police investigate the allegations and prepare a report for submission to the Director of Public Prosecutions or to the county or local police solicitor. The victim company will be required to assist and to make witnesses available.
3. If the evidence is sufficient, charges are drafted and the accused person arrested or summoned to attend the magistrates' court on a certain date and time. Witnesses may also be summoned to attend and, should they fail to do so, may be arrested.
4. If the accused person, prosecution and magistrates agree and are allowed by law to do so, the case will be heard. If the accused person wants to be heard by a higher court—before a jury and the law gives him the right of making this election—he will be committed for trial and released on bail, or kept in custody, to attend the higher court.

    If the prosecution wants the case to be heard by a higher court—which has the power to impose greater penalties—the magistrates must remit it. The magistrates too have the right to forward the case to a higher court. Generally, before a case comes before the magistrates all parties will know whether it is to be heard there or whether it is to be committed for trial before a jury.

There are essentially two ways that these committal proceedings will be dealt with by the magistrates, neither of which needs detailed mention here. For the purpose of this account it will be assumed that the case has been committed for trial to a Crown Court.

5. Witnesses will be bound over to attend the Crown Court. The summonses will be full (in which case the witness must attend) or conditional (when a witness will not have to attend unless he receives further specific instructions).

6. At the Crown Court:

   - the fully bound over witness will report to the court officer;
   - the defendant will be brought into court and the charges read over to him and he will be asked to plead guilty or not guilty.

If he pleads guilty:

   - prosecuting counsel will outline the case;
   - defence counsel will speak in mitigation;
   - the Judge will pass sentence.

If the defendant pleads not guilty:

   - the jury is sworn in subject to objections from defence counsel (cynics would say that people who look reasonably intelligent and capable of understanding the case will be rejected);
   - prosecuting counsel makes his opening speech and calls for his first witness who gives evidence from the witness box, under oath, based on his statement. The witness may be cross-examined by defending counsel, may be examined by the judge and re-examined by prosecuting counsel. He will then be released and may leave the court. Other prosecution witnesses will be called;
   - when all the prosecution witnesses have been heard and when the statements of conditionally bound over witnesses read out, the defence case begins;
   - defending counsel makes his opening speech and calls his witnesses. The defendant may be called to give evidence on his own behalf, from the witness box (under oath) or from the dock (when the evidence is not under oath). The defendant can elect not to give evidence at all;
   - prosecuting and defending counsel make their closing speeches and the judge sums up;
   - the jury retires and returns and gives its verdict;
   - if found guilty, sentence is passed or if not guilty the defendant is released;

- the judge may award costs to the prosecution or, if he is found not guilty, to the defendant.

Criminal prosecution can be a lengthy and difficult process and an accurate, fair and professional investigation is absolutely essential.

CIVIL ACTION

Action through the civil courts may be started by a victim of fraud (the plaintiff):

- to seek recovery of the amount lost or compensation for damages incurred;
- to seek an injunction to prevent further transgressions;
- in certain circumstances, to seek an order requiring a person to comply with a specific order.

Should the opposing party (the defendant) fail to comply he may be penalized for contempt of court.

Thus civil action (or negotiation in the face of it) may be taken to recover funds from:

- the perpetrators before, after or in lieu of criminal or civil proceedings;
- auditors, if they acted negligently;
- bankers, if they failed to maintain appropriate controls;
- security companies, if their staff failed to maintain professional standards;
- computer equipment suppliers, if their equipment failed to operate properly or securely.

Or under a fidelity insurance policy. These options are discussed later.

There are usually important powers under civil law which enable victims to 'discover' documents in the possession of third parties (including the criminals themselves). Orders for discovery require platintiffs and defendants to release all relevant evidence in their possession to the opposing party.

In many cases, criminals will try to move their assets beyond the jurisdiction of the courts or transfer them to third parties against whom action cannot be taken. In these circumstances it is possible for the victim to obtain a blocking order on assets (in the UK these are called Mareva injunctions).

Similarly, many perpetrators will destroy documents prior to discovery. When a party to civil proceedings in the UK believes this might happen he can apply to the court—without his opponent's knowledge—seeking what is called an Anton Pillar order. These orders, which take their name from the company that was first successful in obtaining one, allow the plaintiff's lawyers to enter, search for and seize documents and other evidence specified in the order. If the defendant fails to comply he may be imprisoned for contempt of court.

Anton Pillar orders have an equivalent in other countries and they are particularly powerful tools in corruption investigations (when third party cash books and bank records can be obtained) and in cases of product piracy (when premises suspected to contain contraband stocks or other evidence can be entered and searched).

Many countries have reciprocal powers as far as civil laws are concerned. Thus proceedings started in the USA may be used to obtain Anton Pillar or discovery orders in the UK. Similarly, British plaintiffs can apply through the UK courts to have witnesses deposed on oath in the USA and to produce documents for examination.

Whereas the evidence in criminal proceedings is given almost entirely from the witness box, civil cases may be heard on written affidavit and the attendance of witnesses may not be necessary.

Clearly the civil law is very powerful (in some ways more so than the criminal law) and proceedings might be considered simply to obtain vital documents not otherwise available and to depose witnesses and suspects under oath. It should be noted that evidence obtained under Anton Pillar orders can be used only for the proceedings in which they were issued: they cannot be used in criminal cases unless a release has been obtained from the defendant.

Civil proceedings are started by instructing specialist litigation lawyers who will make the necessary applications to the appropriate court.

In the UK the case will be heard before one or more judges who will decide upon its merits. Unlike the USA where, irrespective of the outcome, each side bears its own costs UK courts normally award costs to the successful party. This fact should be considered in deciding in which jurisdiction a civil action should be started.

NEGOTIATION

The threat of civil or criminal proceedings can be used as a lever to seek a negotiated settlement with criminals, accomplices, receivers and third parties, although care must be taken if this objective is chosen.

First, if it fails, criminals will be prewarned and vital records and other evidence may be destroyed. Secondly, the victim may be exposed to claims of extortion or blackmail if he pushes too hard.

Thus, negotiated settlements should be discussed, in advance, with experienced litigation lawyers.

FIDELITY INSURANCE

Many companies who hold fidelity insurance—against dishonesty by employees—overlook the possibilities of claiming when fraud is suspected. It is true that fidelity insurance settlements can be prolonged and difficult but the benefits are worth pursuing.

Carriers or underwriters often dispute claims on the following grounds:

- the premium has not been paid;
- the accounting system has changed since the policy was issued and proper controls have not been maintained;
- the perpetrator is not an 'employee' as defined in the policy (this usually excludes all part-time and contract workers);
- the employee did not gain personally nor did he act with 'manifest intent to deceive';
- notification of the loss was not made in the proper form or at the proper time;
- the policy does not cover losses of the type in question;
- the claim is insufficiently detailed;
- action by the insured has prejudiced the carrier's chances of recovery from third parties.

Fraud victims can minimize the possibility of having claims rejected by:

- reporting the first suspicions to the carrier in a registered or hand delivered letter. At this point it is not necessary to have completed the investigation. Most policies require a detailed proof of loss within a fixed period but in large cases these deadlines are impossible to achieve. Thus the carrier should be kept informed in writing of progress. Similarly, applications to extend the time for submission of a detailed claim should also be made in writing;
- conducting a full investigation—independent of the carrier—of all the facts as quickly as possible;
- documentating every stage of the investigation, including notes of all interviews and maintaining a chronological file of all documents delivered to the carrier;
- retaining original evidence carefully;
- making no settlements with third parties without the express permission of the carrier.

Ultimately, if settlement is not agreed, it may be necessary for the victim to take legal action against the carrier and friends can quickly become adversaries: caution, good documentation and relentless pursuit of insurance claims are strongly advised.

DISMISSAL

Dismissal of internal thieves may be a desirable outcome of an investigation. To achieve this, the loss, responsibility for it and the method of fraud must be proved to a reasonable degree.

In the UK, a person who believes he has been unfairly dismissed may take his case to a tribunal which may award damages or order reinstatement.

The following acts would, under normal circumstances, constitute adequate grounds for immediate dismissal of an employee:

- conviction by a court for an offence in relation to his job;
- conviction by a court which affects an employee's ability to perform his job (for example, a driving suspension or imprisonment);
- conviction by a court of an offence which, though unconnected with the employer, discredits the reputation of an employee whose integrity is an essential qualification for his job (for example, a bank clerk convicted of fraud on a hotel, say, may be dismissed from the bank);
- admission of guilt by an employee to a criminal offence in relation to his job, or in appropriate cases, involving his reputation.

The dismissal must take place as soon as the facts have been established to the reasonable satisfaction of the employer. An employer who delays his action may be held to have forgiven the employee's misconduct. He may then be accused of unfair dismissal, even though his action is adequately justified by the facts.

The overriding condition of all dismissals is that they were reasonable in the circumstances and at the time they were made. Thus dismissal should not be delayed, pending a decision by a criminal court. It does not matter that the court should eventually find the person not guilty. The test is whether or not the employer acted reasonably at the time.

DEFENSIVE ACTION

Where the objective of an investigation is merely to stop future frauds and to set up more effective defences, the proof of loss is relatively unimportant. So is the responsibility for it, and the intent of the perpetrator. The major point is to determine how the loss occurred and its mechanics. This may be achieved by one or more of the investigative methods outlined later. There are few advantages in adopting this objective because if thieves are not weeded out, they will attack new defences and continue as before.

Factors to be considered in setting objectives

The objectives of any investigation may be constrained by a number of factors, the most common of which are given below.

COMPANY POLITICS

Investigations are contentious and difficult, often made more so by internal company politics. Ideally all companies should have predefined policies on the conduct of investigations.

Decisions taken on a case-by-case basis can be confused by the person-alities of the people involved, sympathy for the perpetrator and self-interest of managers whose trust has been violated. A reason for taking no action in any case can always be found.

Policy should state that all cases of suspected fraud will be fully investigated, reported to the police and subject to civil action for financial recovery. A sample policy is set out in Appendix C.

ADVERSE PUBLICITY

Many victims of fraud decide to take no action because they fear that shareholders and customers will be alarmed by the bad publicity. This attitude is dishonest and self-defeating.

First, if the victim genuinely believes that the truth would cause customers to withdraw their business, deliberate suppression of the facts is deceitful. Secondly, other employees will see that fraud is a rewarding pursuit, with few dangers if detected. Thirdly, and perhaps more importantly for weak corporate victims, the truth usually comes out in the end. The victim then has to face publicity of the fraud and the fact that he tried to conceal it.

A survey conducted for the *Computer Fraud and Security Bulletin* asked a number of people what their attitudes to fraud and publicity were. Some of the results are given in Table 8.2.

Table 8.2 Attitudes to bank frauds

	Yes	No
Would you be alarmed to hear that the bank at which you kept your account had been defrauded?	80	20
Do you believe banks should prosecute offenders?	70	30
Would you be alarmed that your bank was the victim of frequent frauds and never prosecuted because it feared bad publicity?	90	10
Would you withdraw your account if you knew frauds were commonplace and:		
– always prosecuted?	10	90
– never prosecuted for fear of bad publicity?	40	60

The consequences of bad publicity appear to be more important in the minds of corporate politicians than in truth. Failure to prosecute and deal openly with problems is a positive encouragement to fraud: it is the ultimate blank cheque!

POLICE INVOLVEMENT

Another factor that should be considered in setting general policy or the objectives of an investigation is the benefit that might be obtained by reporting suspected frauds to the police. This is an important decision since in many countries victims are not obliged to make a formal report.

However, if the objective is to press for criminal prosecution, the sooner the police are involved the better, simply because no investigator likes to be held responsible for a case that someone else has trampled on.

There may be cases where the police may not be overjoyed at receiving a call for assistance, particularly when the facts are complicated, the accounting system confused or the proof of loss unclear. Technically the police are obliged to follow up every complaint but obviously some are investigated more thoroughly than others.

All police forces are overburdened by reported public and violent crime and it is little wonder if they seem less than anxious to take on a fraud investigation when the victim has been patently neglectful or where he has called them as the final resort.

It is also important to recognize the objectives of the police and law enforcement. Whereas corporate victims wish to have a loss proved down to the last penny, so that they can seek compensation, a conviction is the important outcome for the police and it does not matter greatly whether a criminal is convicted of a $19 000 or a $99 000 fraud. On the contrary, police investigations will often concentrate on those parts of a fraud that can most easily be presented to a jury.

A further point that sometimes acts against reporting suspected frauds to the police is that it may reduce the flexibility of the victim company and tie up management time and resources.

It should also be understood that information will flow almost totally one way. Police are bound by legislation that prevents disclosure of information and they cannot hand over copies of statements or documents to victims or their lawyers without express permission of senior officers. Permission is seldom given until prosecution has been completed. For this reason, a victim may have to conduct its own enquiries in parallel to those being undertaken by the police. This calls for careful planning and close liaison.

Victim companies would be well advised to designate a senior manager through whom all contact with the police is handled. He should retain copies of, and receipts for, all documents handed to the police.

In complex long-term investigations an office on the victim company's premises should be set aside for police use, to which they have access outside normal hours. Consideration should also be given to issuing appropriate police officers with company passes so that they do not have to report to the reception desk on each visit. It can be very off-putting for suppliers and customers to see frequent entries by the Fraud Squad in the victim's reception register.

So far, the disadvantages of police involvement have been discussed. On the plus side (and they are big pluses) are the professionalism, thoroughness and the resources that police have available. Some investigations are just too large for a company to handle without professional assistance.

Other public bodies may be able to help with the investigation of corporate fraud. Where, for example, tax evasion follows from a manipulative fraud involving purchases, the Customs and Excise Department may be interested and provide specialist resources.

The Ministry of Agriculture, Fisheries and Foods, Post Office, the Board of Trade, the Treasury and Inland Revenue also have enforcement sections whose investigators may assist when government and corporate interests coincide.

Thus, a company which believes itself to be the victim of fraud should consider the resources it has available and the professional help that can be called upon.

INVESTIGATIVE RESOURCES

Resources that a company has available should be taken into account in determining the objectives of an investigation; employee skills as well as available manpower are important factors.

When the size or difficulty of a suspected fraud exceeds in-house resources, professional assistance should be sought. To try to tackle a large investigation with insufficient manpower or skills is to court disaster.

External consultants or private investigators may be retained in appropriate cases and providing careful selection is made impressive results can be obtained. Selection criteria for consultants are shown on page 324.

EMPLOYEE MORALE

The effect that an investigation will have on employee morale should be considered. Experience suggests that when an investigation is conducted fairly, few problems arise. When employees believe they are being unfairly victimized, trouble is usually inevitable but it is not unknown for thieves whose detection is imminent to stir up trouble, strikes or militant action, in the hope that the investigation will be called off.

The purpose of a major investigation should be explained to staff and union representatives as soon as it is safe to do so. A union, trade association or management group that condones fraud or is prepared to be used by thieves as a means of protection is in the long run destroying itself.

It is always easy to take the simple course in investigations: not to involve police, not to start criminal prosecution, not to dismiss the dishonest employee, or cut off the criminal customer. Misplaced sympathy for a thief often overrides common sense and sound company strategy, which must be to deter others.

In considering action against dishonest customers the philosophy that 'half a loaf is better than no loaf at all' might be argued as a reason for doing nothing. However, a company that condones fraud on the grounds that volume and sales count for all is digging its own grave. Once one fraud is condoned, others will inevitably spring up. Experience suggests that fraud grows in the garden of corporate weakness, indecision and greed.

A certainty and consistency of response deters fraud: the position of the detected thief—one he usually deserves—should not be allowed to cloud decisions that are in the best interest of the company, its honest and loyal employees, customers and suppliers.

CONSIDER THE WORST CASE

Experience shows that the first suspicions of a fraud are likely to reveal less than 10 per cent of its true extent. Before finally deciding on the objectives of and resources necessary for an investigation consideration should be given to:

- the exact mechanics of the suspected fraud
- how, where, why and who?
- why weren't symptoms discovered earlier?
- the worst case
- what other frauds could the suspects have committed?
- who else could be involved?

The investigation should be directed towards proving or disproving the worst case rather than being limited to the immediate suspicions, simply because the bigger the fraud the greater the financial recovery should be.

ACQUISITION OF RECORDS

A key element in most investigations is to decide how accounts and other evidence can be obtained from third parties. The options are usually restricted to:

- negotiation and requests for assistance in lieu of civil litigation
- civil litigation, including Anton Pillar orders
- pretext or undercover investigations

and will to a large extent depend on the scale of the fraud in question and the positions and likely attitudes of the third parties involved. Practical experience shows that the possibility of obtaining evidence by a direct request or negotiation is much greater than might appear to be the case (see Table 8.3).

Table 8.3   Methods of acquiring third-party records

Records held by:	Reason for cooperation				
	General cooperation	In lieu of civil criminal proceedings	To prevent involvement of police	To prevent termination of business or employment	Resignation allowed in lieu of dismissal
Perpetrators		✓	✓	✓	✓
Accomplices		✓	✓	✓	✓
Customers, suppliers, etc., of the victim company	✓		✓		
Accountants	✓			✓	
Other third parties	✓	✓	✓		

ADMISSIBILITY OF EVIDENCE

Consideration should be given before objectives are finally decided to the problems that could arise over the admissibility of evidence. In some countries evidence can be tainted and rejected if it is not properly obtained. Problems can also arise over computerized records, particularly those derived without human intervention.

In most countries evidence from a computer will be admitted in criminal courts when a responsible person certifies to the best of his knowledge and belief that:

– the evidence (usually a printout) was produced by a computer in the ordinary course of business and during working hours;
– appropriate security measures were in force which prevented unauthorized interference;
– the computer was operating properly at the time.

Interpretation of these conditions is left to the court to decide but reports produced by special audit software would usually be held inadmissible, since they break the 'normal business' rule.

In complex cases where proof depends on computerized records, expert legal opinion should be obtained so that problems of admissibility can be minimized.

ANALYSIS OF EXPOSURE POINTS

A most important piece of preplanning is to examine what is known about the suspected fraud and the thieves involved in it and to try to identify where and how they are most exposed.

Criminals are obviously at their weakest when caught in the commission of a crime. Thus where there are reasons for believing that a fraud is continuing, plans should be made to catch the thieves by surprise:

- when they, accomplices or receivers are in the act of theft, conversion or misrepresentation;
- when they are in possession of stolen goods;
- when they are in the course of doing some other act in connection with the fraud that their normal duties would not require them to do.

Where possible, therefore, the first impact of an investigation should be arranged to catch the criminals at their weak point where interrogation and investigation will stand the highest chance of success.

When more than one thief is caught in the act of dishonesty they should be separated as quickly as possible so that they are unable to learn what their accomplices are saying or will say. Each thief should be questioned individually and should not be given the opportunity to compare stories with accomplices. Their differing explanations will help to establish criminal intent.

Further, any physical or documentary evidence found at the time criminals are first intercepted should be carefully preserved and their explanations of it obtained as soon as possible.

ANALYSIS OF WEAK POINTS IN THE VICTIM'S CASE

Before an investigation gets under way, the victim company should consider what might be the weak points in the logical development of its own case. What untrue, but plausible, explanations might the thieves give for their dishonesty? Can the loss or responsibility for it be confused? When caught in the act or questioned, what explanations might they be able to offer? Ways in which these false explanations can be disproved should be considered in advance.

When these aspects have been considered and objectives decided upon the investigation proper can begin.

Methods of investigation

Quite where or how an investigation should start depends on the particular case and the objectives of the victim. However, there are three important rules. Wherever possible enquiries should be concentrated around the central issues or hub of the fraud. Inexperienced investigators can be too subtle, skate around issues, delay interviewing suspects and fail in every aspect except to alert the criminal that he is under suspicion. The rule is to concentrate on the hub of the fraud and to make sure that each line of enquiry is necessary and timely.

Secondly, investigators would be well advised not to seek the most complex solutions to fraud cases: the rule is to examine the most obvious answer and only when that has been eliminated to go on to more complicated solutions.

Thirdly, if concealment is difficult to unravel, investigators should 'follow the money': determine who benefited at the end of the day and work backwards.

Table 8.4 summarizes a number of investigative methods and gauges their efficiency in proving a loss, guilty knowledge, responsibility and method. For example, the analysis of documents is highly effective in proving a loss and is thus marked with the letter 'H' on the chart.

Table 8.4 Effectiveness of investigation techniques

| Technique | Effectiveness in proving: | | | |
	Intent	Method	Responsibility	Loss
Analysis of documents	M	H	M	H
Schedules	M	H	H	H
Analysis of deviations	H	H	M	L
Observation	M	H	H	M
Expert witness	L	M	M	M
Pretext	H	H	M	L
Interviews with witnesses	H	H	H	M
Interviews with suspects	H	M	M	H

H = highly effective; M = moderate; L = some effect.

By describing investigation methods in self-contained sections, there is a danger that the indefinable skill that all good investigators have—the imagination and instinct to do the right thing at the right time—may be underplayed. With this qualification, the techniques of investigation can be described as shown below.

ACQUISITION AND ANALYSIS OF DOCUMENTS

A thorough and professional examination of documentary evidence (this includes computer files) involved in a suspected fraud is usually essential to

- prove the loss
- establish responsibility and intent
- prove the methods used

All records that have a bearing on the fraud should be securely handled:

- All original documents that could be of any possible interest should be secured at the earliest possible stage of an investigation.
- When documents are first obtained, they should be listed and logged so that details of who found them, when and where can be proved if necessary. Receipts should be given and taken.
- Complete working copies of all relevant documents and printouts of computer files should be used by the investigator.
- Original documents should not be stapled nor should bundles and files be broken up. They should be preserved in the general order in which they were found.
- Original documents should be kept separate from the working copies and should not be released until after the case (and appeal) has been completed.
- Important single documents should be put in transparent plastic bags.
- Documentary exhibits should be assembled with care and accuracy and cross-references and indices should be attached.
- Comments and cross-references should be written on the copies—*never on the originals.*

These procedures will ensure that the integrity of documents is preserved and that their admissibility in court is not prejudiced.

Photocopied working documents (supported where necessary by reference to the originals) may be examined from three fundamental aspects.

The first and most obvious is to detect alterations and forgeries. This analysis will be a broad one, looking for patterns and suspicions rather than for a scientific proof.

There are some general principles:

- All of the documents in the case should be examined by one person (so that logical connections can be made).
- Every entry on every document should have a known and proven explanation (even rough notes and scribbled calculations).
- All documents, waste paper, carbon typewriter ribbons and carbon papers should be examined for:

- erased or crossed out figures
- inconsistent inks and typefaces
- odd notes, phone numbers and calculations
- evidence of old documents reused
- altered photocopy documents
- missing records (from sequential checks)
- mathematically adjusted figures after authorization and posting
- missing blocks and sequences
- colour sets
- changed directors' names and changed addresses
- form numbers and dates of printing
- patterns
- layout of typing (same format for apparently unconnected companies)
- method of writing dates (1st Jan or 1.1, etc.)
- similar folding
- pin holes
- handwriting
- franking machine stamps
- address layout on envelopes
- impressions from other documents
- deviations from procedures

On this preliminary examination notes would be made of those documents which, on their face, appear fraudulent or forged. Depending on the patterns that emerge, more detailed or professional forensic examination may be justified.

Every entry on every document that could be relevant to the suspected fraud should be examined. Rough notes—written on the back of delivery documents, for example—should be followed through and what they relate to established beyond doubt. Formal cross-references should be checked. Before the case comes to court, the victim should be in a position to explain every entry on every documentary exhibit; the connection between one figure and another should be known. Where mistakes have occurred in the accounts, or where inconsistencies appear, the reasons should be known.

Examination of documents always takes time but it is usually time well spent. An interviewer has an enormous advantage when he is armed with evidence of concealment or deviations from procedures.

The second important task is to prepare schedules summarizing important documents and facts. These form a vital part of a fraud investigation and can be used to present complicated evidence in a way that laymen can understand.

Schedules can be prepared and produced in court by any person connected with the investigation: he does not have to be a chartered accountant or a police officer, but he must be accurate and prepared to justify his work.

There are some general rules on preparing schedules:

– When in doubt prepare a schedule.
– Make schedules easy to audit.
– Leave adequate space for additional notes and columns.
– Use colour felt tip pens for cross-referencing, e.g., all green marks are confirmed facts; all red marks need checking, etc.
– If schedules get too wide (too many columns) consider redesigning them in a tabular/vertical form with a separate sheet; one for each transaction if necessary.
– Assemble one set of supporting documents in the order in which they are referred to on schedules.
– The left-hand side of a schedule should be reserved for anchor or confirmed information: such as:

    – declared sales
    – actual banking
    – recorded deliveries
    – formal records

and the right-hand columns used for recording comparative information from different sources:

    – informal notes on sales orders
    – observed deliveries
    – informal records

Discrepancies between the two halves often highlight evidence of fraud and can be referred to in interviews with suspects and witnesses.
– Unusual sources of corroborating information should be scheduled against recorded information. Unusual sources might include:

    – informal records
    – internal non-financial records
    – shift sheets or basic documents
    – suspense items
    – postal records
    – correspondence
    – third-party records

Discrepancies should be noted and acted on as investigative or interview leads.
– All available information should be shown on working schedules. For example, a listing of sales invoices might include formal identification of the invoices plus:

- a note of the colour of the invoice in the file
- whether it is a typed or manuscript document
- the type of handwriting
- whether the document is an original or a copy

By noting what might seem irrelevant points, patterns of fraud may emerge.
- Consider preparing high level summary schedules from working documents but make sure they can be audited.
- Double check the accuracy of schedules before they are produced in court.

In most cases, it will be necessary to produce schedules setting out the amount of the loss. These should be supported by relevant documents, so that every entry can be proved. If the case is to go forward for criminal prosecution, witness statements must be obtained to prove the accuracy of documents on which the loss schedule is based.

For example, where a company suspects that sales at one of its branches have been suppressed, the loss schedule might show:

1. Deliveries from the central warehouse to the branch:

    - invoices listed under product headings
    - dates of deliveries
    - value of deliveries at cost

2. Opening and closing stocks at the branch:

    - under product headings

3. Sales made and declared by the branch:

    - sales invoices listed under product headings
    - dates of sales
    - sales values accounted for to head office

4. Calculation of shortages. To support the loss schedule, the prosecution in a criminal case might have to obtain witness statements producing or proving the following points:

    - all delivery invoices from the central warehouse to branch X
    - the dates and methods of delivery
    - proof of receipt at branch X
    - proof of the dates of delivery
    - value of the deliveries based on price lists
    - all delivery/sales invoices issued by branch X
    - the system for recording sales at branch X

- the banking or remittances made by branch X to its head office
- the statement of account of branch X at head office
- stock figures and schedules

Thus, to support a simple loss schedule, up to a dozen witness statements may be required and possibly thousands of sales and purchase invoices and stock records produced as exhibits.

The schedule of loss should be compiled from the best available figures, using the most accurate method of assessment. In some cases, the best method will be less than perfect: for example, it is difficult to prove the exact losses in market diversion or espionage cases.

Where the schedule of loss is an estimate only, that fact should be made clear. A court or tribunal should never be misled over the accuracy imputed to loss figures—or to any other evidence for that matter.

The third purpose of preparing schedules is to pick out symptoms of concealment, prove guilty knowledge or identify patterns that add to the evidence in the case.

Very often, until all documents, including correspondence, have been examined and scheduled, their true value cannot be estimated. At the earliest stages in an investigation the ultimate purpose of schedules may not be clear. It is not unusual to start out producing a simple schedule of loss only to find in the process that patterns emerge which virtually prove the fraud; guilty knowledge and responsibility.

'When in doubt—schedule' is a good rule for any fraud investigator. The subject of the schedule might be correspondence—a timetable of recorded events—it might be delivery notes compared with sales invoices, or goods inwards passes compared with purchase invoices.

Analysis schedules are also important to establish and illustrate links between apparently unconnected events or people. For example a link chart showing companies and their officers can be prepared as shown in Figure 8.2. Similar formats can be used in other areas in which it is important to prove connected facts.

ANALYSIS OF DEVIATIONS

Fraud is deviant behaviour and criminals often conceal their dishonesty as plausible breaches of rules or procedures. It is thus worth while to identify all deviations from accepted behaviour or procedures and to obtain explanations of them. Firstly, because they may point to direct evidence of fraud and, secondly, because they are important discussion points in interviews with witnesses and suspects.

The method is to list everything known about the fraud in question and to obtain positive external and preferably independent corroboration of every

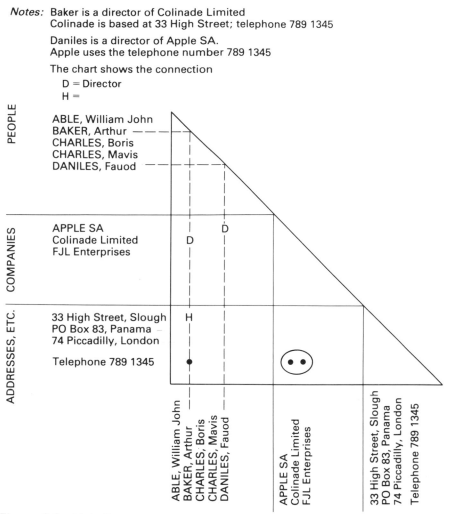

Notes: Baker is a director of Colinade Limited
Colinade is based at 33 High Street; telephone 789 1345

Daniles is a director of Apple SA.
Apple uses the telephone number 789 1345

The chart shows the connection
D = Director
H =

PEOPLE

ABLE, William John
BAKER, Arthur
CHARLES, Boris
CHARLES, Mavis
DANILES, Fauod

COMPANIES

APPLE SA
Colinade Limited
FJL Enterprises

ADDRESSES, ETC.

33 High Street, Slough
PO Box 83, Panama
74 Piccadilly, London

Telephone 789 1345

ABLE, William John
BAKER, Arthur
CHARLES, Boris
CHARLES, Mavis
DANILES, Fauod

APPLE SA
Colinade Limited
FJL Enterprises

33 High Street, Slough
PO Box 83, Panama
74 Piccadilly, London
Telephone 789 1345

Figure 8.2 Link diagram

fact: never assume, but check and double check. Then consider how the fraud was committed and how it was not committed. Consider why the criminals took the course they did rather than other alternatives. Look carefully at all deviations from the position of a perpetrator and identify why they were necessary.

SURVEILLANCE

Surveillance may be used in an investigation to

– prove a loss
– establish responsibility

- prove the method of fraud
- establish guilty knowledge
- identify other thieves or receivers

Visual surveillance

The techniques of static observation were discussed in Chapter 7 and it is not necessary to go into further detail here. However, moving observation—following a thief or his associates—may be necessary to identify other people involved in the fraud and particularly receivers of stolen goods. Mobile observation whether on foot or by vehicle is something that only the police or trained investigators should undertake. Where this form of surveillance is necessary, the case should be passed over to the police or to a reputable professional investigator.

The most likely outcome of observation is a pattern in behaviour different from facts recorded in accounting records. The difference between what actually happened or happens and what is recorded often hits at the heart of fraud. Thus observation should be carried out meticulously and accurate records should be kept. In static observations, closed circuit television and fixed frame photography may be used to establish the necessary standard of proof.

A court may be more impressed if it is able to see moving evidence of theft or conversion than if a witness stands in the witness box and says on oath that he saw such and such happen. Oral evidence of observation is always open to doubt.

Further, events sometimes happen so quickly that human memory alone is not a satisfactory method of recall. A case could hinge on whether 12 or 15 boxes of item X were illegally delivered to the receiver. Thus, besides the evidential benefits of filming, there are operational spin-offs.

Audio surveillance

Telephone subscribers in the UK (and many other countries) are entitled to listen in to conversations by employees. It is thus permissible to attach a covert tape recorder to the telephone of a suspected employee providing the subscriber (i.e., a director of the company paying the telephone bill) agrees.

The evidence obtained is likely to be admissible in court but, because of the civil rights sensitivities, companies would be well advised to seek legal advice before deciding to intercept telephones.

Similarly it is no offence in the UK to covertly tape record conversations even when the party who owns or installs the recorder is not present. For example if a tape recorder brief case is left behind by a visitor and recovered later, conversations recorded during the intervening period will probably be admissible.

Audio surveillance can be invaluable in corruption investigations but should only be considered a possibility after the adverse consequences have been discussed with lawyers.

EXPERT WITNESSES AND FORENSIC EXAMINATION

Forensic and technical examination may be necessary to prove product copying by competitors or interference with control machinery. In some frauds, finger print or handwriting identification may also be considered to prove responsibility for a larcenous theft, false accounts or an extorsive written demand.

The value of and need for expert advice will obviously depend on the nature of the case concerned but there are some general rules:

— Expert testimony is intended to inform and be helpful and not simply to impress the judge with the skill of the witness, nor to bamboozle the jury. The quality of expert testimony is its simplicity, so that what the witness says can be understood by a jury of unqualified laymen.
— Make sure the expert understands exactly what is required of him and what the problem is. Each question should be framed *in writing* and should deal with a single matter upon which an opinion is required.
— Never suggest the result you would like him to achieve; let him make up his own mind.
— Give him a realistic amount of time to study the facts and to form an opinion.
— Ask him to provide an initial report and read this carefully. Clear up any ambiguities.
— Avoid technicalities, acronyms and abbreviations. Write down the expert's statement in the most simple terms.
— If the subject is complex (for example, a computer fraud) consider how charts, diagrams or working models might be used to assist the jury to understand the testimony.
— Submit the draft statement to two or three colleagues who are not familiar with the case. Then question them on their understanding. Revise the statement if necessary.
— Provide a glossary of terms in complex cases.

This procedure should result in clear cut and simple evidence and not, as often happens, in technical gobbledegook that confuses the judge, jury and even other expert witnesses.

PRETEXT INVESTIGATIONS

Fraud victims may conduct enquiries under a pretext to obtain evidence of loss or to prove guilty knowledge: test purchases of counterfeit products are commonplace in both civil and criminal courts.

Some private investigators are expert at arranging and managing more complex pretext investigations as the following example demonstrates:

> X Limited is a wholesaler of chemical products and spends over £500 000 per annum on printing and stationery (much of it on glossy advertising brochures). Management believed that the stationery buyer was receiving large kickbacks from the main printer to place work, accept inflated charges and overlook poor quality materials. An investigator was employed to resolve the suspicions. The investigator obtained copies of the brochures concerned and details of the prices paid for them. Posing as director of a printing company, the investigator called on the buyer and quoted prices substantially less than those being paid to the existing printer. The buyer did not seem interested and said the prices were too expensive and above those already being paid (this was known to be untrue).
>
> The investigator said he was disturbed by the buyer's attitude and that he would write to the managing director enclosing a quotation. Over lunch, the buyer much the better for a couple of bottles of expensive wine, explained that he received a 10 per cent commission from the existing printer. He said that since the investigator's 'company' was cheaper than the existing supplier his commission rates would have to be greater than 10 per cent so that he would not lose money!
>
> At a subsequent meeting, the buyer said that he wanted his commission paid to ABC Limited, which was his wife's company used to launder his commissions.

The nature and efficiency of pretext enquiries vary but should be considered as possible means of obtaining evidence not otherwise available. Careful consideration needs to be given to the pretext used and to ensure that the investigator does not obtain property by deception. For these reasons, pretext investigations should first be considered by litigation lawyers.

INTERVIEWS

Interview techniques can be learned and improved upon, but it always appears far easier to fail than to succeed; usually there are no second chances.

In most investigations, interviews with witnesses, informants and suspects are vitally important but too often victims of fraud, and their professional advisers do not plan in advance and fall at the first hurdle. As a result of failure, they leave themselves and their companies exposed.

Interviews with witnesses and suspects usually fail for one or more of the following reasons:

1. Interviewers do not set clear objectives for the interview and do not plan its general structure, objectives and success criteria in advance.
2. *They do not listen to what the subject is saying and do not watch his reactions.*
3. They fail to hold the interview in private and expect subjects to confess or disclose sensitive information in front of a whole host of people.
4. They give up far too easily: *and often don't try at all.*
5. They try to rush and bluster their way to success and fail to establish empathy with the subject.
6. They tend to get angry—and worse still, show it—when the interview does not go their way.
7. They fail to recognize symptoms of guilt and *innocence.*
8. They allow a subject to succeed with obvious untruths and diversions.
9. They allow prejudices to interfere with their relationship with the subject and with the objectivity of the interview.
10. They do not use techniques that suit their own personality and with which they feel comfortable.
11. They never reach the point where the suspect is asked to admit his guilt.
12. They do not provide the suspect with a good reason to confess.
13. They expect to fail and, having found or more usually built a psychological crutch for their failure, give up.

All of these failings can be corrected by sound methods and practice.

Types of questions

There are a number of ways in which questions can be asked. Open questions require the subject to give a detailed reply. For example:

> 'What did you do next?'
> 'How could this have been done?'

They are useful in interviews with witnesses, since they allow a witness to explain, in detail, exactly what he did, saw or heard.

They may be used with suspects to pin them down to detail but they may lead to 'rambling' explanations and answers that stray off the point. If this happens, the interviewer can change to leading questions or bring the subject back to a relevant point.

Closed and leading questions usually call for 'yes' or 'no' replies or suggest the answer required. For example:

> 'And then you threw the papers in the shredder?'
> 'And he told you to say nothing?'

They are useful in pinning suspects down, but they do not, usually, provide any free flowing replies. Frequently, if the matter results in criminal proceedings, the suggestion is made that words were put into the mouth of the accused.

Negative questions such as:

'You didn't take the money, did you?'

can only bring one answer. Negative questions provide negative answers and should normally be avoided at all costs.

Regressive questions return a suspect's answer verbatim: for example:

Suspect:	'Then I threw the papers in the bin.'
Interviewer:	'Then you threw the papers in the bin.'
Suspect:	'Yes.'
Interviewer:	'Yes, and what next?'
Suspect:	'Then I went out to the pub.'
Interviewer:	'Then you went to the pub.'

This technique usually causes irritation but can be used with good effect against over-confident suspects.

Normally questions should be simply constructed, so that there can be no misunderstanding. Complex questions usually disorientate the suspect but they can lead to disagreement concerning which answer applied to what question.

Transactional analysis and empathy building

This branch of psychology has received much acclaim in explaining the nature of inter-personal relationships. Founded by an American psychologist, Eric Byrne, it examines the basic element of human contact—called a transaction.

In transactions, people adopt one of three roles—parent, adult or child—depending to a large extent upon their perception of the other person.

When one party to a transaction tries to force upon the other a role he does not wish to play, conflict usually arises: it is a crossed transaction. If, on the other hand, an interviewer can adapt his position, he can build on empathy and get the best results from the interview.

The three 'roles' are shown in Figure 8.3.

It is not the intention to cover transactional analysis in depth, simply to point out that investigators and policemen are seen (and usually behave instinctively) as critical parents. Yet this role is only likely to establish rapport, *through domination*, with just those subjects who are prepared to adopt the role of a free or natural child. In all other cases, empathy may be hard to establish.

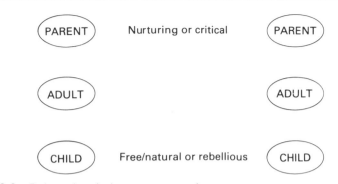

Figure 8.3 Roles taken in human transactions

With fraud suspects, who are usually mature people given responsibility in their jobs (albeit abused), the critical parent approach is likely to create friction rather than empathy. Ideally, the interviewer should adopt the role of an adult and should allow the subject to find a generally equivalent level.

Obvious dangers arise where the subject perceives his role as that of a critical parent and sees the interviewer as a natural child! In such cases, shock tactics may be necessary to change the balance. The major point, however, is that the interviewer recognizes the nature of relationships and is able to change his approach accordingly.

Body language and non-verbal communication

We all recognize body language: the skill is in-built but we may not be aware of its significance. We can tell, instinctively, when a person is hesitant, open, frightened, challenging, happy or sad, simply by looking at him.

The golden rule is to trust the eyes, but question the facial expression.

The signs of stress, which often accompany deception, include:

Gestures Expressions }	exaggerated, pained, rapidly changing
Mannerisms	agitated, fussy, fiddling, hand over mouth, staring, changing levels of eye contact
Proximity	distanced from interviewer, avoidance stance, leans back, arms crossed, remains well outside 'personal space' limits
Physical	sweating, sickness, flushed face, nervous hands, rapidly changing position, rearranges furniture

The interviewer should remain on the look out for signs of stress, when and how they occur. As explained later, in some cases these stress symptoms should be brought to the attention of the subject.

Interviews with witnesses

Interviews with witnesses can be conducted at any stage in an investigation. The object is to obtain information and formal proof which can be used in court, industrial tribunal or for making a claim for recovery.

A witness can be summonsed to give evidence even though he does not want to and has refused to make a written statement, although most lawyers are unhappy about calling a witness without knowing precisely what he is going to say. A written statement has the following value:

- it enables Counsel to understand exactly what the witness will say;
- when the evidence concerned is not challenged by the opposition the statement can be read out without going to the expense of calling the witness in person;
- if the witness fails to stick to his statement he may, with the leave of the trial judge, be questioned by Counsel as a hostile witness.

Thus, the final object of interviews with witnesses is to obtain formal evidence in statement or written form:

- to prove a loss
- to establish responsibility
- to prove a method of fraud
- to establish a suspect's guilty intent
- to obtain expert testimony
- to uncover other crimes/losses

Interviews should be conducted in private in a low key and professional way. The witness should be:

- asked to relate everything he knows about the crime or event in question in his own words; he should not be interrupted. Open questions should be used;
- questioned about specific points in his story;
- asked to produce documents or other evidence in his possession;
- shown case documents and other exhibits to identify them and to refresh his memory;
- asked to go over his story again;
- asked to resolve discrepancies between his first and subsequent statements; and
- what the witness has said should be written down in a statement or proof of evidence.

A proof of evidence is a written account of what a witness says. It may contain hearsay and other details not directly related to the facts in issue. Lawyers can use a proof as the basis for preparing a formal statement (which would omit hearsay, etc.).

Although in both criminal and civil proceedings statements must be made available to the opposing side, this is not usually true of proofs of evidence, providing they are prefaced as follows:

'This Proof of Evidence has been prepared for the Legal Advisers of X Ltd., for information and in contemplation of legal proceedings relating to the matters referred to in it.'

This caveat should establish the privileged nature of the document. It is therefore much safer for inexperienced investigators to obtain proofs of evidence, rather than formal signed statements.

Interviews with suspects

Interviews with suspects are usually necessary to resolve suspicions of fraud one way or the other; to pin down guilt or establish innocence. They call for special interviewing techniques.

It is not essential that a guilty suspect admits his responsibility. Deliberate lies, in the face of overwhelming evidence, will be just as condemning. Moreover, a suspect's continued deceit and denials will be taken into account by a court when considering what sentence to impose.

Every person will admit the truth providing the correct techniques are used. The overwhelming attitude of the interviewer should be an expectation that he will find the truth.

He should be confident and convinced that even the most difficult interviews (perhaps with third parties over whom the victim has no control) are worth the effort. A positive attitude is vital.

Each interview should be planned carefully in advance, using techniques which, in all circumstances, appear to provide the best chance of success. However, there are some general principles.

Place of interviews

Interviews with suspects should either be conducted in a *private room* at a time most convenient to the interviewer, or if the fraud is continuing (and the criminals can be caught in the act) at the scene of the crime.

The room in which a suspect is interviewed can have an enormous effect on the outcome:

- it should be private and unfamiliar to the suspect (never in his own office or home);
- telephones should be disconnected;
- clocks and other distractions should be removed;

- pens, pencils, paper clips and other items which the suspect can use as 'worry beads' should be removed;
- furniture should be arranged so that the suspect and interviewer are always close together and preferably 'sideways on'. They should not be separated by desks or tables;
- seats for any corroborating witnesses should be placed out of the suspect's direct line of sight;
- a table should be placed to the side of the interviewer's chair on which he can place documents;
- *if there are pieces of particularly incriminating evidence (e.g., forged documents, altered accounts) these should be enlarged and pinned to the walls.*

When the plan is to catch the criminals in the act, an office near to the crime scene should be arranged in advance. A hotel room may be suitable. The interviewer needs to be careful in the way he invites a suspect to join him in the interview room, the danger being that the suspect may later claim he was arrested. To avoid this possibility, the exact words used to and by the suspect leading up to this agreement to attend the interview should be recorded.

Selection of the best person to conduct the interview

This might seem an impossible luxury for a company without a security or audit department. Normally the person nominated to conduct an interview is the person who happens to be available or who volunteers.

But it is unrealistic to expect a junior auditor successfully to interview a hard nosed senior vice-president who is suspected of having his hand in the till. It is equally as wrong to expect results from any interview where massive cultural, social, economic or corporate hierarchical gaps exist between the position of a subject and an inexperienced interviewer; either the suspect or the interviewer will be overwhelmed.

Experienced investigators automatically raise or lower their approach depending on the standing of the suspect being interviewed: this skill comes with practice and experience.

The factors governing the selection of the most effective interviewer in any particular case are:

- the position and character type of the suspect;
- the skills and experience of interviewers available;
- the nature and complexity of the fraud suspected.

The chances of success can be improved in any case by:

- making sure that lower class/low intelligence suspects are not overwhelmed;

– having a very senior manager attend as a witness to an interview with a suspect considerably senior to the interviewer.

These measures should ensure that the relationship in the interview is such that the interviewer can maintain the initiative without being overpowering or being overpowered.

The chances of success are further improved when interviews are conducted 'one to one': under no circumstances should a suspect ever be interviewed by more than two people at a time and then the second person should stay out of the suspect's line of sight and should remain silent unless the leading interviewer signals for his assistance.

The problem with having one interviewer acting alone is one of corroboration which can be overcome in one or more of the following ways:

– tape recording the interview;
– taking a written statement;
– writing a file note and having the suspect sign it as correct;
– asking the suspect to repeat his admissions in front of another person.

In the final analysis, the best corroboration of a successful interview is the continued admissions and acceptance of guilt by a suspect, and the tracing of any missing funds—physical evidence which corroborates his admissions.

Interviewer's style

It is impossible to say which techniques will succeed most easily in a particular case (although the odds can be increased by careful preplanning).

It is essential that the interviewer selects and uses techniques with which he feels comfortable and which suit his own personality: forget the tough TV cop image! Most people do not like shouting or getting involved in controversy or arguments and people that do should never be allowed to conduct interviews with suspects.

Successful interviewers are able to create such empathy and confidence that admissions and confessions are almost obligatory. *A low key, professional and persistent style is usually the most effective in all fraud cases.*

However, in most interviews it is essential for the interviewer to state his belief that the suspect is responsible for the fraud, crime or loss in question and to build stress levels to the point where major admissions will be made.

Stages of an interview

Most interviews with suspects follow a predictable pattern as shown in Figure 8.4.

Obviously people have different natural stress levels and some will be terrified at the mere thought of being interviewed. Thus initial nerves cannot

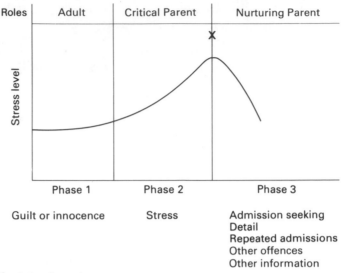

Figure 8.4 Interview phases

be taken as an indication of guilt. Phase 1 should build empathy between the interviewer and the suspect and should make it abundantly clear that the truth is inevitable. Also, if it is not already obvious, questions will be asked in this phase to test the subject's guilt or innocence.

If guilt is likely, phase 2 will build up stress by showing the inevitability of the investigation's outcome until point X is reached. At this point, the suspect will realize that it is in his best interest to confess: voluntarily. The interviewer has to recognize this point and, in phase 3, provide the framework in which the suspect is able to verbalize his guilt.

Techniques for these three phases are discussed later. But the interviewer should preplan how he will handle and phrase stress inducing and admission seeking questions. He should make sure that he feels comfortable with the style chosen and that it fits in with his own personality.

Also at the preplanning stage the interviewer should identify and rehearse techniques that, depending on the evidence available and the character of the suspect, give the greatest chances of success.

Notes and records of interviews

It is important that a full and accurate record of each interview is prepared and retained. Written notes may be taken by the interviewer or a corroborating witness during an interview or immediately afterwards, when the facts are still fresh in his mind.

Taking notes at the time is not recommended simply because it slows down and destroys the flow of an interview and distracts both the subject and the interviewer. Notes made immediately after an interview can be agreed and signed by the people present, including the suspect.

An interview may be tape recorded, with or without the subject's knowledge and the tape and notes made from it may be tendered in evidence, where necessary. It is usually in the best interest of all parties that a tape recording is taken and, to ensure its admissibility, the following procedure is recommended:

- Make sure the interview room is silent with soft sound-absorbing furnishing. Air conditioning and other barely audible noises can completely obliterate a recording and for this reason it is wise to test record and play back before conducting an interview.
- Make sure that the tape recorder is loaded with new batteries.
- Purchase new tape cassettes for the interview and retain the receipt for production in court, if necessary.
- Initial and date each tape immediately prior to loading it into the machine and ask corroborating witnesses to do the same.
- Record on one side of the tape.
- Immediately after the interview has finished, break the recording lugs on both sides of the cassette: this prevents over-recording.
- Take a working copy of each tape as soon as possible: if necessary the copy can be filtered through a spectrum analyser to remove background noise.
- Deliver the original tapes (as soon as possible after the interview has finished) to the company's lawyers and obtain a signed receipt, showing the date and time that the tape(s) were handed over. This should reduce the possibility of accusations that the tape was interfered with.
- Transcribe notes from the copy tapes and check them carefully.

The original tapes should be retained by lawyers until all litigation in connection with the interview has been completed.

General principles of interviews with suspects

The individual techniques described later should be built upon the following main principles. The interviewer should:

- stress that there is limitless time to find the truth;
- take care over the use of emotive words such as 'liar', 'cheat', 'fraud', 'steal', etc., and instead talk about 'not telling the truth', 'losses', 'taken', etc.;
- maintain a logical and calm approach at all times. Do not show signs of temper or frustration. If the suspect makes a major admission the interviewer should not appear surprised or show obvious delight but should say something along the lines 'I'm glad you had the courage to admit to that'. He should then ask further questions of major importance.

- Never underestimate or overestimate a suspect; do not berate or ridicule him.
- Do not engage in humour or sarcasm; remain professional at all times.
- Use language that will be understood by the suspect.
- Give the clear impression that the truth will be discovered.
- Use 'golden nuggets' on past cases to emphasize a point. For example, he might say 'on a similar case I dealt with a couple of years ago . . .'.
- Be absolutely frank with the suspect: if you believe him responsible, say so. If he is not telling the truth, let him know: state anything that 'bothers you'.
- Maintain the initiative throughout the interview and do not let the suspect wander off the point or succeed with obvious lies.
- Keep pencils and note pads out of sight—they will distract both the interviewer and suspect.
- Never try to rush through an interview. If a stage is reached where the interviewer can progress no further he should adjourn for 30 minutes and then try again (rarely will a guilty suspect get up and leave).

Finally, if a full admission is obtained, the suspect should be questioned closely about other frauds. The outcome should be proof of the 'worst case' and not simply the fraud on which there is evidence. *It is also prudent to have admissions repeated as frequently as possible and to establish why the person did what he did and how he felt at the time.* This adds substance to a confession and makes retraction far less likely.

Why people confess to crimes

It is impossible to say what, in the final analysis, causes a person to confess. Over the past five years, analyses of statistics in selected cases suggest which techniques are effective and why. Table 8.5 summarizes the results.

Table 8.5 Reasons for making admissions

Total number interviewed	220
Admissions	195
Percentage	88%
The case could be proved anyway	70%
I wanted to minimize my punishment	40%
I wanted to help the company	10%
I wanted to clear other people	5%
The interviewer trapped me	15%
I felt bad about what I had done	5%
I felt I had no alternative	60%

Ultimately a suspect will do what he believes is in his best interest. It is extremely difficult for a person to lie consistently under persistent and professional interrogation.

Interview techniques

This section outlines the techniques that can be used in interviews with suspects, uncooperative witnesses and informants. To avoid ambiguity, the techniques are written in direct terms. First, it should be stressed that the 'guilty' and 'not guilty' reactions are only general indicators: there will inevitably be exceptions. Secondly, although all of the techniques are legal, they are not necessarily recommended by the author for general application. Finally, it should be stressed that interviews should be conducted fairly and professionally.

Show the exhibits and documentary evidence to the suspect (some highly incriminating ones may be held back until later) and seek his acknowledgement of them. Formal acknowledgement will make it more straightforward to have the document produced in court.

Where a document is of vital significance it should be kept in a transparent document cover. Suspects have been known to try to eat or mutilate them! Never leave a suspect alone in a room with important documents.

Tests of guilt and innocence

1. Arrange incriminating physical evidence, photographs or exhibits prominently, in such a way that the suspect cannot fail to see them.

Not guilty	Guilty
– may not notice – unlikely to ask about them	– will look closely – may comment – if left alone in the room is likely to rummage through them

2. Ask the suspect what he thinks should happen to the thief responsible for the 'blatant fraud'.

Not guilty	Guilty
– usually recommends a hard line – call in the police – may repeat words 'thief' and 'fraud'	– ambivalent – does not wish a 'fuss' to be made – will minimize the crime – unlikely to use emotive words

3. Ask the person whether he thinks the police should be called in.

Not guilty	Guilty
– likely to say 'yes'	– unlikely to say 'yes' – likely to minimize the fraud

4. Outline the evidence in reasonable detail (some major points may be omitted) and imply that the suspect is responsible.

Not guilty	Guilty
– may interrupt and press his views	– will not normally interrupt and will usually defer to the interviewer

5. Point out some, but not all, of the evidence indicating the subject's guilt. He should not be allowed to give an untruthful explanation. The interviewer might say 'just wait a minute, till I've finished'.

Not guilty	Guilty
– unlikely to defer	– will normally defer

6. Point out that you have conducted hundreds of interviews with people in the suspect's position and that you know when people are not telling the truth. Suggest that the subject's behaviour is indicative of guilt.

Not guilty	Guilty
– usually a strong reaction	– usually a poor or low level reaction, often followed by assertions of honour – will usually try to give a non-criminal explanation

7. Obtain full details about the facts, days, events, transactions surrounding the crime in question.

Not guilty	Guilty
– will explain with fairly consistent recollection of facts and detail	– will appear to have inconsistent memory—patchy story. Statements such as 'I can't recall for certain' are indicative of guilt

Guilty subjects will usually try not to get 'pinned down' to explanations that can be used against them later. Answers are likely to lack detail.

8. Ask some questions casually as though the answers were already known.

Not guilty	Guilty
– low level reaction	– nervous reaction – will offer explanation

9. Ask and repeat some questions to which the answers are already known.

Not guilty	Guilty
– reliable, consistent and truthful answers	– deceptive, false or inconsistent answers or admissions of guilt – answers lacking in detail

10. Ask the subject if there is any reason why he should appear totally responsible (or why the evidence points in a particular way).

Not guilty	Guilty
– will not usually change his story – may dispute the facts	– likely to consider – change his story – explain

11. Ask the suspect whether he has ever 'thought' about the crime in question.

Not guilty	Guilty
– No (probably)	– Yes (probably) then ask him to explain further

Note   This apparently strange reaction is straightforward when viewed through the eyes of a criminal. The chances are he has discussed the case with accomplices. He will not give a specific 'no' answer, being fearful that the interviewer may know of these discussions. He is much more likely to keep future options open by admitting that he 'might have discussed' the fraud with someone else. The guilty suspect is likely to state that he cannot remember who he discussed the possibilities with.

12. At various times throughout the interview, show the suspect pieces of incriminating evidence—documents, real evidence, witness statements—and ask for his explanation.

Not guilty	Guilty
– consistent replies	– inconsistent replies – nervous reactions – may accuse witnesses of lying or of trying to 'frame' him – replies lacking in detail – answers such as 'to the best of my knowledge . . .' 'not that I can recall'

13. Repeat indications of responsibility.

Not guilty	Guilty
– denials usually become stronger – consistent explanations	– denials become weaker – inconsistencies – statement such as 'I couldn't have done it' 'there is no evidence' or 'you cannot prove it'

14. If the suspect wanders off the point bring him back to the subject matter directly—'come off it Fred—we don't want to get on to that'.

Not guilty	Guilty
– will continue with his explanation or will object to interference	– will usually defer without objection

15. When the suspect makes assertions such as:

> 'I swear on the Bible that I'm telling the truth'
> 'I have a spotless past record and would not do such a thing'
> 'I'm a very religious man . . . , etc.'

the interviewer should say in the past he has learned that such statements are a direct admission of guilt and that he doesn't care how religious the suspect is: all he is interested in is finding out the truth. Further, that the reasons why the suspect is making such statements is because he knows he is not telling the truth and is dragging religion, etc., into things in order to make a hopeless story more convincing.

16. Ask the subject how he proposes to repay the value stolen.

Not guilty	Guilty
– has no intention of repaying something he has not stolen	– accepts repayment as a possibility – low level reaction – may explain that he has insufficient funds

17. Ask the subject if he would consider resigning.

Not guilty	Guilty
– no	– may discuss the possibility

18. Tell the subject that matters look very serious and that management is considering taking very firm action. Ask him if he would like you to speak on his behalf.

Not guilty	Guilty
– probably a neutral reply	– probably 'yes'

19. Ask the subject whether he thinks Mr X is responsible.

Not guilty	Guilty
– may express an opinion or will not, usually, be too definite	– usually a strong 'no'

Note   These reactions do not apply to organized or violent criminals.

20. Ask the suspect to tell you how he would have committed the crime. Get him to go through exact details step by step and watch for disclosure of facts that only the perpetrator would know. Then ask direct—admission seeking—questions.

Not guilty	Guilty
– normally will not be drawn into such a hypothetical exercise	– will usually discuss – look for the disclosure of facts that only the person responsible would know

21. Observe the subject's reaction generally and his eye contact in particular.

Not guilty	Guilty
– consistent behaviour – may or may not retain good eye contact with the interviewer but is likely to be fairly consistent	– inconsistent behaviour – signs of excessive nervousness – erratic eye contact particularly when he is not telling the truth

Note   Never challenge a suspect's ability to 'look you in the eye'.

Stress inducing questions

1. Ask the subject—at the start of the interview—if he knows why he is being questioned.

Not guilty	Guilty
– will explain	– may explain but is more likely to say 'no'

2. A person who should know why he is being interviewed where, for instance, overt enquiries have been made for some time but replies 'no' should be asked 'but didn't so and so explain to you' or 'weren't you aware of such and such facts'.

Not guilty	Guilty
– will explain what he really knows	– psychological effect on being 'caught out' in a minor lie will shake his confidence

3. Move your chair very close to the suspect (so that you are within his personal space) then ask a question that indicates his guilt is obvious. For example: 'I can see this has been worrying you, how much did you get for the goods?'

Not guilty	Guilty
– usually a low level reaction – may joke about 'pressure'	– will move his chair away – nervous reaction – may confess – may plead illness

4. Ask the subject to be very careful, then point out a fact or piece of evidence that points to his guilt.

Not guilty	Guilty
– will deny, usually very strongly	– will explain

5. Create a verbal vacuum by saying something like 'I know you did . . . if you are not prepared to be absolutely honest with me I suggest you say nothing'. Then interviewer should remain silent.

Not guilty	Guilty
– will usually remain silent	– will break the silence with an explanation

6. At certain points in the interview, the interviewer should say: 'I don't want you to be nervous about what I am going to say'—then reveal facts which indicate the suspect's guilt and ask a direct, admission seeking question.

7. At various times the interviewer should say: 'Would you please repeat that, I am not sure I heard you correctly'.

8. If the suspect shows signs of guilt:

    – acute nervousness
    – fidgeting hands/feet
    – sweating
    – dry mouth and difficulty in swallowing
    – nervous pulses in his neck

point these out to him, either by looking directly at the offending movement or by saying 'this has been bothering you hasn't it . . .' then ask a direct question as though his guilt were beyond all doubt.

9. Repeat 'stress inducing phrases' such as:
   - 'I hope that's true'
   - 'Be careful how you answer this'
   - 'Don't be worried about this, but . . .'
   - 'Take your time: I want you to make sure . . .'

Not guilty	Guilty
·– will not worry	– pensive
– prompt replies	– thoughtful
– detailed replies	– lacking detail

10. Rapidly changing from one major point to another or stopping the interview—at selected points—to take notes increases stress.

Admission seeking questions

1. The suspect should be given a morally acceptable excuse for his crime and told that anyone in his circumstances may have done the same thing. The effect of the crime may be minimized by the interviewer. Accomplices in the crime may be condemned or the company blamed for tempting people into crime.
2. The subject should be urged to tell the truth; the hopelessness of denials should be stressed. Challenge his honour to tell the truth. 'The only decent thing to do . . . take it on the chin, etc.' The effect of continuing with crime (on him and his family) should be pointed out. 'This has to stop somewhere Joe . . . why not make the break now and get off to a fresh start.' It's not the end of the world.
3. Point out that there is limitless time in which to find out the truth and that whatever else happens it is your/the company's intention to get to the bottom of the matter.
4. Against the presssures which society, the company and his family, etc., have put on him, compliment the subject on his intelligence in planning his criminal scheme . . . 'Bad luck that things went wrong . . . wasn't your fault . . . but now is the time to tell the truth . . .'.
5. Ask the suspect the reasons why he committed the crime. Show that you know he did it . . . just seek his motives.
6. Ask the suspect a question in the hope that he will try to mislead you. If he does, lead him on to even greater deception, then disclose the proof you

have. Ask him why he tried to mislead; emphasize the seriousness of not telling the truth and then ask him about a major issue in the case that it is essential for you to prove. Tell him not to let himself down further by not being truthful.

7. Early on, the interviewer should state that he knows the suspect is responsible . . . the evidence is overwhelming. Or he may say 'Our investigations show that you are obviously responsible'. After the assertion the interviewer should say absolutely nothing (the pregnant pause). If the subject speaks (perhaps to explain) it is fairly certain that he will make an admission.

The assertion may be softened with a morally acceptable solution or of an offer of help. 'It's obvious that you are responsible.' 'Shall we act sensibly and try and sort it out?' Or 'The company is taking a very dim view of this: do you want me to speak up on your behalf?'

8. Use levers and wedges.

Great care must be taken to ensure that confessions are not extracted unfairly. However, subject to discussion with litigation lawyers, pressure may be applied to a suspect. The exact nature will vary from case to case but it is acceptable to stress the inevitability of the investigation, its consequences on family and friends, etc.

Untruthful and uncooperative suspects

1. If the suspect says: 'I'm saying nothing . . . you prove it', point out that he has to say nothing, that the people serving on juries are not fools, and when given the chance to offer a reasonable explanation the person says nothing they will draw their own conclusions. The interviewer should then give an actual example of when this happened; when a previous suspect said nothing and how foolish the person looked. If the suspect continues to refuse to answer questions the interviewer should then ask formal questions, pull out his notebook and each time—while the suspect refuses to answer—say: 'To that question Mr X said nothing'. It is extremely difficult for the suspect to remain silent in this situation.

2. Alternatively, the interviewer should terminate the formal interview and the suspect should be engaged in general conversation. If the suspect has been arrested before, he should be asked what he told the police on that occasion, what happened, etc. The interviewer should then gently turn to the current investigation and to questions and statements with which the subject is likely to agree.

3. If the suspect threatens to get up and leave, tell him that he is perfectly entitled to do so. Explain that his unwillingness to face the facts will be unlikely to help him in the long run; that the truth of the case will come out. You should state that you are not prepared to waste time on the

suspect. Then say, 'If you are not prepared to tell me the truth, I suggest you say nothing'.

Note   The guilty subject is most unlikely to walk out. He will also break the silence.

4. If the suspect continues to tell lies, take a written statement from him with all the deceptions in it (the more outrageous the better) then point out how damaging the statement is to him and how foolish it makes him appear. Then offer to let him substitute a fresh statement. But do not destroy the original.
5. A dishonest/deceitful suspect should be asked: 'What would you think if someone told you [repeat his explanation]. You wouldn't believe it, would you?'

Not guilty	Guilty
– no reaction – angry reaction	– pause or 'no'

Counterattacks and responses

Often during an interview a suspect will strongly counterattack. The interviewer should be prepared for this and should not panic or abdicate control (see Table 8.6).

Table 8.6   Counterattacks and responses

Statement by suspect	Reaction by interviewer
'Are you calling me a liar?'	'I have not called you a liar but it is obvious that you are not telling the truth. Now why did you . . .?' (Ask a direct question on a key area)
'That is libel and I am going to get you for this'	'I am not getting involved in what you might not do. Threats will get you nowhere. Now why did you . . .?' (Ask direct question)
'I am going to call my lawyer'	'That's up to you to decide. If you think trying to deceive your lawyer is going to help go ahead. I assure you we are going to find the truth one way or the other'
'You are accusing me'	'I am trying to find the truth and the evidence is perfectly clear . . . what did you do with the money?' (Or another direct question)
'You can't prove that'	'It would be very unsafe for you to jump to that conclusion. We intend to take as much time over this as necessary and believe me, one way or the other, the facts will come out'

Establish the size of the loss

1. Ask the suspect and:
   - agree the date when the fraud started;
   - agree the place where offences took place, e.g., office or safe from which money stolen, address where meeting took place, etc.;
   - agree the average frequency (once a week, etc.);
   - agree the average amount stolen each time;
   - reconfirm the above facts, with the suspect, then get him to agree your calculations of the total amount lost.
2. Seek to recover stolen goods or the 'fruits' of the fraud and always try to trace physical evidence as a result of an interview.

Taking a statement of admission

It is an overriding condition that all admissions against a person's self-interest for use in *criminal proceedings* are voluntary. In various countries, different rules have been set down by the courts to guide police officers and other investigators on the actions that, if followed, will lead a court to accept a confession as having been made without fear or promise, etc. In the UK these guidelines are called the Judges' Rules.

Businessmen, accountants and others—whose main job is not the investigation of crime—do not have to give a caution when they interview a person suspected of crime. But the caution must be given at the appropriate stage by security officers and other people whose job regularly involves crime investigation.

Statements should then be taken down at the person's dictation; he should not be prompted, although questions to remove ambiguities may be asked. He should be asked to read through the statement and should initial all alterations (some mistakes in the body of the statement and initialled by the suspect are not necessarily a bad thing).

The person should write and sign the following declaration at the end of the statement:

> 'I have read the above statement and I have been told that I can correct, alter or add anything I wish. This statement is true, I have made it of my own free will.'

If the person refuses to sign this declaration, a note should be made by the interviewer and signed by him and any witnesses.

The data and time that the statement was commenced, time it was completed and timings of any breaks taken during the writing of the statement should be added to the statement by the investigator.

Conclusions on interviewing

The techniques outlined in this part are legally correct and normally effective. As stated, initially, each organization must decide, in advance, how firm it will be with dishonesty and fraud and be prepared to defend that stance against public scrutiny.

Reviewing investigation results

At or towards the end of an investigation, and before a final report is prepared, evidence should be reviewed by experienced litigation lawyers to determine whether it is sufficient to meet the original objectives. As a result of this review, further enquiries might be necessary.

Report

The final report of the investigation may have to serve a number of different purposes.

For complex cases the report might be structured as follows:
Management overview

- a brief summary of the case and details of the people involved
- recommended action

Chronology

- a detailed diary of events of the fraud, cross-referenced to documentary exhibits

Investigation diary

- a detailed account of steps taken in the investigation including interviews with suspects and third parties

Analysis of documentary exhibits

- detailed explanation of every important entry on all documents

Appendices

- these should consist of copies of the main exhibits, preferably bound separately from the report

The sensitivity of an investigation report is likely to be extremely high and the possible damage, if it were to fall into the wrong hands, immeasurable.

The report should, therefore, be given protection both before, during and after preparation, and should be released only to people who have a genuine need to see it. It should be addressed to the company's legal advisers and, where possible, covered by a clause that establishes its privileged nature.

Where a case is to go forward for prosecution, schedules and exhibits may be arranged in the following order.

ORIGINAL EXHIBITS

- Loose documents should be placed in individual transparent document bags, marked on the outside with the witness's exhibit number.
- Books, computer printouts and other bulky records should be labelled on the outer cover with the exhibit number and name of witness who produced them.
- Physical evidence should be labelled with the name of the witness and exhibit number.

COPY EXHIBITS

These are exhibits that would be given to the jury as working copies and attached to the company's internal report.

- They should be bound into easily manageable folders, interleaved between witnesses' names and arranged in the order that witnesses are to be called to give their evidence.
- They should be indexed by witness and by name of document, i.e.,

    Exhibit Smith 1   page 76
    Sales Invoice 117   page 76

- Schedules should be kept as simple as possible and where comparison between them and supporting exhibits is necessary they should be bound up separately or kept loose.
- Photographs of large real exhibits should be found in separate folders.
- Statements made by the accused person should be included among the original exhibits and should be copied. However, the copies should not be included in the binders for the jury. Only when the admissibility of the statement has been decided by the court should jury copies be handed round. To include a statement in binders is to prejudge its admissibility.
- Witness statements would not normally be issued to the jury, but a number of copies may be required for counsel and for the judge. They should be bound in the same witness order as the exhibits and should be interleaved.

It is essential that copies of exhibits and statements are consistently marked, numbered and labelled. Ideally, numbers should be placed on the plastic envelopes protecting original exhibits and then copied intact, thus guaranteeing consistency of the copies.

Filing papers

When the objectives of an investigation do not call for prosecution, a similar standard of professionalism should be applied to documentation and reporting. Even when the papers are to be filed with no action taken upon them, an accurate fully documented report may prove vital at a later date.

9. Defensive systems

Rule 9:   The easiest way to make money is to stop losing it

If crime is to be controlled, the solution cannot be left to law enforcement bodies of security and police; parents, educators, politicians, and all law abiding people must share the responsibility. But prevention of corporate fraud is a corporate responsibility.

Defensive rationale

In Chapter 1 the factors that motivate criminal behaviour were discussed:

- an opportunity
- an economic or psychological need
- a moral justification
- a low chance of detection

Often defences are concentrated on reducing the opportunities for fraud through physical barriers, procedures and systems. Yet it is surely more efficient to attack the problem on all fronts—reducing the economic and psychological needs, moral justifications and increasing the chances of detection—rather than to rely only on preventive controls. If the causal factors are interdependent, then so are the countermeasures.

In some circumstances, the more elaborate the preventive controls, the more sophisticated the criminals become. Total reliance on before-the-fact controls can lead to a spiralling battle which the victim is almost certain to lose, simply because not all opportunities can be removed and preventive controls cost money.

A balance has to be struck between flexibility of business operation, costs and before-the-fact defences. If controls are too strict, business is interrupted and employees lose interest. If they are too weak, thieves walk straight through them. The balance between prevention and restriction is critical and almost impossible to achieve unless preventive controls are finely tuned and backed up by other measures.

Where a company has a system to detect frauds it can accept lower standards of conventional preventive security. Thieves and employees who see an opportunity will be well aware of their chance of detection should they exploit it. Detection, therefore, serves a deterrent purpose and discriminates against criminals. The threat of detection does not restrict innocent people.

Removal or reduction of the economic or psychological justifications for fraud also allows before-the-fact controls to be relaxed. In an honest, happy and efficient company, opportunities are less likely to be exploited and to be reported when they occur. The interrelationship of before and after-the-fact controls and the climate that a company creates within and radiates externally are vitally important to security and loss control. Remove all opportunities, all motives, and make sure the criminal believes he will get caught and all security problems will be solved. This Utopian solution is, of course, unobtainable but it is possible for companies to work in the right general direction—to attack fraud with an integrated defence.

Defences should be layered and should commit a criminal to a course of criminal conduct for which there is no innocent explanation. This fact should be made obvious to him before he sets out on crime. In fraud, this rationale should not just be restricted to the theft act stage but should apply to misrepresentations, concealments and conversions. The attractiveness of, say, a calculator is not so high if the company's name is engraved indelibly on the case, simply because it becomes more difficult to convert. It puts the criminal at risk if he wishes to dispose of it.

Defences should be viewed from the position of a would-be thief—the rule is to 'think like a thief', first to identify his opportunities and secondly to devise controls that will deter him.

Security on a day-to-day basis can succeed only if controls are totally self-enforcing or if all employees:

– understand the risks in the areas in which they operate;
– know what the company's security objectives are;
– know what is expected of them;
– have confidence in the adequacy and consistency of controls;
– understand that non-compliance will be penalized.

The starting point in all cases is formation of company policy.

Company policy and strategy of control

The culture of an organization is set by top management. When the directors are themselves less than honest or tolerate unacceptable standards of behaviour, employees at all levels are more easily able to justify their own transgressions.

It is essential for top management to define standards which it expects the company to follow. Emphasis should be placed on the word 'follow', for management itself should lead.

Further, the impression that a company creates with outsiders has a direct bearing on its exposure to fraud. Where a company is seen to have sloppy controls and disinterested staff it is tempting others to steal its assets. A company that is in reality efficient and vigilant and gives the clear perception of being so, is far less likely to attract thieves and far more likely to detect them.

Senior management is responsible for setting the framework, for allocating resources, and for creating the environment in which controls can work effectively (see Figure 9.1).

Figure 9.1 Framework of effective security

Strategy can be implemented in the following ways:

- Company-wide procedures, based on an effective policy.
- Setting standards of minimum security at all company locations.
- Specific additional controls in individual areas, commensurate with special risks.

These, which can be considered as mechanics of control, are described later.

Security policy should be determined by senior management and issued to all employees. It should cover the following aspects.

RESPONSIBILITIES FOR SECURITY

Policy should clearly assign responsibilities. Security is a line management obligation, and this fact should be made clear on all job descriptions. In larger organizations, line managers may be assisted by a specialist corporate security adviser or external consultant, but this should not detract from the prime responsibility of line managers to maintain proper security over the operations and assets with which they are entrusted.

In larger organizations, a corporate security adviser should be responsible for:

- risk analysis
- setting security standards and objectives
- investigations
- compliance auditing

- liaison with authorities
- physical security surveys
- advising on and centralizing the purchase of security hardware and services
- security education and training programmes

He should report directly to a member of the board and preferably to the chairman or financial director. Under no circumstances should corporate security report to personnel or general line management simply because the interests of these functions often conflict with security. The most senior member of management is in the *only* position to determine the relative priority of security against other issues.

The choices that an organization has for professional security advice are summarized on Figure 9.2 and the final decision needs to be made with care.

In some cases, even when a professional security adviser has been appointed, help from specialist consultants is justified; for example, to review computer security or to assist in a major investigation.

Clearly, external consultants are placed in an exceptional position of trust and their appointment should be handled along the following lines:

1. Before approaching consultants, the services required should be carefully defined: preferably in a written assignment specification.
2. A list of consulting firms that have an established track record in conducting the type of work required should be prepared.
3. Trade and business references should be taken up for short-listed firms.
4. A director or senior partner of the consulting firm should be interviewed so that exactly what is wanted may be explained to him. The potential client should listen carefully to what the consultant says. He may suggest different lines of approach to those originally identified. These should be carefully considered.
5. If first impressions are favourable, the consultants should be asked to prepare a written proposal containing:

   - a list of the firm's resources and skills;
   - details of the services to be provided and the time required to perform them;
   - the names and qualifications of the staff who will be used on the assignment, with an indication of the part they will play;
   - an outline method of approach and fee budget;
   - names and addresses of at least two previous clients and permission to contact them.

6. A written contract should be signed by the client and the consulting firm. This should include a confidentiality clause, terms of payment and timetables.

Responsibility for security laid to:	Advantages	Disadvantages	Suitability
AN EMPLOYEE			
– existing business manager, without previous security experience; either full or part time	– low cost – familiar with company culture and procedures	– not professional advice, may not be cost effective, will tend to be hardware and equipment orientated; possibly not a defence in depth – may not be committed to security ideals and may be looking to a career outside security; because of this may not be independent of business lines – requires extensive training in security – may not be accepted by law enforcement bodies, other companies' security advisers probably unable to conduct investigations; may not be taken 'seriously' by other employees, particularly dishonest ones	– small companies with minor security risks – branches of a multiple company to support a professional corporate security adviser
– retired government official trained in security but with little commercial experience	– needs commercial training in security subjects – low cost – independent (i.e., should have unbiased approach to fraud and other investigations)	– may need extensive training in commercial subjects and practices – may be seen as a 'private police force' and may be unable to integrate into the company or become acceptable to other managers – may be inflexible and unable to learn – may be looking for a 'quiet life' after a distinguished first career	– small or medium companies – careful selection of the 'right' candidate – under day-to-day control and guidance of senior business manager
– trained security adviser recruited from another company	– needs little or no training in technical security subjects or commercial operations – low or medium cost	– may have a preconceived and unvarying approach to security based upon his experience with previous employers – may be in a conflict of interests situation	– possibly the most cost effective source of corporate security advice for major companies
A CONSULTANT			
– external security consultant	– low cost – independent and cost conscious – results orientated – fully trained in best methods and experienced in their application	– may have conflicting interests in the supply of security services/hardware/insurance; the consultant should be free of all such ties – may not be available when required because of the demands of other clients – needs regular contact with company manager(s)	– most cost effective answer for small and medium sized companies – useful external advice and security audit for major companies – careful selection is necessary

Figure 9.2 Professional security: sources

7. The client should decide which employees will work with the consultants. It is advisable to appoint a senior manager who, if necessary, can call for detailed advice from subordinates.

The benefits to be obtained from using specialist consultants are shown on Figure 9.2.

BUDGETS FOR SECURITY AND CONTROLS

Department and other senior managers should be required to budget for security. The budget should include the cost of implementing company-wide procedures as well as security improvements, consulting services and manpower (such as security guards).

Costs of disclosed losses, frauds and defalcations should be charged to the budgets of the appropriate managers and credit should be given for recoveries. Performance against security budgets should be taken into account in assessing managers for salary and promotion purposes.

The corporate security adviser should be provided with a central budget for special projects and company-wide controls.

MINIMUM STANDARDS OF PROTECTION

Senior managers in conjunction with the corporate security adviser or external consultants, should determine the minimum standards of protection required at all company facilities.

This might include company-wide procedures on:

- recruitment and pre-employment screening
- conflicts of interest
- classification and protection of information
- reporting of incidents
- conduct of investigations
- computer security
- contingency planning

as well as minimum standards of physical security and access control.

CONDUCT OF INVESTIGATIONS

The policy should state the company's intention to prosecute all cases of suspected dishonesty, to make reports to the police and to seek restitution. It should also set out the obligation of all employees to cooperate in internal and police investigations.

A sample security policy is found in Appendix C.

Company-wide procedures

Management policy on security can be implemented, to a large extent through the following company-wide procedures.

EMPLOYEE SELECTION

It is in the best interests of any organization to select and retain honest, efficient and suitable employees.

Selection should not be confused with recruitment. Whereas recruitment is concerned with attracting applications, selection involves making a choice. The costs involved in choosing the wrong candidate are enormous. Research carried out in 1963 by the Sales Executive Club of New York established that the average cost of hiring and training a salesman was $8289 and that almost half the recruits left their employers before the end of their first year. These obvious costs to the employer in selecting an unsuitable employee are the beginning, not the end of the problem.

Security problems and requirements in employee selection

Statistics indicate that many enterprises engage staff without making even the most elementary checks into their background or suitability.

Accurate figures are not available to show the true rates of criminal recidivism, although there have been cases where people who have been convicted of serious criminal offences have been exposed to further temptation simply because the company hiring them failed to check.

Perhaps the most alarming example concerned the killer, Graham Young. This man had been convicted of poisoning his parents and was sentenced to life imprisonment in a mental institution. Some years later he was released on parole and sent to work in a paint factory just outside London. His background did not come to the attention of his new employers—indeed, they did not even know he was on parole. The result? A number of his fellow employees were poisoned. Young was imprisoned again for life.

Professor Derek McClintock of Edinburgh University reports that, in the UK, one man in three and one woman in eight will be convicted of a criminal offence at some time in their lives. A study by the Sperry Rand Corporation on 6398 job applications between July 1960 and 1969 in the USA showed the results set out in Table 9.1.

The table shows that over 10 per cent of the job applicants had major derogatory data in their backgrounds, including convictions for serious criminal offences.

These statistics do not imply that people who have been previously convicted of a criminal offence should not be employed. But with certain exceptions, brought about in the UK by the Rehabilitation of Offenders Act, a company has the right to evaluate the risk it is taking. The employer also has a responsibility to existing employees to ensure that their safety and welfare is not prejudiced by the employment of undesirable people.

From the job applicant's point of view, it is better that his background should be known and verified. When a person is engaged without his record being known he is constantly at risk of blackmail and in fear that he might lose his job should the true facts come to light.

Perhaps some employers place too much weight on the absence of a criminal conviction as a qualifying factor in employment. Experience suggests that large corporate losses often arise from first-time offenders.

Couple this fact with society's obligation to rehabilitate criminals and the value of conviction records as a predictive factor in employment screening can be put into its proper context. It is one of many considerations.

Possibly more dangerous than the convicted criminal in the long run is the job applicant who falsifies his educational qualifications or job experience. What have been termed 'degree mills' offer unqualified people apparently genuine qualifications on payment of a fee. The *Sunday Times* gave a detailed

Table 9.1 Reasons for rejecting job applicants

Applicant category	Total investigations	Major derog.	Minor derog.	Total and %	
Shop and office	3228	369	132		
Technical	2665	185	72		
Management	420	50	26		
Miscellaneous	85	10	7		
Totals	6398	614	237		
False employment information		28	15	43	5.05
Previous record of job hopping		12	0	12	1.40
Unexplained gaps in employment		3	1	4	0.47
False information, education, military, etc.		138	11	149	17.50
Dishonourable discharge		4	0	4	0.47
Criminal record		103	29	132	15.51
Alcoholism		32	0	32	3.76
Drug addiction		0	0	0	0.00
Sexual perversion		9	0	9	1.05
Unsatisfactory employment		185	101	286	33.60
Physical and mental illness		30	3	33	3.76
Coercion or hostage		7	5	12	1.40
Fighting or uncontrolled temper		3	0	3	0.35
Subversive record		10	0	10	1.17
Poor credit risk		36	7	43	5.05
Company disloyalty		8	6	14	1.65
Miscellaneous		6	59	65	7.63
		614	237	851	100.00

Source: Timothy J. Walsh, Harris and Walsh New York, 'The case for applicant investigations', *Industrial Security Magazine*, October 1966.

exposé of these so-called universities, of which there are some 27 in Britain alone and another 180 worldwide. The *Sunday Times* report stated:

> Some degree mills offer a BA for as little as £28 and a PhD for £56. For £100 one enterprising college will bestow the title of Professor Emeritus. The scale of charges at Britain's leading degree mill 'Sussex College of Technology' is a little higher, BA—£80, MA—£98, doctorate—£120, and PhD—£155.

An American company offers Master Mariner certificates for as little as £10.

Table 9.2 Reasons for falsification of application forms

Reason for faking	Total reasons (%)	Most important reason (%)
1. It is probably possible to tell what the employer is looking for, and in order to get the job I will answer the questions in such a way as to appear favourable in the eyes of the employer.	39.7	47.2
2. It is probably not possible to tell which answer is really the honest one. Of those that are more or less honest I will pick the one that will present the most favourable picture of myself.	18.6	20.7
3. It seems that everyone else will fake so I must also if I want the job.	16.6	9.2
4. The employer has no right to know the honest answer so I will fake.	5.2	5.6
5. A certain answer is more socially desirable, apart from any personal quality needed to get the job, and I will fake in order to present myself as socially valued and an acceptable person.	19.6	17.3

Issued by the Republic of Minerva, they could enable an unqualified seaman to become the master of a super tanker. The applicant's previous job and educational records are the foundation on which any salary offer is built. Yet evidence shows that a number of job applicants will deliberately falsify their backgrounds. Research carried out by R. H. Larson and D. M. Swarthort for their MA thesis at Michigan State University suggested the main reasons for falsification of application forms (see Table 9.2).

During the 1972 American Presidential election, it was alleged that a chauffeur had infiltrated the Democratic headquarters to pick up secret information. How successful infiltration has been in industry is a matter of conjecture, but it would appear to be relatively easy to penetrate most companies' security systems simply by applying for employment.

The differential association theory mentioned in Chapter 1 may have spin-offs that did not form part of the original work of Sutherland. He submitted that where in a closed society a person perceived a balance of criminality over good then he too would be tempted towards crime. There is another choice open to the person put in an environment where criminality pervades and that is to leave it—to get out before he too becomes involved. The dishonest employees in a company are likely to corrupt the good ones or to force them to leave.

Another reason for checking on the job applicant is consistency. What is the point of building sophisticated security barriers to keep out undesirable third parties if employment practices allow equally unknown third parties unrestricted access simply because they happen to apply to work for the company or are sent along by an employment agency?

A company should not be ashamed of checking the background of potential employees—provided, of course, that care is taken not to infringe civil liberties or to discriminate unfairly on grounds of race, religion, colour and, now in the UK, sex.

For these five reasons:

- protection of existing employees
- selection of truly the best applicant
- protection of assets and information
- creation and maintenance of an honest company culture
- consistency

an employer should select employees with care.

Legal restraints and requirements

Laws governing privacy and access to government information vary from country to country but generally there is no prohibition on an employer making the most rigorous checks into the background of a potential employee.

A job applicant must take cognizance of the law. If he attempts to gain employment by way of a false application form or oral misrepresentation then he may be at risk of prosecution. If the deception does not come to light until after he has been engaged, employment may be terminated.

Previous employers and others who are called on to supply references must also be aware of the law. In most countries laws of slander (verbal, untrue and malicious statements) and libel (malicious and untrue written statements) have to be considered.

However, genuine commercial references may be privileged and a referee has little to fear in providing an honest reference, even if it is derogatory.

The nature and limitations of pre-employment checks

The reasons for checking into the job applicant's background are clear and generally accepted, although the degree and depth of check seem to vary from company to company and country to country.

Checks fall into one of two types. The first, and most common, examines the applicant's background and past performance so that a judgement on how he will perform in the future can be made. On the face of things this may seem a logical approach—the leopard does not change his spots. How distinct the spots depends on the contrast with their environment.

The environment in which the applicant has lived and worked will have an effect on his recorded reputation. Unfortunately, social class and colour may influence the previous record of a job applicant.

Although statistics to illustrate discrimination on grounds of social class are rare, research conducted by Wolfgang and Cohen, 1972,* involving 1698 people, biased towards the upper socio-economic class, showed that two-thirds of all men interviewed and one in ten of women had committed a serious criminal offence without being arrested. The studies indicated that people in the lower socio-economic groups were most likely to be prosecuted and convicted.

The effects of race and colour are more clear cut. In the USA it is accepted by the courts that the use of arrest records in selection unfairly discriminates against black people—since a larger proportion live in high crime, ghetto areas and are more likely to be arrested (*Gregory* v. *Litton*). To what extent the same bias applies in Europe—if at all—has still to be established.

Another factor which can mislead is the policy of the company for whom a job applicant has previously worked. Some companies refuse to prosecute or report internal crimes to the police. Others, for fear of libel action, will not give derogatory references; yet others will not dismiss but instead will allow a thief to resign. Thus, the policy of previous employers will determine how accurately good or detrimental information is recorded against a person's name. In one company a thief may be allowed to resign; in another company, for exactly the same offence, another man may be prosecuted and imprisoned. Their behaviour has been the same, but their records are entirely different.

For these reasons, past records should not be taken as an infallible measure of future performance or as a reliable means of choice between candidates.

The second type of pre-employment check, which tries to evaluate the 'inner man', is based on psychological tests and responses.

Although psychological analysis has a sound scientific base and may predict future performance and behaviour with acceptable accuracy, it is not a tool generally used in pre-employment screening. The reasons for this vary from cost to social acceptability. Thus, on one hand, historical checks can be unreliable and, on the other, possibly more meaningful methods are unacceptable.

Given this general background, what can an employer do to ensure that job applicants are suitable, honest and trustworthy, and will fit into the organization?

In the final analysis, the course chosen by any organization will depend on the sensitivity of its operation and on its culture and management style.

* *Crime and Race*, Institute of Human Relations Press.

Management policy

Pre-employment checks should never be carried out other than under the full authority of the board of the company concerned; neither should checking go beyond what is laid down in the policy. Policy should consider the following questions.

1. What should be the extent of the pre-employment screening programme?

   - Should it apply to all employees?
   - Should it apply to temporary staff?
   - Should it apply to contractors' staff, particularly cleaners?
   - Should checks be made on existing employees prior to internal promotions?

2. Who should administer the programme?
3. What vital factors should be checked?
4. Should different checks be made according to the importance and criticality of the job?
5. What areas cannot be checked?
6. How should the vital checks be made?

Company policy should be based on the answers to these questions. The policy should be brought to the attention of management and, where appropriate, discussed with union and staff representatives.

Definition of job categories

The next step, within management policy, is to define the qualities and qualifications required for, and the sensitivity of, each job within the organization.

The following points should be considered for each job:

1. The exact description and title.
2. The essential educational and professional qualifications and job skills.
3. The sensitivity of the job and the potential to damage the company through fraud, sabotage or dishonesty.
4. The highest position that an outstanding incumbent could be expected to reach during his career.
5. The derogatory data that would debar employment in the particular position and in the highest position to which the applicant might aspire.
6. The protective or legal agreements that are necessary.
7. Whether agency or temporary staff might be allowed to fill the job.

This should help to identify high risk jobs.

Application forms

All job applicants should be required to complete an application form. The questions asked on it should be aimed at collecting all the information required to verify suitability and honesty of the candidate.

For the most critical positions a detailed application form is essential. For positions of low sensitivity another form may be used which requires less detail. Application forms should be designed and laid out with care; questions for their own sake or padded application forms impress no one. For each question, the person drawing up the application form should satisfy himself on the following points.

1. Is the question necessary to identify the applicant?
2. Is the question necessary to assess his qualifications, suitability, experience, honesty or reliability?
3. Is the question fair and unambiguous?
4. Is the question legal? Has the company the right to ask it?
5. Will the information be used? Is it capable of being checked?
6. Will the result of the check have a bearing on the selection of the applicant?
7. Are all the questions on the form based upon an analysis of the job in question and on its sensitivity?

A genuine applicant will not resent completing a detailed form. People who have something to hide may show more reluctance and fail to pursue their applications, perhaps alleging that the forms intrude upon their privacy or civil liberties. However viewed, a detailed application form can only benefit the company and its existing employees.

The questions most frequently asked on employment forms (taken from British and American surveys) are listed on Table 9.3 (page 334), together with the likely decisions based on replies to background checks.

Table 9.3 Questions frequently asked on employment applications forms

Percentage of forms asking question	Information	Finding	Decision Management	Others
	Identification details			
100	Full name	False	Reject	Reject
17	Previous names	False	Reject	Reject
100	Sex	False	Reject	Reject
74	Date of birth	False	Reject	Reject
33	Place of birth	False	Reject	Reject
15	Citizenship	False	Reject	Reject
2	Passport number	False	Explain	Explain
22	Social security number	False	Explain	Explain
11	Physical description	False	Explain	Explain
9	Enclose current photograph	Wrong person	Reject	Reject
100	Current address	False	Reject	Reject
40	Years at address	False	Confront	Explain
15	Previous address	False/omit	Explain	Explain
37	Home telephone number	False	Explain	Explain
26	Person to contact in emergency	Does not exist	Reject	Reject
	Education			
20	Names of schools attended	False	Reject	Reject
20	Dates of attendance	False/wrong	Confront	Explain
20	Name of university attended	False	Reject	Reject
20	Dates of attendance	False/wrong	Confront	Explain
100	Qualifications obtained	False/inflated	Reject	Reject
30	Name of teacher to whom reference can be made	Never existed	Reject	Reject
	Results of checks made by company			
	– Unexplained gaps in schooling		Explain	Explain
	– Record of insubordination		Consider	Consider
	– Record of violence/theft		Confront	Confront
	– Record of drug abuse/alcoholism		Confront	Confront
	– Record of truancy		Confront	Confront
	Financial information			
15	*Total family income	False	Confront	Explain
15	*Regular monthly outgoings	False	Confront	Explain
15	*Name and address of banker	False	Reject	Reject
7	*Credit cards held	False	Confront	Confront
9	*Names/addresses of creditors	False	Confront	Confront
	+ *Results of company checks into financial position*			
	*Excess of outgoings over salary offered		Reject	Reject
	*Unreliable credit record		Reject	Reject

Table 9.3—*Continued*

Percentage of forms asking question	Information	Finding	Decision Management	Others
	Miscellaneous information			
11	*Details of criminal convictions	Disclosed		
	*Serious within past 5 years	Disclosed	Reject	Reject
	*Serious over 5 years	Disclosed	Consider	Consider
	*Minor or juvenile (not repeated)	Disclosed	Accept	Accept
	*Serious within past 5 years	Undisclosed	Reject	Reject
	*Other	Undisclosed	Reject	Reject
	Personal and family			
20	*Personal referees	Derogatory	Confront	Confront
13	*Wife's employment			
	*With competitor	Disclosed	Consider	Consider
	*With competitor	Undisclosed	Reject	Reject
24	*Membership of clubs, hobbies	False	Consider	Explain
40	*Membership of trade union, professional ass.	False	Confront	Confront
20	*Possession of driving licence	False	Reject	Reject
0	*Other company directorships or possible conflicts of interest	Disclosed	Consider	Consider
		Concealed	Reject	Reject
	Family			
39	*Marital status	False	Reject	Reject
20	*Number of children	False	Explain	Explain
15	*Names of children	False	Explain	Explain
17	*Dates of children's birth	False	Explain	Explain
15	*Number of dependants	False	Explain	Explain
9	*Date and place of marriage	False	Confront	Confront
7	*Wife's maiden name	False	Confront	Confront
11	*Wife's date of birth	False	Explain	Explain
4	*Details of previous marriages	False	Confront	Explain
4	*Names and addresses of parents	False	Confront	Confront
	+ *Company checks into family background*			
	*Unstable family or relationships		Reject	Reject
	Housing			
17	*Owned/rented/furnished	False	Reject	Confront
7	*Name and address of landlord	False	Confront	Explain
	+ *Company checks into house ownership*			
	False or derogatory information		Confront	Confront

Table 9.3—*Continued*

Percentage of forms asking question	Information	Finding	Decision Management	Others
	Employment history			
43	Name/address of present employer	False	Reject	Reject
24	Length of employment	False	Confront	Confront
61	Work responsibilities	False	Explain	Explain
31	Salary record	False	Confront	Confront
10	Name of company referee	Derogatory	Reject	Reject
20	Reasons for leaving previous employers			
	= resignation	False	Reject	Reject
	= redundant	False	Reject	Reject
	= dismissed	True	Explain	Explain
	+ *Company checks on employment*			
	Job hopping		Confront	Explain
	Unexplained gaps in employment		Confront	Confront
	Unsatisfactory performance		Confront	Confront
	Company disloyalty/ subversion/dishonesty/ insubordination		Reject	Reject
	Undisclosed covenants not to compete with previous employers		Reject	
	Health			
20	Physical disabilities affecting job	Concealed Disclosed	Reject Consider	Reject Consider
11	Name/address of doctor	False	Explain	Explain
11	Surgical operations	Concealed	Explain	Explain
	+ *Company checks of health* Undisclosed information affecting job performance		Confront	Confront

* Based on research by J. M. Carroll in *Sources of Information*, Security World Publishing Co., California.

Column 1 shows the percentage of companies that ask the sort of question shown in column 2, for example 17% of the companies surveyed ask applicants to state their previous names.

Column 3 sets out what the adverse answer to a question, or the adverse result of a check might be and column 4 the likely acceptance or rejection decision depending on the type of vacancy concerned and its sensitivity divided, generally, into management or labour.

The decision whether to accept or reject an application will, of course, be determined under the general policy of the company concerned.

False replies to questions on the application form or undisclosed derogatory data can, in our view, be placed on an acceptance or rejection scale as shown on Table 9.4.

Table 9.4 Decisions on derogatory information

Reject	Confront	Consider	Explain	Accept
– False material information on the application				Totally honest reply
– Concealed derogatory data				

Thus important derogatory factors or false answers should result in rejection or a serious discussion (*confront*) with the applicant in order to resolve the question concerned. The shades of these decision possibilities are shown in columns 4 and 5 on Table 9.3.

Application forms should also set out some words of caution. Many applicants do not realize the serious criminal implications of false declarations and it is in everyone's interests to clarify the position.

A recommended form of wording is set out below.

'Thank you for your interest in ABC Limited. It is a very special company; we care very much about our employees, customers and suppliers and we intend to maintain the very highest professional standards throughout the organization. If you join us, we are sure that you will agree with our philosophy and with our professional objectives.

Because we intend to maintain these high standards, coupled with close and friendly team work, we must have absolute honesty in all of our dealings. There can be no secrets between members of our team and no surprises. For this reason, we urge you to complete the form fully and accurately. Take your time and if you have any questions or problems, please ask us. Do not put down information unless you are sure it is correct.

The fact that something may have happened in your past that you now regret, need not debar your employment with us. But we do need to know where we stand and to be absolutely honest with each other.

Before starting work with us, we will need to see your birth certificate . . ., etc.

Good luck; we hope to have you working with us.'

The closing certificate, signed by the applicant, reads as follows:

> 'I certify that the above replies are true, complete and correct. I know that it is a criminal offence to attempt to obtain employment by deception and that any misrepresentation of a material fact will be cause for cancellation of consideration, or dismissal.'

A clear, comprehensive and well structured application form is essential. In some cases, companies have two forms. The first is a general background form and the other a 'security clearance' supplement.

Method of checking application forms

Consideration should be given, at the policy formation stage, as to how details shown on application forms can be verified. The most common methods, their advantages and disadvantages are summarized on Table 9.5.

Table 9.5   Methods of verifying information

Method	Major disadvantages	Effectiveness rating (relative order)	Cost rating (relative order)	Speed (relative order)
Written references	– do not check in depth – libel implications – easily forged	6	1	2
Telephone references	– do not check in depth – slander implications	7	2	2
Personnel department interviews	– subjective/inconsistent – do not check in depth – easily overcome	8	3	1
Polygraph examination	– social/moral implications – privacy and civil liberties issues – effect on candidate	3	4	3
Psychological testing	– unacceptable except for the most senior staff	4	7	2
PSE examination	– social/moral/privacy and civil liberties problems – not tested to reliability – need qualified analyst	5	5	3
Handwriting analysis	– not generally accepted as reliable	4	6	2
Weighted application blanks	– reliability not proved	5	3	1
Positive vetting	– confrontation situation	1	7	8
Investigation	– slow	2	6	7

Note   1 = best, most cost effective or fast.

In most cases, where the job concerned is sensitive or important, organizations would be well advised to pass responsibility for background checking to an outside agency. The advantages of this are:

- it relieves management of a burden usually outside its area of skill;
- the agency should have the ability to check in depth, if necessary using 'field visits', direct and indirect techniques;
- external checking is usually more cost effective and thorough;
- should the agency fail, responsibility for negligence can be claimed. Under these circumstances the employer may be able to make substantial recoveries.

However, should an organization decide to keep the programme completely 'in house', we suggest the following procedure in addition to the normal recruitment and personnel action.

Interviews and follow up

1. When a candidate attends a preliminary interview, he/she should be given an application form and should be told that because of:

   - the importance of the position concerned
   - the fact that a suitable applicant can expect rapid promotion
   - fidelity or other insurance requirements

   his/her background has to be thoroughly checked.
2. The candidate should be asked to complete the application form in full and return it to the recruiting manager as soon as possible. He/she should be told that if his/her name is added to the short list, he or she will be required to produce originals of his or her birth certificate, driving licence, passport, educational and professional qualifications as well as a current photograph.

   It should be explained that derogatory information in a candidate's background may not debar him/her from employment providing he/she declares it honestly and openly on an application form. However, he/she should be cautioned that any attempt to mislead will be uncovered and could lead to serious consequences.
3. When a short list has been prepared, written references should be taken up and the candidate asked to attend a further interview and to bring his/her certificates and other papers with him/her.
4. After any second interview by personnel, and if the candidate is generally suitable, he/she should be asked to attend a further 'briefing' with the company's security adviser.

Security interview

The security adviser (or a member of personnel department responsible for security) should see the candidate alone in a quiet room.

The interviewer should explain the company's policy on business and professional ethics and the reasons why backgrounds of short-listed candidates have to be checked.

1. The interviewer should ask to inspect all of the candidate's certificates looking closely for:

    − alterations of names, dates, particularly on photocopies
    − additions
    − differences from details shown on application form

    He should verify the following aspects:
    (a) From the applicant's birth certificate:

    − verify full names
    − verify date and place of birth
    − verify parents' name

    (b) From the applicant's passport:

    − verify citizenship
    − confirm date and place of birth
    − identify from photograph
    − note overseas visits and visas
    − note signature
    − note children's and spouse's names
    − note height, colour of hair and eyes
    − note occupation

    (c) From the applicant's marriage certificate:

    − verify date and place of marriage
    − verify full names
    − verify spouse's name
    − verify spouse's date and place of birth

    (d) From the applicant's driving licence:

    − check validity and endorsements
    − confirm full name and signature

The interviewer should then ask the candidate's permission to take and retain photocopies of all documents and certificates.

The interviewer should then work through the application form line by line, trying to 'flesh out' and add details to the replies given. He/she should be on the look out for:

- obvious attempts to mislead
- conflicting answers
- acute nervousness over a particular question or subject
- answers lacking in detail or depth
- unexplained gaps in employment
- unwillingness to answer or be 'pinned down' to facts
- highly emotional reactions

Any of these symptoms should be brought to the attention of the candidate, in a relaxed and friendly way, and further explanations sought.

For highly technical jobs consideration should be given to the possibility of conducting an 'aptitude test' rather than merely relying on recorded information, certificates and past references.

External verification

The application form and all supporting detail including copy documents should be passed to a security adviser or external investigator who by telephone contact and personal visits should check all or some of the following records.

1. Inspect rating or housing list or building society register:

   - confirm house ownership
   - note valuation of house (rating)
   - note name and address of landlord

2. Contact last school or university:

   - verify dates of attendance
   - verify course(s) attended and qualifications, *as well as the status of college*
   - verify reputation
   - check with named teacher or tutor

3. Visit the last (or last but one, if still employed) employer, telephone and write to previous employers for past 10 years or since the age of 18, whichever is the shorter:

   - verify duration of employment
   - confirm photographic identification
   - verify work responsibilities
   - verify position held and promotion obtained
   - verify salary record
   - verify reasons for leaving

- check sickness record
- check family background and details
- check eligibility for re-employment
- check reputation for work, honesty, reliability, stability
- check absence of covenants not to compete/existing legal agreement
- check prior employment from previous employer's records
- check educational qualifications
- examine previous employer's file of application forms and work reports
- check with, if possible, a named manager or supervisor

4. Contact doctor:

- verify health record
- verify surgical records
- verify family numbers and names

5. Contact bankers:

- verify financial stability
- verify outgoings and income
- check credit rating

6. Write to credit card companies:

- verify financial stability

7. Check with neighbours:

- verify family details
- verify spouse's occupation
- verify dates of residency
- check reputation/family stability
- note other background information

8. Check electoral roll:

- confirm residency
- confirm family name
- note other occupiers of address
- note names of immediate neighbours

9. Check telephone directory:

- confirm telephone number

Acceptance or rejection decisions

If answers given on the application form do not tie into the results of these checks the candidate should be asked to attend a further interview (or the interviewer should arrange to see him at home) and he/she should be closely questioned about the discrepancies.

Based on these external checks and interviews a brief clearance report should be submitted to the personnel or other manager who will take the decision to hire or reject. A copy of the report should be retained in a confidential security file.

Comments on the recommended system

The system outlined may, at first, seem tedious and off-putting. It works extremely efficiently in practice and does not deter suitable applicants. In fact many candidates have said they were encouraged by the efficiency and thoroughness of organizations using this method.

The cost, whether through an outside agency or internally, works out at less than £100 per applicant; a small cost to pay considering the down side possibilities of poor selection and the investment that the company will make in the candidate.

PERSONNEL POLICIES AND PROCEDURES

Fair, open and efficient personnel procedures have a major effect on a company's exposure to fraud.

Job descriptions

All job descriptions and contracts of employment should contain a section on security responsibilities. As a minimum, they should state:

> ... is responsible for maintaining security over all aspects of his work and for compliance with company security policy and procedures. Failure to observe these policies and procedures will be subject to disciplinary action.

In addition, job descriptions should allow all employees to discuss matters of a security nature with the corporate security adviser without reference to their normal line management.

For particularly sensitive jobs, contracts of employment should refer specifically to compliance with policies on conflicts of interest, assignment of patents, etc.

Legal agreements

Reference was made in the discussion of pre-employment screening to legal agreements with employees. The agreements most commonly encountered in industry are given in Table 9.6.

Table 9.6 Agreements with employees

Type of agreement	Purpose
Conflict of interest	To restrict an employee from entering into a second job whose interests might conflict with those of the company
Patents	To assign all inventions and patents discovered and designed by an employee to the employer
Secrecy	To prevent the employee from dislosing sensitive company information
Non-competitive	To prevent the employee—on termination—from joining a competitor or from setting up his own company
Search consent	To require the employee to submit to search (both personal and vehicles) when entering or leaving company premises
Termination agreements	To ensure that the employee has returned all company property and information prior to termination

Clearly agreements of the sort described in Table 9.6 do not prevent the employee from doing anything. The existence of a conflicts of interest agreement does not physically prevent an employee from starting up his own company and selling goods to his employer's customers. Legal agreements are essentially after-the-fact controls; they give the company the right of redress should a person commit an act detrimental to its interests. Their use is therefore limited, but they can serve a deterrent purpose. They draw the employee's attention to a course of conduct which he knows he should not embark upon and they deny him the chance to provide a plausible excuse for dishonesty. The ex-employee who retains company records can have little excuse when his termination agreement is shown to him or read over to a court.

Laws in some countries prevent agreements being used. For example, in the UK restrictive covenants on termination of employment are usually limited in scope and duration. Further, some agreements involve labour laws and practices—search consents are not generally used in Europe. So where a company believes that a certain type of legal agreement might be beneficial, it should first check that its introduction would be lawful and an acceptable labour practice.

Legal agreements with suppliers, customers and other business contacts can make a direct contribution to reducing the opportunities for misrepresentative frauds and particularly corruption. Agreements that give audit or other inspection rights may serve to deter market diversions, bribery, corruption and other external frauds. Obviously the time to negotiate such agreements is at or before normal commercial arrangements are concluded, when the supplier or customer is anxious to close the business.

Employee education

Another element in creating the right climate is to lay down—without ambiguity—the practices that will be tolerated and those that will not. A clear line should be drawn between acceptable business conduct, short cuts and fraud, so that an employee who oversteps the line cannot claim it was done by mistake.

Further, those acts which are considered to be criminal offences should be brought to the notice of all staff. The line should be drawn between what is considered a bribe and what can be accepted as a genuine gift or perk.

Corruption and exposing oneself to suspicion of corruption are almost equal sins; the dangers should be pointed out to all employees and they should be discouraged from putting themselves in a position where their self-interest could conflict with the interests of their company.

Good security comes from an employee knowing that if he commits fraud he will be detected (certainty of detection), prosecuted (certainty of action), and that he will be treated no differently from anyone else (including the managing director) found in a similar position (uniformity of action).

Security education also has an important part to play in alerting employees to the possibilities and methods of fraud to which they and the company may be exposed.

The risks of industrial espionage should be included—where appropriate—in a security education programme. Points that might be brought to the attention of employees include:

- the need to safeguard classified or sensitive documents and information
- the need to take care in informal discussions while travelling or in hotels or at conference
- the need to take care in disposing of scrap paper, typewriter ribbons and dictating tapes
- the need to lock up document containers at night and while premises are being cleaned or left unattended
- the need to challenge unidentified people walking in or around company premises
- the need to search rooms immediately after visitors have left to detect the forgotten briefcase/tape recorder
- the need to call back all people asking for commercially sensitive information over the telephone (after checking the number given in the telephone directory)

The awareness and interest of employees can make an important contribution to security.

The education programme can be implemented through some or all of the following methods:

- booklets on business ethics and security policies
- induction training of new employees
- security presentations at management meetings
- reading files for senior managers
- articles in house magazines
- films and video tapes
- security newsletters
- posters
- reports and letters
- notices (on photocopiers and in conference rooms)
- programmed learning texts
- management development reviews

The object is to increase the profile of security, so that controls are integrated naturally into the life blood of the organization.

Supervision

Top management sets the standards and framework of security but the first line of supervision implements it. Interest and awareness at this level play an important part in reducing fraud opportunities, concealment courses and justifications for committing crime. Thus supervisors should be specially trained in all aspects of security.

Incentives

Some companies offer incentives to employees in departments or branches whose losses, fire or safety records meet predetermined standards. There is evidence to suggest that safety incentives work in reducing reported accidents—whether they reduce actual accidents is a matter of conjecture. How many accidents go unreported so that safety bonuses should not be lost is open to debate!

Therefore, in evaluating incentive schemes a company should consider whether the bonus or prize conditions can be defeated by misrepresentations of fact—by failure to report or manipulation of performance records. If there is a chance of this happening then *ad hoc* or unannounced awards might be considered in lieu of a formal programme.

A company should not invite dishonesty or inaccurate reporting no matter how well intentioned the objectives.

Deterioration in performance

Each employee's progress in the company should be monitored and reported upon in a routine way. Annual performance reports allow an employee to discover how he is progressing and how he should improve. They also allow him to judge and revise his personal aspirations. This is not to suggest that performance should be spied upon—rather that an approach of concerned interest be adopted. Often junior employees are reluctant to come forward when things are troubling them. It is in the company's interest that 'on-the-job' worries and personal problems are identified and remedied quickly.

Deterioration in performance, demeanour or attitude is often the first warning signal. To ignore such symptoms is fair to neither the employee nor the company.

Prompt action should be taken to prevent an unhappy or dissatisfied climate being created. In such a climate, employees generally are able to rationalize dishonesty and disloyalty.

Termination procedures

Employees who decide to terminate their employment are a valuable source of information which most companies fail to develop.

An employee who has given satisfactory service and resigns always has a reason. At worst, it might be that he feels the whole company environment is dishonest and that he can stand it no longer. At best, it may be because he just wants a change. His reasons for leaving should be researched. He should be interviewed by a senior employee (not his normal manager) and debriefed on security, safety and personnel procedures. File notes should be prepared in all cases.

PROTECTION OF INFORMATION

The object of commercial as well as international espionage is to obtain target information in a form such that its validity cannot be in doubt, without its owner realizing it has been stolen or compromised.

Therefore business spies normally seek written self-validating information and they are careful to conceal its loss. Often the caution they exercise is not necessary because their victims do not take proper care and are certainly not in a position to know that their information has been copied or stolen.

There are two main lines of defence against industrial espionage:

- classification and protection of information
- electronic sweeping for listening devices

These are discussed below: sample policy documents are set out in Appendix A.

Information classification and protection

Records' management systems vary from the highly complex controlled by a computer to one-drawer cabinets kept locked in a manager's office.

The starting point is to set down a standard method of classification, depending on the sensitivity or value of the information concerned.

The following classifications are adequate for most companies:

Top secret
Information requiring the highest level of protection.
Proprietary
Highly sensitive commercial information.
Private
Sensitive information of a personal nature.

In addition, it may be prudent to identify and secure two other categories:

Vital
Records that would be required to resume functional activities or establish legal title to assets following an emergency.
Financial
Applies to information and records which entitle the holder to the opportunity of financial gain.

Information may be classified under more than one heading as shown on Table 9.7.

Table 9.7 Information classification

Sensitivity class	Financial	Vital
Top secret		
Proprietary		
Private		

Responsibilities for protecting information should be clearly assigned. Management—probably in conjunction with the corporate security adviser—should set down the minimum standards of protection for each classification.

Electronic sweeping for listening devices

Eavesdropping equipment can be detected by physical searches or by electronic sweeping. 'Sweeps' using broadband radio receivers, field strength meters and similar devices may detect transmissions emitted from radio 'bugs' and simple microphones. Although there are many devices on the market that promise to detect bugs and microphones, their value is limited and they would be unlikely to reveal anything but the most amateur attempts. It is dangerous to rely on them.

For this reason, it is not worth explaining the various sweeping methods and equipment. It is more sensible for a company to seek assistance from private security firms that carry out defensive sweeps using advanced equipment.

Having made this suggestion it is also necessary to give a warning that not all companies that offer this service are what they seem. Some are as equally willing to plant bugs as they are to detect them. Selection should be made with great caution.

Further, a company that believes itself the target of commercial espionage should decide, before employing a private firm, what its objectives are. Are they simply to remove the bug, should one exist, with the minimum of fuss or should it be fed with false information to mislead the opposition and force him into disclosure? The objectives will determine the sweeping method.

Although it is difficult for a company to detect eavesdropping equipment without outside assistance, steps can be taken to make it more difficult for a would-be spy to plant his equipment. Conference and other rooms in which sensitive meetings take place should be secured. Basic preventive security and common sense can reduce the risks significantly.

REPORTING LOSSES AND OTHER INCIDENTS

Another factor in creating the proper climate is openness about mistakes and losses. Frauds and other possible security violations that come to light should never be swept under the carpet but should be reported in writing to senior management. An employee (except in the most unusual circumstances) should not be treated too severely because a fraud has been detected in his area of operation—unless, of course, there is reason to believe he was involved in it.

He might not be blamed for the fact that fraud has occurred but he should be dismissed or severely reprimanded for concealing a loss. A company-wide procedure on the reporting of incidents should cover the following points.

1. The type of incidents to be reported:
   - robberies, burglaries, frauds, hold-ups, etc.
   - fires, sabotage and other overt acts
   - breaches of safety codes
   - unexplained losses
   - unfair competitive activity

2. The timing of the report:
   - immediately by telephone or telex
   - followed up by a written report as soon as possible

3. The names of the people to whom incidents should be reported:

- legal adviser
- company secretary
- corporate security adviser

Some companies' reporting procedures only come into operation when the loss exceeds a certain limit. In practice these are poor. First, an employee who does not wish to make a report may say later, when it is discovered, that he thought it was below the limit. He has an excuse for not reporting. Second, many large frauds are discovered as a result of minor discrepancies. Third, it is genuinely difficult to calculate the size of a fraud, particularly in its early days. If reporting is delayed until the true picture is known, vital evidence may be lost.

In larger organizations a preprinted incident reporting form should be used:

- prepared in triplicate by the employee who discovers the incident;
- the top copy should be sent immediately and directly to the corporate security adviser, the second copy should be sent simultaneously to the employee's department manager; the third copy should be retained by the employee initiating the report;
- the corporate security adviser should liaise with the employee and his manager and should decide what action should be taken;
- the corporate security adviser should be held accountable for any follow-up investigation (in line with company policy) for claiming against fidelity or other insurance and instituting recovery action;
- he should inform the department manager and the employee when and how the incident was resolved.

In addition, each year departmental managers should prepare a summary of all incidents reported; nil returns should be required.

The corporate security adviser should include statistics on reported incidents in his annual review of security for the board of directors.

FIDELITY INSURANCE

Fidelity insurance is a fall-back that may reduce the criticality of a loss.

In negotiating cover, the following aspects should be considered:

1. Cover is normally provided for dishonest loss caused by employees of the insured (not suppliers, contractors, etc.). Stock losses without proof of dishonesty by employees are excluded.
2. There are basically three types of cover:

> (a) Individual or collective   The names of people insured must be set out in the policy.
> (b) Positions   The positions insured (e.g., chief accountant) must be shown in the policy.
> (c) Unnamed and floating   Covers all employees.

3. Subject to any deductible amounts specified in the policy, cover is in force from its inception to cancellation. Losses arising during the life of the policy and discovered within 18 months of its termination are also covered.
4. The indemnity provided under a floating policy is reduced by the total amount of admitted claims. The policy will usually contain an option whereby full cover, from the date of discovery of loss, may be reinstated for the remaining period of the insurance.
5. The policy may contain an interlocking clause, which extends cover when a policy is transferred from one carrier to another.
6. Cover usually extends to the cost of auditors/professional fees incurred solely for the purpose of submitting or quantifying a claim. Investigation and litigation costs are not covered.
7. An agreed system of check must be maintained and immediate notice given to the insurer of any material changes. Failure to do so may forfeit the protection of the policy.

There are two other aspects of insurance that require special attention.

It is wise to ensure that protection extends to 'directors'. It is a principle of fidelity insurance that carriers will not protect a person against defrauding himself and will not insure owners or majority shareholders of a business. This exclusion is sometimes worded so as to apply to all directors whether they are shareholders or not. In some policies, the mere fact that a job title includes the word 'director' can be enough to exclude cover. Wherever possible, all working directors should be insured for fidelity purposes and a side letter obtained to this effect.

Fidelity insurers are not obliged to pay out against a claim. Although the majority of carriers are fair and settle claims quickly, there are others who will prevaricate. They are entitled to do this if in doubt about a claim's bona fides. It can also make good financial sense for the carrier to delay payment; usually his legal fees are more than offset by interest savings.

Thus, the prudent applicant should insist that if a disputed claim is finally judged valid, all legal fees will be reimbursed by the carrier, together with commercial interest from the date of filing.

EMERGENCY PLANNING

Another essential part of company-wide security procedures is the provision of back-up facilities and emergency planning.

Clearly such arrangements are essential in today's violent world. The destruction of an electricity generator might close down a plant and throw thousands temporarily out of work. Back-up is therefore usually linked to overt and violent risks, although it does have its part to play in minimizing the criticality of extorsive crimes.

The starting point is to identify critical functions (computers are an obvious example) on which the organization depends for continuity of operations. The next step is to provide the minimum back-up hardware necessary to reduce the criticality of loss to a tolerable level. The minimum procedures necessary to transfer operations back-up or standby resources should be written down and tested on a regular basis.

Preventive security

What barriers criminals perceive as making a target too difficult or an opportunity too risky is a question that criminologists, police and security people would like to solve. In the absence of a definitive answer, any defence measures are speculative. They may work in some cases and fail in others.

Because of this uncertainty, defences should be layered so that, should one fail, a second may succeed. There is, of course, a limit to the number of different layers of defence that a company can consider. Costs and flexibility of commercial operations are primary considerations.

Preventive security may be defined as security hardware and systems that reduce the opportunities for crime by physical and psychological barriers. The physical barriers may deny a criminal the access he needs to steal, and the psychological barriers may deter him. The most obvious psychological defence is the certainty of detection.

The objectives of preventive security in a fraud context are:

- to prevent the opportunity for larcenous thefts by controlling access of people and vehicles to premises and physical assets
- to commit a criminal to a course of conduct for which there is no innocent excuse and to make this position obvious to him before he commits the crime, in the hope that he will be deterred

These objectives are quite narrow, but they reflect the true value of preventive security in minimizing the risk of fraud. Against frauds that rely on deception—misrepresentation or manipulation—preventive security is not a complete or effective countermeasure. Its value can be explained by examining the two divisions of preventive security: physical security and security systems.

PHYSICAL SECURITY

The layout of commercial premises can favour or deter crime and yet security considerations are often ignored in the construction of new factories and offices. The basic design of premises can simplify access controls and can create psychological barriers that deter crime.

In recent times two significant developments in building security have occurred. These are the techniques of controlled space and perceptual security.

Controlled space

An American architect—Oscar Newman—researched the subject of controlled space and his book, *Defensible Space*,* describes design features in American housing projects that reduced ambient crime rates by staggering amounts.

Newman reasoned that certain crimes were more likely in physical areas that criminals perceived as being public—as not being under the control or natural surveillance of one person or group of persons. Robberies, muggings and other violent crimes were significantly higher in areas that criminals perceived as public than they were in similar areas that they believed were under control.

The idea of controlled space—responsibility for defined physical areas—is the counterpart of the book-keeping principle of accountability.

When a person is held responsible for a certain task, he is likely to try to discharge it properly and efficiently. He is unlikely to allow others to commit crime involving his own direct responsibilities. Thus, thieves will seldom steal assets they are accountable for (unless they are also able to conceal the loss or provide a plausible excuse).

Newman's work would suggest that controlled space planning might be used in the design of commercial premises to reduce the vulnerability to larcenous thefts. Large premises could be divided into small areas (by physical, psychological or procedural barriers) so that accountability is increased, access controlled and the chance of larcenous acts reduced.

Figures 9.3 and 9.4 show how alterations might be made to a reception area in line with Newman's theory.

At this time, so little is known about the success rate of controlled space planning in industrial design that it should not be used as the sole method of defence. On the other hand, the technique, used discreetly, appears to have a significant and yet low cost effect in reducing internal and external larcenous frauds.

* Architectural Press, London, 1976.

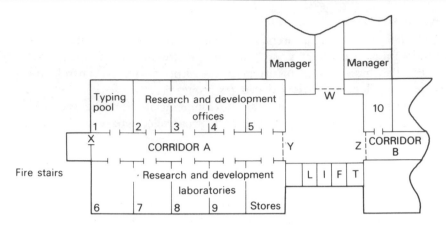

W, X, Y and Z are self-closing fire doors

Figure 9.3 Floor plan—eighth floor of high rise block

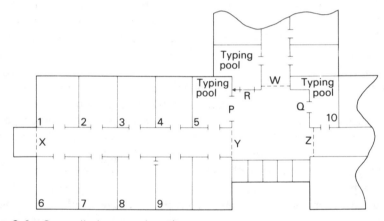

Figure 9.4 Controlled space alterations

Perceptual security

The objective of perceptual security techniques is to make defences appear as effective as possible. To some extent, they cheat a thief, by leading him to believe that his chances of success are lower than they really are.

At a basic level, an automatic switch that turns on lights in an empty house could be defined as a perceptual security control.

In industrial situations, perceptual security techniques might best be used to support existing physical barriers: so that the barriers would look more effective than they really were. Perceptual defences would be chosen because they would be cheaper than their real or true counterpart. For example, dummy television cameras or infrared alarm posts might be mounted inside a perimeter fence to give the impression of high security.

Conventional security design

Although the techniques of controlled space and perceptual security are new and to some extent unproven, there are other well established design features that can reduce security risks. To many criminals opportunity is synonymous with access: if access can be controlled, opportunities can be reduced. Access can be gained in a number of ways, varying from simple trespass to violent penetration of security barriers.

The efficiency of a barrier can be measured from the length of time it resists attack. The longer it takes a criminal to break through, climb over or under, the more secure a barrier is.

As important as the materials used are the design and positioning of the barrier itself. Put in a poor position, even a barrier made from high security materials will be of little use. Placed in a position where to overcome it a criminal would be conspicuous, even a weak barrier may be highly effective. Defences should be appropriate to the risk. In the design stage, or in reviewing the physical security of premises, the 'bullseye' principle should be used to concentrate defences around the most vulnerable or sensitive areas.

The principle can be applied by first identifying the most important rooms or areas within premises. These may be called exclusion areas and access into them should be controlled as tightly as possible. The sensitivity of areas can be identified from:

- the nature of the work performed
- the nature of documents handled and stored
- the criticality of the operation
- the importance of personnel

Examples of exclusion areas:

- computer centres, telex and mail rooms
- cashier's office
- research and development laboratories
- boardroom and directors' offices
- telephone and communications frame room

Immediately adjacent to an exclusion area would be a layer, access into which should be restricted (see Figure 9.5).

Access into a restricted area would be controlled, but not as tightly as into an exclusion area. Some business functions may call for protection and yet not warrant exclusion—these could be located in a restricted area.

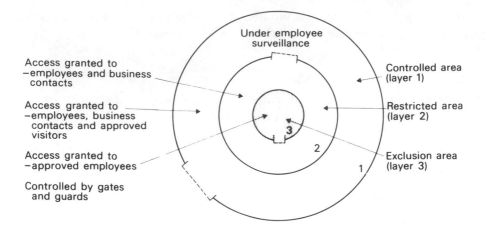

Access granted to
−employees and business
  contacts

Access granted to
−employees, business
  contacts and approved
  visitors

Access granted to
−approved employees

Controlled by gates
  and guards

Figure 9.5   Access levels

Examples of restricted areas:

− photocopying centres
− conference rooms
− receiving and shipping bays

Finally, outside the restricted area—and inside the perimeter—would be controlled areas.

Within any perimeter there might be a number of exclusion areas, each with its own restricted surround.

But from a cost point of view the fewer exclusion areas the better. For this reason it is often advisable to concentrate all high risks into one exclusion area, as shown in Figure 9.6.

In high risk businesses, the barrier forming the outer layer might be a chain link fence, gates and a guard. The barriers between the controlled and restricted areas (layer 2) may be building walls. The division between a restricted area and an exclusion area (layer 3) might be internal walls and doors.

Within an exclusion area there may be further security controls: locked document cabinets or safes, for example.

In some cases it might be difficult, too costly or impossible to construct a suitable physical barrier at any one of the layers mentioned. Where access control is difficult or ineffective, the speed and certainty of response to a violation should be increased. Response may be in the form of an alarm or the intervention of an employee or a security guard.

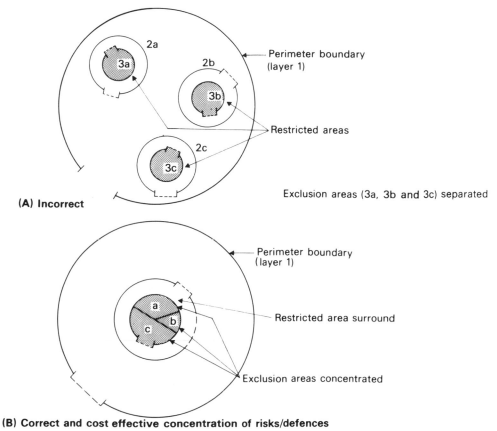

(A) Incorrect

(B) Correct and cost effective concentration of risks/defences

Figure 9.6   Concentration of risks and protection

Generally speaking, the greater the negative difference between the response and delay times the better. The net security value of a barrier might be calculated from the formula below.

Net security value = response time *less* delay time

$$n = r - d$$

For example:

	Delay factor from barrier (d)	Response time (r)	Net security value (n)
System 1 (worst system)	15 mins	20 mins	+ 5 mins
System 2	2 mins	1 min	− 1 min
System 3 (best system)	7 mins	1 min	− 6 mins

This trade-off between delay and response times is an important consideration. The net security value is the amount of time a criminal has available
before his crime will be discovered. The design objective is to keep this time
as low as possible and preferably negative.

Security hardware

Security hardware is an obvious part of a company's defence but so far as
fraud is concerned its use is limited in the ways shown in Table 9.8.

Table 9.8 Effects of security hardware

	Purpose
Guard services	– to respond to and prevent larcenous and opportunist crimes – to control the movement of goods, people and vehicles in and out of company premises – to ensure that transactions involving the movement of goods are recorded on basic documents – to conduct spot checks
Locks, safes and cabinets	– to reinforce the protection of assets and business information – to delay a criminal
Alarms, closed circuit television	– to supervise personnel and vehicular movements – to reinforce access controls – to create psychological deterrents – to respond to violations
Security seals	– to detect and prevent tampering with control equipment and assets
Shredders	– to destroy unwanted copies of sensitive information
Scramblers	– to encipher sensitive communications: voice, telex and computer links

Security hardware can be used to reinforce preventive controls, to delay, to
commit criminals to a course of criminal conduct incapable of innocent
explanation and to increase the chances of detection. It can be used as part of
an integrated defence.

These and other preventive security principles are summarized in the
Handbook of Security.*

– Protective measures must be so designed that, when a breach of security
occurs, this fact is known as quickly as possible.
– Security measures should be commensurate with the threat.

* Noel Currer Briggs, Peter Hamilton and A. D. Norman, *Handbook of Security*, Kluwer Harrap,
London, 1975.

- Risks should be concentrated.
- The criterion of access is need.
- It is not one measure that will give security but the sum of all practical and possible measures.
- That which protects must itself be protected (e.g., a safe or a burglar alarm should be protected against interference).
- All security systems should contain an element of surprise for the criminal.
- While the strongest barrier should be that closest to the target, the most effective burglar alarm (or other response) is that which gives the earliest warning.

One further principle may be added:

- Defences should be arranged so that to overcome them the criminal is made conspicuous, and this fact should be obvious to him before he attempts his crime.

SECURITY SYSTEMS

One defensive link or one piece of hardware is rarely sufficient to provide a total answer to a security problem. An important part of any corporate defence is its security systems. These may be purely software procedures or they may support and reinforce particular pieces of hardware.

The systems that are most relevant to fraud prevention are set out in Table 9.9.

Being essentially before the fact, systems tend to place restrictions on normal commercial operations. For that reason they should be selected and introduced with care—the overriding consideration being their relevance and effectiveness in reducing real risks.

CONCLUSIONS ON PREVENTIVE SECURITY

Access controls and barriers have only a medium effect on preventing and detecting internal frauds, simply because employees, to do their jobs, need unrestricted access to their places of work.

However, controls into discrete areas within perimeter boundaries can significantly reduce the chance of fraud; they may, for example, keep the record control function separated from the custodianship of assets.

Similarly, business contacts need access to premises, and for this reason first layer and second layer access controls are of only low or medium effect in countering frauds in categories C1, 2 and 3, and in CDE4.

Security hardware and systems reduce the risk of external and larcenous frauds and commit the movement of goods to basic records. They force criminals to conceal and yet restrict the availability of a concealment course.

Table 9.9 Security systems

Name of system	Purpose
Lock and key control	To reinforce hardware defences by ensuring that the integrity of locks and keys is not compromised by inefficient practices
Guard scheduling	To ensure that security guards are properly and effectively employed and trained
Cash handling	To ensure that cash in transit and on commercial premises is handled properly
Personnel identification	To ensure that people are given access to those areas they need to enter; to reinforce basic access controls and 'layering'
Vehicle identification	To ensure that vehicle movements are properly controlled
Espionage defences	To ensure that commercial information is adequately protected
Emergency planning	To ensure that contingency plans exist to protect company employees and property against bombs, bomb threats and extorsive crimes and natural disasters
Security education	To advise employees of permissible conduct and to make them aware of possible methods of fraud

They increase detection chances and create psychological barriers. For these reasons preventive security forms an essential link in the fraud prevention chain.

Accounting controls

The number and diversity of accounting systems is as wide and diverse as business itself. Because of this, no practical purpose would be served in setting our specific systems descriptions. Here general principles will be examined.

THE ROLE OF ACCOUNTING SYSTEMS IN FRAUD PREVENTION

Accounting systems and controls have the following roles to play in fraud prevention and detection.

1. They ensure that transactions are recorded on controlled source documents, thereby making it less easy to carry out negative manipulations.
2. They ensure that thefts result in recognizable account/inventory discrepancies—a desirable position.
3. They ensure that responsibility for losses can be pinned down.

4. In defining proper procedures they remove the chance of plausible excuses being advanced to cover dishonesty.
5. They ensure speedy identification of losses.
6. In setting controls they establish psychological barriers that are likely to deter fraud.

Accounting controls make the manipulation stage of fraud more difficult and hazardous to a thief. They create psychological barriers and increase the chance of detection.

THE SCOPE OF ACCOUNTING CONTROLS

Each accounting system should be comprehensive and should record all assets and all transactions of the company concerned. This may seem an obvious statement, but many companies do not have an accurate record of exceptional transactions nor of their intangible assets and information.

If accurate and complete records are not maintained, thieves can steal without the loss coming to light. Controls should force losses and thefts into the open.

DEFINED SYSTEMS

All accounting systems should be formalized in accounting manuals. Copies should be issued against signature to all people responsible for or involved in the operation of the system or subsystem. Only those parts of the manual that a person needs for this current job should be issued to him.

The overall design of accounting systems should avoid the creation of exceptions to basic routines. The fewer exceptions to a system the less likely it is for a genuine mistake to occur and the smaller the chance of fraud. These simple measures make sure that transactions are handled consistently. In knowing what their jobs are and should be, employees are less able to provide a plausible excuse for dishonesty when, in the course of a fraud, they deviate from accounting practice.

All systems should be designed to prevent the concealment of fraud by negative means: by omission of an entry or destruction of a record. Systems should be such that an employee who commits fraud can only conceal it by creating a false entry or record. This may sound naive, but systems that allow the concealment of fraud by omission make detection difficult and proof of guilty knowledge to a court almost impossible. The thief can always say that he forgot to make an entry or that the record was lost.

Where the accounting system is such that to commit and conceal fraud a false record or entry has to be created, the examination of the record itself and its impact on other records may make the fraud obvious. Also, in court the false record may establish criminal intention.

Defined accounting systems also have a preventive aspect. Before committing fraud thieves weigh up their chances of escape or of being able to provide a plausible excuse. When they see that a system forces them to record their dishonesty, they may be deterred.

To a thief there is a world of difference, in fact and psychologically, between tearing up a delivery note—so that sales income can be stolen—and writing out a false credit note for subsequent conversion. In the latter case the false credit note is lingering evidence of guilt.

The accounting manual should also define authority levels for employees and should determine the procedure for making inter-account adjustments and bad debt, stock and other write-offs.

PHYSICAL CONTROLS

The maximum possible use should be made of gate controls to ensure that all goods movements—both out and in—are recorded on controlled basic documents (see Figures 9.7 and 9.8). This is an essential factor in preventing the concealment of fraud by negative means and retroactive positive manipulations of source documents (for example, the creation of false goods-in records to back up a false credit in a supplier's ledger account).

All movements should be supported by a pass. For goods delivered the pass might comprise a copy of the sales invoice or purchase return note and for goods inwards it may simply be a numerically controlled goods received note.

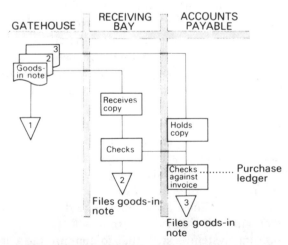

The creation of a false credit in the purchase ledger will call for retroactive manipulation of the goods inwards notes (and filing of appropriate copies at 1, 2 and 3) or collusion between the gatehouse, goods receiving and accounting staff.

Figure 9.7 Goods inwards flow chart

The fundamental principle is to ensure that goods are not removed from the premises without being recorded (preventing negative manipulations) and that accounts are not credited for goods that are not received (purchase inflations).

The physical layout of the gatehouse area should allow the guards or other controllers sufficient time and space to check.

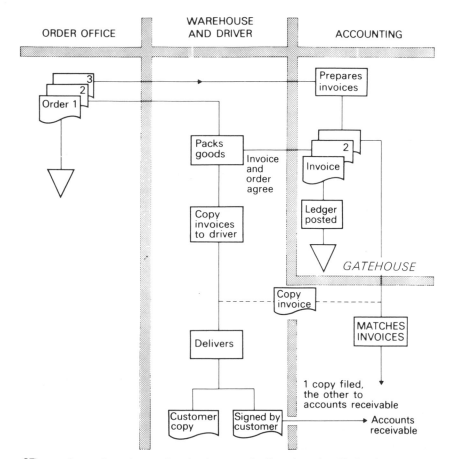

●The warehouse dispatches goods only when an order (from the order office) and sales invoices (from accounting) are received and agree. Thus, the transaction is split before the goods are allowed to move.

● One copy of the sales invoice is received by the gatehouse in advance of the goods being dispatched. It is tied up with a further copy produced on exit from the premises by the driver of the delivery vehicle. Thus, when transactions are suppressed that fact should become obvious from the possession by the gatehouse of only the first copy of the sales invoice.

To suppress a transaction after the goods have been authorized to move, a thief would have to destroy the copy orders (held in the order office and in accounting) and the gatehouse copy invoice.

Figure 9.8   Goods outwards flow chart

CONTROLS OVER INVENTORIES AND THE MOVEMENT OF GOODS

Goods in transit and inventories are highly exposed to larcenous theft and manipulative frauds. The following controls are recommended.

Deliveries outwards

- The routes of delivery drivers should be changed as frequently as possible.
- Log sheets/mileometers should be closely controlled and should establish accountability after the event.
- Sealed containers/pallets/boxes should be prepacked by an independent person so that drivers do not have to 'break bulk' for individual customers. Wherever possible vehicles should be dispatched with full loads.
- Time schedules should be made tight to prevent off route diversions to receivers.
- Drivers should never be allowed to swap routes and loads with colleagues.
- Drivers should not be allowed to load their own vehicles without an independent check.
- Drivers should not be allowed to take preloaded vehicles home overnight.
- Drivers should be required to obtain a signature for all deliveries on an approved company form and should never be allowed to give 'informal or temporary' receipts.
- Drivers should never be allowed to divert a load without first obtaining permission from management.

Deliveries inwards

- A gate keeper should maintain a chronological record of all vehicle movements.
- Goods should be checked on the vehicle before unloading.
- After unloading, high value goods should be retained in a sterile area for double checking.
- Receipts should never be signed in advance of checking. Checkers should take their time.
- Discrepancies should be reported before a receipt is given and before the vehicle concerned is allowed to leave the premises.
- Management should carry out spot checks.

Factories, warehouses and weighbridges

- Parking spaces for employees' cars should be kept away from storage areas, shipping and receiving bays.
- Weighbridges and other control machinery should be secured against interference.
- Weighbridge operators should be instructed in operating procedures.

Automatic exit and entry gates should be connected by logic circuits to weighbridges. In high risk situations, weighbridges should be kept under closed circuit television/video control.
- Weighbridges should be properly maintained and regularly inspected by qualified engineers. A written log of these inspections should be retained.

Inventory control

- All valuable inventories should be kept in secure premises and should be controlled by perpetual stock records. All movements in and out should be recorded on serially numbered documents.
- All adjustments to book stocks as a result of physical checks should be carefully controlled and audited.

Senior management should carry out regular spot checks on all aspects of inventory control.

ACCOUNTABILITY

The systems should pin down responsibility for losses, whether accidental or fraudulent. In large companies fraud can sometimes escape detection because of the size of the operation and nothing more. It is then difficult to prove that Smith was responsible for a particular act rather than Jones.

Although, as mentioned in Chapter 7, thieves are often reluctant to blame a colleague when they are responsible for a theft, they are often prepared to let guilt rest with a group of employees in the certain knowledge that the proprietors of the company will never be able to identify the true culprit.

This idea of accountability, of pinning down responsibility, is an important one. It can be achieved in many different ways, for example:

- by defining areas of responsibility in accounting manuals;
- by defining areas of responsibility on job descriptions.

The principle can also be used in larger organizations to reduce the possibility of fraud concealment:

- by allocating assets to small operating centres (for example, instead of saying that the company has 350 lathes of type ABC, each department that has a lathe of this type would have it listed on its own separate inventory);
- by allocating costs to the smallest possible cost centres (for example, fraud might be concealed by posting consequential debits to an advertising budget: when this is a corporate account the inflation may not be noticed, but when the advertising charges are written back to small cost centres the fraud may be obvious).

The principle can also be applied to individual transactions and in appropriate circumstances documents should have space for entry of signatures and dates. Managers should ensure that the people responsible sign for goods, tools and cash or acknowledge—by signature—the fact that they have done or checked something.

The requirement to give a signature has a before- and an after-the-fact benefit. Before the fact, it causes a person tempted to commit a fraud to pause: will he have a plausible excuse if his signature is entered? Can he claim it was a mistake?

If he thinks not, then he may be deterred. After the fact, a signature pins down responsibility; it is a good detection aid and often invaluable as proof of criminal intent.

As an extension of the accountability principle, systems should be designed to give an immediate or prompt indication that a loss has occurred. Other measures outlined in this section will ensure that a larcenous fraud will result in an account/inventory discrepancy. It follows that recognition of this fact should be as prompt as possible. If the loss is identified on the day it occurs, the trail is still warm. If the loss is not recognized until six months later the trail will have gone cold, records been destroyed, plausible explanations worked out and the chance of proof severely limited.

The 'immediacy of response' principle can be achieved by routinely checking the most critical or vulnerable assets. In the oil industry, for example, stocks are taken once or twice a day and frauds that result in account/inventory discrepancies are quickly identified.

CONSISTENCY AND UNIFORMITY

It is essential that similar units or branches of a company process transactions in a uniform and standard way. Accounting and systems manuals should ensure this consistency but occasionally companies allow unit managers to adopt informal systems and to use non-standard forms. These introduce the possibility of concealing fraud by preparing a plausible excuse and facilitating negative manipulations. The use of informal records may distort central accounting figures to such an extent that inter-branch comparisons of performance—and monitoring for fraud symptoms—becomes meaningless.

It is essential, therefore, that within similar units of a company uniformity of processing is maintained. Surprise audits and spot checks should reinforce this requirement.

RECORD INTEGRITY

Systems should be designed to make the maximum use of numerical sequences and colour codes. Numerical sequences can be used to detect and prevent negative manipulations and retroactive positive manipulations on basic documents. For example, a missing delivery note on a sequential check may indicate suppressed sales income. Also, where a false purchase invoice has been created, it may be necessary for the thief to support it by retroactively creating a false goods inwards note. If the sequence of these notes is intact then the manipulation may not be possible.

Colour coding of documents also serves a security purpose. Colours enable supervisory staff to detect the presence of documents and copies that should not be with the person in whose control they are found. For example, if, because of a controlled separation of responsibilities, all blue copies of sales invoices act as the gate pass and a blue copy is found with the warehouse clerk—or in his waste bin—then further investigation might be warranted. Thus colour coding can assist in the separation of responsibilities. Colour coding of documents, in yearly batches, can also prevent manipulations involving reuse of old documents. For example, where disbursement cheques are colour coded each year, substitution of an old cheque to conceal a disbursement fraud would be that much more difficult.

Books and records should have the same degree of protection as the merchandise and transactions they record. This principle applies to:

- formal books and records
- computer tapes and disks
- new and unused forms (particularly money-generating, numerically controlled sales records)
- old records
- records in the course of processing

The separation of responsibilities concept should ensure that as few people as possible have access to assets *and* to a cogent concealment course. When documents are left insecure, the possibility that a person who has access to assets could obtain access to a concealment course—particularly a negative one—is strong. Proper protection of records reduces this risk.

All accounting records should be completed in ink or ballpoint pen (i.e., not pencil) and they should be dated and initialled or signed by the person making them.

Alterations to records should be initialled by the person making the alteration. Figures should be crossed through, and not obliterated. On important documents, the reason for the alteration should be entered on the document—preferably on the face. If there is insufficient room the entry can be made on the reverse side.

When a manager detects an incorrect money-generating document he should not return it to the creator unless he first retains a photocopy. It is not unknown for documents returned for alteration (when in fact they have been fraudulent) to be lost in the mail system.

ROTATION OF DUTIES

From time to time—without advance notice—the duties of employees should be rotated: clerk X should take over clerk Y's job, and so forth. Such changes are most practical when clerk Y is due to take his holidays but the fact that some thieves are reluctant to go absent still holds true and in these circumstances more positive action to rotate jobs should be taken.

It is, of course, essential to ask rotated employees to report matters they cannot resolve to a senior manager and not to the previous incumbent. The number of detection chances that have been lost because the newly rotated employee asked for the advice of his predecessor (who then further conceals his fraud) are too numerous to contemplate.

SEPARATION OF DUTIES

It is a fundamental accounting principle that the custodianship of assets and the records that control them should be separated. In small organizations, separation is not always possible but it is nevertheless a principle worth striving towards.

In a fraud context the separation should be between theft opportunities and the availability of a concealment course. When a thief has access to assets, either direct or contrived, and access to a concealment course, fraud risks are increased.

Separation can take place by *function* or by *transaction stages*. Separation by function is essentially an organizational division—for example, separation of the cashier's function from sales and purchases ledger control. Extreme care should be given to functional separations. The division should be between assets and records. People in charge of assets should have no uncontrolled access to *any* records, not just those that refer to the assets under their control. In Chapter 2 an example of a lapping fraud was given and it was clear that many financial accounts can be used to conceal the account/inventory discrepancy; not just the records relating to the particular real asset stolen. The theft of cash may be concealed in a personal ledger, in stock accounts or in expenses.

Separation within transactions is probably more effective and a more practical solution for smaller organizations. Each transaction can be divided into a series of stages, no one person having control over or authority to handle the whole. The critical point in the separation is the stage where goods move: delivery from company premises for sales and receipt into company premises for purchases. So far as sales are concerned, suppression is not usually possible until authority to release the goods has been given and effected; if sales documentation is suppressed before this stage then the goods will not move and the fraud is frustrated. Therefore, separation should take place around the critical point of goods movements.

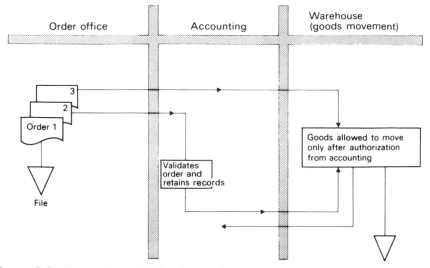

Figure 9.9 Separation of duties (correct)

Figure 9.9 shows a system in which separation occurs before goods release. Thus, no one person has the ability to suppress transaction.

In the system shown in Figure 9.10, however, a person working in the warehouse or in accounting has the ability to suppress all copies of the invoice after the goods have been released.

The same principle applies—though it is perhaps less effective—to purchases. Here the critical point is receipt of goods and separation of duties

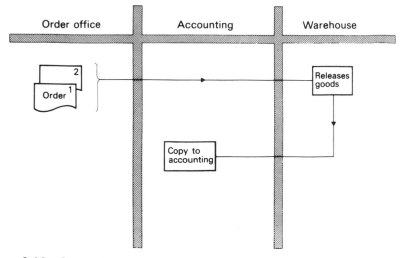

Figure 9.10 Separation of duties (incorrect)

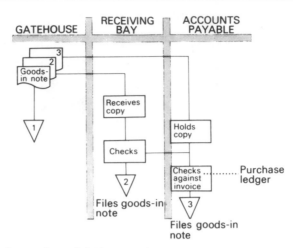

Figure 9.11   Separation of duties: purchases

should ensure that purchase invoices are not forwarded for posting to a ledger account unless they are supported by a serially numbered and signed goods inwards note. This system is shown in Figure 9.11.

Most transactions can be separated, to prevent both positive and negative manipulations, by the use of 'locked-in' copies of basic documents. The principle is to lock in an anchor document against which later processing can be checked. The locked-in documents are not available to accounting staff.

THIRD-PARTY INTERVENTION AND CORROBORATION

When transactions or movements of goods are invariably committed to serially numbered source documents, a large number of fraud possibilities are reduced. Manipulations up the accounting stream expose a thief to danger; missing documents should be noticed and a falsely created document may stand out. A common danger area is negative manipulation by income suppression.

A way of ensuring that transactions are recorded is to use the principle of third-party intervention. Here the automatic response of a customer or other third party is used to make sure that sales are recorded. The object is to ensure that a customer reports a transaction to the company, whether or not it is suppressed by an employee.

Prize schemes—based on the production of a company form—guarantee cards, and other documents that a customer is obliged to return to the company to obtain a benefit may be used to check on the completeness and accuracy of recorded entries.

For this to be an effective control, the customer—whether the sale to him

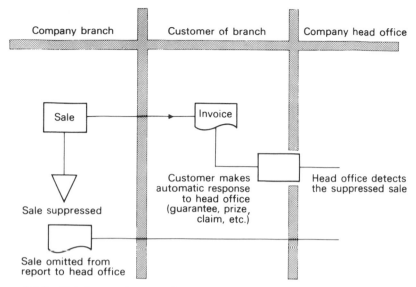

Figure 9.12 Third-party intervention

was formally recorded or not—must respond automatically to the company (see Figure 9.12).

The technique can be used to test for and prevent frauds involving market diversions and sales suppressions at company branches.

AUTHORIZATION

All documents that require authorization should be authorized at a time when the pertinent facts can be checked. After authorization, the documents should not be returned to the person who prepared them, but should be handed to an independent third party for finalizing, as shown in Figure 9.13.

The basic documents on which the case for authorization was made should be perforated or otherwise marked to prevent reuse.

EXCEPTION REPORTS

Some of the critical point techniques discussed in Chapter 7 can be used on a regular basis to monitor high risk areas. Probably the most important are computer produced exception reports which list out—on a routine basis—transactions that could be symptomatic of fraud.

Besides producing lists of transactions worthy of further investigation, a routine computer surveillance program serves a deterrent purpose. The fact that the company is using its computer in this way will soon get around and help to create uncertainty in the minds of potential criminals.

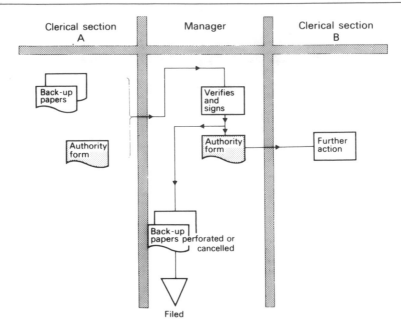

Figure 9.13 Authorization process

DISBURSEMENTS

Conversion is usually the most important element in systematic frauds. Thus, tight control over disbursements is essential:

- Cheques should be properly authorized at the time pertinent facts can be verified.
- Pre-signed cheques should be absolutely prohibited.
- Blank cheques should be controlled.
- Blank spaces on cheques should be obliterated.
- All cheques should be crossed 'not negotiable'.

It is also important to ensure that cheques cancelled after clearance are carefully examined and retained securely.

INCOMING FUNDS

Incoming funds are exposed to conversion and manipulation. The following controls are recommended:

- Mailrooms and mail transmission systems should be controlled.
- Details of incoming cheques should be recorded at the earliest possible moment.
- Cheques should be endorsed with a company stamp as soon as possible after receipt.
- Cash suspense accounts should be closely controlled.

CONTRACTS AND TENDERS

One of the most sensitive areas in many businesses is the handling of bids and tenders made or received by the company. They are dangerous from an espionage point of view as well as being vulnerable to fraud.

Bids made by the company

1. Policy and discussions on pricing information should be restricted on a need-to-know basis.
2. One senior manager should be made accountable for preparing a bid; he should be responsible for its security.
3. Where a complex bid cannot be compiled by one manager without assistance, he should see that it is subdivided in such a way that no junior employee is in a position to assess the final figures or terms.
4. The bid should be typed up without sensitive figures or amounts being shown.
5. Immediately before the bid is due for submission the manager should enter in the final figures by hand.
6. The bid should be delivered by courier immediately before the deadline.
7. The manager or deputy delivering the bid should try to be present when all the other bids are opened or should wait until the result is announced.

Tenders received by the company

1. Specific details should be circulated to regular contractors and the deadline for receiving offers stated.
2. Replies should be addressed to the company's bank in sealed envelopes.
3. Letters should not be opened by the bank.
4. At the deadline time, the letters/offers should be opened in the presence of a senior manager. Each page of each tender should be initialled or marked by him.
5. A record should be kept of all companies entering a tender, their price and other details. This should be inspected from time to time by senior managers to see if patterns indicating 'rigging' exist.

Management spot checking also creates uncertainty in the criminal mind and serves both a preventive and a detective purpose.

ENFORCEMENT

No control system can be effective if it is not enforced. It is vital that all levels of management carry out sufficient checks to ensure that the system defined in the accounting manuals is being properly used and that it is effective and relevant to existing business needs.

Particular attention should be paid to the bona fides of:

– cancelled sales documentation
– cancelled goods outwards passes
– out of sequence goods inwards passes
– misplaced colour coded documents

Managers and auditors should discuss the system with employees who have to use it and should follow up unusual transactions and events that may be symptomatic of fraud.

Special defences against misrepresentations

Somewhere between conventional accounting controls and security systems are a small group of techniques that can best be described as general countermeasures. In this section we will see how they can be used to combat misrepresentations. The measures are part accounting, part security, but mainly common sense.

Some terms which will be used in describing the elements of misrepresentation require definition.

A *central issue* is a fact, event or material condition forming part of a transaction, the accuracy of which causes a victim to act.

A *transaction* is a sale, purchase, investment or other business activity into which a victim may enter.

A *point of business* is the stage in the transaction where a central issue is represented. It is the point at which the victim or his agent decides to enter into a transaction. The point of business may be the cashier's desk in a bank or the office in which applications for loans are received. It is the point in time and the place at which misrepresentations take effect.

In most transactions there will be one or more central issues. In banking the central issue may be the commercial reputation of the potential borrower; in industry it might be the creditworthiness or true commercial standing of an enterprise or the right of a person to dispose of property offered for sale. These central issues are what misrepresentative frauds are all about; by falsifying them a thief is able to gain an advantage. On the other side, if the potential victim is able to prove that a central issue has been falsified he can prevent or detect fraud.

Thus, within commercial organizations a determination should be made of the central issues of all transactions that might be vulnerable to misrepresentative frauds. These issues will normally come under the control of employees at the point of business.

The accurate identification of all vulnerable points of business, possible transactions and the central issues that might affect a company is the first and fundamental step in defending against misrepresentative frauds.

The second essential is the training of employees who might be exposed to such frauds.

Defences against misrepresentative frauds should be as obvious as possible and should make a criminal believe—before he embarks on fraud—that he will be detected. This, of course, is not easy to do because at the early stages of a transaction the victim may not be able to distinguish a criminal from a legitimate customer or contact. Although the victim may be confused, the thief will be well aware of the risks of detection. These perceived risks will apply only to a thief; they will not affect or deter a legitimate contact. Thus, everything that a company does in mounting its defences against misrepresentative frauds—whether by accounting, para-accounting or security—should be inclined towards making a criminal uncertain. The fact mentioned in Chapter 5, that thieves are most open to detection at the time of making a misrepresentation, holds true in the majority of cases. Whether the thief is a small-time crook trying fraudulently to obtain credit or an international fraudsman seeking false export subsidies or premium refunds, the principle remains the same. At the time they are making a misrepresentation—when they come face to face with the victim at the point of business—they will be nervous and aware of the risk of detection. If they see this risk as high, they may be deterred.

Forms or contracts containing central issue clauses should be worded clearly; they should commit a criminal to a course of criminal conduct incapable of innocent explanation. Appropriate wording will take misrepresentations from civil into the criminal courts, and will increase the victim's chance of recovery. More important, forms and contracts that commit a criminal to expose his intended dishonest course and leave him without an excuse may deter him.

These three objectives:

- identification of vulnerable transactions
- high profile defences
- criminal prosecution

are important in fighting all misrepresentative frauds.

It should never be forgotten that frauds involving the misrepresentation of commercial and personal realities almost always result in overt account/inventory discrepancies. After the thief has left the premises the loss is often abundantly obvious; speed and a fast escape are his stock in trade. The more he can be delayed, the more the potential victim checks, the more likely the thief is to be deterred. Moreover, within reasonable limits, a genuine customer or contact is unlikely to be affected or deterred by controls.

DEFENCES AGAINST COMMERCIAL MISREPRESENTATION

Many frauds in categories A, B, C, D, E and F2 rely on the victim being deceived by misrepresentation. The deception may be before, after or contiguous with an act of theft.

The majority of deceptions involving commercial realities occur before or at the same time as a theft act. For example, the thief deceives a cashier into believing his cheques are good immediately before he takes possession of cash.

In long firm frauds, as a result of elaborate falsifications of commercial or personal realities, the victim is induced to part with goods on credit. The deception is prior to and contiguous with the act of theft.

Criminals are able to succeed in misrepresentations of commercial realities for one and sometimes more of four reasons. First is the victim's greed: attracted by the thought of a sale, new account, larger commission or some other advantage, the victim or his agent is led on by the thief. The second is speed: invariably the thief imposes a time limit on the victim's acceptance of the transaction. The third reason why criminals succeed is because of the victim's ignorance: the fact that he is unaware of the fraud possibilities in a given transaction. The fourth reason is when an employee of the victim company works in collusion with an external thief.

It follows, therefore, that if potential victims suppress their own greed, take time to check out the central issues of vulnerable transactions and educate staff, most misrepresentative frauds can be prevented.

To advise the management of a company that it should not be too greedy is possibly offensive; yet, when it comes to misrepresentations, but for the greed of the victim many frauds would fail. The victim's greed is exacerbated by the demand for speed. Claims like 'If you don't complete the contract by Friday we will take our business elsewhere', are almost certain in misrepresentative frauds. Their object is to rush the victim into a transaction without time to make adequate checks. The fact that a time limit has been imposed, particularly when the person concerned is not closely known to the victim, should in itself be grounds for extra care. These days, with the international nature of trade, the speed and rush demands of a thief may be assisted by physical distance. The home base of the criminal may be so distant that the victim does not have the time or the means to check the central issue of a vulnerable transaction. The golden rule is not to enter into possible loss transactions without making all necessary checks into the truth of the central issues represented. If there is any doubt, the transaction should be delayed or declined. Where a company is exposed to misrepresentative frauds involving commercial realities, and most companies are, it should preplan its organization in such a way that essential representations, the central issues, can be checked quickly and effectively. Contacts should be established with government departments, other companies and trade associations, so that, where necessary, verifications and investigations can be made with the minimum of delay.

Second, on long-term transactions and contracts, the company concerned might reasonably require access to a continuing method of verification. A contract may give the company the right to audit its supplier's expenses where 'on cost' contracts are involved or to examine a customer's sales and other records where market diversions are suspected.

Third, all forms and documents should clearly identify the central issues. If it is permissible within the law to do so, sales invoices might be endorsed 'for sale within such and such an area only'; cartons might be similarly marked. Such endorsements will assist in establishing guilty intent if the terms of the central issues are not complied with. This step—which also removes the opportunity for a plausible explanation—may act as a deterrent to fraud.

Fourth, the education, training and awareness of employees at the point of business are essential parts of the defence. They are discussed later under personal misrepresentations.

DEFENCES AGAINST PERSONAL MISREPRESENTATIONS

The central issue of these frauds is the falsification of a personal identity, the fact that the thief claims to be someone he is not. The falsification of identity may stand alone, and be sufficient to achieve a fraud, or it may form part of a larger scheme involving commercial deceptions or account manipulations. The best defence is to make it clear to the thief that he will be identified. In most misrepresentative frauds, the loss soon comes to light; the thief relies on anonymity to avoid apprehension. Make it clear to a thief that he will be identified and he may be deterred.

In the USA, closed circuit television cameras in banking halls have reduced the impact of cheque frauds simply because thieves realize before they cash stolen cheques that evidence of their true identity—a photograph—will be left behind.

As an alternative, a company may decide to make a full and detailed verification of the customer's identity before the transaction in question is entered into. Whether conventional means of before-the-fact verification— such as personal references, identity cards—are used or whether closed circuit or point-of-sale devices are installed does not matter overmuch from a preventive point of view. What does matter is the fact that, before attempting a personal misrepresentation, the thief realizes his chances of successful escape are low.

Employees who make judgements on the company's behalf at a time when the central issues—either commercial or personal—are represented should be given instruction in the most likely methods of fraud and in the checks that they should automatically carry out.

This training can normally be arranged through the police or a local reputable security company. There are also a number of books* which deal with misrepresentative frauds and these are worth reading. The newspapers, too, often describe frauds in detail. Circulating copies of relevant reports reminds employees of the risks and alerts them to fashionable methods of fraud.

DEFENCES AGAINST PHYSICAL MISREPRESENTATIONS

Physical misrepresentations fall into one of two types. First, those that are intended to conceal an account/inventory discrepancy by misrepresenting the true value of a real inventory. The second type misrepresents the accuracy of measuring or control equipment.

Whereas commercial and personal misrepresentations mostly concern external thieves, the falsification of physical realities normally involves company employees or business contacts—people with access to machinery and stocks.

Misrepresentations of stock can be prevented, or the vulnerabilities reduced, by:

– good housekeeping—keeping stock areas clean, tidy and well laid out;
– binning, palletizing and containerizing small items into countable units;
– maintaining perpetual inventories and carrying out regular stock checks;
– writing stock adjustments on to routine management records and investigating high loss areas;
– controlling inventories by quantity and value.

Physical misrepresentation involving control equipment is less easy to counter and there are only a few general principles that can be outlined here, so diverse are the types of control machinery in use.

Most of the control machinery used in industry and commerce measures a physical condition or quantity: weighbridges—weight, flow meters—bulk liquids, cash registers—amounts of money.

These physical measurements may be looked upon as central issues. Vulnerabilities can be assessed by establishing how the central issues can be misrepresented. How can weight be misrepresented? How can flow of bulk be suppressed? How can cash be under-recorded? Answers to these questions will determine the possible points and methods of interference. The physical defences around and on control machinery should be such that interference is made obvious—a broken seal, missing nut or regular machine failure should be followed up as indications of fraud or misuse.

In addition to interference with the machinery itself, it is possible that

* Mary Carey and George Sherman, *A Compendium of Bunk or How to Spot a Con Artist*, Charles C. Thomas, Springfield, Illinois. 1975. Robert Farr, *The Electronic Criminals*, McGraw-Hill, 1975.

there are ways of misusing a support system so that even when the machinery is performing normally and accurately, a central issue can still be misrepresented. Such falsifications are essentially accounts orientated—manipulations—and are not dealt with here. However, the point should be borne in mind that most control machinery can be defeated either by mechancial interference and deliberate breakage or by systems avoidance or manipulation.

CONCLUSION ON DEFENCES AGAINST MISREPRESENTATIONS

Of the three misrepresentation types, those involving the falsification of commercial and personal realities are probably the most dangerous and most prevalent. They are also the most preventable. The measures outlined have a high impact in reducing misrepresentative frauds involving business contacts, opportunists and organized criminals. These are fraud categories not adequately countered by other defences.

Finally, as a defensive back-up, senior management can monitor the records relating to vulnerable transactions, so as to detect frauds that might have escaped the eye of or involved employees at the point of business.

Ideally, the reports should be based on exception formats and might show:

- the frequency of bad cheques accepted (by name of the employee at the point of business)—the regular appearance of one employee's name might be an indication of carelessness or his complicity in fraud;
- the frequency of bad debts (by sales representative area)—for the same reason as that given above;
- the ratio of cancelled life insurance policies (in sales representative's order) or cancelled hire purchase agreements—to detect false commission earning policies;
- frequency of machine failure or replacement of seals—usually control machinery that has been interfered with has a poor breakdown record.

The records that might be produced will depend on the type of business conducted and on the source data from which exception reports can be compiled.

Detection

The role of detection in fraud prevention cannot be overstated. It provides the safety net should before-the-fact controls be overcome and assists in creating a climate of honesty. In the final analysis it is a deterrent.

Whether this deterrent is provided by internal auditors, security investigators or other managers does not matter too much. The important fact is that its presence and effect is known to all staff and business contacts.

Conclusion

Just as there are no easy answers to fraud detection, prevention calls for care and preplanning; equally it calls for discretion and selection. Since many of the available controls can restrict normal commercial operations, they should only be employed when they genuinely counter a real or highly probable fraud risk. Defences should always be commensurate with the risk and should be as cost effective as possible.

10. Computer security and fraud defences

Rule 10:   If computer security is made simple, no one will believe it

The protection of computers has attracted more attention than any other aspect of security and it is not the intention of this book to add further to the esoteric mechanics of control that are already available. Rather, the purpose is to set a workable framework on which risks and controls in individual systems can be evaluated.

Perceptions of risks and controls

People's attitudes to security and their perception of risks vary widely, depending to a large extent on their *direct* personal experience (see Figure 10.1). Thus different people can have completely different views of risks in the same system and the controls necessary to counter them.

Similarly, risks vary from place to place, from one system to another and from time to time; there are no set solutions to computer security.

Risk evaluation: background and methods

Computer fraud risks were discussed in detail in Chapter 6 and it is not necessary to repeat them here. However, it is important to examine alternative methods of risk evaluation, their advantages and limitations.

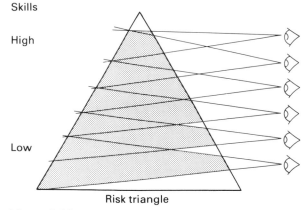

Figure 10.1 View of risks

Figure 10.2 Balance of risks and controls

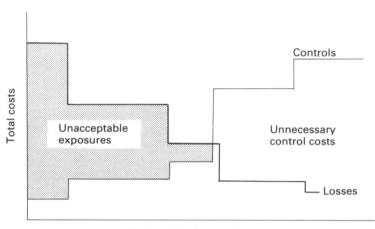

Phases in losses and controls

Figure 10.3 Over- and under-protection

It is a fundamental principle of security that risks and controls should be in approximate balance (see Figure 10.2). When this balance is unequal the organization concerned will either face risks against which it is unjustifiably exposed or incur unnecessary control costs (see Figure 10.3).

Various formalized methods of risk evaluation have been developed to help arrive at the proper balance and to try to justify the cost of controls.

Users can be led into complex risk evaluation exercises which do little except waste an enormous amount of time. The truth is that there are minimum standards that should be present in even the most elementary systems: these minimum or *baseline* controls are set out later.

Thus security can be improved to a baseline level without the need for any risk evaluation.

Present imbalance (see Figure 10.4):

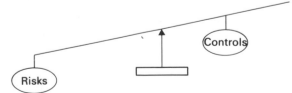

Figure 10.4 Imbalance between risks and controls

Baseline improvements (see Figure 10.5):

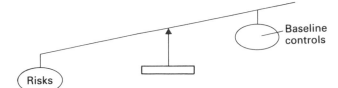

Figure 10.5 Effect of baseline controls

Thus risk evaluation is needed only to identify and justify controls above the baseline. In many cases the difference between baseline and optimum controls will be marginal.

Optimum balance of risks and controls (see Figure 10.6):

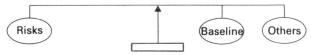

Figure 10.6 Optimum balance

Risks in each computer system are unique and result from a combination of inherent and modifying factors. Inherent risks, common to all computer systems, arise from the following factors:

– invisibility of transactions processed by computer;
– absence of separation in duties, particularly in smaller systems;
– user dependency on the continuing availability of computer resources;
– concentration of assets and information in one easily identifiable place;
– difficulty of 'proving' computer records in civil and criminal litigation.

However, modifying factors are more significant because they determine the unique combination of risks in individual systems.

The factors include:

National environment

– economic and social pressures on employees
– political factors
– national crime rates
– efficiency of public police forces and security

Physical location of computer equipment

– in an urban or suburban area
– in a green field site or multi-tenancy, high rise building

Applications processed

- high risk financial transactions
- government or commercial processing
- in-house programming or bought-in packages
- facilities' management or dedicated operations
- private and confidential or open house management style

Financial controls

- small profit and cost centres
- discrete or global budgetary controls
- high or low profit accountability
- structured or loose general ledger headings

Company image and ethics

- clear management policies
- statements on business ethics and conflicts of interests
- policies for the protection of information
- organizational structure

Personnel policies

- pre-employment screening
- well defined supervisory controls
- employee training
- policies on prosecution and dismissal
- employee morale and staff turnover rates

Because inherent and modifying factors interact to produce unique exposures in each system, methods of risk identification and quantification appear to be necessary to ensure that the proper controls are in place.

RISK IDENTIFICATION

There are essentially two methods of identifying risks: objectively or subjectively.

Objective methods examine past incidents and, based upon their frequency and costs, future losses are predicted. Because many covert incidents are never reported, objective methods are unreliable and understate the scale of computer frauds.

Subjective methods take account of past experience but are primarily based on the 'best guess' of what could go wrong in a particular system. If not carefully managed, subjective assessments may lack credibility.

Risks are spread across various ranges of probability and criticality and methods have been developed to rank or assess their relative importance. There are two methods of assessment: quantitative and qualitative.

Quantitative methods rank the significance of risks based on a calculation of their estimated annual costs (EAC):

Estimated annual cost = Probability × Criticality
(EAC)   = P   × C

Thus it is possible *in theory* to attach estimates of probability and criticality to all identified risks and to calculate their costs on an annual basis. For example see Table 10.1.

Table 10.1 Calculation of estimated annual costs

Risk	P once in (n) years	C $	EAC $ p.a.
Major fire	10	100 000	10 000
Flood	20	10 000	500
Major fraud	8	400 000	50 000
Major terrorist attack, etc.	100	1 000 000	10 000

Since EAC figures are built on rough predictions of probability and criticality they are seldom accurate. This fact does not deter some supporters of quantitative risk assessment, who argue that it is also possible to justify the cost of individual controls by estimating their savings, again calculated on an annualized basis. For example they might argue that a new security system, costing say $100 000, was justified because it reduced the probability of a certain type of fraud from once in 8 years to once in 20, thus:

Existing EAC = 1/8 × 400 000 = 50 000
Reduced EAC = 1/20 × 400 000 = 20 000
Savings   = 30 000 p.a.

Management might be pursuaded to spend 100 000 based on a 'payback period' of slightly more than 3 years!

Although quantitative methods appear sophisticated, they are imprecise and it is quite impossible to justify the cost benefits of controls based on theoretical 'savings'.

Qualitative methods of risk assessment make no attempt to calculate EACs but simply place systems in one or more broad classifications. Typically these would include those shown in Table 10.2.

Table 10.2 Classification of systems

System considered exposed to	Classified as
Loss unavailability of systems resources, resulting in processing delays of serious financial significance	VITAL
Disclosure release of information of value or having privacy or statutory protection requirements without authority	PROPRIETARY
Modification alteration of data resulting in a financial loss	FINANCIAL

Management would then decide that systems classified as *vital* should, among other things, be provided with standby hardware: in those classified *proprietary*, password files should be encrypted and so on.

Thus the differences between quantitative and qualitative methods of assessment can be summarized as shown in Table 10.3.

Table 10.3 Quantitative and qualitative methods of risk evaluation

	Quantitative	Qualitative
Risks identified by:	Usually objective methods	Usually subjective methods
Risks quantified by	Annual cost (EAC) based on estimates of probability and criticality	Broad classifications
Controls determined	By annual savings	By management standards according to each class
Control costs justified	By annual savings	By management in line with agreed classifcations and controls
Uniformity across systems obtained by	Individual risk	Classifications and control standards
Auditability	Individual basis	Against agreed control standards

In practice, qualitative methods appear to work effectively in large organizations providing they are sufficiently granular to ensure that protection is consistent between different systems. The main objections are that too much is left to the judgement of management and that costs and the efficiency of controls cannot be justified in financial terms. Quantitative methods imply unattainable accuracy and involve enormous effort with limited practical value.

PRINCIPLES OF RISK MANAGEMENT

Whichever method is used, risk identification is a starting point rather than being an end in itself and principles of risk management have to be considered. There are four main methods of dealing with identified risks.

Risk acceptance

Identified risks may be accepted, without the need for further controls, under the following circumstances:

- the cost of controls exceeds the predicted cost of risks;
- controls would place unworkable restrictions on necessary business operations;
- risks are highly improbable or of little consequence.

It is clearly essential that risk acceptance decisions are elevated to the proper management levels. It should not, for example, be left to a junior operator to decide what level of standby hardware is necessary.

Risk transfer

Risks, once identified, may be transferred to a third party: usually an insurance company. Transfer usually applies to risk of low probability but high criticality. Clearly the premium charged by the insurance carrier will be greater than its own estimate of the corresponding EACs.

Risk avoidance

Strategic changes can be made to operations so that risks are avoided: for example a high risk research and development application might be removed from a mainframe (which has dial-up facilities) to a dedicated mini computer.

Risk reduction

Risks, once identified, may be reduced by introducing additional controls which cut back on their probability or criticality or ideally on both.

The methods of risk management can be summarized as shown in Table 10.4.

Table 10.4   Methods of risk management

	Probability	
Criticality	High	Low
Low	Reduction Acceptance	Acceptance
High	Reduction Avoidance Transfer	Avoidance Transfer

Recommended method of approach

This chapter proposes a practical and workable compromise between quantitative and qualitative methods of risk evaluation which takes the alternative methods of risk management into account. The starting point is the appointment of a project team.

APPOINTMENT OF A COMPUTER SECURITY PROJECT TEAM

It would be an exceptional person who would claim that he could solve all security problems by himself. In most companies, computer security is a compromise: either security and audit people struggling with technology or computer people trying to learn accounting and security as they go along. The most effective way of using these resources is to coordinate them in a computer security project team.

Ideally the team should consist of:

- a senior accountant
- a senior programmer
- an internal audit representative
- the security adviser or external consultant *experienced in investigations*
- user department representatives

and it should have direct access to a board member.

Precise terms of reference should be prepared and approved by senior management. The most important of these is to decide whether the team has to review risks and controls in one system or whether it is to set standards for general application in a number of installations throughout the organization.

Either way, it is often difficult to identify the boundaries of any computer system, since apparently different applications share common environments and hardware components (see Figure 10.7).

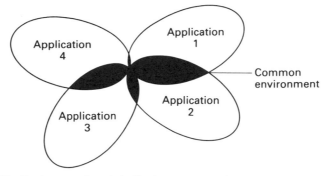

Figure 10.7 Environment and dedicate component

The team should take realistic decisions on the boundaries of the systems under review. This can be done by breaking them down for analysis purposes into identifiable hardware and software components in shared *environments* and components *dedicated* to specific applications. Clearly the security over components in the shared environment must be commensurate with the requirements of its most highly sensitive application.

Wherever possible, deadlines should be set and the team held accountable for meeting them.

ECLECTIC RISK EVALUATION

The first task of the team is to identify risks in the system or systems under review. The broad cross-section of skills in the team should ensure that most possibilities are considered (see Figure 10.8).

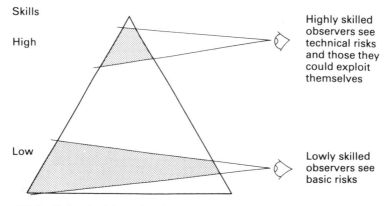

Figure 10.8 Eclectic risk evaluation

The team should consider accidental, natural and deliberate risks and use the best available methods of assessing their probability and criticality as shown in Table 10.5.

Table 10.5   Sources of information

	Overt	Covert
Accidental	Published reports Internal statistics	Subjective analysis
Natural	Insurance statistics	
Deliberate	Previous experience	Vulnerability charts, etc.

Members of the team should be issued with sets of analysis sheets similar to that shown in Figure 10.9 and a reference table of the type shown in Figure 10.10 (on page 392). Each member should be asked to complete analysis sheets, showing the risks they perceive in as much detail as possible and particularly the methods of fraud and the components concerned.

Estimates of probability and criticality for each risk should be taken from the reference table and the appropriate figures, together with the broad estimated annual cost entered on the analysis sheet. For example, if an event was thought likely to occur once in 20 years with a possible criticality of 100 000 the EAC would be read off the reference table as 5000.

Analysis sheets should be summarized and brainstormed by the team. This will inevitably result in some additional risks being identified and others eliminated as impracticable. Further discussion might be necessary to produce the final catalogue of risks. This, which should obviously be handled securely, will present the best subjective estimate of all risks in the system concerned.

A summary chart may be completed along the lines of Figure 10.11 (page 393). This allocates the broad EACs taken from the analysis sheets to specific components.

On the example analysis sheet (Figure 10.9), F21 identifies a risk of fraud in the accounts payable system with an estimated probability of once in 20 years and a criticality of £100 000. This produces a broad EAC of £5000. The components which have to be overcome for this fraud to succeed are terminals, bought ledger and cancelled cheques. The summary chart (Figure 10.11) apportions the EAC of £5000 to these components on a best guess

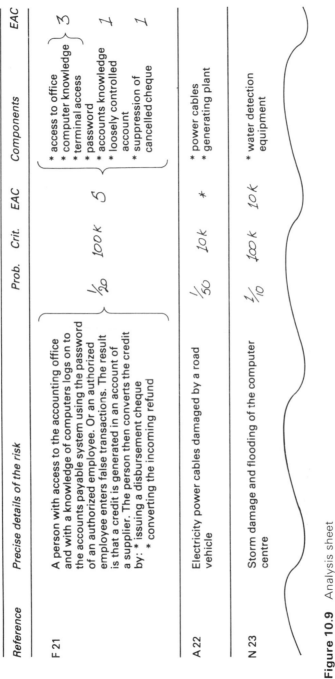

Reference	Precise details of the risk	Prob.	Crit.	EAC	Components	EAC
F 21	A person with access to the accounting office and with a knowledge of computers logs on to the accounts payable system using the password of an authorized employee. Or an authorized employee enters false transactions. The result is that a credit is generated in an account of a supplier. The person then converts the credit by: * issuing a disbursement cheque * converting the incoming refund	1/20	100k	5	* access to office * computer knowledge * terminal access * password * accounts knowledge * loosely controlled account * suppression of cancelled cheque	3 1 1
A 22	Electricity power cables damaged by a road vehicle	1/50	10k	*	* power cables * generating plant	
N 23	Storm damage and flooding of the computer centre	1/10	100k	10k	* water detection equipment	

Figure 10.9 Analysis sheet

FREQUENCY OF EXPECTED OCCURRENCE

Criticality	Examples of risks by criticality	Times per day 10	Times per day 1	Times per week 1	Times per year 1	25	5	10	20	50	100	200	300	400
1		40	4											
100		400	40	1										
1000	Inout frauds		400	40	1									
10000	Purchase fraud			400	10	4	2	1						
100000	Master file fraud				100	40	20	10	5 (Risk FD1 — EAC)	2	1			
1000000	One-time fraud				1M	400	200	100	50	20	10	5 (Risk FD2 — EAC)	3	5
2000000	Terrorist attack				2M	800	400	200	100	40	20	10	10	5
3000000	Bombing				3M	1M	600	300	150	60	30	15	10	7
4000000	Fire				4M	2M	800	400	200	80	40	20	10	10
5000000	Wire transfer fraud				5M	2M	1M	500	250	100	50	25	15	10
6000000	National strike				6M	3M	1M	600	300	120	60	30	20	15
7000000					7M	3M	2M	700	350	140	70	35	20	15
8000000					8M	3M	2M	800	400	160	80	40	25	20
9000000								900	450	180	90	45	30	25
10000000								1M	500	200	100	50	30	25

The matrix shows approximate EACs in thousands. Thus a risk with a probability of 1 in 25 years and criticality of £100000 has an EAC of £40K.

In some cases, EAC figures have been rounded.

Figure 10.10 Reference table

	Covert: Deliberate						S1	S2	Covert: Accidental				TOTAL EAC OF COMPONENTS
	F1	F2	F3	F4	F21	F22			C1	C2	C3	C4	
(a) COMPUTER EQUIPMENT													
CPU													
Back-up CPU													
Terminals					3	(1)				ADD ACROSS ROWS			4
Terminals						1							1
Other terminals													
RJE points													
Comms lines						(2)							2
...continue from worksheet detail													
(b) ACCOUNTING RECORDS													
Bought ledger					1	1							2
Nominal ledger													
Cash book													
Blank cheques													
Cancelled cheques					1								1
...continue from worksheet details					(5)	(5)							10

Figure 10.11 Summary chart

principle as follows: terminals (3000), bought ledger (1000) and cancelled cheques (1000).

When all risks have been entered the total for each component can be added across the summary chart, to show the broad EACs of all risks to which they are exposed.

In practice, there are seldom major problems in agreeing factors of probability and criticality in the wide groupings shown on the reference table. Although the figures finally produced are naturally 'fuzzy' they are a good guide to risks and to the areas where controls could be applied most effectively.

SELECTION OF CONTROLS

Many textbooks contain lists of possible controls. The art is to ensure that those selected are appropriate to the risks in the system concerned.

Thus the team should select those controls they believe most appropriate to the components highlighted on summary charts. The decision to recommend a particular control will depend on collective judgement of the broad EACs rather than on precisely quantified savings.

Finally, action plans should be prepared for the phased implementation of improvements. These will be made up of a combination of baseline and other controls.

BASELINE CONTROLS

Baseline controls are considered the minimum required in any computer system, irrespective of the finer points of risk evaluation and risk management.

The concept of baselines was introduced in an excellent report entitled *Computer Crime*, sponsored by the Department of Justice. It sets out 82 controls which the authors considered appropriate to all computer systems. To make the report even more relevant to commercial operations, the controls have been added, rearranged and edited as follows.

Management policies
1. Policies on controls should be defined by senior management.
2. All employees should be required to maintain security of data processing resources under their control. Guidelines should be issued by management on the standards expected. The responsibility for security should be incorporated on job descriptions and contracts of employment. Compliance with security procedures should be a factor on which suitability for promotion is based: deliberate non-compliance should result in dismissal.
3. All employees should sign undertakings on conflicts of interest, misuse of

computer resources, the protection of classified information and the reporting of security violations.
4. All job applicants should be screened prior to employment. The screening process should be controlled by security rather than by personnel.
5. Data should be classified and protected according to its sensitivity.
6. Insurance should be held for all computer activities including

- asset loss protection
- business interruption
- expense of contingency recovery
- fraud

Insurance should be considered to be a 'fall back' when security fails. It is normally prudent to obtain cover against losses of low probability and high criticality.

The problems described in connection with fidelity insurance (Chapter 7) apply equally to newer types of computer crime policies. Special care should be taken over the following aspects:

(a) If possible the same carrier should be used for both fidelity and computer crime insurance.
(b) If an important risk is not directly included in the policy (e.g., computer driven telex machines) a side letter should be obtained from the carrier confirming cover.
(c) Risks should not be doubly protected under both fidelity and computer crime policies or, if they are, premium reductions should be negotiated.
(d) All policies should contain a precise definition of the term 'employee'.
(e) Interlocking arrangements should be negotiated when a change of carrier is contemplated.
(f) Policies should be negotiated outside the preprinted standard, when appropriate.
(g) Verbal assurances on the scope of coverage should not be accepted. All policy conditions should be carefully documented.
(h) A system should ensure that the carrier is advised of any changes to accounting or computer controls. This is essential.
(i) Cover should be extended to working 'directors'.
(j) If cover is conditional on a risk management survey, the consultant should be retained jointly by the applicant and the carrier.

Physical security
1. Buildings housing computer facilities should be unobtrusive and give the minimum indication of their purpose. Notice boards should not draw

attention to the physical location of computer facilities. However, physical barriers and security systems should be reasonably visible to deter intruders.

2. All important functions should be included in a protected environment. Supporting equipment, such as air conditioning, power and telecommunications lines should also be secured.

3. Buildings should be designed so that access to sensitive areas is restricted.

4. Physical access points should be limited to the lowest number possible, consistent with safety. Openings should be controlled by one of the following:

   - sign in and out logs
   - manned control points (e.g., receptionist/guard)
   - mechanically or electronically operated doors
   - mantraps and turnstiles
   - alarmed emergency exits

5. All persons authorized to enter sensitive areas should be required to wear a badge or pass bearing their photograph. Different colour codings can be used for different areas: temporary badges should be issued to visitors.

6. Loading docks (for the receipt of goods) and mail rooms should be secure. Vehicles and persons should not be allowed to enter secured areas until they have been identified and their bona fides established.

7. Communication lines should be secured, particularly at main distribution frames and junction boxes.

8. Sensitive areas should be fully secured when unoccupied.

9. Hazardous and combustible material should be stored in a protected area, remote from data processing equipment.

10. Emergency procedures should be developed, tested and practised on a regular basis.

11. Smoking, eating and drinking should be prohibited in computer areas. Rules should be strictly enforced.

12. A back-up power supply—independent of the public utility—should be available.

Terminal and access controls

1. Terminal access should be physically restricted. Terminals should be located in locked rooms and power should be disabled during unattended periods. Terminal locks should be considered.

2. Terminal hardware identifiers should be used in appropriate cases.

3. All external and third-party users should be required to sign a legal agreement indicating their understanding of security policies.

4. Strict control should be applied to dial-up facilities.

5. The transactions that a user can process should be limited.
6. Requests for changes in access levels or modes of access should be approved through a formal system.
7. Terminal log on protocols should give the minimum amount of information to prevent attempts at unauthorized access. Feedback and help calls should be kept to a minimum. Repeated unsuccessful attempts at log on should be reported as violations.
8. Every sensitive file should be protected by a password. File access should be further restricted by mode of access (e.g., read only).
9. The password file should be kept in encrypted form.
10. Users should be allowed to change their passwords at any time.
11. Passwords should be managed under a secure system: with enforced changes on a periodic basis.
12. A record should be kept to establish the identity of passwords and users: including the dates of use and the resources to which access was allowed.
13. Data bases should be controlled to restrict users to access only that data they need to perform their jobs.
14. Similar restrictions should be applied to the fields in a data base that any employee is allowed to update.
15. On a periodic but random basis, communications between the CPU and remote terminals should be monitored and file names and contents examined.

Manual controls
1. Users should be formally assigned responsibility for the accuracy, safekeeping and dissemination of the data they handle.
2. Dissemination of incomplete or obsolete data should be restricted.
3. Unwanted sensitive output should be destroyed under secure conditions.
4. Data base updates should be carefully controlled and audited after the event.

Operations security
1. All computer operators should be issued with a unique identification/user code. These codes should be used to establish accountability for processing.
2. Financially sensitive applications (e.g., those producing cheques or negotiable instruments) should be run under top security conditions. This might include the disabling of external communications during processing or other isolation mechanisms.
3. All faults and failures should be logged. The log should be reviewed by a member of management.
4. Systems activity logs should be maintained and reviewed to detect

unauthorized running. Console logs should be written to magnetic tape and on continuous paper, each entry should be numbered to detect omissions and destruction of pages. All logs should show the names of the operators on duty.

5. Computer processing should be made as automatic as possible through the maximum use of job set-up, job control, and automated library programs.

6. Consideration should be given to using a separate machine for test purposes. A formal system should be used to approve the transfer of programs from test to production libraries.

7. The use of current or sensitive data for test purposes should be prohibited.

8. Systems utilities should be carefully controlled:

   (a) Identify the restricted and engineers' utilities available on the system.
   (b) Establish what commands can be used to:

   (i) compromise passwords, particularly when the system is being loaded or reset;
   (ii) directly alter data or amend files;
   (iii) remedy systems crashes by resetting flags and registers;
   (iv) disregard/override/rewrite input file balances and control totals;
   (v) suppress entries on systems logs;
   (vi) increase privilege levels to data and programs.

   (c) Consider storing restricted utilities offline and establish a close control over loading and use.
   (d) Ensure that customer engineers' diskettes are properly secured.
   (e) Establish close control over outside personnel working in the computer room so that engineers and analysts are not left unsupervised.
   (f) Restrict access to the system console.
   (g) Remove signposts to files that hold information which could be fraudulently manipulated, i.e., change the names of directories and payroll files so that they cannot be readily identified when listed out.
   (h) Encrypt sensitive data on disk so that it cannot be accessed without authority.
   (i) Establish effective manual controls to interface with computer totals.

9. 'Fast and dirty' fixes, which can be used to make changes to programs (e.g., DITTO or Superzap) should be monitored carefully. Programs and data files which have been temporarily amended should be considered suspect until formal and audited maintenance procedures have been complied with.

10. Tape management and library controls should be efficient and auditable.
11. Production programs should be checked from identifiers against an approved inventory. Separate lists should be maintained for production and test libraries.
12. Audit programs should be kept offline, outside the data processing centre.
13. To ensure independence and non-interference with audit programs, auditors should consider running their work on a computer not associated with the system under test (e.g., on a timesharing service).
14. Every piece of equipment that is separately powered should have a circuit breaker in its electrical supply. Circuit breakers should be clearly labelled.
15. Emergency 'power off' switches should be located alongside exits. Back-up power supplies should be regularly tested.
16. Magnetic tape erasure and line monitoring equipment should be kept under secure conditions. A request for their use should be submitted and a record kept after the event. (This equipment should not be available in back-up stores!)
17. Back-up files, programs and documentation should be maintained off site under secure conditions and preferably not under the control of computer operators.
18. A written disaster plan should be prepared and tested. Responsibilities should be assigned covering major and minor disasters. Priority processing should be identified.
19. Couriers (both the company and individuals) should be checked out before engagement. Systems should be provided to establish accountability for all items handed to and received from couriers. All items should be transmitted in locked containers. All users should be informed immediately a particular courier's services have been terminated. Couriers should be required to carry special identification badges.
20. Output awaiting collection should be secured.

Program development and maintenance

1. Owners and users should be responsible for setting out control requirements at the program design stage.
2. Auditors should be involved in the design of controls and the formal approval of systems.
3. A quality control or peer group should review new applications and documentation for compliance with specifications. The group should also test programs prior to final acceptance.
4. All changes to programs should be logged in a permanent record.

5. Data file and program names should not be set out in user documentation. Alternative names for files, etc., should be used in their place.
6. Computer program libraries should be protected as should all associated documentation. Source listings should be signed out to the control of individual programmers, when needed.

Computer systems controls

1. To the greatest extent possible, vendor supplied programs should be used without modification.
2. All proposed program changes should be reviewed in advance for their positive and adverse consequences.
3. Data bases containing sensitive personal information should be designed to prevent compromise.
4. Highly sensitive data should be encrypted both in storage and transmission.
5. Exception reports should be designed to indicate automatically deviations from expected activity.
6. Validation of all input should be carried out in application programs and through the operating system.

COMPUTER AUDIT

Effective auditing can also reduce the possibilities of fraud. The Institute of Internal Auditors summarized various techniques in a series of manuals by the title: *Systems Auditability and Control.*

The main techniques and their effectiveness or limitations in uncovering frauds are summarized below.

Area audit selection

Method

A risk profile matrix is developed for each company computer installation. Risk exposure scores are attributed so that high risk installations and systems can be identified.

Uses

General management tool to identify 'auditable units'. The technique has limited use in fraud detection unless related to a full risk analysis.

Scoring

Method

Key areas in applications are weighted for risk content so that high risk systems can be identified. The audit benefit can be calculated in terms of payback.

Uses
General management tool.

Multi-site audit software

Method
Audit programs are developed centrally and used at dispersed computer centres. It provides a standard audit approach requiring limited audit and data processing skills by its users.

Problems
It is vital that the tactical routines are valid and that the integrity of audit programs is not compromised.

Competency centres

Method
Audit programs are developed and used centrally: copies of dispersed files are received at a central point for checking.

Problems
It is necessary to establish that the correct files have been sent for examination. The technique also poses problems with the security of files in transit and is restricted by the fact that local operations staff are not subject to interview.

Systems development controls

Method
Auditors are actively engaged in the development of new systems and advise on controls and the audit trails required.

Problems
It is sometimes suggested that this technique diminishes the independence of auditors.

Systems development life cycles

Method
Auditors and owners set down 'check points'. As systems development progresses auditors verify that these check points have been passed and achieved. Audit involvement also extends through the life cycle (running and maintenance) of the system.

Problems

None.

Systems acceptance review group

Method

The review group usually consists of DP staff, owners and auditors. New systems are checked against standards before being taken into use.

Problems

Care has to be taken with the initial risk evaluation, particularly in respect of covert risks and the controls necessary to deal with them.

Base case systems evaluation

Method

A standard body of test data is applied to new systems to ensure that programs operate satisfactorily.

Problems

Limited use in detecting or preventing fraud.

Control flowcharting

Method

Systems are written out on control flow charts. Control points are identified and evaluated. Useful in picking up the accounts in which fraud is likely to have an impact.

Problems

Using this technique one is unable to check that program coding is correct at the machine or object level.

Audit guide

Method

A checklist is used to identify significant audit points in new and current systems. The technique ensures that important control points are not overlooked.

Problems

Efficiency depends on the completeness of the checklist.

Post-installation audit

Method

Formal tests, consisting of one or more of the tactical methods described later, are carried out soon after the system has become operational.

Problems

More use in detecting errors than fraud.

Test data

Method

Dummy or test data is fed into the application under test and the output compared with predetermined results. The technique is intended to check the accuracy and logic of coding.

Problems

Test data is unlikely to contain the specific data item that would 'trigger' a fraudulent routine or branch.

Integrated test facility

Method

Dummy entities (customers, suppliers, etc.) are set up and dummy transactions fed through the applications under test to check the integrity of programs.

Problems

Inefficient in detecting fraud. Extremely dangerous in practice since it may be difficult to distinguish dummy transactions from fraudulent ones (at least in the mind of jurors if fraud is discovered).

Parallel simulation

Method

Duplicate live transactions are run through a standard audit copy of the application under test. Output is compared with that produced by the operational version of the program.

Problems

Difficult to maintain a fully up-to-date version of standard programs: otherwise it is an excellent audit method and may detect fraudulent program patches.

Transaction selection

Method

Based on parameters determined by auditors, transactions are automatically selected and printed out for detailed verification.

Problems

None, and providing parameters are correctly selected this can be a useful fraud detection method.

Embedded data collection

Method

Data collection modules are embedded in application programs. Parameters can be set so that transactions are tagged for special verification.

Problems

None. It can be an effective method of detecting fraud.

Extended records

Method

Software extracts details of various processes and transactions including conditional branches and decision points for manual verification.

Problems

Good systems design should produce the same results.

Generalized audit software

Method

Software packages, which can be written and controlled by auditors, extract, reform, cross-check and total data in application files and data bases. Almost unlimited use.

Problems

Selection of areas to be audited: otherwise an excellent technique.

Snapshot auditing

Method

Captures and prints out pictures of selected areas of computer memory that contain data elements involved in important decision points. May be parameter driven.

Problems

Not easily used by auditors. Mainly a systems debugging tool.

Tracing

Method

Software traces the paths followed by a program during execution. It points out branches infrequently or incorrectly used. Conditional branches are flagged.

Problems

Mainly a debugging tool for programmers.

Mapping

Method

This software tool monitors program execution and shows how and in which order program steps were executed and the time taken to execute them. It highlights unused and inefficient code and conditional branches.

Problems

Mainly used as a debugging tool.

Job accounting and data analysis

Method

A software package, usually part of the operating system, that captures and records the resources used by an application.

Problems

Can be difficult to analyse complex logs. When job accounting files are held on disk, incriminating entries may be easily erased.

Disaster testing

Method

Computer resources are withdrawn without notice so that contingency plans can be tested.

Problems

Useful: however may be difficult to organize except during quiet periods, thus giving unrealistic results.

Code comparison

Method

Program code is verified, step by step, usually at source level to check its validity.

Problems

Programs need to be checked at object or machine level unless there is total control over compilations.

Black box

Method

Audit is limited to an examination of input and output.

Problems

Not usually considered elegant by auditors but the technique can be very effective when focused on the symptoms of conversion.

Crash log audit

Method

Special checks are made on every systems crash or initial program load (during which time security may be exposed).

Problems

Normally when a system fails all logging is disabled. This technique, therefore, has limited value.

Object code comparison

Method

Without prior warning a copy is taken of the object program to be tested. The related source listing is examined for all conditional branches coding logic. The source program is recompiled and compared by computer with the copy of the object program. Differences are printed out and verified.

Problems

This method is most effective in uncovering fraudulent modification of programs.

Conclusions

The framework set out in this chapter should result in practical controls, commensurate with the risks in individual systems. But in the final analysis computer security is a matter of determination by top management. The problems are not insoluble.

Appendix A. Corporate fraud checklist

Introduction and summary of contents

INTRODUCTION

This checklist has been compiled to highlight weaknesses in controls that could be exploited by dishonesty. It is divided into 11 sections. The scoring from each section should be transferred to the evaluation on pages 418–420, where suggestions for improvements in controls are made.

The savings to be made from loss prevention are enormous. It is reckoned that the 'average company' loses between 2 and 5 per cent of gross turnover as a result of dishonesty. We believe these figures are conservative.

Bottom line benefits from reducing losses can be calculated as follows. You may wish to make these calculations for your own company.

Enter last year's gross turnover	A	_____
Enter 2 per cent of the above	B	_____
Enter last year's profits	C	_____
Calculate: $\dfrac{A \times C}{B \times 2}$ equals	D	_____

D shows the amount by which turnover would have to be increased to make a contribution equivalent to cutting losses by half!

CONTENTS

Section	Contents
1	Company policy
2	Personnel
3	Accounting
4	Preventive security
5	Purchases
6	Goods received
7	Control equipment
8	Marketing
9	Delivery transport
10	Computer security
11	Other controls

1. Company policy and standards

1.	Does the company have a loss control and security policy and a person responsible? Does it set objectives and allocate a security budget?	YES NO	0 100
2.	Is this responsibility given to a senior manager with direct access to the board?	YES NO	0 50
3.	Are all employees required to report losses, suspected frauds and other incidents under this policy?	YES NO	0 50
4.	Is this incidents reporting policy always enforced?	YES NO	0 20
5.	Does this policy extend to all areas of the company's business and to all locations?	YES NO	0 20
6.	Does the company have a written policy on business ethics and dishonesty? Is the policy enforced, invariably, whether the offender is a senior manager, a shop steward or an office cleaner?	YES NO	0 50
7.	Are people suspected of dishonesty invariably reported to the police?	YES NO	0 50
8.	Have vital company functions and supplies been backed up or duplicated so that should a prime resource fail, alternative arrangements can be turned to?	YES NO	0 30

Total this part

Please transfer this score to page 418, etc.

2. Personnel policies

1.	Does the company have a formalized system for checking on the suitability of job applicants?	YES NO	0 20
2.	Would it defend in public its right to make such checks?	YES NO	0 30
3.	What is the average length of service of employees?		
	– less than 1 year		10
	– 1 to 5 years		5
	– over 5 years		0
4.	Are employees allowed to engage in part-time jobs without company permission?	YES NO	30 0

5.	Does the company require all employees to disclose their interests in other companies?	YES NO	0 20
6.	Is there a formal scheme requiring employees in sensitive or senior jobs to make an annual declaration of private commercial interests, whether held directly or indirectly?	NO YES	20 0
7.	Is there a written policy on the personal use of telephones, photocopiers, mail and other company resources?	NO YES	30 0
8.	Is the performance of each and every employee monitored by his manager and his progress discussed openly with him?	YES NO	0 10
9.	Does the company have a grievance system for all employees, which allows them to discuss work problems freely and without adverse personal reports?	YES NO	0 5
10.	Do employees working in sensitive jobs sign agreements with the company over secrecy, assignment of copyright and trade secrets?	YES NO	0 30
11.	Are employees who resign from the company interviewed about their reasons for leaving?	YES NO	0 10

Total this part

3. Accounting policy

1.	Are all accounting systems written down in company manuals and agreed and understood by the people who have to use them?	YES NO	0 20
2.	When new systems are being designed is the vulnerability to fraud considered?	YES NO	0 10
3.	Are all costs and incomes written into small, self-contained cost and profit centres or are accounts prepared in large departmental sections? – small centres – large departments		0 20
4.	Are employees allowed to design and use their own unofficial records and forms?	YES NO	10 0
5.	Are all company records classified according to their sensitivity? – secret – private – vital	YES NO	0 30

6.	Is someone made responsible for seeing that classification standards are properly and uniformly enforced?	YES NO	0 20
7.	Are reports of exceptional transactions produced for management inspection?	YES NO	0 5
8.	Does internal audit check the action taken on such exception reports?	YES NO	0 5
9.	Are some transactions dealt with outside the formal accounting systems?	YES NO	10 0
10.	Is the accounting system sufficiently discrete and accurate to point up stock or cash shortages?	YES NO	0 30

Total this part

4. Preventive security

1. Is access to all company premises controlled on a 'need to enter' basis or can people walk in off the street without being checked or challenged?
    - controlled   0
    - can walk in   30

2.	Have trespassers been detected on company premises?	YES NO	0 5

3. Have security guards written instructions on their rights to:
    - evict trespassers
    - refuse entry
    - search   YES   0
    - arrest?   NO   20

4.	Are vehicles controlled and their entry and exit recorded on a gate/car park pass?	YES NO	0 5
5.	Are privately owned motor cars allowed to park inside the perimeter of manufacturing or distributing plants?	YES NO	20 0
6.	If 'yes' to 5 above, are such vehicles subject to random search?	YES NO	0 20
7.	Do security guards know what to do if a driver refuses to allow his vehicle to be searched?	YES NO	0 10

8.	Are all warehouses under the direct control of a supervisor or accountable person?	YES NO	0 20

Total this part

5. Purchases

1.	Does company policy require all purchases over a certain value to be made on the authority of a senior manager?	YES NO	0 5
2.	Is there a method of checking that employees do not avoid their purchasing authorities by splitting large invoices into smaller amounts, within their approval levels?	YES NO	0 20
3.	Are buyers allowed to be entertained by potential or actual suppliers?	YES NO	10 0

4.	What limits are set on hospitality payments at Christmas, etc.?
	  – none
	  – nominal
	  – £100
			30
			5
			20

5.	Are buyers required to report attempted bribery or supplier dishonesty?	YES NO	0 10
6.	Has a buyer made such a report within the last year?	YES NO	0 50
7.	Are invitations to tender for company business opened on a predetermined date, in the presence of an independent senior manager?	YES NO	0 30
8.	Are capital purchases—including land—and buildings both home and overseas—checked prior to contract to ensure that employees have not used inside information to their advantage?	YES NO	0 20
9.	Are all costs written into the budgets/accounts of the smallest possible units, so that excesses will be noticed quickly?	YES NO	0 30

Total this part

6. Goods received

1.	Are goods received checked for quantity and quality before the driver of a delivery vehicle is allowed to leave?	YES NO	0 10
2.	Is there an occasional double check on the quantity and quality of goods received?	YES NO	0 20
3.	Are copies of goods received notes used as a basis for authorizing purchase invoices?	YES NO	0 20
4.	Does a receptionist or security guard keep a chronological and intact record of all deliveries?	YES NO	0 10
5.	If there is no gatehouse check, does the goods received checker keep a list of receipts in a serially numbered book?	YES NO	0 10
6.	Are shortages quickly noticed and followed up?	YES NO	0 20
7.	Are trends and patterns in shortages monitored, that is shortages from one particular supplier or involving one delivery driver?	YES NO	0 10
8.	Are detailed stock records—of each line of goods dealt in—kept and reconciled against physical stocks?	YES NO	0 50
9.	Are all stock checks recorded in permanent record?	YES NO	0 10
10.	Is this record kept securely?	YES NO	0 10
12.	Are stock turnover periods—for each product line—monitored?	YES NO	0 10

Total this part

7. Control, mechanical and accounting machinery

1.	Has the vulnerability to fraud of control machinery been evaluated?	YES NO	0 20
2.	Is such machinery prone to malfunction or breakdown?	YES NO	30 0
3.	Do employees who use the machines complain that they are unreliable or inaccurate?	YES NO	20 0
4.	Is someone responsible for checking that control machinery has not been interfered with?	YES NO	0 10

5.	Have signs of interference been found?	YES	10
		NO	0
6.	Are supervisors aware of the possible interference methods?	YES	0
		NO	10
7.	Have the machines been tested for error/malfunction outside their normal performance accuracy, for example, at extremely fast or slow flow rates, extreme temperature, etc.?	YES	0
		NO	30
8.	Is it possible to frustrate the effect of control machinery by:		
	– destroying its printout		
	– winding back mechanical counters		
	– interfering with the recording mechanism		
	– entering false input	YES	0
	– winding on through counter capacity?	DON'T	
		KNOW	30

Total this part

8. Marketing

1.	Are references taken up on all new customers by other than the sales department?	YES	0
		NO	10
2.	Does a senior sales or credit manager visit the premises of all new customers?	YES	0
		NO	10
3.	Are credit limits set by other than the sales department and are they strictly enforced?	YES	0
		NO	10
4.	Does the company have different price schedules for different classes of customers?	YES	10
		NO	0
5	Are controls adequate to prevent manipulation of different price schedules by customers and sales staff?	YES	0
		NO	20
6.	Are products considered to be 'brand leaders'?	YES	20
		NO	10
7.	Has the sales force been asked to watch for unfair competitive practices?	YES	0
		NO	10
8.	Does someone coordinate and analyse this information?	YES	0
		NO	5
9.	Do competitors consistently undercut on prices of the same goods?	YES	10
		NO	0

10.	Is much of the company's income dependent on intangibles, such as licence, royalty and other fees?	YES	20
		NO	0

Total this part

9. Delivery transport

1.	Are the delivery routes of your drivers varied from day to day or do they have regular routes?		
	– varied day to day		0
	– regular		20
2.	Can drivers predict what deliveries they are likely	YES	20
	to make two or three days ahead?	NO	0
3.	Are detailed work records specifying:		
	– mileage covered		
	– customers served		
	– quantities of goods delivered	YES	0
	submitted by all drivers?	NO	10
4.	Are customers' complaints of short deliveries fol-	YES	0
	lowed up by an in-depth investigation?	NO	10
5.	If drivers are allowed to refuel their vehicles out-		
	side company premises, are they required to sub-	YES	0
	mit a proper invoice?	NO	10
6.	Are m.p.g. figures kept for each vehicle?	YES	0
		NO	20
7.	Does an independent person load all delivery trucks or do drivers do their own loading?		
	– independent		0
	– drivers		20
8.	Are spot checks made on quantities loaded?	YES	0
		NO	20
9.	Are drivers required to sign for the accuracy of	YES	0
	their loads before they leave company premises?	NO	20
10.	If a customer is unable to accept all of the goods loaded for him, are drivers allowed to divert to		
	another customer without first obtaining permis-	YES	20
	sion?	NO	0

Total this part

10. Computer security

1. Who is responsible for ensuring that the company's computer systems, mini computers and computer based control machinery are not exposed to fraud and other risks?

– the computer manager	15
– the chief accountant	15
– the security officer	15
– a committee of the above plus line management representatives	0

2. Are standards for system design, new applications, changes, etc., written down in a company manual and invariably followed?

	YES	0
	NO	20

3. Are new systems and system changes looked at from a fraud vulnerability point of view?

	YES	0
	NO	20

4. Are responsibilities within computing separated between various functions?

	YES	0
	NO	10

5. Are all computer costs charged back to users?

	YES	0
	NO	30

6. Are program testing costs similarly written back into a small and controlled budget?

	YES	0
	NO	20

7. Is rejected data clearly listed and followed up or is it transferred into suspense accounts for subsequent manual adjustment?

– listed	0
– into suspense accounts	20

8. Are all exceptions to financial programs properly controlled?

– suspense accounts		
– adjustment codes	YES	0
– fixed pricing codes	NO	30

9. Are all amendments to financial master files documented, printed out for checking by user departments and authorized in writing?

	YES	0
	NO	30

10. Are all highly sensitive programs run during normal business hours under close supervision?

	YES	0
	NO	20

11. Are dial-up facilities closely monitored?

	YES	0
	NO	30

12. Are real time entries backed up by adequate logs and user department printouts and balances?

	YES	0
	NO	20

13. Have experienced analysts (from outside the

company) been asked to test the security of the company's main systems?	YES	0
	NO	10
14. Are all employees who are dismissed or resign their computing jobs released immediately?	YES	0
	NO	10

Total this part

---

11. Other controls and checks

1. Are company waste paper, carbon, typewriter ribbons, etc.
   - shredded 0
   - burned 0
   - collected by ordinary waste collection service? ... 20

2. Are sensitive offices checked for the presence of electronic eavesdropping equipment?   YES 0   NO 10

3. Not all frauds are long term and planned. What are the possibilities of the company being the victim of a one-time, large scale 'rip-off' in which the thief relies on a fast escape?
   - low 0
   - high 30
   - don't know 30

4. Are staff at the point of business given training to spot fraudulent transactions?   YES 0   NO 10

5. Has the company been the victim of large fraud (over £50 000), if so how was it detected?
   - by company auditors 0
   - by police 10
   - by security 10
   - by accident 50
   - don't know 100

6. Were the people responsible prosecuted?   YES 0   NO 50

7. Were all company departments told about the fraud so that they would know what to look out for?   YES 0   NO 10

8. Were defences reviewed to prevent the fraud being repeated?   YES 0   NO 30

9. Have contingency plans been drawn up to enable the company to respond—without panic—to extortion, bomb threats, or kidnapping?   YES 0   NO 20

10.	Have these plans been tested and accepted by the police?	YES NO	0 10
11.	Are unusual sources of income: — rents — royalties and licence payments — bad debt dividends — scrap sales — company cars — unwanted fixed assets — redundant stocks properly controlled? Would shortages be noticed?	YES NO	0 20
12.	When large errors are found in sales invoices (underbilling) or purchases (overbilling) or in cash or stock shortages, are the possibilities of fraud investigated?	YES NO	0 20
13.	Have 'errors' of the type described been found in your company? If so, was the beneficiary of the error made to repay?	NO YES	20 0
14.	Has adequate fidelity insurance cover been obtained for all company operations?	YES NO	0 50
15.	Is there a system to make sure that cover remains valid even when staff and systems change?	YES NO	0 40

Total this part

Corporate fraud evaluation

Section number	Level	Indicates
1	100 plus	**Company policy and standards** This score suggests that the company does not take loss control seriously. *Security is an attitude* that spreads from the top of an organization down. If top management does not give the lead with a security and loss control policy, it cannot be surprised if lower levels of management and employees display a 'couldn't care less' attitude.
2	50 plus	**Personnel policies** This score indicates that the company could be infiltrated with ease. Honest people are a company's greatest asset and dishonest or grossly inefficient ones its greatest weakness. Efficient and fair personnel policies that stimulate morale and company loyalty can have a great effect on all aspects of a company's operations; including security. Moreover, an efficient company is less likely to attract the attention of either internal or external thieves and is more likely to detect them should they be tempted.
3	40 plus	**Accounting policy** A sound and formalized accounting policy—which pinpoints losses and responsibility for them—is an essential defensive element. When accounts are loosely defined and sloppily controlled, errors are more likely to occur and not be noticed, fraud is more easily concealed and downright dishonesty more easily glossed over as a misunderstanding or mistake. A score of 40 plus on this part should serve as a warning that the company's accounts are not properly controlled.
4	40 plus	**Preventive security** Good preventive security ensures that thieves cannot walk in off the street and rob, steal or bomb. Uncontrolled access is an invitation to external dishonesty and a threat to the safety of staff. A score in excess of 40 should lead you to question and review the value of the company's security defences.

Section number	Level	Indicates
5	50 plus	**Purchases** Purchases are one of the easiest and, therefore, most common avenues of internal, external and collusive fraud. Inflation of true costs to cover bribes paid to buyers is difficult to detect unless they are charged to small and efficient cost centres where the inflations should be noticeable. A score of 50 plus indicates a potential problem.
6	40 plus	**Goods received** Short delivery of goods is a common method of fraud, simply because too many companies fail to check on the quality and quantity of goods invoiced and supposedly delivered to them. The receiving company has the right to check and should not be put off or sign a delivery note until *sure* the correct quantity and quality has been delivered. Records of checks on stocks should be kept in a permanent record to which the regular stockkeeper should not have access.
7	30 plus	**Control equipment, etc.** Most companies rely on machinery (weighbridges, flow meters, cash tills, etc.) to measure or control goods received, in stock or delivered. Through some quirk in human nature, people assume that such machines must be accurate. In fact, they can be manipulated quite easily. A score of 30 plus should cause your company to check.
8	40 plus	**Marketing** Unfair competition is not usually discovered until too late! A score of 40 or over indicates that the company would be an easy victim of competitor fraud.
9	40 plus	**Delivery transport** Even in the most sophisticated frauds, thieves need to gain possession of goods or a tangible interest of value; in many cases this means the delivery of goods into their custody. Control over deliveries can, therefore,

Section number	Level	Indicates
		frustrate such defalcations and can also reduce the problem of driver dishonesty.
10	50 plus	**Computer security** Computers must be viewed in the total company context and not as a self-contained unit or self-contained problem. A score of 40 plus and the company may be merely 'picking' at the subject and not defending in depth.
11	50 plus	**Other controls and checks** These general points evaluate the company's awareness to special risks. Criminals hit the weak points; a score in excess of 50 indicates some fairly conventional weaknesses that could be exploited quite easily.

SUMMARY

The time to act on security is before the disaster. Prevention is better than cure.

Appendix B

NOTES

The following questionnaire was developed by FACT FINDER INTERNATIONAL based on over 20 years experience in commercial and computer fraud investigation and prevention. The questions, divided into ten blocks, cover the key aspects of the "Differential of Opportunity Theory" and have alongside them scores, depending on the significance of the job attribute in relation to fraud and other security risks. There is a degree of overlap between some of the questions; this is deliberate.

We suggest the form should be completed in the following way:

- assemble full details about the job in question

- if possible discuss its practical aspects with people who have held the position in the past

- work through the questionnaire, block by block, circling the points total appropriate to each question. *More than one points entry can be made against each question*

- total up the points for each block

- transfer the points to the Appraisal page 9

- multiply the points by the weighting factors shown on page 9

- enter the final points total

- the sensitivity total should be used to determine the depth of pre employment screening necessary - the levels are shown - the higher the points total, the more sensitive the job

We recommend that any job producing a total of 600 points or more should never be filled unless the background of the candidate has been thoroughly checked by positive vetting methods.

If Fact Finder International Limited is used in the checking process and gives clearance, Fidelity Insurance cover is automatically given to the candidate, usually at rates significantly lower than otherwise available.

CHECK LIST
1 Reporting Lines

FACT FINDER
INTERNATIONAL
LIMITED
© London 1982

		Points	Remarks
A Position reports to	Board Level	5	
	Board Level -1	4	
	Board Level -2	3	
	Other	1	
B Immediate manager has the following number of people reporting to him	1 to 5 employees	2	
	6 to 12 employees	4	
	more than 12	5	
C The position has the following number of people reporting to it	1 to 5 employees	2	
	6 or more	4	
	Contractors	5	
	none	2	
TOTAL OF THIS SECTION			

Transfer total to page 9

2 Profession or Occupation

	Points	Remarks
FINANCIAL		
Financial control : general	5	
Financial record keeping	4	
Cashier	5	
Contracts Management	9	
Sales Accounting	6	
Bought Ledger accounting	7	
Other	4	
COMPUTING		
Systems Analyst	7	
Programmer	7	
Operator	5	
Other	5	
STAFF		
Auditor	8	
Security Manager	8	
Legal Adviser	5	
Personnel	7	
SECRETARIAL		
Board level secretary	8	
Board level - 1 or 2 secretary	7	
Other personal secretary	5	
Typing pool	3	
Filing staff	3	
GENERAL MANAGERIAL		
Sales Manager	8	
Sales Representative	5	
Support services	7	
Purchasing or Contracts Manager	9	
Buyer	7	
Purchasing Support	6	
Manufacturing Manager	3	
Warehouse Manager	5	
Transport Manager	6	
Advertising, Sales & Promotions	6	
COMMUNICATIONS		
Computer Terminal Operator	5	
Telex Operator	6	
Communications Engineer /Manager	7	
LABOUR AND WORKERS		
Transport Drivers	6	
Warehouse Operator	5	
Receiving - Goods In - staff	6	
Manufacturing	1	
Other	1	
TOTAL OF THIS SECTION		

Transfer total to page 9

2

3 Nature of Supervision & Control

	Points	Remarks
A ROUTINE WORK		
policy setting and innovation	7	
innovation within general policy	5	
follows written policy	3	
B LOCATION OF JOB		
in single occupancy office or from home	4	
office shared with one other person	2	
'open' office or work area.	0	
remote from company head office	1	
travelling (mainly)	3	
overseas or remote base	5	
TOTAL OF THIS SECTION		

4 Skill and Qualification Level

	Points	
A Degree or equivalent as a background qualification (entry level)	5	
B Degree or equivalent for specific daily duties	8	
C Other	2	
TOTAL OF THIS SECTION		

5 Authority Levels

		Enter reduced points for shared authority
A Has authority to sign for a *single transaction* on his own of :		
up to £1,000	5	
up to £10,000	7	
over £10,000	9	
TOTAL OF THIS SECTION		

Transfer all totals to page **9**

3

6 Discretion (EITHER FORMAL OR CONTRIVED)

	Points	Remarks
A Is able to exercise discretion in favour of *third parties* with significance to them of:		Enter reduced points for shared authority
up to £10,000 p.a.	5	
up to £100,000 p.a.	7	
over £100,000 p.a.	10	
B Is able to exercise discretion in favour of employees:		
to recruit	4	
promote	6	
dismiss	3	
C Is able to quote for sales contracts and select vendors		
under a formal bidding system	5	
on own authority	10	
D Is able to quote sales prices		
under a formal and written system	3	
on own authority	8	
TOTAL FOR THIS SECTION		

Transfer total to page 9

7 Control Responsibility

		Enter reduced points for shared authority
A Approves expenditure		
up to £500 per instance	3	
up to £10,000 per instance	5	
more than £10,000	9	
B Directly controls annual cost budget of		
up to £10,000	5	
up to £100,000	7	
more than £100,000	9	
C Establishes Sales Prices to customers		
on formal price list	3	
to individual customers	5	
allocates scarce products	7	
D Controls special allowances/rebates etc	7	
E Controls income or revenue directly of		
up to £100,000	4	
up to £1,000,000	5	
more than £1,000,000 p.a.	8	

7 Control Responsibility CONTINUED

	Points	Remarks
F Controls bank records		Enter reduced points for shared authority
daily reconcilliations	5	
supervises accounts generally	4	
money or funds management:		
foreign exchange	9	
issue of disbursement cheques	8	
daily bankings (cash and cheques)	9	
manages EFTS operation	10	
G Controls Customer or Supplier Accounts		
liaises and visits premises	7	
responsible for statements	5	
responsible for approving invoices	8	
responsible for credit notes	5	
H Controls Trading and Investment of Funds		
Pension funds	8	
Investments	7	
Commodity and General Trading	8	
Commodity or Financial Futures	9	
I Controls Contractor or third party work records and invoices		
approves invoices	8	
allocates emergency contracts	9	
allocates 'local' contracts	9	
J Controls or handles physical movement of goods/inventories		
goods inwards or returns	7	
despatch and replacement	8	
warehouse inventories	6	
TOTAL OF THIS SECTION		

Transfer total to page 9

8 Custody and Control of Records and Computer Resources

A Has access to:		Enter reduced points for shared authority
blank cheques or equivalent	5	
returned cheques	3	
unopened incoming mail	3	
sealed outgoing mail (after approval)	5	
outgoing cheques/approved payment forms	7	
despatch notes	4	
purchase orders	3	
suspense account journal vouchers	7	

8 Custody and Control of Records and Computer Resources CONTINUED

	Points	Remarks
B Has access to:		
computer terminals	3	
systems console	7	
major computer hardware	5	
data files (prime or backup)	4	
programs and documentation	5	
communication or 'test key' codes	9	
TOTAL OF THIS SECTION		

Transfer total to page 9

9 Access to Premises and Physical Assets

A Key holding		Enter reduced points for shared authority
is a key holder to a main building	3	
holds keys to general office areas	2	
holds keys to major computer facilities	8	
holds keys to money safe	6	
B Goods		
has unrestricted access to inventories	6	
C Equipment		
has access to critical or sensitive equipment whose compromise or damage could :		
*seriously disrupt company operations	8	
*cause serious inconvenience to third parties	5	
D Classified Information		
has direct access to information concerning:		
*investment plans	8	
*trade secrets or patents	8	
*research and development	8	
*personnel records	5	
*bidding and tendering plans	5	
*market strategies, pricing policies	5	
TOTAL OF THIS SECTION		

Transfer total to page 9

10 Associated Legal Agreements

Some companies require employees in sensitive
positions to sign agreements prior to engagement.
These are an indication of the sensitivity of the jobs
concerned and the possible adverse consequences
of a breach or failure to comply. If an employee
has to (or on reflection should) sign any of the
following agreements, the points shown should
be added.

	Points	Remarks
Assignment of Patent, Trade Mark or Proprietary rights to the employer	8	
Covenants not to compete	8	
Conflicts of interests	6	
Business ethics policy	6	
Annual financial statement	9	
TOTAL OF THIS SECTION		

Transfer total to page **9**

WEIGHTING FACTORS

BLOCK	HEADING	S SCORE	W WEIGHT	S times W FACTOR
1	REPORTING LINES		10	
2	PROFESSION OR OCCUPATION		8	
3	SUPERVISION		8	
4	QUALIFICATION		5	
5	AUTHORITY		20	
6	DISCRETION		20	
7	CONTROL RESPONSIBILITY		15	
8	CUSTODY OF RECORDS ETC.		12	
9	PHYSICAL ACCESS		7	
10	LEGAL AGREEMENTS		2	

Total Appraisal Points

APPRAISAL

POINTS TOTAL	RISK LEVEL	LEVEL OF CLEARANCE RECOMMENDED
up to 200	Low	Standard Reference checks/interview
201 - 400	Medium	Negative Vetting
401 - 600	Medium/High	Basic Positive Vetting
600 +	HIGH	FULL POSITIVE VETTING FIDELITY INSURANCE RECOMMENDED

FACT FINDER
INTERNATIONAL
LIMITED
© London 1982

Appendix C. Recommended security policy

Background and purpose

This recommended security policy is based on two fundamental principles:

1. The company has the right to protect its assets and an obligation to provide a secure environment for employees.
2. All employees are expected to observe the highest standards of ethical, personal and professional conduct.

These principles will be assisted by the observance of the following procedures as well as through specific controls at individual locations.

Responsibilities

GENERAL PRINCIPLES

Each employee is responsible for maintaining security over all aspects of his or her work and for ensuring that assets, resources and information entrusted to him or her are properly protected. Compliance with this policy will be a factor in determining an employee's suitability for promotion. Conversely, employees who disregard this policy or fail to observe their responsibilities will be liable to immediate dismissal. In addition to their normal reporting channels, employees have the right to discuss matters of a security nature with the corporate security adviser, without reference to their line manager.

SENIOR MANAGEMENT RESPONSIBILITIES

The senior manager at each location and in each division is responsible for ensuring that the following procedures are maintained.

Recruitment

The backgrounds of all potential employees must be verified prior to engagement. This includes full- and part-time employees, contractors and consultants. Detailed procedures are set out in . . .

Information classification and protection

All sensitive information must be classified and protected in accordance with board procedures. See . . .

431

Approval of new investments

The corporate security adviser should be informed in writing before any investment involving the disbursement of funds greater than £500 000 is made. He is responsible for providing such advice as he deems necessary to ensure that the board's assets are properly protected.

Data security

All data processing resources must be protected in accordance with the board's guidelines. In cases of difficulty or where defined standards cannot be complied with, appropriate managers are responsible for advising the corporate security adviser in writing and without delay.

Emergency and contingency planning

Each manager is responsible for ensuring that procedures for dealing with bombs, bomb threats and other emergencies are complied with and known to all employees under his or her control. Managers are also responsible for identifying any critical resource, service or process which if lost or compromised could seriously hinder the continued operations of the company. Standby or alternative sources should be identified and appropriate plans prepared and tested. The corporate security adviser should be consulted, where necessary.

Reporting incidents

All incidents of a security nature must be reported to the corporate security division, either in writing or via the *hot line*.

Other procedures

In addition managers are required to maintain and budget for the minimum standards of security laid down by the board and summarized in . . . All managers can call for assistance from the corporate security adviser at any time.

RESPONSIBILITIES OF CORPORATE SECURITY

The corporate security adviser is responsible for:

- advising management on all aspects of security
- setting down standards to be maintained
- conducting surveys and investigations
- liaising with police and other law enforcement bodies
- assisting managers and employees in the discharge of their security responsibilities

These responsibilities do not detract from nor diminish the prime obligation of all employees and line managers to maintain security.

RESPONSIBILITIES OF EMPLOYEES

Each employee is responsible for maintaining security over all aspects of his or her work:

- reading and complying with procedures and local practices
- drawing risks, deviations from procedures and suspected fraud to the attention of management and/or the corporate security adviser
- assisting corporate security in the conduct of investigations

If any employee has any doubts over what his or her responsibilities under this policy might be, he or she should not hesitate in contacting his/her manager or the corporate security adviser.

Cases of suspected fraud

The company will not tolerate dishonesty of any kind. It is an invariable policy to dismiss dishonest employees without notice, to press for prosecution and to make financial recovery through the civil courts.

Conduct of investigations

The corporate security adviser is responsible for conducting investigations into all suspected losses and incidents of a security nature. Employees are required to assist by making available all relevant information and cooperating in interviews. Failure to comply with this requirement may lead to dismissal.

Interpretation

If any employee has any questions in regard to this policy he or she should not delay in discussing them with his or her manager or with the corporate security adviser.

Reading List

General security

Bridges, C. and Bugg, D., *Burglary Protection and Insurance Surveys*, Stone and Cox, London, 1975. Excellent reference book on locks and physical security.

Hamilton, Peter *et al.*, *Handbook of Security*, Kluwer Harrap, London. A high level, updated manual on all aspects of security. Slightly more theoretical than the *Protection of Assets Manual*, but still very good value and highly recommended.

Oliver, Eric and Wilson, John, *Practical Security in Commerce and Industry*, Gower, London, 1982 (Revised). Considered to be a standard text for the security practitioner although more directed towards nuts and bolts rather than security management or fraud prevention.

Walsh, Timothy J. and Healey, Dick, *Protection of Assets Manual*, Merritt, Santa Monica, Cal., 1974. A comprehensive and regularly updated manual on all aspects of security. Essential reading for any professional security practitioner.

Wright, Ken, *Cost-effective Security*, McGraw-Hill, London, 1972. A good reference book, written at a management level.

Computer security

Carroll, John M., *Computer Security*, Security World Publishing Co., Los Angeles, CA, 1977. Very good introduction and highly recommended reading.

Krauss, Leonard A. and MacGahan, Aileen, *Computer Fraud and Counter-measures*, Prentice-Hall, Englewood Cliffs, NJ, 1979. Probably the best of the lot!

Leibholz, Stephen and Wilson, Louis, *User's Guide to Computer Crime*, Chilton Book Company, Radnor, PA, 1979. One of the best books written on computer fraud and security. Originally published in 1974, but still of value.

Norman, Adrian R. D., *Computer Insecurity*, Chapman & Hall, London, 1983. Contains interesting case studies in Europe.

Parker, Donn B., *Manager's Guide to Computer Security*, Reston Publishing Company, Reston, VA, 1983. Donn Parker was among the first researchers to recognize the risks involved in computer processing. He has written extensively on his research and this book is a good summary. The book contains some interesting ideas and useful policy documents.

General fraud

Bequai, August, *White-collar Crime*, Lexington Books, Lexington, MA, 1978. Disappointing!

Kroll, Jules B. (editor), *Crimes Against Business*, Arno Press Inc., *New York Times*, 1980. Comprehensive analysis of cases reported in the press: worldwide.

Other useful references

Chambers, Andrew, *Internal Auditing*, Pitman, London, 1983. A very good practical guide to auditing.

Gorrill, B. E., *Effective Personnel Security Policies*, Dow Jones-Irwin, Homewood, IL, 1980. This is an outstanding book. It should be compulsory reading for every manager.

Inbau, Fred and Reid, John E., *Criminal Interrogation and Confessions*, Williams and Wilkins, Baltimore, MA, 1970. The best reference work available on the conduct of investigative interviews. Built on years of practical experience.

Kepner and Tregoe, *The Rational Manager*, Kepner Tregoe Inc., NJ, 1979. A textbook on problem solving and decision making. Good background for the security practitioner.

Newman, Oscar, *Defensible Space*, Architectural Press, London, 1974. An eye opening book on the interrelationships of building design and crime.

Glossary

ACCOUNT

A distinct chronological accumulation—*in balanced books*—of entries relating to an asset, liability, income or expense.

ACCOUNTING RECORD OR RECORD

See RECORDS.

ACCOUNT/INVENTORY DISCREPANCY

The difference that arises between a real inventory and its related account as a result, *inter alia*, of fraud, theft, embezzlement, accidental loss or removal. Such discrepancies are often referred to as 'wastage', 'stock losses' or 'shortages'. Discrepancies may be concealed by manipulation of accounts or by misrepresentations of physical or commercial realities. The concealment of an account/inventory discrepancy is referred to as primary manipulation or primary misrepresentation.

When a consequential debit is cleared from the real account in which it arose, further manipulation may be necessary before it can be absorbed in final accounts. This further concealment is referred to as secondary manipulation.

CLOSELY CONTROLLED ACCOUNT

An account (either real, nominal or personal) in which the accumulation of consequential debits (or discrepancies with real inventories) will almost certainly be noticed. Consequential debits are usually fraudulently manipulated into loosely controlled accounts before being absorbed or written off in final accounts.

COMPANY

Used in this text to describe any corporate body, including government departments, tax authorities, companies (in the strict legal sense), firms, partnerships and individuals engaged in commerce.

COMPUTER PROGRAM

A complete sequence of instructions for a job to be performed by a computer. Programs may be *executive* (operating systems), which are loaded into the machine to operate the main logic and processing units, or *application*, which govern and direct transaction data and specific jobs.

CONCEALMENT

An element of fraud (one of three, i.e., theft act, concealment or conversion) which is intended to disguise or delay the recognition of an account/inventory discrepancy (primary), to achieve a theft, to avoid blame or to provide the thief with a plausible excuse for his dishonesty.

Concealment may take place through the manipulation of accounts and records or by misrepresentation of a physical, commercial or personal reality. Concealment may be before, after or contiguous with a theft act or a conversion.

CONSEQUENTIAL DEBIT

When a real asset is stolen a theoretical or notional credit should be posted to its associated account so that the account and inventory agree. If the account is not credited an account/inventory discrepancy arises which in a closely contolled situation should cause a fraud to come to notice. If, however, the account for the asset stolen is falsely credited, the consequential or counterpart debit must also be posted into another account, otherwise the trial balance will be distorted. In theory the consequential debit should be posted to the personal account of the thief, but in fraud this is his last wish since he does not intend to pay for the goods stolen.

The clearance of a consequential debit is an essential part of the primary concealment process.

When a consequential debit arises in other than a real account (e.g., an expense or income account) manipulation may transfer—fraudulently—the debit into a loosely controlled nominal account which will be closed to profit and loss at the year end.

CONTROL MACHINERY

A generic term used throughout this text to represent all the various devices used in commerce to check on the quantity or value of an inventory. Under this heading are included cash registeres, weighbridges, ticket machines, flow meters, scales and dials, interference with which enables an account/inventory discrepancy to be concealed or a theft to be achieved. Interference with such equipment is usually classed as the misrepresentation of a physical reality and may be before, after or contiguous with a theft act.

CONVERSION

An element of fraud in which the asset stolen by a thief or the false credit manipulated by him is converted into something else he would prefer to possess. The most frequent conversions are:

Item 'stolen'	Converted to
– false accounting credit	– goods or cash or disbursement cheque
– stolen goods	– cash
– stolen cheque	– cash

Even in internal management frauds where the thief has almost unrestricted access to accounting records, he may not be able to conceal the impact of conversion on proportional, historical and other trends and ratios.

CRIME*

An intentional act that violates the prescription and proscriptions of the criminal law under which no legal excuse applies and where there is a state with the power to codify such laws and to enforce penalties in response to their breach. This definition says several things:

1. There is no crime without law and without a state to punish a breach.
2. There is no crime where the act is justified by the law.
3. There is no crime without intention.
4. There is no crime where the 'offender' is deemed to be incompetent—that is, without capacity.

Not all frauds can be classed as crime. In this text 'fraud' is used to include crimes and those acts through which companies may lose by the non-criminal dishonesty of 'thieves'. For example, theft of trade secrets through the use of a hidden tape recorder is not a crime; it is, however, a fraud and those that commit it are referred to as 'thieves' even though they may not be at risk of prosecution under the criminal law.

CRIMINAL

One who commits crime. 'White collar criminal' is a term widely used to refer to management class thieves who may have limited access to assets and control equipment but general access to accounting records. An embezzler could be classed as a white collar criminal.

'Blue collar or operations criminal' refers to a thief (whether internal or external to the victim company) whose job brings him into routine contact with physical assets and inventories but whose access to accounting records is possibly limited.

---

* See Gwynn Nettler, *Explaining Crime*, McGraw-Hill, New York, 1974.

DETECTION

The picking up of fraud symptoms in situations in which no prior suspicion exists. It is the initiating action from which investigation follows.

ENTRY

A deliberate writing or input into an account or on to an accounting record. Entries into accounts are 'posted'.

FALSE CREDIT

A manipulated accounting entry intended to counter an existing consequential debit (to conceal it) or to assist to achieve a theft without further concealment. A false credit can be failing to enter a debit.

FORGERY

The dividing line between a manipulated document and a forged one is fine.

A manipulated document has an accounting purpose and tells a lie about an aspect of the business: asset, liability, income or expense. It has no intrinsic value. A forged document tells a lie *about itself* and it could, if genuine, have a value of its own. For example:

- share certificates
- paper currency
- bonds

have a value. They are part of a company's *inventory* and are not accounting records.

FRAUD

Any behaviour by which one person intends to gain a dishonest advantage over another. A fraud may not be a crime. Corporate fraud refers to those frauds in which a company is involved.

INVENTORY

A factual, real asset as distinct from its related account; examples—cash, stocks, finished goods, debtors.

INVESTIGATION

That stage between the detection of fraud symptoms and their resolution. The resolution may be criminal prosecution or some other course.

LAPPING

A manipulative fraud in which consequential debits are temporarily concealed by irregular and improper transfers between accounts. Also known as 'teeming and lading'.

LARCENOUS FRAUDS AND LARCENOUS THEFTS

Unconcealed thefts. Thefts may remain unconcealed because:

– concealment is not possible
– concealment is not necessary

LONG FIRM FRAUDS

Commercial frauds in which a thief buys goods on credit and then disappears without paying. Often involve organized conspiracies.

LOOSELY CONTROLLED ACCOUNT

An account which is not controlled sufficiently to reveal an account/inventory discrepancy (or in which consequential debits may be accumulated without the risk to a thief of detection). The accounts may be real (when they have a related inventory), expense or income (when the accumulation of debits is written off to profit and loss), or personal (when the debtor or creditor does not check his account or is himself involved in fraud).

MANIPULATION

A branch of fraud concealment in which falsification of accounts and accounting records take place. The manipulation may be primary (to conceal an account/inventory discrepancy or to conceal a consequential debit) or secondary (to provide the thief with a plausible excuse or to avoid blame).

MISREPRESENTATION

The counterpart of manipulation is the concealment process. The falsification may be primary (to conceal an account/inventory discrepancy by inflating the value of the inventory so that it agrees with its associated account) or secondary (to avoid blame or to provide a plausible excuse).

The misrepresentation may be of a physical, commercial or personal reality (see Chapter 2) and may be before, after or contiguous with a theft or conversion.

NEGATIVE MANIPULATION

Falsification of an accounting record or account by the deliberate omission of an entry or the destruction of a record (as opposed to positive manipulation where a false entry or document is created). Frauds involving the suppression of sales are usually concealed by negative manipulations. For example, the destruction of cash sales invoices.

Negative manipulations may achieve primary and secondary concealment objectives. They are especially dangerous because they leave no 'audit trail'.

PLAUSIBLE EXCUSE

An excuse created by a thief, usually in advance of a fraud or theft, which enables him to pass off dishonesty as an accident or some other non-criminal omission. Probably the most common method of fraud concealment: often too readily accepted by the victims. For example, a supplier who deliberately 'double bills' for the same shipment (as a means of fraud) may provide an excuse that the computer failed or that a junior clerk made a mistake.

PRIMARY MANIPULATION

See MANIPULATION and CONCEALMENT.

REALITY

A real life physical, commercial or personal fact, as distinct from recorded information in correspondence and accounts. An inventory (e.g., cash held or stock) is a physical reality. The identification of a person is a personal reality. The standing of a company is a commercial reality.

Most realities have at least one 'central issue'. A central issue is a pivot of fundamental fact on which certain commercial transactions are based. For example, the central issue in a banking transaction may be the true identity of a person presenting a cheque. Misrepresentative frauds are concerned with falsification of central issues before, after or during a theft act as a means of concealment or of theft achievement.

RECORDS

Any document, magnetic tape, punched card, computer file or equivalent, used for recording the activities of a business. An account is a record; a record is not necessarily an account.

RETROSPECTIVE MANIPULATION

Manipulation of source documents, correspondence or memoranda to support existing or proposed false credits or concealed debits in accounts. For example, if a thief has a false credit already created in the purchase ledger, he may decide to post it into an account in which he has an interest. To support this false entry he may have to create (retrospectively) false goods inwards passes, warehouse notes, etc. Retrospective manipulations are backwards down the accounting chain from balanced accounts to source documents and correspondence.

THEFT ACT

One of the three elements of fraud, concerned with the physical movement of an asset or the removal or reduction of an interest. Theft acts are manifested in physical and behavioural ways.

THIEF

A person or company who commits or plans fraud (not necessarily a criminal in the strict legal sense).

UNRECORDED CREDIT

A manipulative process of negative type. The net effect of failing to post a genuine debit to an account is an unrecorded credit.

UNRECORDED DEBIT

The reverse of an unrecorded cedit.

VALUE ADDED TAX (VAT)

A UK sales tax.

Index

Access to fraud opportunities, 24, 146–156
Access levels, 356
Account/inventory discrepancy, 25, 26, 80, 134
Accountability:
  assets, 95
  in accounting controls, 365–366
Accounting controls, 214, 360–374
  accountability in, 365–366
  colour coding of documents, 367
  consistency and uniformity in, 366
  defined systems, 361–362
  enforcement of, 373
  numerical sequences in, 366
  overall design of, 361
  physical controls, 362–363
  record integrity, 366–367
  role in fraud prevention, 360
  rotation of duties, 368
  scope of, 361
  separation of duties, 368
  third-party intervention and corroboration, 370
Accounting manipulations, invigilation of, 236
Accounting policy, checklist, 409
Accounting principles, 74
Accounting records, 69–80
Accounting systems:
  formalized, 361–362
  in fraud prevention, 360
Accounts:
  budgetary, 76
  closing of, 76–77
  control, 76
  double entry, 74–77
  final (see Final accounts)
  management, 76
  nominal, 75
  personal, 75, 77
  real, 75

suspense (see Suspense accounts)
(see also Computer processing)
Adding machine, 112–113
Admission, reasons for making, 306
Admission statement, 317
Age effects, 5
Agents provocateurs, rules covering, 249
Anomie theory, 220
Anton Pillar order, 277, 278
Application forms, falsification of, 329
Architects, 110
Assets, 69, 210–212, 227
  accountability, 95
  at risk, 225
  uncontrolled, 93
Audit (see Computer audit)
Auditing:
  irrelevant, 10
  (see also Critical (or key point) auditing)
Auditors:
  internal, 10
  obligations of, 9
Authority levels, 221
Authorization of documents, 371
Average collection period, 70

Back-up facilities, 351–352
Balance sheet, 69, 77
Bank account, 125, 128
  cross-firing between, 129
  induced errors involving, 238
Bank frauds, 2
  attitudes to, 281
  reporting, 3
Bank losses from fraud, 5, 15
Bank robbery, 15
Bank statements, 117, 128
Behavioural symptoms of fraud, 104
Binoculars, use in detection, 246
Blackmail, 255

Blame avoidance, 130–132
  by external criminals, 131–132
  by internal criminals, 131
Bleepers, 245–246, 260
Body language, 299
Book-keeping, 173
Bottlenecks, security implications of, 143
Brainstorming, 222
Bribery, 108
  and corruption, 111, 203, 345
Briggs, Noel Currer, 358
Briston, Richard, 10
British Leyland, 102
'Bug' detection, 348
Bulk liquid stocks, spot checks on, 265–266
Business competitors, 227
Business intelligence:
  in fraud detection, 254–267
  information involved, 256
  prime objective of, 254
Byrne, Eric, 298

Cameras, use in detection, 246
Card access system, 154–155
Carey, Mary, 378
Cash, detection of shortages, 261
Cash books, 210
Cash inventory, 117
Cash payments, 210
Cash sales to credit sales ratio, 72
Central issue, definition, 374
Check Book, 2
Checklist for corporate fraud, 407–420
Cheques, 127
  conversions, 96–98
  cross-fired, 129
  disbursement, 117, 205
  doctored, 205
  examining, 200, 205
  incoming, 209–210
  stolen, 137
Civil action, 277–278
Cohen, 331
Collusion, 261
  and fraud risk, 229
  detection of, 260
  indications of, 228
  theories of minimum and maximum, 24, 28
Commercial realities:
  misrepresentation of, 137–138, 375, 376
  spot checks on, 262–264
Commission, 123

Communication:
  non-verbal, 299
  use in detection, 246–247
Communication channels, 168–169
Company informants, use in detection, 253
Company policy, 9
  and standards, checklist, 408
Compendium of Bunk or How to spot a Con
    Artist, 378
Competitors:
  and business intelligence, 254
  monitoring, 256
Computer audit, 400–406
Computer courses for prisoners, 2
Computer Crime, 394
Computer fraud, 6, 18, 99, 139–189
  access to systems, 146–156
  accounting objectives of, 156
  attitudes to, 141
  background to, 139–140
  card access system, 154–155
  definition, 140
  deliberately induced errors, 155
  dial port and network access, 148–149
  elements of, 91
  extortion and sabotage, 183–184
  failures, errors and poor adjustments, 169–
    171
  falsification of transaction data, 156–166
  falsification of transaction entry codes,
    166–168
  file names, 149–150
  front panel operations, 155
  hardware changes, 182–183
  input falsification, 157
  job control manipulation, 181–182
  mainstream, 146–185
  mainstream manipulation methods, 156–
    185
  manipulation of master files, 171–172
  motivation for, 18–21
  nature and extent, 140
  nature and risks, 143–146
  output manipulation, 175–177
  passwords, 87, 150–152
  preventive defences, 143
  privacy infringements, 184
  program patches, 178–181
  programs, 183
  prosecution, 3
  reaction to, 141
  restricted utilities, 177–178

smash and grab, 146
statistics, 4
symptoms of, 166, 168, 171, 175; 178, 181
systematic, 146
theft of resources, 184–186
unconventional methods, 183–187
Computer Fraud and Security Bulletin, 2, 10, 24, 152, 281
Computer input, 117, 127
Computer operating system weaknesses, 153–154
Computer processing, 80–90
  application programs, 83–85
  basic components, 81
  basic operations, 81
  compilers, 84
  conditional statements, 84
  crashes, 89
  customer billing, 89
  data files and data bases, 85–86
  data protection methods, 86
  error correction and adjustments, 89
  falsification of output, 88
  hardware failures, 89
  interpreter, 84
  journalling, 88
  object programs, 83
  operating systems, 81–83
  packaged programs, 85
  passwords, 87, 150–152
  queuing, spooling and printing, 87–88
  security, 83
  supervisory mode, 82
  systems console, 88
  terminals and remote access, 86–87
  user mode, 82
Computer programs, back-up media and programs, 90, 178–181, 183
Computer risks, 139, 383
  categories of, 144
  covert, 144–145
  criticality of, 144
  nature of, 144
  overt, 144–145
  probability of, 144
  (*see also* Risks)
Computer security, 141, 142, 153, 381–406
  baseline controls, 394–402
  controls, 394
  management policies, 394–402
  manual controls, 397

operations security, 397–399
physical security, 395–396
program development and maintenance, 399–400
project team appointment, 388–389
terminal and access controls, 396–397
Computer systems, 140
Computer terminal simulation programs, 152–153
Concealment, 25–27, 78, 105–138, 189
  availability of course of, 229
  investigating, 259
  logic of, 106
  opportunities for, 107
  secondary, 130–132
  theory, 25–27
  (*see also* Manipulation; Misrepresentation)
Concentration, security implications of, 143
Conflict of interest agreement, 344
Consequential debits, 107, 214, 215
Console log suppression, 155
Consultant services, 324–325
Contingency planning, 432
Contracts, 373
  of employment, 343
Control machinery, interference with, 136–137, 216
Control strategy, 322–326
  implementation of, 323
Control systems, 132
  equipment used for, 134
  interference with, 134–137
Controlled areas, 356
Controlled space technique, 353
Controls, 321–322, 356
  budgets for, 325–326
  computer security, 394
  efficiency of, 228–229
  perceptions of, 381
Conversion, 96–104, 189, 240
  investigating, 259
  of cheques, 96–98
  of false accounting credits, 98–99
  of stolen goods, 99–104
  symptoms of, 104
Corporate fraud (*see* Fraud)
Correspondence, 80
Correspondence files, examining, 208
Corruption (*see* Bribery and corruption)
Costs:
  fraud, 2–3
  security, 7

Counters, 134
Created checks:
  and induced errors, 236–238
  in criminal targeting, 268
Credit balance, 75
Credit cards, 137
Credit control, 121, 123
Credit entry, 74, 75
Credit notes, 123
  examining, 208
Credibility gap, 2
Cressey, Donald R., 15, 16
Crime:
  acceptable, 17–18
  attitude in dealing with, 16
  condoned, 94
  justifying, 18
  white collar, 15
Crime statistics, 3–5
Criminal Law Act 1967, 273
Criminal motivation, 14–22
  aspirations and practical theories of, 21
  external pressures, 22
Criminal offences, 345
Criminal targeting as fraud detection tech-
    nique, 267–269
Criminals:
  external, 29, 131–132, 226
  internal, 131, 132, 226, 227
  international, 3, 25
  organized, 14, 29
  professional, 130
  schooling, 2
Critical (or key point) auditing, 191–218
  analysis working sheet, 197–198
  extent of, 194
  historical proportional and intercompany
      analysis, 195–198
  method of approach, 195
  period of, 195
  planning, 193–195
  probability of detection, 192–194
  problems arising from, 191–192
  specific tests, 198–218
  staff selection, 194
Crown Court, 276
Current assets, 69
Current ratio, 70
Customs and Excise Department, 283

Data bases, 85–86
Data files, 85–86

Data protection methods, 86
Data security, 432
Debit balance, 75, 123
Debit entry, 74, 75
Defensible Space, 353
Defensive systems, 321–380
'Degree mills', 327–328
Deliveries inwards controls, 364
Deliveries outwards controls, 364
Delivery notes, 112, 228
Delivery transport, checklist, 414
Detection, 321
  basic rules, 189
  purpose and benefits of, 188–191
  role in fraud prevention, 379
  techniques of, 10, 188–269
Detection aids, 245–246, 260, 348
Deviations theory, 27
Dial port number, 148
Dial-up facilities, 169
Differential association theory, 15–16, 329
Differential of opportunity theory, 23–25
'Dirty tricks', 256
Disbursement cheques, 117, 205
Disbursements, 115–124
  controls, 372
  fraud symptoms, 119
  induced errors involving, 237
Dismissal, 270, 331
  grounds for, 279–280
  overriding condition of, 280
Dispatch notes, 119–121
Documents:
  alterations and forgeries in, 288–289
  authorization of, 371
  colour coding of, 367
  examination of, 288–289
  handling of, 288
Double entry accounts, 74–77
Dun and Bradstreet, 151
Durkheim, Emile, 21

Eavesdropping equipment, 348, 349
Education programme, 345–346
Electronic sweeping for listening devices,
    348–349
Elements of fraud (see Fraud elements)
Emergency planning, 351–352, 432
Employee education, 345
Employee performance reports, 347
Employee selection:
  acceptance or rejection decisions, 342–343

comments on recommended system, 343
interviews and follow up, 339
legal restraints and requirements, 330–331
management policy, 332
pre-employment checks, 330–331
procedures of, 326–343
security aspects, 340
security problems and requirements in, 327–330
Employees:
  job rotation of, 266
  legal agreements with, 343
  responsibilities of, 431, 433
Employment, termination of, 347
Entity verification tests, 199
Errors, induced, as detection technique, 236
Espionage, industrial, 3, 227, 345, 347
Ethical standards, 6
Evidence:
  admissibility of, 285
  documentary, 288
  incriminating, 302
Exceptions, 130, 371
Exclusion areas, 355
Exhibits, 319
Expert witnesses, 295
Export conversions, 230
Extortion, 183

Factory controls, 364–365
False credit, 26, 91, 98–99, 105, 107, 114, 156, 158, 362
Fidelity insurance, 278–279, 350–351
File names, 149–150
Films, use in detection, 247
Final accounts, 69
  impact of fraud on, 77–78
  measurements of performance from, 70
  preparation of, 71
Financial problems, 16
Financial ratios, 69–74, 197
  improvement of, 73
  interdependence, 73
  methods of improving, 74
Finger prints, 264, 295
First-time offenders, 15–17
Forensic examination, 295
Ford Motor Company, 11–12
Fraud:
  attitudes to, 6–10

behavioural symptoms of, 104
critical areas of, 258
dealing with, 7
definition, 1
divisions in, 28–29
evidence of, 250
final factors in, 68
impact of, 196, 232
inevitability of, 14
losses due to, 5
motivating factors, 321
nature of, 14
opportunities for, 228
opportunist, 95
pattern of, 25
pre-conditions for, 233
predictability, 68
probabilities of, 142
problem of, 1–13
scale of, 6–7
'small', 6, 94
subdivisions in, 30
suspicion of, 270
symptoms of, 191, 221, 270
Fraud categories, 30
  A1 internal-management-larcenous, 30–32
    characteristics of, 32
    definition, 30
    examples, 31–32
  A2 internal-management-misrepresenta-tive, 32
    characteristics of, 33
    definition, 32
    examples, 32
  A3 internal-management-manipulative, 33–37
    characteristics of, 36
    examples, 34–36
  B1 internal-operations larcenous, 37
    characteristics of, 38
    definition, 37
    examples, 37–38
  B2 internal-operations-misrepresentative, 38–40
    characteristics, 40
    definition, 38
    examples, 39–40
  B3 internal-operations-manipulative, 41–42
    characteristics of, 42
    definition, 41
    example, 41–42

Fraud categories—*contd.*
  AB4 internal-management or operations-
      extorsive, 42–44
    characteristics, 44
    definition, 42
    examples, 42–43
  C1 external-business contacts-larcenous,
      44–45
    characteristics of, 45
    definition, 44
    examples, 44–45
  C2 external-business contacts-
      misrepresentative, 45–48
    characteristics of, 48
    definition, 45–46
    examples, 46–48
  C3 external-business contacts-
      manipulative, 49–50
    characteristics of, 50
    definition, 49
    examples, 49–50
  D1 external-opportunist-larcenous, 50–51
    characteristics of, 51
    definition, 50
    example, 51
  D2 external-opportunist-
      misrepresentative, 51–53
    characteristics of, 53
    definition, 51–52
    examples, 52–53
  D3 external-opportunist-manipulative,
      53–56
    characteristics of, 55
    definition, 53
    examples, 54–55
  E1 external-organized-larcenous, 56–58
    characteristics of, 57–58
    definition, 56
    examples, 56–57
  E2 external-organized-misrepresentative,
      58–59
    characteristics, 59
    definition, 58
    examples, 58–59
  E3 external-organized-manipulative, 59–60
    characteristics of, 60
    definition, 59
    example, 59–60
  CDE4 external extorsive, 60–63
    characteristics, 63
    definition, 60
    examples, 60–62

Fraud checklist, 407–420
Fraud elements (*see also* Concealment; Con-
    version; Theft act), 91–138, 143, 189
Fraud exposures, categories of, 68
Fraud-free profile, 231
Fraud prevention, 10, 190, 264
    approach to, 238–239
    basic principles of, 239
    benefits of, 12
Fraud risks (*see* Risks)
Fraud theories, 23–28
Fraud types, 4
Funds recovery, 272, 277

Gate controls, 362–363
Goods, induced errors involving, 237
Goods inwards notes, 362
Goods movement, spot checks on, 260
Goods movements controls, 364
    recording, 362
Goods, received, checklist, 412
Goods received notes, 112
Guarantee cards, 80
    in criminal targeting, 269
Guilt, tests of, 307
Gullibility fill, 2

Hamilton, Peter, 358
Handbook of Security, 358
Handbook of White Collar Crime, 4
Honesty categories, 4

Incentive schemes, 346
Incident reporting, 349–350, 432
Income:
    from unusual sources, 207
    induced errors involving, 237
    under recording, 261
Incoming funds, controls, 372
Industrial espionage, 3, 227, 345, 347
Informants, company, use in detection, 253
Information classification and protection (*see
    also* Business intelligence), 347–349,
    431
Infrared alarms, 355
Innocence, tests of, 307
Insurance, 4, 145, 278–279, 350–351
International criminals, 25
Interviews, 296–318
    admission seeking questions, 314
    admission statement, 317
    best person to conduct, 302–303

body language in, 299
chances of success, 303
counterattacks and responses, 316
empathy building, 298
failures in, 296–297
general principles of, 305–306
notes and records of, 304–305
place of, 301–302
stages of, 303–304
stress inducing questions, 312
style of, 303
techniques, 307
tests of guilt and innocence, 307
transactional analysis, 298
.types of questions, 297–298
with suspects, 301, 305–306
with witnesses, 300–301
(*see also* Employee selection)
Inventory control, 17, 92, 100, 210–212, 365
Inventory inflation, 134
Investigations, 270–320
acquisition of records, 284
acquisition and analysis of documents, 288–289
admissibility of evidence, 285–286
adverse publicity due to, 281
analysis of deviations, 292–293
analysis of exposure points, 286
analysis of weak points, 286
company politics in, 280–281
conduct of, 326, 433
criminal targeting, 268–269
effectiveness of techniques, 287
employee morale effects, 283–284
factors to be considered in setting objectives, 280–286
flow chart, 270
methods of, 287–318
need for secrecy, 270–272
objectives of, 270–280
police involvement in, 281–283
pretext, 296
reasons for conducting, 272
report, 318
resources available, 283
reviewing results, 318
schedules in, 289–292
starting point for, 270
surveillance in, 293–295
(*see also* Undercover investigations)
Investments, 432

Invigilation:
as detection technique, 231–239
impacts of, 234–236
method of operation and problem areas, 233–238
of account manipulations, 236
preventive, 238–239
Invoice splitting, 202
Invoice verification, 200

Jails, 2
JCL language, 181–182
Job applicants, reasons for rejecting, 328
Job applications, 333
falsifications in, 327
method of checking, 338
Job categories, definition of, 332
Job control manipulation, 181–182
Job descriptions, 343
Job rotation of employees, 266
Job sensitivity analysis, 218–222, 421–429
level of day-to-day supervision, 220
method of approach, 218
reporting levels, 218
Journal records, 155
Journal vouchers, 123, 127
Judges' Rules, 274

Labour practices, 344
Lapping frauds, 34–35, 210, 212, 368
Larson, R. H., 329
Ledger structure, 76
Ledger verifications, 201
Legal agreements with employees, 343
Legislation, 11, 12
Line tapping methods, 149
Link chart, 292
Listening devices, 348–349
Logic tree, 233
Long firm frauds, 121
Loss reporting, 349

Machinery, fraudulent interference of, 136, 264
Machinery controls, checklist, 412
McClintock, Derek, 327
Mail references in fraud detection, 218
Management:
attitude of, 7, 229
preventive investigations, 239
Management reports, 114
Management responsibilities, 431

Manipulation, 91, 96, 105–133
  accounting, 236
  computer output, 175–177
  detecting, 132–133
  general impacts of, 108
  job control, 181–182
  marketing, 206–209
  negative, 157, 159
  object of, 115
  of master files, 121, 171–172
  of records, 132
  positive, 157, 159
  primary, 105–130
  sales, 206–209
  secondary, 113
  suspense account, 172–175
  use of term, 26
  (see also under Computer fraud)
Manipulative frauds, 30
  in accounts receivable, 119
  involving bank accounts, 128–130
  involving intangible services and expenses,
    115
  involving miscellaneous accounts, 128–130
  involving purchases, 108–115
  involving receipts, 124–128
Manipulative objectives, 109, 116, 118, 120,
    126
Mareva injunctions, 277
Markers, stolen goods, 260
Marketing:
  checklist, 413
  manipulations, 206–209
Master files, alteration of, 122
Media Metrics Inc., 151
Microphones, 246, 348
Miranda Ruling, 274
Misrepresentation, 96, 105, 133–138, 240
  elements of, 374
  of commercial realities, 137–138, 375, 376
  of packaged stocks, 265
  of personal realities, 137, 375, 377–378
  of physical realities, 133–137, 378–379
  special defences against, 376–379
  symptoms of, 138
  use of term, 26
Misrepresentative frauds, investigating, 259

NCSS, 150–151
Negotiated settlement, 278
Net profit to sales ratio, 72
Net worth, 69

Nettler, Gwynn, 3, 21
Network Security Management Limited, 21,
    153
Newman, Oscar, 353
Norman, A. D., 358

Observation, 240
  as detection technique, 239–248
  equipment, 246
  from building, 243
  from vehicle, 243–245
  methods and problems, 240–246
  mobile, 240, 294
  record details, 247
  record verification, 247–248
  scene illumination, 241–242
  scene selection, 240–241
  selection of position, 243
  static, 240
  traffic flow effects, 242
  (see also Surveillance)
One-time frauds, 95, 130, 146, 222
Order splitting, 111, 202
Overseas markets, 230

Packaged stocks:
  misrepresentation of, 265
  spot checks on, 265
'Passing off' offences, 268
Passwords, 87, 150–152
Patents, 344
Paying in slips, 125–127, 209, 210
Payment record, 118
Payment request, 117
Payroll frauds, 212
Perceptual security, 354
Personal accounts, 124
Personal characteristics, 221
Personal expenses, 111
Personal misrepresentations, 137
Personal realities:
  misrepresentation of, 137, 375, 377–378
  spot checks, 263–264
Personal travelling expenses, 80
Personnel files, examining, 212
Personnel policies, checklist, 408
Personnel procedures, 343
Physical realities:
  misrepresentations of, 133–137, 378–379
  spot checks on, 264–266
Place of work effects, 220
Plausible excuses, 132

Point of business, definition, 374
Police involvement in investigations, 281–283
Polygraph tests, 5
Premium payments, reasons for, 204
Preventive security, 352–360
  checklist, 410
  definition, 352
  objectives of, 352
  physical security, 353–359
  value of, 352
Pricing file, 121
Prisoners, computer courses for, 2
Privacy infringements, 184
Product statistics, 114
Profit and loss account, 69, 76
Prosecution, 3, 270, 273–277
  police involvement, 282
  procedure of, 274–277
  reasons for and against, 273–274
Protection, minimum standards of, 326
Psychological sabotage, 255
Psychological tests, 331
Purchase frauds, tests for, 198
Purchase invoice, 112, 113
Purchase ledger, 362
Purchase orders, 108
  open files of, 112
Purchase records, 109, 116
Purchase returns suppression, 202
Purchase statistics, 79
Purchases, induced errors involving, 237
Purchases policy, checklist, 411
Purchasing fraud symptoms and loosely controlled accounts, 113
Purchasing statistics, 114

Quick ratio, 70
Quotations for contract work, 110

Radio monitoring, 260
Radio transmitter, 3
Receipts, 124–128
  fraud symptoms, 127–128
Records, 69–80
  access to, 221
  acquisition of third-party, 284
  alterations to, 367
  computerized, 285, 286
  day-to-day, 74
  informal and personal, 80
  statistical, impact of fraud, 78–80

stock, 78
transportation, 78
Recruitment policy, 431
References, 331
Rehabilitation of Offenders Act, 327
Reliability of business competitors, 229
Remote sensors, 261
Reports:
  of fraud, 2–3
  sales, 79
Restricted areas, 355, 356
Risk(s), 6
  computer related, 139
  cost estimation, 385
  criticality, 230
  factors affecting, 229
  high risk areas, 63–67
  percentages of, 381
Risk acceptance, 387
Risk activities, 221–222
Risk analysis, 218
Risk analysis sheet, 390
Risk areas, 63–67, 220, 230
  monitoring, 371
Risk assessment, qualitative methods of, 386
Risk avoidance, 387
Risk concentration, 356
Risk evaluation:
  eclectic, 389
  methods of, 381–384
  quantitative and qualitative methods of, 386
Risk identification, 384, 390
  eclectic, 389–394
  principles of, 387
Risk quantification, 385
Risk reduction, 387
Risk schedule, 222
Risk sources, 29
  accidental, natural and deliberate, 390
Risk transfer, 387
Ruder, Brian, 10

Sabotage, 183
Sales fraud symptoms, 124
Sales invoices, 363
  second (off-record), 207
Sales ledger, 210
  examining, 208
Sales manipulations, 206–209
Sales orders, 119–120
Sales record, 120

Sales reports, 79
Sales revenue, 119
Sales statistics, 213
Sales suppression, 261
Schedules, 319
  general rules on preparing, 290–292
  in investigations, 289–292
Search consent, 344
Secrecy, 344
Security:
  and personnel issues, 8–9
  budgets for, 325–326
  company-wide procedures, 326–352
  computer, 141, 142
  computer processing, 83
  effective, 8
  employee selection, 340
  framework of, 323
  irrelevant, 141
  job description, 343
  laxity in, 11
  object of, 7
  perceptual, 354
  physical, 1
  preventive (see Preventive security)
  professional sources, 325
  responsibilities for, 323–325
  supervision of, 346
Security adviser, 323–324, 340, 343, 432–433
Security costs, 7
Security design, 355
Security education, 345
Security exposures, 143
Security hardware, 358
Security policy, 326, 431–433
Security risks, attitudes to, 142
Security seals, 137
Security systems, 359
Security value calculation, 357–358
Sensors, 134
Sherman, George, 378
Short delivery frauds, 112
Skill levels, minimum and maximum collusion, 24
Skill requirements, 220
Skills of employees and managers, past and future, 20
Smash and grab frauds (see One-time frauds)
Source documents, 74, 76
Sperry Rand Corporation, 327

Spot checks:
  bulk liquid stocks, 265–266
  commercial realities, 262–264
  completeness of recorded income, 261–262
  general principles of, 258–259
  movement of goods, 260
  packaged stocks, 265
  personal realities, 263–264
  personnel selection for, 258
  physical realities, 264–266
  potential for, 262
  problems of, 257
  selection of areas for, 258
  surprise element, 260
  through staff rotation, 266–267
  use in fraud detection, 257
  value of, 267
Statistical information, 79
Statistical records, 124
  analysis of, 213
  impact of fraud, 78–80
Stealing (see Theft act)
Stock control, 210–212
Stock records, 78
Stolen goods:
  conversion of, 99–104
  conversion through dishonest third party, 100–104
  markers, 260
  methods of laundering, 100
  outlets for, 230
  receiver is customer of victim, 103
  receiver is independent of victim, 103–104
Surveillance, 240
  audio, 294–295
  criminal targeting, 268–269
  in investigations, 293–295
  mechanical, 245
  short-term, 245
  visual, 294
  (see also Observation)
Surveyors, 110
Suspects:
  interviews with, 301
  untruthful and uncooperative, 315
Suspense accounts, 75, 123, 172–175, 215, 216
Sutherland, Edwin O., 15, 16
Swarthort, D. M., 329
Systems Auditability and Control, 400

Tape recording, 3, 294, 302, 305
Targeting, criminal, as fraud detection technique, 267–269
Tax evasion, 2, 283
Telephone billing records, 80
Telephone interceptions, 294
Television cameras, 246, 263, 355
Tenders, 110, 373
Termination agreements, 344
Termination procedures, 347
Theft act, 6, 91–96, 189, 240
    computer resources, 184
    concealment of, 25–26, 96
    condoned losses, 94
    creative checks of, 236
    definition, 92
    justifying, 16
    losses not detected, 92
    symptoms of, 104
    unconcealed, 92
Third party intervention, 370
Tobacco Advisory Board, 267
Transaction, definition, 374
Transaction data, 122
Transaction entry codes, 214
Transactional analysis, 298
Transport costs, examining, 217
Transport records, 78
Travelling expense claims, 80
Trip devices, 245–246
Turnover to inventory ratio, 72

Ultraviolet crayon, 261
Undercover agent:
    as potential supplier, 253
        liaison with company, 253
        placing in position, 251–253
Undercover investigations, 248–254
    basic rules, 251–253
    circumstances recommending use of, 249
    disadvantages of, 248–249
    roles of, 250–269
    sources available for, 249–250
    value of, 252–254
Underground books, 2
Unfair competition, 254–255
    special checks for, 208
Unfair practices, 256
Unfair trading, 256

Veriprint Corporation, 264
Vouchers, 75–76
Vulnerability:
    elements of, 224
    measurement of, 225
    method of ranking, 224
Vulnerability charts, 222–231, 233, 258
    example of use of, 230–231
    method of completing, 225
    uses of, 224

Warehouse controls, 364–365
Weighbridge controls, 364–365
Wire tapping, 2
Wireless and Telegraphy Act, 3
Witnesses, interviews with, 300–301
Wolfgang, 331

Young, Graham, 327